Student Solutions Manual

Lawrence Tenenbaum
McGill University

Judith Watson
Capilano University

Marcela Porporato
York University

Anita Smale
CA

Maureen P. Gowing
University of Windsor

Cost Accounting
A Managerial Emphasis

Fifth Canadian Edition

Charles T. Horngren
Stanford University

George Foster
Stanford University

Srikant M. Datar
Stanford University

Maureen P. Gowing
University of Windsor

Pearson Canada
Toronto

ISBN-13: 978-0-13-611021-7
ISBN-10: 0-13-611021-5

Vice President, Editorial Director: Gary Bennett
Developmental Editor: Diliana Chopova
Production Editor: Cheryl Jackson
Production Coordinator: Andrea Falkenberg

1 2 3 4 5   13 12 11 10 09

Printed and bound in Canada.

Contents

CHAPTER 1
MANAGEMENT ACCOUNTANTS:
THEIR VITAL ROLE IN STRATEGIC AND OPERATING DECISIONS

1-2 Financial accounting is constrained by generally accepted accounting principles. Management accounting is not restricted to these principles. The result is that:

- management accounting can include assets or liabilities (such as "brand names" developed internally) not recognized under GAAP, and
- management accounting can use asset or liability measurement rules (such as present values or resale prices) not permitted under GAAP.

1-4 The business functions in the value chain are:

- *Research and development*—the generation of, and experimentation with, ideas related to new products, services, or processes.
- *Design of products, services, and processes*—the detailed planning and engineering of products, services, or processes.
- *Production*—the coordination and assembly of resources to produce a product or deliver a service.
- *Marketing*—the process of promoting and selling products or services to customers or prospective customers.
- *Distribution*—the mechanism by which products or services are delivered to the customer.
- *Customer service*—the support activities provided to customers.

1-6 A successful management accountant requires general business skills (such as understanding the strategy of an organization) and people skills (such as motivating other team members) as well as technical skills (such as using computer software). Accountants also analyze costs throughout the value chain and co-ordinate cost reductions to assure no impairment to the product that customers demand.

1-8 Planning decisions are made in choosing goals. Control decisions are made when implementing the planning decision(s) and evaluating personnel and operations with respect to the goal(s).

1-10 The three guidelines are:

(a) The cost/benefit approach that assures the improvement in quality of the data provides a benefit to the managers that exceeds the cost of improvement.
(b) Sensitivity to the balance of information that not only supports decisions to improve profits and motivates honest effort to achieve those profits but also is understandable.
(c) There are different costs to achieve different purposes.

1-12 The new controller could reply in one or more of several ways:

(a) Demonstrate to the plant manager how he or she could make better decisions if the plant controller was viewed as a resource rather than a dead weight. In a related way, the plant controller could show how the plant manager's time and resources could be saved by viewing the new plant controller as a team member.

(b) Demonstrate to the plant manager a good knowledge of technical aspects at the plant. This approach may involve doing background reading. It certainly will involve spending much time on the plant floor speaking to plant personnel.

(c) Show the plant manager examples of the new plant controller's past successes in working with line managers in other plants. Examples could include:
  - assistance in preparing the budget,
  - assistance in analyzing problem situations, and
  - assistance in submitting capital budget requests.

(d) Seek assistance from the corporate controller to highlight to the plant manager the importance of many tasks undertaken by the new plant controller. This approach is a last resort but may be necessary in some cases.

1-14 The SMAC sets standards of ethical conduct for management accountants. The four areas in which standards of ethical conduct exist for management accounts are:

1) Mastery of specific intellectual skill acquired by education and training.
2) Acceptance of duties to society (i.e., protection of the public) as a whole in addition to duties to the employer or client.
3) An outlook that is essentially objective.
4) A high standard in the conduct and performance of personal service.

1-16 (10 min.) Cost, management, and financial accounting.

1. Financial accountants wait until a transaction occurs, classify it according to GAAP, then estimate its financial value in full compliance with accounting standards to communicate the information to external parties in a standardized way. Management accountants use financial accounting information to classify the estimates of financial value using a variety of techniques. The classification is intended to filter relevant costs to inform an internal decision maker.

2. All accountants are members of a profession and are bound by professional duty to act with integrity. Their duty is to report estimates that do not materially misstate the economic value of the company.

1-18 (15 min.) **Value chain, supply chain, and key success factors.**

Change in Management Accounting	Link
a.	Total value-chain analysis
b.	Key success factors (quality) or Total value-chain analysis
c.	Dual external/internal focus
d.	Continuous improvement
e.	Customer satisfaction is priority one

1-20 (15 min.) **Value chain and classification of costs, fast food restaurant.**

Cost Item	Value Chain Business Function
a.	Production
b.	Distribution
c.	Marketing
d.	Marketing
e.	Marketing
f.	Production
g.	Design
h.	Customer service

1-22 (15 min.) **Problem solving, scorekeeping, and attention directing.**

Because the accountant's duties are often not sharply defined, some of these answers might be challenged.

a. Scorekeeping
b. Attention directing
c. Scorekeeping
d. Problem solving
e. Attention directing
f. Attention directing
g. Problem solving
h. Scorekeeping, depending on the extent of the report
i. This question is intentionally vague. The give-and-take of the budgetary process usually encompasses all three functions, but it emphasizes scorekeeping the least. The main function is attention directing, but problem solving is also involved.
j. Problem solving

1-24 (15 min.) **Management accounting guidelines.**

1. Cost-benefit approach
2. Behavioural and technical considerations
3. Behavioural and technical considerations
4. Different costs for different purposes
5. Behavioural and technical considerations
6. Cost-benefit approach

1-26 (15 min.) **Planning and control decisions.**

The plan or budget communicates the financial goals the organization will achieve while control arises from feedback on how well the plan has been achieved and reasons why the plan has not been achieved.

1. Annual financial statements communicate what was achieved. The annual report is a standardized control report on financial performance. It is feedback on what the organization accomplished.
2. Internal periodic reports of financial performance are control reports.
3. The report of losses suffered from a storm is a financial report that is a control report. Externally the insurer will use the report to estimate the amounts it will reimburse Softmoc according to the insurance contract. Internally the managers will use the report to modify their plan and generate the most appropriate response to an unanticipated event.

    The actual event will also initiate review of the adequacy of the insurance coverage relative to its cost. These new data will be used in subsequent plans for future insurance coverage and its cost.
4. Weekly reports of the total quantity of particular shoes sold are feedback. They are control reports internally because a comparison can be made with the plan to determine if the plan was achieved and if not, why not. They are control reports for the supplier for the same reasons.
5. Studies of new business development opportunities communicate planned costs and revenue.

1-28 (15 min.) Planning and control decisions; Internet company.

1. **Planning decisions**
   a. Decision to raise monthly subscription fee
   c. Decision to upgrade content of online services
   e. Decision to decrease monthly subscription fee

   Control decisions
   b. Decision to inform existing subscribers about the rate of increase—an implementation part of control decisions
   d. Dismissed the VP of Marketing—performance evaluation and feedback aspect of control decisions

2. Planning decisions at WebInfo.com focus on organizational goals, predicting results under various alternative ways of achieving those goals, and then deciding how to attain the desired goal, for example:

   (a) WebInfo.com could have the objective of revenue growth to gain critical mass.
   (b) It could have the objective of increasing operating income.

   Many Internet companies in their formative years make revenue growth (and subscriber growth) their primary goal.
   Control focuses on deciding on, and taking actions that implement, the planning decision, and deciding on performance evaluation and the related feedback that will help future decision making. For example, WebInfo.com will

   (a) communicate the new rates to advertisers.
   (b) communicate the new price to marketing representatives.

1-30 (15 min.) Management accounting guidelines.

1. Cost-benefit approach
2. Behavioural and technical considerations
3. Different costs for different purposes
4. Cost-benefit approach
5. Behavioural and technical considerations
6. Cost-benefit approach
7. Behavioural and technical considerations
8. Different costs for different purposes
9. Behavioural and technical considerations

1-32 (30-40 min.) Governance and end-of-year actions.

1. The possible motivations for the snack foods division president wanting to take end-of-year actions include:

   (a) Management incentives. Gourmet Foods may have a division bonus scheme based on one-year reported division earnings. Efforts to front-end revenue into the current year or transfer costs into the next year can increase this bonus.

   (b) Promotion opportunities and job security. Top management of Gourmet Foods likely will view those division managers that deliver high reported earnings growth rates as being the best prospects for promotion. Division managers who deliver "unwelcome surprises" may be viewed as less capable.

   (c) Retain division autonomy. If top management of Gourmet Foods adopts a "management by exception" approach, divisions that report sharp reductions in their earnings growth rates may attract a sizable increase in top management oversight.

2. Several of the "end-of-year actions" clearly are in conflict with these requirements and should be viewed as unacceptable by Taylor:

   (b) The fiscal year-end should be closed on midnight of December 31. "Extending" the close falsely reports next year's sales as this year's sales.

   (c) Altering shipping dates is falsification of the accounting reports.

   (f) Advertisements run in December should be charged to the current year. The advertising agency is facilitating falsification of the accounting records of Gourmet Foods as well as falsifying its own records.

The other "end-of-year actions" occur in many organizations and may fall into the "grey" to "acceptable" area. However, much depends on the circumstances surrounding each one:

1-32 (cont'd)

(a) If the independent contractor does not do maintenance work in December, there is no transaction regarding maintenance to record. The responsibility for ensuring packaging equipment is well maintained is that of the plant manager. The division controller probably can do little more than observe the absence of a December maintenance charge.

(d) In many organizations sales are heavily concentrated in the final weeks of the fiscal year end. If the double bonus is approved by the division marketing manager, the division controller can do little more than observe the extra bonus paid in December.

(e) If advertising is reduced in December, the advertising cost in December will be reduced. There is no record falsification here.

(g) Much depends on the means of "persuading" carriers to accept the merchandise. For example, if an under-the-table payment is involved, it is clearly unethical. If, however, the carrier receives no extra consideration and willingly agrees to accept the assignment, the transaction appears ethical.

Each of the (a), (d), (e) and (g) "end-of-year actions" may well disadvantage Gourmet Foods in the long-run. The divisional controller is well advised to raise this issue in meetings with the division president. However, if Gourmet Foods has a rigid set of line/staff distinctions, the division president is the one who bears primary responsibility for justifying division actions to senior corporate officers.

3. If Taylor believes that Ryan wants her to engage in unethical behaviour, she should first directly raise her concerns with Ryan. If Ryan is unwilling to change his request, Taylor should discuss her concerns with the Corporate Controller of Gourmet Foods. She could also initiate a confidential discussion with a SMAC adviser, other impartial adviser, or her own lawyer. Taylor also may well ask for a transfer from the snack foods division if she perceives Ryan is unwilling to listen to pressure brought by the Corporate Controller, CFO, or even President of Gourmet Foods. In the extreme, she may want to resign if the corporate culture of Gourmet Foods is to reward division managers who take "end-of-year actions" that Taylor views as unethical and possibly illegal.

CHAPTER 2
AN INTRODUCTION TO COST TERMS AND PURPOSES

2-2   A *cost object* is anything for which a separate measurement of costs is desired. Examples include a product, a service, a project, a customer, a brand category, an activity, a department, and a program.

2-4   Direct costs of a cost object are costs that are related to the particular cost object and that can be traced to it in an economically feasible way. Indirect costs of a cost object are costs that are related to the particular cost object but cannot be traced to it in an economically feasible way.

2-6   *Direct materials costs:* The acquisition costs of all materials that eventually become part of the cost object (say, units finished or in process) and that can be traced to that cost object in an economically feasible way. Acquisition costs of direct materials include freight-in (inward delivery) charges, sales taxes, and custom duties.

   Direct manufacturing labour costs: The compensation of all manufacturing labour that is specifically identified with the cost object (say, units finished or in process) and that can be traced to the cost object in an economically feasible way. Examples include wages and fringe benefits paid to machine operators and assembly-line workers.

   Indirect manufacturing costs: All manufacturing costs considered to be part of the cost object (say, units finished or in process) but that cannot be individually traced to that cost object in an economically feasible way. Examples include power, supplies, indirect materials, indirect manufacturing labour, plant rent, plant insurance, property taxes on plants, plant amortization, and the compensation of plant managers.

   Prime costs: All direct manufacturing costs. In the two-part classification of manufacturing costs, prime costs would comprise direct materials costs. In the three-part classification, prime costs would comprise direct materials costs and direct manufacturing labour costs.

   Conversion costs: All manufacturing costs other than direct materials costs. One group of conversion costs can be direct manufacturing labour costs separate from all remaining indirect costs of manufacturing. The second group of conversion costs can be simply all indirect costs of manufacturing including direct manufacturing labour cost. The definition of a conversion cost will change depending on the relevance of the direct manufacturing labour cost.

2-8   No. Service sector companies have no inventories and, hence, no inventoriable costs.

2-10   A cost driver is the cause of a cost. The Pareto principle is an alternative expression of materiality that says for many events, 80% of the effects arise from 20% of the causes. This means management accountants will focus on the 20% of causes that result in 80% of the costs first.

2-12   The *relevant range* is the range of the cost driver in which a specific relationship between cost and driver is valid. This concept enables the use of linear cost functions when examining cost-volume-profit (CVP) relationships as long as the volume levels are within that relevant range.

2-14   To execute a lean management strategy that will continue to fulfill a value proposition for customers, the features of the output unit, whether a good or a service, must match what is demanded at a price customers are willing to pay.

2-16 (20-30 min.)   Inventoriable costs vs. period costs.

1.   *Manufacturing-sector companies* purchase materials and components and convert them into different finished goods.

Merchandising-sector companies purchase and then sell tangible products without changing their basic form.

Service-sector companies provide services or intangible products to their customers—for example, legal advice or audits.

Only manufacturing and merchandising companies have inventories of goods for sale.

2.   *Inventoriable costs* are all costs of a product that are regarded as an asset when they are incurred and then become cost of goods sold when the product is sold. These costs for a manufacturing company are included in work-in-process and finished goods inventory (they are "inventoried") to build up the costs of creating these assets.

Period costs are all costs in the income statement other than cost of goods sold. These costs are treated as expenses of the period in which they are incurred because they are presumed not to benefit future periods (or because there is not sufficient evidence to conclude that such benefit exists). Expensing these costs immediately best matches expenses to revenues.

3.
   (a) Spring water purchased for resale by Sobeys—inventoriable cost of a merchandising company. It becomes part of cost of goods sold when the mineral water is sold.
   (b) Electricity used at a Toyota assembly plant—inventoriable cost of a manufacturing company. It is part of the manufacturing overhead that is included in the manufacturing cost of a truck finished good.
   (c) Amortization on Google's computer equipment—period cost of a service company. Google has no inventory of goods for sale and, hence, no inventoriable cost.
   (d) Electricity for Sobeys store aisles—period cost of a merchandising company. It is a cost that benefits the current period and is not traceable to goods purchased for resale.

2-16 (cont'd)

    (e) Amortization on Toyota's assembly testing equipment—inventoriable cost of a manufacturing company. It is part of the manufacturing overhead that is included in the manufacturing cost of truck finished good.

    (f) Salaries of Sobeys marketing personnel—period cost of a merchandising company. It is a cost that is not traceable to goods purchased for resale. It is presumed not to benefit future periods (or at least not to have sufficiently reliable evidence to estimate such future benefits).

    (g) Water consumed by Google's engineers—period cost of a service company. Google has no inventory of goods for sale and, hence, no inventoriable cost.

    (h) Salaries of Google's marketing personnel—period cost of a service company. Google has no inventory of goods for sale and, hence, no inventoriable cost.

2-18 (20 min.) Direct and indirect costs, effect of changing the classification of a cost item.

1.   *Direct costs* are costs that are related to the particular paper products (Supreme, Deluxe, or Regular) and can be traced to each one in an economically feasible (cost-effective) way.

       Indirect costs are costs that are related to the particular paper products (Supreme, Deluxe, or Regular) but cannot be traced to each one in an economically feasible (cost-effective) way.

2.   Energy costs of $108 million can be traced to each individual production line. This tracing will result in a more accurate assignment of costs to products than when the $150 million of indirect manufacturing costs ($20 million of which is fixed) is allocated using direct manufacturing labour costs at each line. The $108 million in energy costs does not have an identical relationship to direct manufacturing labour costs for each product line as is assumed when the direct manufacturing labour cost allocation base is used in Exercise 2-17:

		Supreme	Deluxe	Regular	Total
1.	Direct energy costs	$45.00	$25.00	$38.00	$108.00
2.	Direct manuf. labour cost	14.00	28.00	8.00	50.00
3.	Ratio of 1. to 2.	3.214	0.893	4.750	2.160

The Supreme and the Regular product line present energy-intensive usage vis-à-vis their direct manufacturing labour cost content. The result is that these product lines will be undercosted when the Exercise 2-17 unit cost numbers are used. (The Deluxe product line will be overcosted.)

2-18 (cont'd)

3.

	Supreme	Deluxe	Regular
Direct materials costs	$ 84.00	$ 54.00	$ 62.00
Direct manuf. labour costs	14.00	28.00	8.00
Direct energy costs	45.00	25.00	38.00
Indirect manuf. costs	20.00	15.00	7.00
Total manuf. costs	$163.00	$122.00	$115.00
Fixed costs allocated at a rate of $20 ÷ $50 (direct mfg. labour) equal to $0.40 per dir. manuf. labour dollar (0.40 × $14; 28; 8)	5.60	11.20	3.20
Variable costs	$157.40	$110.80	$ 111.80
Kilograms produced	80	120	100
Cost per kilogram	$1.9675	$0.9233	$1.1180

The unit cost amounts are:

		Supreme	Deluxe	Regular
1.	Exercise 2-18	$1.9675	$0.9233	$1.1180
2.	Exercise 2-17	1.7500	1.3833	0.9400
	Ratio of 1 to 2	1.1243	0.6675	1.1894

As predicted in requirement 2, the tracing of the higher-than-average energy costs to Supreme and Regular results in an increase in reported unit costs for these product lines.

11

2-20 (15-20 min.) Classification of costs, merchandising sector.

Cost object: DVD section of store

Cost variability: With respect to changes in the number of DVDs sold

There may be some debate over classifications of individual items. Debate is more likely as regards cost variability.

Cost Item	D or I	V or F
A	D	F
B	I	F
C	D	V
D	D	F
E	I	F
F	I	V or F
G	I	F
H	D	V

2-22 (20-25 min.) Computing cost of goods manufactured and cost of goods sold.

Schedule of Cost of Goods Manufactured
For the Year Ended December 31, 2009
(in thousands)

Direct materials used		$ 106,800
Direct manufacturing labour costs		38,400
Indirect manufacturing costs:		
Property tax on plant building	$ 4,200	
Plant utilities	20,400	
Amortization of plant building	14,700	
Amortization of plant equipment	14,700	
Plant repairs and maintenance	19,200	
Indirect manufacturing labour costs	27,600	
Indirect materials used	12,200	
Miscellaneous plant overhead	5,200	118,200
Manufacturing costs incurred during 2009		263,400
Add beginning work-in-process inventory, Jan. 1, 2009		25,000
Total manufacturing costs to account for		288,400
Deduct ending work-in-process inventory, Dec. 31, 2009		32,200
Cost of goods manufactured		$256,200

2-22 (cont'd)

Schedule of Cost of Goods Sold
For the Year Ended December 31, 2009
(in thousands)

Beginning finished goods, Jan. 1, 2009	$ 37,400
Cost of goods manufactured (above)	256,200
Cost of goods available for sale	293,600
Ending finished goods, Dec. 31, 2009	44,800
Cost of goods sold	$248,800

2-24 (10 min.) **Variable costs and fixed costs behaviour.**

Choice (b)

Since indirect fixed manufacturing costs will not increase, and marketing and other period costs will remain the same with the special order, only the revenue and the variable manufacturing costs will be affected by the special order. If the revenue from the special order is greater than the variable costs of the special order, then the operating income will increase and the special order should be undertaken. The increase in operating income is calculated as:

Revenue ($13.20/unit × 20,000 units)	$264,000
Variable manufacturing costs	
($9.90/unit unit × 20,000 units)	198,000
Increase in operating income	$ 66,000

2-26 (10 min.) **Total costs and unit costs.**

1. Total cost, $4,800. Unit cost per person, $4,800 ÷ 500 = $9.60

2. Total cost, $4,800. Unit cost per person, $4,800 ÷ 2,000 = $2.40

3. The main lesson of this problem is to alert the student early in the course to the desirability of thinking in terms of total costs rather than unit costs wherever feasible. Changes in the number of cost driver units will affect total variable costs but not total fixed costs. In our example, it would be perilous to use either the $9.60 or the $2.40 unit cost to predict the total cost because the total costs are not affected by the attendance. Instead, the student association should use the $4,800 total cost. Obviously, if the musical group agreed to work for, say $4.80 per person, such a unit variable cost could be used to predict the total cost.

2-28 (20 min.) **Labour cost, overtime, and idle time.**

1.(a) Total cost of hours worked at regular rates

42 hours × 12 per hour	$ 504.00
42 hours × 12 per hour	504.00
43 hours × 12 per hour	516.00
40 hours × 12 per hour	480.00
	2,004.00
Minus idle time (5.2 hours × $12 per hour)	62.40
Direct manufacturing labour costs	$1,941.60

(b) Idle time = 5.2 hours × 12 per hour = $62.40

(c) Overtime and holiday premium.

Week 1: Overtime (42–40) hours × Premium, $6 per hour	$ 12.00
Week 2: Overtime (42–40) hours ×Premium, $6 per hour	12.00
Week 3: Overtime (43–40) hours × Premium, $6 per hour	18.00
Week 4: Holiday 8 hours × Premium, $12 per hour	96.00
Total overtime and holiday premium	$138.00

(d) Total earnings in May

Direct manufacturing labour costs	$1,941.60
Idle time	62.40
Overtime and holiday premium	138.00
Total earnings	$2,142.00

2. Idle time caused by equipment breakdowns and scheduling mix-ups is an indirect cost of the job because it is not related to a specific job.

Overtime premium caused by the heavy overall volume of work is also an indirect cost because it is not related to a particular job that happened to be worked on during the overtime hours. If, however, the overtime is the result of a demanding "rush job," the overtime premium is a direct cost of that job.

2-30 (30 min.) **Budgeted income statement.**

1.

Target ending finished goods, Dec. 31, 2010	12,000 units
Forecasted sales for 2010	122,000 units
Total finished goods required in 2010	134,000 units
Beginning finished goods, Jan. 1, 2010	9,000 units
Finished goods production required in 2010	125,000 units

2-30 (cont'd)

2.	Revenues (122,000 units sold × $4.80)		$585,600
	Cost of units sold:		
	Beginning finished goods, Jan. 1, 2010	$ 20,970	
	Cost of goods manufactured	281,250[a]	
	Cost of goods available for sale	302,220	
	Ending finished goods, Dec. 31, 2010	27,000[c]	275,220
	Gross margin		310,380
	Operating costs:		
	Marketing, distn., and customer-service costs	204,700	
	Administrative costs	50,000	254,700[d]
	Operating income		$ 55,680

Supporting Computations

a.

	Manufacturing Costs for 125,000 Units		
	Variable	Fixed	Total
Direct materials costs	$175,000[b]	$ –	$175,000
Direct manufacturing labour costs	37,500	–	37,500
Plant energy costs	6,250	–	6,250
Indirect manufacturing labour costs	12,500	16,000	28,500
Other indirect manufacturing costs	10,000	24,000	34,000
Cost of goods manufactured	$241,250	$40,000	$281,250

b. Direct materials costs = 250,000 kg × $0.70 per kg = $175,000.

c. The average unit manufacturing costs in 2010 is $281,250 ÷ 125,000 units = $2.25. Finished goods, December 31, 2010 = 12,000 × $2.25 = $27,000.

d.

Variable mktg., distn., and customer-service costs, 122,000 × $1.35	$164,700
Fixed marketing, distn., and customer-service costs	40,000
Fixed administrative costs	50,000
	$254,700

2-32 (30 min.) Flow of inventoriable costs.

		(in millions)
1.	Direct materials inventory, Aug. 1, 2009	$ 90
	Direct materials purchased	360
	Direct materials available	450
	Deduct direct materials used	375
	Direct materials inventory, Aug. 31, 2009	$ 75
2.	Total manufacturing overhead costs	$ 480
	Subtract: Variable manufacturing overhead costs	250
	Fixed manufacturing overhead costs	$ 230

3.	Total manufacturing costs		$1,600
	Deduct:		
	Direct materials used	$375	
	Manufacturing overhead	480	855
	Direct manufacturing labour costs		$ 745

4.	Work-in-Process inventory, Aug. 1, 2009	$ 200
	Total manufacturing costs	1,600
		1,800
	Deduct cost of goods manufactured (moved into FG)	1,650
	Work-in-Process inventory Aug. 31, 2009	$ 150
5.	Finished goods inventory Aug. 1, 2009	$ 125
	Cost of goods manufactured (moved from WIP)	1,650
	Goods available for sale	$1,775
6.	Goods available for sale in August (from req. 5)	$1,775
	Deduct cost of goods sold	1,700
	Finished goods inventory, Aug. 31, 2008	$ 75

2-34 (25-30 min.) Income statement and schedule of cost of goods manufactured.

Powell Corporation
Income Statement
For the Year Ended December 31, 2009
(in millions)

Revenues		$1,140
Cost of goods sold:		
Beginning finished goods, Jan. 1, 2009	$ 70	
Cost of goods manufactured (below)	762	
Cost of goods available for sale	832	
Ending finished goods, Dec. 31, 2009	55	777
Gross margin		363
Marketing, distribution, and customer-service costs		288
Operating income		$ 75

Powell Corporation
Schedule of Cost of Goods Manufactured
For the Year Ended December 31, 2009
(in millions)

Direct materials costs:		
Beginning inventory, Jan. 1, 2009	$ 15	
Purchases of direct materials	390	
Cost of direct materials available for use	405	
Ending inventory, Dec. 31, 2009	20	
Direct materials used		$385
Direct manufacturing labour costs		120
Indirect manufacturing costs:		
Indirect manufacturing labour	60	
Plant supplies used	12	
Plant utilities	36	
Amortization—plant, building, and equipment	96	
Plant supervisory salaries	6	
Miscellaneous plant overhead	42	252
Manufacturing costs incurred during 2009		757
Add beginning work in process inventory, Jan. 1, 2009		10
Total manufacturing costs to account for		767
Deduct ending work in process, Dec. 31, 2009		5
Cost of goods manufactured		$762

17

2-36   (25-30 min.)   Income statement and schedule of cost of goods manufactured.

Chan Corporation
Income Statement
For the Year Ended December 31, 2009
(in millions)

Revenues		$350
Cost of goods sold:		
Beginning finished goods, Jan. 1, 2009	$ 40	
Cost of goods manufactured (below)	204	
Cost of goods available for sale	244	
Ending finished goods, Dec. 31, 2009	12	232
Gross margin		118
Marketing, distribution, and customer-service costs		90
Operating income		$ 28

Chan Corporation
Schedule of Cost of Goods Manufactured
For the Year Ended December 31, 2009
(in millions)

Direct material costs:		
Beginning inventory, Jan. 1, 2009	$ 30	
Direct materials purchased	80	
Cost of direct materials available for use	110	
Ending inventory, Dec. 31, 2009	5	
Direct materials used		$105
Direct manufacturing labour costs		40
Indirect manufacturing costs:		
Plant supplies used	6	
Property taxes on plant	1	
Plant utilities	5	
Indirect manufacturing labour costs	20	
Amortization – plant, building, and equipment	9	
Miscellaneous manufacturing overhead costs	10	51
Manufacturing costs incurred during 2007		196
Add beginning work in process inventory, Jan. 1, 2009		10
Total manufacturing costs to account for		206
Deduct ending work in process inventory, Dec. 31, 2009		2
Cost of goods manufactured (to income statement)		$204

2-38 (15-20 min.) Cost classifications and the income statement.

1.

Foxwood Company
Income Statement
For the Year Ended December 31, 2009

Revenues		$1,360,000
Cost of goods sold:		
Beginning finished goods, Jan. 1, 2009	$ 100,000	
Cost of goods manufactured (see below)	960,000	
Cost of goods available for sale	1,060,000	
Ending finished goods, Dec. 31, 2009	150,000	910,000
Gross margin		450,000
Operating costs:		
Marketing and promotion	$ 60,000	
Marketing salaries	100,000	
Shipping costs	70,000	
Customer-service costs	100,000	330,000
Operating income		$ 120,000

Foxwood Company
Schedule of Cost of Goods Manufactured
For the Year Ended December 31, 2009

Direct material costs:		
Beginning inventory, Jan. 1, 2009	$ 40,000	
Direct materials purchased during 2009	460,000	
Cost of direct materials available for use	500,000	
Ending inventory, Dec. 31, 2009	50,000	
Direct materials used		$450,000 (V)
Direct manufacturing labour costs		300,000 (V)
Indirect manufacturing costs:		
Sandpaper	2,000 (V)	
Materials–handling costs	70,000 (V)	
Lubricants and coolants	5,000 (V)	
Miscellaneous indirect manufacturing labour	40,000 (V)	
Plant leasing costs	54,000 (F)	
Amortization—plant equipment	36,000 (F)	
Property taxes on plant equipment	4,000 (F)	
Fire and casualty insurance on plant equipment	3,000 (F)	214,000
Manufacturing costs incurred during 2009		964,000
Add beginning work in process inventory, Jan. 1, 2009		10,000
Total manufacturing costs to account for		974,000
Deduct ending work in process inventory, Dec. 31, 2009		14,000
Cost of goods manufactured (to income statement)		$960,000

2-38 (cont'd)

2. Direct materials unit cost = Direct materials used ÷ Units produced
$$= \$450,000 \div 900,000 = \$0.50$$

Plant leasing unit cost = Plant leasing costs ÷ Units produced
$$= \$54,000 \div 900,000 = \$0.06$$

3. The direct materials costs are variable, so they would increase in total from \$450,000 to \$500,000 (1,000,000 x \$0.50). However, their unit costs would be unaffected: \$500,000 ÷ 1,000,000 units = \$0.50.

In contrast, the plant leasing costs of \$54,000 are fixed, so they would not increase in total. However, if the plant leasing costs were assigned to units produced, the unit costs would decline from \$0.060 to \$0.054: \$54,000 ÷ 1,000,000 = \$0.054.

4. The explanation would begin with the answer to requirement 3. As a consultant, you should stress that the unitizing (averaging) of costs that have different behaviour patterns can be misleading. A common error is to assume that a total unit cost, which is often a sum of variable unit costs and fixed unit costs, is an indicator that total costs change in a wholly variable way as the level of production output changes. The next chapter demonstrates the necessity for distinguishing between cost behaviour patterns. You must be especially wary about unit fixed costs. Too often, unit fixed costs are erroneously regarded as being indistinguishable from unit variable costs.

5. DML is 33% (\$300,000 ÷ \$910,000) of total COGS. This is a material amount based on the normal financial accounting guideline that suggests materiality thresholds of 5% to 10%. Because DML is material it should be classified as a prime rather than a conversion cost. Total conversion costs are \$214,000, less than the DML. To include DML in the conversion cost would distort the relationship between the contribution to costs made by direct and those made by indirect costs. This would misrepresent the material and efficient causes of the cost of each output unit.

2-40 (20-25 min.) Labour-cost ethics, governance.

1. No. The direct manufacturing labour costs are not 20% or greater of total manufacturing costs.   Direct manufacturing labour costs are $410,000 which are 16.4% of total manufacturing costs, $410,000 ÷ $2,500,000 = 16.4%

2. Bob Zixson can ask the controller to reclassify at least two of the costs that are currently reported as indirect manufacturing costs to direct manufacturing labour costs. The most logical are the fringe benefits and some of the overtime costs, particularly if it can be argued that some of the overtime was directly caused by jobs. The fringe benefits are logical because they are not only the largest, but can be argued to be a part of normal cost of manufacturing labour. Fringe benefits related to direct manufacturing labour costs together with some of the overtime premium could bring the total direct manufacturing labour cost over the minimum $500,000.

   Justification for reclassifying vacation and sick time is similar to that of fringe benefits — that it is a normal cost of labour since it is part of and can be traced to the direct manufacturing labourer's payment. It is harder to justify reclassifying idle time, since it is difficult to identify a specific job that the idle time relates to. Idle time is also the smallest cost item.

3. The controller should not reclassify overhead costs as direct manufacturing labour costs just so the firm can reap tax benefits particularly if the changes would violate the company's policy of computing direct manufacturing labour costs. The idea of cost classification is to allow internal (and external) decision making by clarifying what each cost item represents. Also, if costs in only the Costa Melon plant are reclassified, it will be harder for Zix to evaluate the Costa Melon plant, when compared to Zix's other plants. Nevertheless, some of the arguments presented in requirement 2 can be justified and could prompt a reevaluation of Zix's direct manufacturing labour classifications.

CHAPTER 3
COST-VOLUME-PROFIT ANALYSIS

3-2 The assumptions underlying the CVP analysis outlined in Chapter 3 are:

1. Changes in the level of revenues and costs arise only because of changes in the number of product (or service) units produced or sold.
2. Total costs can be divided into a fixed component and a component that is variable with respect to the level of output.
3. The behaviour of total revenues and total costs is linear (straight-line) in relation to output units within the relevant range.
4. The unit selling price, unit variable costs, and fixed costs are known.
5. The analysis either covers a single product or assumes that a given revenue mix of products will remain constant as the level of total units sold changes.
6. All revenues and costs can be added and compared without taking into account the time value of money.

3-4 *Contribution margin* is computed as revenues minus all costs that vary with respect to the output level.

Gross margin is computed as revenues minus cost of goods sold.

Contribution-margin percentage is the total contribution margin divided by revenues.

Variable-cost percentage is the total variable costs (with respect to units of output) divided by revenues.

Margin of safety is the excess of budgeted revenues over breakeven revenues.

3-6 Breakeven analysis denotes the study of the breakeven point, which is often only an incidental part of the relationship between cost, volume, and profit. Cost-volume-profit analysis is a more comprehensive term than breakeven analysis.

3-8 An increase in the income tax rate does not affect the breakeven point. Operating income at the breakeven point is zero and thus no income taxes will be paid at this point.

3-10 Examples include:

Manufacturing—substituting a robotic machine for hourly wage workers.

Marketing—changing a sales force compensation plan from a percentage of sales dollars to a fixed salary.

Customer service—hiring a subcontractor to do customer repair visits on an annual retainer basis rather than a per visit basis.

3-12 Operating leverage describes the effects that fixed costs have on changes in operating income as changes occur in units sold and hence in contribution margin. Knowing the degree of operating leverage at a given level of sales helps managers calculate the effect of fluctuations in sales on operating incomes.

3-14 A company with multiple products can compute a breakeven point by assuming there is a constant mix of products at different levels of total revenue.

3-16 (10 min.) CVP analysis computations.
Contribution Margin column is not a requirement, it is shown for illustration purposes.

Case	Revenues	Variable Costs	Fixed Costs	Total Costs	OI	CM ($)	CM%
a	$3,000	$2,290	$250	$2,540	$460	$710	23.67%
b	18,500	7,400	1,300	8,700	9,800	11,100	60.00%
c	$10,600	7,420	3,200	10,620	(20)	3,180	30.00%
d	9,450	5,670	2,500	8,170	1,280	3,780	40.00%

Case a: Revenues – Total Costs = Operating Income
$3,000 – Total Costs = $460, Total Costs = $2,540
Total Costs = $2,540 = Variable Costs + Fixed Costs
$2,540 = $250 + Variable Costs, Variable Costs = $2,290
CM = Revenues – Variable Costs = $3,000 - $2,290 = $710
CM % = CM/Revenues = $710/$3,000 = 23.67%

Case b: Total Costs = Variable Costs + Fixed Costs
$8,700 = $7,400 + Fixed Costs, Fixed Costs = $1,300
Revenue – Total Costs = OI
Revenue - $8,700 = $9,800, Revenue = $18,500
CM = Revenues – Variable Costs = $18,500 - $7,400 = $11,100
CM % = CM/Revenues = $11,100/$18,500= 60.00%

Case c: CM % = CM/Revenues
30% = CM/$10,600, CM = $3,180
CM = Revenues – Variable Costs
$3,180 = $10,600 – Variable Costs, Variable Costs = $7,420
Total Costs = Variable Costs + Fixed Costs
Total Costs = $7,420 + $3,200 = $10,620
OI = Revenues – Total Costs = $10,600 - $10,620 = ($20)

3-16 (cont'd)

Case d: Total Costs = Variable Costs + Fixed Costs
$8,170 = Variable Costs + $2,500, Variable Costs = $5,670
OI = Revenues – Total Costs = $9,450- $8,170 = $1,280
CM = Revenues – Variable Costs = $9,450 - $5,670 = $3,780
CM % = CM/Revenues = $3,780/$9,450= 40.00%

3-18 (10 min.) CVP analysis, income taxes.

1. Monthly fixed costs = $60,000 + $70,000 + $10,000 $\qquad$ = $\qquad$ $140,000

Contribution margin per unit = $26,000 – $22,000 – $500 $\qquad$ = $\qquad$ $ 3,500

$$\text{Breakeven units per month} = \frac{\text{Monthly fixed costs}}{\text{Contribution margin per unit}} = \frac{\$140,000}{\$3,500 \text{ per car}} = 40 \text{ cars}$$

2. Tax rate $\qquad$ 40%

Target net income $\qquad$ $63,000

$$\text{Target operating income} = \frac{\text{Target net income}}{1 \text{ - tax rate}} = \frac{\$63,000}{(1-0.40)} = \frac{\$63,000}{0.60} = \$105,000$$

$$\text{Quantity of output units required to be sold} = \frac{\text{Fixed costs + Target operating income}}{\text{Contribution margin per unit}} = \frac{\$140,000 + \$105,000}{\$3,500} =$$

70 cars

3-20 (20 min.) Gross margin and contribution margin.

1.

Ticket sales ($20 × 500 attendees)		$10,000
Variable cost of dinner ($10[a] × 500 attendees)		$5,000
Variable invitations and paperwork ($1[b] × 500)		$500
Contribution margin		4,500
Fixed cost of dinner	6,000	
Fixed cost of invitations and paperwork	2,500	8,500
Operating profit (loss)		$ (4,000)

[a] $5,000/500 attendees = $10/attendee
[b] $500/500 attendees = $1/attendee

2.

Ticket sales ($20 × 1,000 attendees)		$20,000
Variable cost of dinner ($10[a] × 1,000 attendees)		$10,000
Variable invitations and paperwork ($1[b] × 1,000)		$1,000
Contribution margin		9,000
Fixed cost of dinner	6,000	
Fixed cost of invitations and paperwork	2,500	8,500
Operating profit (loss)		$ 500

3-22 (35–40 min.)   CVP analysis, changing revenues and costs.

1a. SP $= 8\% \times \$1,000 = \$80$ per ticket
  UVC $= \$35$ per ticket
  UCM $= \$80 - \$35 = \$45$ per ticket
  FC $= \$22,000$ a month

$$Q = \frac{FC}{UCM} = \frac{\$22,000}{\$45 \text{ per ticket}} \qquad = 489 \text{ tickets (rounded up)}$$

1b. $$Q = \frac{FC + TOI}{UCM} = \frac{\$22,000 + \$10,000}{\$45 \text{ per ticket}} = \frac{\$32,000}{\$45 \text{ per ticket}}$$
$$= 712 \text{ tickets (rounded up)}$$

2a. SP $= \$80$ per ticket
  VCU $= \$29$ per ticket
  UCM $= \$80 - \$29 = \$51$ per ticket
  FC $= \$22,000$ a month

$$Q = \frac{FC}{UCM} = \frac{\$22,000}{\$51 \text{ per ticket}} \qquad = 432 \text{ tickets (rounded up)}$$

2b. $$Q = \frac{FC + TOI}{UCM} = \frac{\$22,000 + \$10,000}{\$51 \text{ per ticket}} = \frac{\$32,000}{\$51 \text{ per ticket}}$$
$$= 628 \text{ tickets (rounded up)}$$

3a. SP $= \$48$ per ticket
  VCU $= \$29$ per ticket
  CMU $= \$48 - \$29 = \$19$ per ticket
  FC $= \$22,000$ a month

$$Q = \frac{FC}{UCM} = \frac{\$22,000}{\$19 \text{ per ticket}} \qquad = 1,158 \text{ tickets (rounded up)}$$

3b. $$Q = \frac{FC + TOI}{UCM} = \frac{\$22,000 + \$10,000}{\$19 \text{ per ticket}}$$

$$= \frac{\$32,000}{\$19 \text{ per ticket}} \qquad = 1,685 \text{ tickets (rounded up)}$$

3-22 (cont'd)

4a. The $5 delivery fee can be treated as either an extra source of revenue (as done below) or as a cost offset. Either approach increases CMU $5:

SP   = $53 ($48 + $5) per ticket
VCU   = $29 per ticket
CMU   = $53 – $29 = $24 per ticket
FC = $22,000 a month

$$Q = \frac{FC}{CMU} = \frac{\$22,000}{\$24 \text{ per ticket}}$$

= 917 tickets (rounded up)

4b. $$Q = \frac{FC + TOI}{CMU} = \frac{\$22,000 + \$10,000}{\$24 \text{ per ticket}}$$

$$= \frac{\$32,000}{\$24 \text{ per ticket}}$$

= 1,334 tickets (rounded up)

The $5 delivery fee results in a higher contribution margin, which reduces both the breakeven point and the tickets sold to attain operating income of $10,000.

3-24 (20 min.) **CVP exercises.**

	Revenues	Variable Costs	Contribution Margin	Fixed Costs	Budgeted Operating Income
Orig.	$15,000,000^G	$10,800,000^G	$4,200,000	$2,400,000^G	$1,800,000
1.	15,000,000	10,296,000	4,704,000	2,400,000	2,304,000
2.	15,000,000	11,304,000	3,696,000	2,400,000	1,296,000
3.	15,000,000	10,800,000	4,200,000	2,544,000	1,656,000
4.	15,000,000	10,800,000	4,200,000	2,256,000	1,944,000
5.	16,500,000	11,880,000	4,620,000	2,400,000	2,220,000
6.	13,500,000	9,720,000	3,780,000	2,400,000	1,380,000
7.	16,800,000	12,096,000	4,704,000	2,592,000	2,112,000
8.	15,000,000	10,260,000	4,740,000	2,520,000	2,220,000

^G stands for given.

3-26 (10 min.) **CVP, margin of safety.**

1. At the breakeven point:

$$\text{Fixed Costs} = \$323,850$$
$$\text{Contribution Margin Percentage} = \text{CM/Sales}$$
$$= \$323,850/\$2,159,000$$
$$= 15\%$$

2.

CM Percentage		= (Unit Selling Price – Unit VC)/Unit SP
	15%	= (USP - $17)/USP
	0.15USP	= 1.00USP - $17
	$17	= 0.85USP
	USP	= $20

3.

Revenues, 140,000 units × $20	$2,800,000
Breakeven revenues	2,159,000
Margin of safety	$ 641,000

3-28 (15 min.) **Gross margin and contribution margin, making decisions.**

1. Revenues $800,000
    Deduct variable costs:
        Cost of goods sold $384,000
        Sales commissions   96,000
        Other operating costs   32,000   512,000
    Contribution margin $288,000

2. Contribution margin percentage = $\dfrac{\$288,000}{\$800,000} = 36.00\%$

3. Incremental revenue (25% × $800,000)   = $200,000
    Incremental contribution margin
        (36% × $200,000) $72,000
    Incremental fixed costs (advertising)   24,300
    Incremental operating income $47,700

    If Mr. Saunders increases his advertising, the operating income will increase by $47,700 converting an operating loss of $44,700 to an operating income of $3,000.

Proof (Optional):
Variable Other Operating Costs = $32,000/$800,000 = 4% of sales

Revenues (125% × $800,000) $1,000,000
Cost of goods sold (48% of sales)   480,000
Gross margin   520,000

Operating costs:
Store rent   61,200
Salaries and wages $212,000
Sales commissions (12% of sales)   120,000
Amortization of equipment and fixtures   19,200
Other operating costs:
    Variable (4% of sales)   40,000
    Fixed   64,600   517,000
Operating income $ 3,000

29

3-30 (30 min.) CVP, international cost structure differences.

1a.

	India	China	Canada
Selling Price	$ 47.50	$ 47.50	$ 47.50
VC-Manufacturing	$ 5.20	$ 9.50	$ 19.30
VC-Distribution	$ 21.80	$ 18.40	$ 6.20
Total Variable Costs	$ 27.00	$ 27.90	$ 25.50
Unit CM	$ 20.50	$ 19.60	$ 22.00
Fixed Costs	$6,400,000	$4,400,000	$10,200,000
B/E point b/a (units)	312,196	224,490	463,637

B/E point in revenues (Units

1b. *$47.50)

	India	China	Canada
	$14,829,310	$10,663,275	$22,022,757

2.

	India	China	Canada
Volume	1,350,000	1,350,000	1,350,000
Total CM (Volume*UCM)	$ 27,675,000	$ 26,460,000	$ 29,700,000
Less Fixed Costs	$6,400,000	$4,400,000	$10,200,000
Forecasted OI	$ 21,275,000	$ 22,060,000	$ 19,500,000

China has the lowest breakeven point—it has the lowest fixed costs ($4,400,000) and its variable cost per unit ($27.90) is only marginally higher than India. While Canada has a higher per unit CM, the fixed costs are more than double those of China. The higher fixed costs add risk to operating in Canada (leverage).

3. China's OI = $19.60 per unit less Fixed Costs of $4,400,000
   Canada's OI = $22.00 per unit less Fixed Costs of $10,200,000

$19.60X - $4,400,000	=	$22.00X - $10,200,000
$5,800,000	=	$2.40X
X	=	2,416,666.667 (or 2,416,667)

Proof and India's Operating Income at same sales volume

	India	China	Canada
Unit CM	$ 20.50	$ 19.60	$ 22.00
Volume	2,416,666.667	2,416,666.667	2,416,666.667
Total CM (Volume * UCM)	$49,541,667	$ 47,366,667	$ 53,166,667
Less Fixed Costs	$6,400,000	$4,400,000	$10,200,000
Forecasted OI	$43,141,667	$ 42,966,667	$ 42,966,667

(Note: India's forecasted OI is slightly higher at this volume)

3-32 (30 min.) CVP, revenue mix

Zyrcon

1.

	Weighted	Alien Predators	Vegas Pokermatch
Revenue		$89	$59
Variable Manufacturing Costs		18	12
Variable Marketing Costs		27	16
Total Variable Costs		45	28
Unit CM		$44	$31
Sales Mix		40%	60%
Weighted CM	$36.20	$17.60	$18.60

Breakeven in total units	=	Fixed Costs/Weighted CM
	=	$18,750,000/$36.20
	=	517,956 units
40% of 517,596	=	207,183 units of Alien Predators
60% of 517,596	=	310,773 units of Vegas Pokermatch

Proof:

Total CM – Fixed Costs = OI

($44 * 207,183) + ($31 * 310,773) - $18,750,000 = OI

$9,116,052 + $9,633,963 - $18,750,000 = OI

OI = $15   (difference due to rounding of units)

2.

	Weighted	Alien Predators	Vegas Pokermatch
Revenue		$89	$59
Variable Manufacturing Costs		18	12
Variable Marketing Costs		27	16
Total Variable Costs		45	28
Unit CM		$44	$31
Sales Mix		25%	75%
Weighted CM	$34.25	$11.00	$23.25

Breakeven in total units	=	Fixed Costs/Weighted CM
	=	$18,750,000/$34.25
	=	547,446 units
25% of 547,446	=	136,862 units of Alien Predators
75% of 547,446	=	410,584 units of Vegas Pokermatch

Proof:

Total CM – Fixed Costs = OI

($44 *136,862) + ($31 *410,584) - $18,750,000 = OI

$6,021,928 + $12,728,104 - $18,750,000 = OI

OI = $32   (difference due to rounding of units)

3-32 (cont'd)

2.	Weighted	Alien Predators	Vegas Pokermatch
Revenue		$89	$59
Variable Manufacturing Costs		18	12
Variable Marketing Costs		27	16
Total Variable Costs		45	28
Unit CM		$44	$31
Sales Mix		60%	40%
Weighted CM	$38.80	$26.40	$12.40

Breakeven in total units	=	Fixed Costs/Weighted CM
	=	$18,750,000/$38.80
	=	483,248 units
60% of 483,248	=	289,949 units of Alien Predators
40% of 483,248	=	193,299 units of Vegas Pokermatch

Proof:
Total CM – Fixed Costs = OI
($44 *289,949) + ($31 *193,299) - $18,750,000 = OI
$12,757,756 + $5,992,269 - $18,750,000 = OI
OI = $25 (difference due to rounding of units)

2.	Weighted	Alien Predators	Vegas Pokermatch
Revenue		$89	$59
Variable Manufacturing Costs		18	12
Variable Marketing Costs		27	16
Total Variable Costs		45	28
Unit CM		$44	$31
Sales Mix		50%	50%
Weighted CM	$37.50	$22.00	$15.50

Breakeven in total units	=	Fixed Costs/Weighted CM
	=	$18,750,000/$37.50
	=	500,000 units
50% of 500,000	=	250,000 units of Alien Predators
50% of 500,000	=	250,000 units of Vegas Pokermatch

3-32 (cont'd)

Proof:
Total CM – Fixed Costs = OI
($44 *250,000) + ($31 *250,000) - $18,750,000 = OI
$11,000,000 + $7,750,000 - $18,750,000 = OI
OI = $0

3.	40%/60% Mix	25%/75% Mix	60%/40% Mix	50%/50% Mix
Weighted CM	$36.20	$34.25	$38.80	$37.50
Unit Sales	750,000	750,000	750,000	750,000
Total CM	$27,150,000	$25,687,500	$29,100,000	$28,125,000
Fixed Costs	18,750,000	18,750,000	18,750,000	18,750,000
OI	$8,400,000	$6,937,500	$10,350,000	$9,375,000

3-34 (40 min.) Alternative cost structures, uncertainty, and sensitivity analysis.

1. Contribution margin assuming fixed rental arrangement = $50 – $30 = $20 per bouquet
   Fixed costs = $5,000
   Breakeven point = $5,000 ÷ $20 per bouquet = 250 bouquets

   Contribution margin assuming $10 per arrangement rental agreement
   = $50 – $30 – $10 = $10 per bouquet
   Fixed costs = $0
   Breakeven point = $0 ÷ $10 per bouquet = 0
   (i.e. EB makes a profit no matter how few bouquets it sells)

2. Let x denote the number of bouquets EB must sell for it to be indifferent between the fixed rent and royalty agreement.

   To calculate x we solve the following equation.
   $$\$50x - \$30x - \$5,000 = \$50x - \$40x$$
   $$\$20x - \$5,000 = \$10x$$
   $$\$10x = \$5,000$$
   $$x = \$5,000 ÷ \$10 = 500 \text{ bouquets}$$

   For sales between 0 to 500 bouquets, EB prefers the royalty agreement because in this range, $\$10x > \$20x - \$5,000$. For sales greater than 500 bouquets, EB prefers the fixed rent agreement because in this range, $\$20x - \$5,000 > \$10x$.

3-34 (cont'd)

3. If we assume the $5 savings in variable costs applies to both options, we solve the following equation for x.

$50 x - $25 x - $5,000 = $50 x - $35 x

$25 x - $5,000 = $15 x

$10 x = $5,000

$x = $5,000 \div 10 per bouquet = 500 bouquets

The answer is the same as in Requirement 2, that is, for sales between 0 to 500 bouquets, EB prefers the royalty agreement because in this range, $15 x > $25 x - $5,000. For sales greater than 500 bouquets, EB prefers the fixed rent agreement because in this range, $25 x - $5,000 > $15 x.

4. Fixed rent agreement:

Bouquets Sold (1)	Revenue (2)	Fixed Costs (3)	Variable Costs (4)	Operating Income (Loss) (5)=(2)–(3)–(4)	Probability (6)	Expected Operating Income (7)=(5)×(6)
200	200×$50=$10,000	$5,000	200×$30=$ 6,000	$ (1,000)	0.20	$ (200)
400	400×$50=$20,000	$5,000	400×$30=$12,000	$ 3,000	0.20	600
600	600×$50=$30,000	$5,000	600×$30=$18,000	$ 7,000	0.20	1,400
800	800×$50=$40,000	$5,000	800×$30=$24,000	$11,000	0.20	2,200
1,000	1,000×$50=$50,000	$5,000	1,000×$30=$30,000	$15,000	0.20	3,000
Expected value of rent agreement						$7,000

Royalty agreement:

Bouquets Sold (1)	Revenue (2)	Variable Costs (3)	Operating Income (4)=(2)–(3)	Probability (5)	Expected Operating Income (6)=(4)×(5)
200	200×$50=$10,000	200×$40=$ 8,000	$2,000	0.20	$ 400
400	400×$50=$20,000	400×$40=$16,000	$4,000	0.20	800
600	600×$50=$30,000	600×$40=$24,000	$6,000	0.20	1,200
800	800×$50=$40,000	800×$40=$32,000	$8,000	0.20	1,600
1,000	1,000×$50=$50,000	1,000×$40=$40,000	$10,000	0.20	2,000
Expected value of royalty agreement					$6,000

EB should choose the fixed rent agreement because the expected value is higher than the royalty agreement. EB will lose money under the fixed rent agreement if EB sells only 200 bouquets but this loss is more than made up for by high operating incomes when sales are high.

3-36 (15-20 min.)   Uncertainty, CVP.

1. King pays Couture $3.2 million plus $6.75 (25% of $27.00) for every home purchasing the pay-per-view. The expected value of the variable component is:

Demand (1)	Payment (2) = (1) × $6.75	Probability (3)	Expected payment (4) = (2) × (3)
250,000	$ 1,687,500	0.05	$ 84,375
300,000	2,025,000	0.10	202,500
350,000	2,362,500	0.20	472,500
400,000	2,700,000	0.40	1,080,000
500,000	3,375,000	0.15	506,250
1,000,000	6,750,000	0.10	675,000
			$3,020,625

The expected value of King's payment is $6,220,625 ($3,200,000 fixed fee + $3,020,625).

2. USP = $27.00
    UVC = $9.00 ($6.75 payment to Couture + $2.25 variable cost)
    UCM = $18.00
    FC = $3,200,000 + $1,300,000 = $4,500,000

$$Q = \frac{FC}{UCM} = \$4,500,000/\$18 = 250,000$$

If 250,000 homes purchase the pay-per-view, King will break even.

3-38 (15-20 min.) CVP analysis, service firm.

1. Revenue per package $9,200
    Variable cost per package   6,340
    Contribution margin per package $2,860

    Breakeven (units) = Fixed costs ÷ Contribution margin per package
                       = $1,287,000/$2,860   =   450 package tours

2. Contribution margin ratio = $\dfrac{\text{Contribution margin per package}}{\text{Selling price}}$ = $2,860/$9,200

    =31.09%

    Units needed to achieve target income= (Fixed costs + target OI) ÷UCM
                            = ($1,287,000 + $214,500)/$2,860 = 525 packages

    Revenues to earn $214,500 OI = 525 tour packages × $9,200= $4,830,000

    Or

    Revenue to achieve target income   = (Fixed costs + target OI) ÷ CM ratio
                                       = ($1,287,000 + $214,500)/.3109
                                       = $4,829,527 (rounding difference)

3. Fixed costs = $1,287,000+ $40,500= $1,327,500

    Breakeven (units) = $\dfrac{\text{Fixed costs}}{\text{Contribution margin per unit}}$

    Contribution margin per unit   = $1,327,500 /450

                                     = $2,950 per tour package

    Desired variable cost per tour package = $9,200– $2,950 = $6,250

    Because the current variable cost per unit is $6,340 the unit variable cost will need to be reduced by $90 to achieve the breakeven point calculated in requirement 1.

    Alternate Method: If fixed cost increases by $40,500 then total variable costs must be reduced by $40,500 or $40,500/450 or $90 per package tour.

3-40 (30 min.) CVP, target income, service firm.

1.

Revenue per child	$600
Variable costs per child	200
Contribution margin per child	$400

$$\text{Breakeven quantity} = \frac{\text{Fixed costs}}{\text{Contribution margin per child}}$$

$$= \frac{\$5,600}{\$400} = 14 \text{ children}$$

2.

$$\text{Target quantity} = \frac{\text{Fixed costs} + \text{Target operating income}}{\text{Contribution margin per child}}$$

$$= \frac{\$5,600 + \$10,400}{\$400} = 40 \text{ children}$$

3.

Increase in rent ($3,000 – $2,000)	$1,000
Field trips	1,000
Total increase in fixed costs	$2,000
Divide by the number of children enrolled	÷ 40
Increase in fee per child	$ 50

Therefore, the fee per child will increase from $600 to $650.

Alternatively,

$$\text{New contribution margin per child} = \frac{\$5,600 + \$2,000 + \$10,400}{40} = \$450$$

New fee per child = Variable costs per child + New contribution margin per child
= $200 + $450 = $650

3-42 (20-30 min.) CVP, shoe stores.

1. UCM (SP – UVC = $30 – $21)	$ 9.00
a. Breakeven units (FC ÷ UCM = $360,000 ÷ $9 per unit)	40,000
b. Breakeven revenues	
(Breakeven units × SP = 40,000 units × $30 per unit)	$1,200,000

3-42 (cont'd)

2. Pairs sold	35,000
Revenues, 35,000 × $30	$1,050,000
Total cost of shoes, 35,000 × $19.50	682,500
Total sales commissions, 35,000 × $1.50	52,500
Total variable costs	735,000
Contribution margin	315,000
Fixed costs	360,000
Operating income (loss)	$ (45,000)

3. Unit variable data (per pair of shoes)	
Selling price	$ 30.00
Cost of shoes	19.50
Sales commissions	0
Variable cost per unit	$ 19.50
Annual fixed costs	
Rent	$ 60,000
Salaries, $200,000 + $81,000	281,000
Advertising	80,000
Other fixed costs	20,000
Total fixed costs	$ 441,000
UCM, $30 – $19.50	$ 10.50
a. Breakeven units, $441,000 ÷ $10.50 per unit	42,000
b. Breakeven revenues, 42,000 units × $30 per unit	$1,260,000

4. Unit variable data (per pair of shoes)	
Selling price	$ 30.00
Cost of shoes	19.50
Sales commissions	1.80
Variable cost per unit	$ 21.30
Total fixed costs	$ 360,000

3-42 (cont'd)

UCM, $30 – $21.30	$ 8.70
a. Break even units = $360,000 ÷ $8.70 per unit	41,380 (rounded up)
b. Break even revenues = 41,380 units × $30 per unit	$1,241,400

5. Pairs sold	50,000
Revenues (50,000 pairs × $30 per pair)	$1,500,000
Total cost of shoes (50,000 pairs × $19.50 per pair)	$ 975,000
Sales commissions on first 40,000 pairs (40,000 pairs × $1.50 per pair)	60,000
Sales commissions on additional 10,000 pairs	
[10,000 pairs × ($1.50 + $0.30 per pair)]	18,000
Total variable costs	$1,053,000
Contribution margin	$ 447,000
Fixed costs	360,000
Operating income	$ 87,000

Alternative approach:

Breakeven point in units = 40,000 pairs
Store manager receives commission of $0.30 on 10,000 (50,000 – 40,000) pairs.
Contribution margin per pair beyond breakeven point of 10,000 pairs
= $8.70 ($30 – $21 – $0.30) per pair.
Operating income = 10,000 pairs × $8.70 contribution margin per pair = $87,000.

3-44 (30 min.) Uncertainty and expected costs.

1.

Monthly Number of Orders	Cost of Current System
300,000	$1,000,000 + $40(300,000) = $13,000,000
400,000	$1,000,000 + $40(400,000) = $17,000,000
500,000	$1,000,000 + $40(500,000) = $21,000,000
600,000	$1,000,000 + $40(600,000) = $25,000,000
700,000	$1,000,000 + $40(700,000) = $29,000,000

Monthly Number of Orders	Cost of Partially Automated System
300,000	$5,000,000 + $30(300,000) = $14,000,000
400,000	$5,000,000 + $30(400,000) = $17,000,000
500,000	$5,000,000 + $30(500,000) = $20,000,000
600,000	$5,000,000 + $30(600,000) = $23,000,000
700,000	$5,000,000 + $30(700,000) = $26,000,000

Monthly Number of Orders	Cost of Fully Automated System
300,000	$10,000,000 + $20(300,000) = $16,000,000
400,000	$10,000,000 + $20(400,000) = $18,000,000
500,000	$10,000,000 + $20(500,000) = $20,000,000
600,000	$10,000,000 + $20(600,000) = $22,000,000
700,000	$10,000,000 + $20(700,000) = $24,000,000

2. Current System Expected Cost:

$13,000,000 × 0.1	= $	1,300,000
17,000,000 × 0.25	=	4,250,000
21,000,000 × 0.40	=	8,400,000
25,000,000 × 0.15	=	3,750,000
29,000,000 × 0.10	=	2,900,000
		$ 20,600,000

Partially Automated System Expected Cost:

$14,000,000 × 0.1	= $	1 ,400,000
17,000,000 × 0.25	=	4,250,000
20,000,000 × 0.40	=	8,000,000
23,000,000 × 0.15	=	3,450,000
26,000,000 × 0.1	=	2,600,000
		$19,700,000

3-44 (cont'd)

Fully Automated System Expected Cost:

$16,000,000 × 0.1 = $ 1,600,000
18,000,000 × 0.25 =   4,500,000
20,000,000 × 0.40 =   8,000,000
22,000,000 × 0.15 =   3,300,000
24,000,000 × 0.10 =   2,400,000
                    $19,800,000

3. Dawmart should consider the impact of the different systems on its relationship with suppliers. The interface with Dawmart's system may require that suppliers also update their systems. This could cause some suppliers to raise the cost of their merchandise. It could force other suppliers to drop out of Dawmart's supply chain because the cost of the system change would be prohibitive. Dawmart may also want to consider other factors such as the reliability of different systems and the effect on employee morale if employees have to be laid off as it automates its systems.

3-46 (20–25 min.)   Sales mix, two products.

1.   Sales of standard and deluxe carriers are in the ratio of 150,000 : 50,000. So for every 1 unit of deluxe, 3 (150,000 ÷ 50,000) units of standard are sold.

Contribution margin of the bundle = 3 × $6 + 1 × $12 = $18 + $12 = $30

Breakeven point in bundles = $\dfrac{\$1,200,000}{\$30}$ = 40,000 bundles

Breakeven point in units is:

Standard carrier:	40,000 bundles × 3 units per bundle	120,000 units
Deluxe carrier:	40,000 bundles × 1 unit per bundle	40,000 units
Total number of units to breakeven		160,000 units

Alternatively,

Let Q = Number of units of Deluxe carrier to break even

   3Q = Number of units of Standard carrier to break even

Revenues – Variable costs – Fixed costs = Zero operating income

$$\$20(3Q) + \$30Q - \$14(3Q) - \$18Q - \$1,200,000 = 0$$
$$\$60Q + \$30Q - \$42Q - \$18Q = \$1,200,000$$
$$\$30Q = \$1,200,000$$
$$Q = 40,000 \text{ units of Deluxe}$$
$$3Q = 120,000 \text{ units of Standard}$$

The breakeven point is 120,000 Standard units plus 40,000 Deluxe units, a total of 160,000 units.

2a.   Unit contribution margins are: Standard: $20 – $14 = $6; Deluxe: $30 – $18 = $12
      If only Standard carriers were sold, the breakeven point would be:
      $1,200,000 ÷ $6 = 200,000 units.

2b.   If only Deluxe carriers were sold, the breakeven point would be:
      $1,200,000 ÷ $12 = 100,000 units

3. Operating income = Contribution margin of Standard + Contribution margin of Deluxe - Fixed costs
      = 180,000($6) + 20,000($12) – $1,200,000
      = $1,080,000 + $240,000 – $1,200,000
      = $120,000

Sales of standard and deluxe carriers are in the ratio of 180,000 : 20,000. So for every 1 unit of deluxe, 9 (180,000 ÷ 20,000) units of standard are sold.

Contribution margin of the bundle = 9 × $6 + 1 × $12 = $54 + $12 = $66

Breakeven point in bundles = $\dfrac{\$1,200,000}{\$66}$ = 18,182 bundles (rounded up)

3-46 (cont'd)

Breakeven point in units is:

Standard carrier:	18,182 bundles × 9 units per bundle	163,638 units
Deluxe carrier:	18,182 bundles × 1 unit per bundle	18,182 units
Total number of units to breakeven		181,820 units

Alternatively,

Let Q = Number of units of Deluxe product to break even

9Q = Number of units of Standard product to break even

$$\$20(9Q) + \$30Q - \$14(9Q) - \$18Q - \$1,200,000 = 0$$
$$\$180Q + \$30Q - \$126Q - \$18Q = \$1,200,000$$
$$\$66Q = \$1,200,000$$
$$Q = 18,182 \text{ units of Deluxe (rounded up)}$$
$$9Q = 163,638 \text{ units of Standard}$$

The breakeven point is 163,638 Standard + 18,182 Deluxe, a total of 181,820 units.

The major lesson of this problem is that changes in the sales mix change breakeven points and operating incomes. In this example, the budgeted and actual total sales in number of units were identical, but the proportion of the product having the higher contribution margin declined. Operating income suffered, falling from $300,000 to $120,000. Moreover, the breakeven point rose from 160,000 to 181,820 units.

3-48 (20 min.) CVP, cost structure differences, movie production (continuation of 3-47).

1. Contract A

Fixed costs for Contract A:

Production costs	$32,000,000
Fixed salary	50,000,000
Total fixed costs	$82,000,000

Unit variable cost = 8% + 8% + 18% = 34% or $0.34 per $1 revenue marketing fee

Unit contribution margin = $0.66 per $1 revenue

(a) Breakeven point in revenues $= \dfrac{\text{Fixed costs}}{\text{Unit contribution margin per \$1 revenue}}$

$$= \$82,000,000/\$0.66$$
$$= \$124,242,425 \text{ (rounded)}$$

Breakeven point in box office sales $= \$124,242,425/0.65$
$$= \$191,142,192 \text{ (rounded)}$$

3-48 (cont'd)

Contract B
    Fixed costs for Contract B:

Production costs	$32,000,000
Fixed salary	8,000,000
Total fixed costs	$40,000,000

Unit variable cost = $0.18 per $1 revenue fee to Parimont Productions
[3%+3%+8%+8%] $0.22 per $1 revenue residual to directors/actors
                    $0.40 per $1 revenue

Unit contribution margin = $0.60 per $1 revenue

Breakeven point in revenues = $40,000,000/$0.60 = $66,666,667 (rounded)
Breakeven point in box office sales = $66,666,667/0.65
                            = $102,564,103 (rounded)

Difference in Breakeven Points
Contract A has a higher fixed cost and a lower variable cost per sales dollar. In contrast, Contract B has a lower fixed cost and a higher variable cost per sales dollar. In Contract B, there is more risk-sharing between Panther and the actors that lowers the breakeven point, but results in Panther receiving less operating income if the film is a mega-success.

2.

Contract A:

Revenues, 0.65 × $280,000,000	$182,000,000
Variable costs, 0.34 × $182,000,000	61,880,000
Contribution margin	120,120,000
Fixed costs	82,000,000
Operating income	$38,120,000

Contract B:

Revenues, 0.65 × $280,000,000	$182,000,000
Variable costs, 0.4 × $182,000,000	72,800,000
Contribution margin	109,200,000
Fixed costs	40,000,000
Operating income	$69,200,000

3-48 (cont'd)

Contract A has a higher breakeven point than Contract B, because it has a higher level of fixed costs and a lower unit contribution margin. This means after breakeven is reached, under Contract A, $0.66 of every additional revenue dollar will contribute to OI, but under Contract B only $0.60 of every additional revenue dollar will contribute to OI. However, the fixed costs for Contract A are significantly higher than for Contract B.

At the predicted level of box office receipts, Contract B is the more lucrative contract.

The point of indifference (in terms of revenue to Panther) (not required in question)
($1.00- $0.34R) - $82,000,000 =   ($1.00- $0.40) - $40,000,000
$0.66R - $0.60R   = $42,000,000
              R   = $700,000,000

It seems highly unlikely the film will gross enough box office receipts to generate $700 million of revenue to Panther. Panther should select Contract B.

3-50 (30 min.) Choosing between compensation plans, operating leverage. (CMA adapted)

1. We can recast Marston's income statement to emphasize contribution margin, and then use it to compute the required CVP parameters.

Marston Corporation
Income Statement
For the Year Ended December 31, 2008

	Using Sales Agents		Using Own Sales Force	
Revenues		$26,000,000		$26,000,000
Variable Costs				
Cost of goods sold — variable	$11,700,000		$11,700,000	
Marketing commissions	4,680,000	16,380,000	2,600,000	14,300,000
Contribution margin		$9,620,000		$11,700,000
Fixed Costs				
Cost of goods sold — fixed	2,870,000		2,870,000	
Marketing — fixed	3,420,000	6,290,000	5,500,000	8,370,000
Operating income		$3,330,000		$ 3,330,000
Contribution margin percentage ($9,620,000 ÷ 26,000,000; $11,700,000 ÷ $26,000,000)		37%		45%
Breakeven revenues ($6,290,000 ÷ 0.37; $8,370,000 ÷ 0.45)		$17,000,000		$18,600,000
Degree of operating leverage ($9,620,000 ÷ $3,330,000; $11,700,000 ÷ $3,330,000)		2.89		3.51

2. The calculations indicate that at sales of $26,000,000, a percentage change in sales and contribution margin will result in 2.89 times that percentage change in operating income if Marston continues to use sales agents and 3.51 times that percentage change in operating income if Marston employs its own sales staff. The higher contribution margin per dollar of sales and higher fixed costs gives Marston more operating leverage, that is, greater benefits (increases in operating income) if revenues increase but greater risks (decreases in operating income) if revenues decrease. Marston also needs to consider the skill levels and incentives under the two alternatives. Sales agents have more incentive compensation and hence may be more motivated to increase sales. On the other hand, Marston's own sales force may be more knowledgeable and skilled in selling the company's products. That is, the sales volume itself will be affected by who sells and by the nature of the compensation plan.

3-50 (cont'd)

3. Variable costs of marketing = 15% of Revenues
    Fixed marketing costs = $5,500,000

Operating income = Revenues − $\begin{matrix} \text{Variable} \\ \text{manuf. costs} \end{matrix}$ − $\begin{matrix} \text{Fixed} \\ \text{manuf. costs} \end{matrix}$ − $\begin{matrix} \text{Variable} \\ \text{marketing} \\ \text{costs} \end{matrix}$ − $\begin{matrix} \text{Fixed} \\ \text{marketing} \\ \text{costs} \end{matrix}$

Denote the revenues required to earn $3,330,000 of operating income by R, then

$$R - 0.45R - \$2,870,000 - 0.15R - \$5,500,000 = \$3,330,000$$
$$R - 0.45R - 0.15R = \$3,330,000 + \$2,870,000 + \$5,500,000$$
$$0.40R = \$11,700,000$$
$$R = \$11,700,000 \div 0.40 = \$29,250,000$$

3-52 (25 min.) CVP, sensitivity analysis.

Contribution margin per corkscrew = $4 − 3 = $1
Fixed costs = $6,000
Units sold = Total sales ÷ Selling price = $40,000 ÷ $4 per corkscrew = 10,000 corkscrews

1. Sales increase 10%

Sales revenues 10,000 × 1.10 × $4.00	$44,000
Variable costs 10,000 × 1.10 × $3.00	33,000
Contribution margin	11,000
Fixed costs	6,000
Operating income	$ 5,000

2. Increase fixed costs $2,000; Increase sales 50%

Sales revenues 10,000 × 1.50 × $4.00	$60,000
Variable costs 10,000 × 1.50 × $3.00	45,000
Contribution margin	15,000
Fixed costs ($6,000 + $2,000)	8,000
Operating income	$ 7,000

3. Increase selling price to $5.00; Sales decrease 20%

Sales revenues 10,000 × 0.80 × $5.00	$40,000
Variable costs 10,000 × 0.80 × $3.00	24,000
Contribution margin	16,000
Fixed costs	6,000
Operating income	$10,000

3-52 (cont'd)

4. Increase selling price to $6.00; Variable costs increase $1 per corkscrew

Sales revenues 10,000 × $6.00	$60,000
Variable costs 10,000 × $4.00	40,000
Contribution margin	20,000
Fixed costs	6,000
Operating income	$14,000

Alternative 4 yields the highest operating income. If TOP is confident that unit sales will not decrease despite increasing the selling price, it should choose alternative 4.

3-54 (30 min.) CVP, nonprofit event planning.

1. Computation of fixed costs.

	Hotel	University
Rental cost of venue	$2,700	$ 7,000
Permits	0	500
Chamber administration/marketing	5,000	5,000
Entertainment	4,000	4,000
	$11,700	$16,500

Computation of contribution margin per person:

	Hotel	University
Selling (ticket) price per person	$175	$175
Catering cost per person	110	75
Contribution margin per person	$65	$100

$$\text{Breakeven point} = \frac{\text{Fixed costs}}{\text{Unit contribution margin}}$$

Breakeven point for Hotel venue = $11,700/$65 = 180 tickets

Breakeven point for University venue = $16,500/$100 = 165 tickets

3-54 (cont'd)

2.   Operating Income Projections with 100 attendees and 250 attendees

Hotel

Attendees	100	250
Ticket Price	$175	$175
Total Revenues	$17,500	$43,750
VC @ $110	11,000	27,500
CM	6,500	16,250
Fixed Costs	11,700	11,700
Operating Income	$(5,200)	$4,550

University

Attendees	100	250
Ticket Price	$175	$175
Total Revenues	$17,500	$43,750
VC @ $75	7,500	18,750
CM	10,000	25,000
Fixed Costs	16,500	16,500
Operating Income	$(6,500)	$8,500

The Hotel venue has higher variable costs per person and lower fixed costs. In contrast, the University venue has lower variable costs per person and higher fixed costs.

3.   Requirement 2 gives the operating income equation for each venue. Setting these two equations equal and solving for Q gives the level of ticket sales at which the operating incomes for the two venues are equal:

$$\$175Q - \$110Q - \$11,700 = \$175Q - \$75Q - \$16,500$$
$$\$100Q - \$65Q = \$16,500 - \$11,700$$
$$\$35Q = \$4,800$$
$$Q = 137 \text{ (rounded)}$$

Above 137, the University venue will yield higher operating income (or a lower operating loss) than the hotel venue.

3-54 (cont'd)

Proof:

	Hotel	University
Attendees	137.14286	137.14286
Ticket Price	175	175
Total Revenues	24,000	24,000
VC @ $110; $75	15,086	10,286
CM	8,914	13,714
Fixed Costs	11,700	16,500
Operating Income	(2,786)	(2,786)

3-56 (20-30 min.) CVP under uncertainty.

1. (a) At a selling price of $120, the unit contribution margin is ($120 – $60) = $60, and it will require the sale of ($240,000 ÷ $60) = 4,000 units to break even. The sales in dollars are $480,000 and there is a 2/3 probability of equalling or exceeding this sales level—that is, that 2/3 of the area under the graph exists between $480,000 and $720,000.

   (b) At a selling price of $84, the unit contribution margin is ($84 – $60) = $24, and it will require the sale of ($240,000 ÷ $24) = 10,000 units to break even. At the lower price, the sales in dollars are $840,000 and there is a 2/3 probability of equalling or exceeding this sales volume.

   Therefore, if you seek to maximize the probability of showing an operating income, you are indifferent between the two strategies.

2. $$\text{Expected operating income} = \left[\left(\begin{array}{c}\text{Selling} \\ \text{price per unit}\end{array} - \begin{array}{c}\text{Variable} \\ \text{cost per unit}\end{array}\right) \times \left(\begin{array}{c}\text{Expected} \\ \text{sales} \\ \text{level}\end{array}\right)\right] - \left(\begin{array}{c}\text{Fixed} \\ \text{costs}\end{array}\right)$$

   At a selling price of $120:

Expected revenues	=	$540,000 ($120 × 4,500)
Expected operating income	=	[($120 – $60) × 4,500] – $240,000
	=	$30,000

3-56 (cont'd)

At a selling price of $84:

Expected revenues   = $900,000 ($84 × 10,715)
Expected operating income   =   [($84 – $60) × 10,715] – $240,000
                                     = $17,160

A selling price of $120 will maximize the expected operating income.

3-58 (15-20 min.) Short-run pricing, budgeting, capacity constraints.

1. Per kilogram of hard cheese:

Milk (10 liters × $1.50 per liter)	$15
Direct manufacturing labour	5
Variable manufacturing overhead	3
Fixed manufacturing cost allocated	6
Total manufacturing cost	$29

If Tillsonburg can get all the Holstein milk it needs, and has sufficient production capacity, then, the minimum price per kilo it should charge for the hard cheese is the variable cost per kilo = $15+5+3 = $23 per kilo.

2.   If milk is in short supply, then each kilo of hard cheese displaces 2.5 kilos of soft cheese (10 litres of milk per kilo of hard cheese versus 4 litres of milk per kilo of soft cheese). Then, for the hard cheese, the minimum price Tillsonburg should charge is the variable cost per kilo of hard cheese plus the contribution margin from 2.5 kilos of soft cheese, or,

$$\$23 + (2.5 \times \$8 \text{ per kilo}) = \$43 \text{ per kilo}$$

That is, if milk is in short supply, Tillsonburg should not agree to produce any hard cheese unless the buyer is willing to pay at least $43 per kilo.

3-60 (20-25 min.)   Governance, CVP, cost analysis.

1. (a) USP = $68
       UVC = $28.50 ($19.25+ $9.25)
       UCM = $39.50
       FC   = $25,000,000
       Q   = FC/UCM
            = $25,000,000/$39.50
            = 632,912 monthly treatments (rounded up)

   (b) USP = $68
       UVC = $19.25
       UCM = $48.75
       FC   = $25,000,000
       Q   = FC/UCM
            = $25,000,000/$48.75
            = 512,821 monthly treatments (rounded up)

2. Diba believes that the $9.25 per monthly visit should be included in the variable costs per visit. His argument is that a product like "Vital Hair" has a positive probability of attracting product litigation. By excluding any allowance for the possible event, the assumption is that it will be zero.

   Diba faces an integrity issue. His report to the Executive Committee will understate his expected cost estimates when he takes Kelly's advice. His report likely will be seen by those not attending the Executive Committee meeting. Moreover, even those attending the meeting may not remember any verbal comments Diba makes at the meeting.

   One possibility Diba should have explored is reporting the $19.25 per treatment variable cost in the breakeven computations as well as including qualifications in the report about possible product litigation costs.

3. Diba likely has been placed in a compromised situation. He may feel Kelly deliberately set him up to avoid the $9.25 amount being reported to the Executive Committee. At a minimum, he should directly confront Kelly with his concerns. If she is unresponsive, he faces a very tough dilemma. His options are:
   (a) Stay in his current position and be more determined next time to have his concerns registered.
   (b) Report his concerns to Kelly's immediate superior.
   (c) Resign.

   If he selects (a), it would be useful to show Kelly the Code of Professional Ethics and stress how her behaviour has put him in a difficult ethical situation.

3-62 (35 min.) Deciding where to produce.

	Peona		Modine	
Selling price		$150.00		$150.00
Variable cost per unit				
Manufacturing	$72.00		$88.00	
Marketing and distribution	14.00	86.00	14.00	102.00
Contribution margin per unit (CMU)		64.00		48.00
Fixed costs per unit				
Manufacturing	30.00		15.00	
Marketing and distribution	19.00	49.00	14.50	29.50
Operating income per unit		$ 15.00		$ 18.50
CMU of normal production (as shown above)		$64		$48
CMU of overtime production ($64 – $3; $48 – $8)		61		40

1.

Annual fixed costs = Fixed cost per unit × Daily production rate × Normal annual capacity ($49 ×400 units × 240 days; $29.50 × 320 units × 240 days)	$4,704,000		$2,265,600	
Breakeven volume = FC ÷ CMU of normal production ($4,704,000 ÷ $64; $2,265,600 ÷ 48)	73,500	units	47,200	Units

2.

	Peona	Modine
Units produced and sold	96,000	96,000
Normal annual volume (units) (400 × 240; 320 × 240)	96,000	76,800
Units over normal volume (needing overtime)	0	19,200
CM from normal production units (normal annual volume × CMU normal production) (96,000 × $64; 76,800 × 48)	$6,144,000	$3,686,400
CM from overtime production units (0; 19,200 × $40)	0	768,000
Total contribution margin	6,144,000	4,454,400
Total fixed costs	4,704,000	2,265,600
Operating income	$1,440,000	$2,188,800
Total operating income		$3,628,800

3-62 (cont'd)

3.   The optimal production plan is to produce 120,000 units at the Peona plant and 72,000 units at the Modine plant. The full capacity of the Peona plant, 120,000 units (400 units × 300 days), should be used because the contribution from these units is higher at all levels of production than is the contribution from units produced at the Modine plant.

Contribution margin per plant:	
Peona, 96,000 × $64	$ 6,144,000
Peona 24,000 × ($64 – $3)	1,464,000
Modine, 72,000 × $48	3,456,000
Total contribution margin	11,064,000
Deduct total fixed costs	6,969,600
Operating income	$ 4,094,400

The contribution margin is higher when 120,000 units are produced at the Peona plant and 72,000 units at the Modine plant. As a result, operating income will also be higher in this case since total fixed costs for the division remain unchanged regardless of the quantity produced at each plant.

CHAPTER 4
JOB COSTING SERVICES AND GOODS

4-2 In a *job costing system,* costs are assigned to a distinct unit, batch, or a lot of a product or service. In a *process costing system*, the cost of a product or service is obtained by using broad averages to assign costs to masses of similar units.

4-4 Similar to question 4-3, separating costs by departments may result in grouping overhead costs that have similar cause and effect relationships. For example, the nature of overhead costs in a heavily automated department are likely to differ from the types of overhead costs incurred in a labour intensive department. Separating these costs into two pools will allow for selection of different cost drivers and should result in improved cost allocation, leading to improved pricing and decision making.

4-6 Three major source documents used in job-costing systems are (1) job cost record or job cost sheet, a document that records and accumulates all costs assigned to a specific job, (2) materials requisition record, a document used to charge job cost records and departments for the cost of direct materials used on a specific job, and (3) labour-time record, a document used to charge job cost records and departments for labour time used on a specific job.

4-8 Two reasons for using annual budget periods are:
   a. The numerator reason—the longer the time period, the lesser the influence of seasonal patterns, and
   b. The denominator reason—the longer the time period, the lesser the effect of variations in output levels on the allocation of fixed costs.

4-10 A construction firm can use job cost information (a) to determine the profitability of individual jobs, (b) to assist on bidding on future jobs, and (c) to evaluate professionals who are in charge of managing individual jobs.

4-12 Debit entries to Work-in-Process Control represent increases in work in process. Examples of debit entries are: (a) direct materials used (credit to Materials Control), (b) direct manufacturing labour billed to job (credit to Wages Payable Control), and (c) manufacturing overhead allocated to job (credit Manufacturing Overhead Allocated).

4-14 A service company might use budgeted costs rather than actual costs to compute direct labour rates because it may be difficult to trace some costs to jobs as they are completed.

4-16 (10 min.) **Job order costing, process costing.**

a. Job costing
b. Process costing
c. Job costing
d. Process costing (unless specialty)
e. Job costing
f. Process costing
g. Job costing
h. Job or process (depending on production)
i. Process costing
j. Process costing
k. Job costing

l. Job costing
m. Process costing
n. Job costing
o. Job costing
p. Job costing
q. Job costing
r. Process costing
s. Job costing
t. Process costing
u. Job costing

4-18 (20 - 30 min.) **Job costing; actual, normal, and variation from normal costing.**

1.   Actual direct-cost rate for professional labour = $58 per professional labour-hour

$$\text{Actual indirect-cost rate} = \frac{\$744,000}{15,500 \text{ hours}} = \$48 \quad \text{per}$$

professional labour-hour

Budgeted direct-cost rate
for professional labour $= \dfrac{\$960,000}{16,000 \text{ hours}} = \$60$ per professional labour-hour

$$\text{Budgeted indirect-cost rate} = \frac{\$720,000}{16,000 \text{ hours}} = \$45 \text{ per professional labour-hour}$$

	(a) Actual Costing	(b) Normal Costing	(c) Variation of Normal Costing
Direct-Cost Rate	$58 (Actual rate)	$58 (Actual rate)	$60 (Budgeted rate)
Indirect-Cost Rate	$48 (Actual rate)	$45 (Budgeted rate)	$45 (Budgeted rate)

4-18 (cont'd)

2.

	(a) Actual Costing	(b) Normal Costing	(c) Variation of Normal Costing
Direct Costs	$58 × 120 = $ 6,960	$58 × 120 = $ 6,960	$60 × 120 = $ 7,200
Indirect Costs	48 × 120 = 5,760	45 × 120 = 5,400	45 × 120 = 5,400
Total Job Costs	$12,720	$12,360	$12,600

All three costing systems use the actual professional labour time of 120 hours. The budgeted 110 hours for the Pierre Enterprises audit job is not used in job costing. However, Chirac may have used the 110 hour number in bidding for the audit.

The actual costing figure of $12,720 exceeds the normal costing figure of $12,360 because the actual indirect-cost rate ($48) exceeds the budgeted indirect-cost rate ($45). The normal costing figure of $12,360 is less than the variation of normal costing (based on budgeted rates for direct costs) figure of $12,600, because the actual direct-cost rate ($58) is less than the budgeted direct-cost rate ($60).

4-20 (20 -30 min.) Job costing, normal and actual costing.
1.

$$\text{Budgeted indirect-cost rate} = \frac{\text{Budgeted indirect costs}}{\text{Budgeted direct labour-hours}} = \frac{\$8,000,000}{160,000 \text{ hours}}$$

$$= \$50 \text{ per direct labour-hour}$$

$$\text{Actual indirect-cost rate} = \frac{\text{Actual indirect costs}}{\text{Actual direct labour-hours}} = \frac{\$6,888,000}{164,000 \text{ hours}}$$

$$= \$42 \text{ per direct labour-hour}$$

These rates differ because both the numerator and the denominator in the two calculations are different—one based on budgeted numbers and the other based on actual numbers.

4-20 (cont'd)

2a.

	Laguna Model	Mission Model
Normal costing		
Direct costs		
Direct materials	$106,450	$127,604
Direct labour	36,276	41,410
	142,726	169,014
Indirect costs		
Assembly support ($50 × 900; $50 × 1,010)	45,000	50,500
Total costs	$187,726	$219,514

2b.

	Laguna Model	Mission Model
Actual costing		
Direct costs		
Direct materials	$106,450	$127,604
Direct labour	36,276	41,410
	142,726	169,014
Indirect costs		
Assembly support ($42 × 900; $42 × 1,010)	37,800	42,420
Total costs	$180,526	$211,434

3.   Normal costing enables Anderson to report a job cost as soon as the job is completed, assuming that both the direct materials and direct labour costs are known at the time of use. Once the 900 direct labour-hours are known for the Laguna Model (June 2010), Anderson can compute the $187,726 cost figure using normal costing. Anderson can use this information to manage the costs of the Laguna Model job as well as to bid on similar jobs later in the year. In contrast, Anderson has to wait until the December 2010 year end to compute the $180,526 cost of the Laguna Model using actual costing.

4-22 (20-30 min.) Job costing, accounting for manufacturing overhead, budgeted rates.

1. Budgeted manufacturing overhead divided by allocation base:

Machining overhead $\dfrac{\$1,800,000}{50,000}$ = $36 per machine-hour

Assembly overhead: $\dfrac{\$3,600,000}{\$2,000,000}$ = 180% of direct manuf. labour costs

4-22 (cont'd)

Machining department, 2,000 hours × $36	$72,000
Assembly department, 180% × $15,000	27,000
Total manufacturing overhead allocated to Job 494	$99,000

2.

	Machining	Assembly
Actual manufacturing overhead	$2,100,000	$ 3,700,000
Manufacturing overhead allocated,		
55,000 × $36	1,980,000	—
180% × $2,200,000	—	3,960,000
Underallocated (Overallocated)	$ 120,000	$ (260,000)

4-24 (20-30 min.) Job costing, journal entries.

1. & 2.
This answer assumes COGS given of $4,020 does not include the write-off of overallocated manufacturing overhead.

1. (1) Materials Control   800
          Accounts Payable Control   800
     (2) Work-in-Process Control   710
          Materials Control   710
     (3) Manufacturing Overhead Control   100
          Materials Control   100
     (4) Work-in-Process Control   1,300
          Manufacturing Overhead Control   900
          Wages Payable Control   2,200
     (5) Manufacturing Overhead Control   400
          Accumulated Amortization—buildings and
            manufacturing equipment   400
     (6) Manufacturing Overhead Control   550
          Miscellaneous accounts   550
     (7) Work-in-Process Control   2,080
          Manufacturing Overhead Allocated   2,080
          ($1.60 \times \$1,300 = \$2,080$)
     (8) Finished Goods Control   4,120
          Work-in-Process Control   4,120
     (9) Accounts Receivable Control (or Cash)   8,000
          Revenues   8,000
    (10) Cost of Goods Sold   4,020
          Finished Goods Control   4,020
    (11) Manufacturing Overhead Allocated   2,080
          Manufacturing Overhead Control   1,950
          Cost of Goods Sold   130

4-24 (cont'd)

2.

Materials Control

Bal. 12/31/2009	100	(2)	Issues		710
(1) Purchases	800	(3)	Issues		100
Bal. 12/31/2010	90				

Work-in-Process Control

Bal. 12/31/2009	60	(8)Goods completed	4,120
(2) Direct materials	710		
(4) Direct manuf. labour	1,300		
(7) Manuf. overhead allocated	2,080		
Bal. 12/31/2010	30		

Finished Goods Control

Bal. 12/31/2009	500	(10) Goods sold	4,020
(8) Goods completed	4,120		
Bal. 12/31/2010	600		

Cost of Goods Sold

(10) Goods sold	4,020	(11) Adjust for overallocation	130
Bal. 12/31/2010	3,890		

Manufacturing Overhead Control

(3) Indirect materials	100	(11) To close	1,950
(4) Indirect manuf. labour	900		
(5) Amortization	400		
(6) Miscellaneous	550		
Bal.	0		

Manufacturing Overhead Allocated

(11) To close	2,080	(7) Manuf. overhead allocated	2,080
		Bal.	0

4-26 (20-30 min.) Job costing, unit cost, ending work in process.

1. Budgeted MOH $=$ $\dfrac{\text{Budgeted annual MOH}}{\text{Budgeted annual DL hours}}$

   $=$ \$3,780,000/[35,000*12]

   $=$ \$3,780,000/420,000

   $=$ \$9 per direct labour-hour

Cost of Job A701:

Direct materials	$ 80,000
Direct manufacturing labour	287,000
Manufacturing overhead allocated	184,500*
Total cost	$551,500

*Budgeted rate $9 × 20,500 direct manufacturing labour-hours = $216,000

2. Per-unit cost $= \dfrac{\text{Total cost of the job}}{\text{Number of units in the job}}$

   $=$ \$551,500/2,500 $=$ \$220.60 per unit

3.
Finished Goods Control	551,500	
Work-in-Process Control		551,500

4. The work in process consists of Job A702 only:

Direct materials	$ 92,000
Direct manufacturing labour	219,000
Manufacturing overhead allocated	131,400†
Work in process May 31	$442,400

†Budgeted rate of $9 × 14,600 direct manufacturing labour-hours

4-28 (35 minutes) Journal entries, T-accounts, and source documents.

1.

   (1) Direct Materials Control   124,000

           Accounts Payable Control   124,000

Source Document: Purchase Invoice, Receiving Report

Subsidiary Ledger: Direct Materials Record, Accounts Payable

   (2) Work-in-Process Control [a]   122,000

           Direct Materials Control   122,000

Source Document: Material Requisition Records, Job Cost Record

Subsidiary Ledger: Direct Materials Record, Work-in-Process Inventory, Records by Jobs

   (3) Work in Process Control   80,000

        Manufacturing Overhead Control   54,500

           Wages Payable Control   134,500

Source Document: Labour Time Records, Job Cost Records

Subsidiary Ledger:, Manufacturing Overhead Records, Employee Labour Records, Work-in-Process Inventory Records by Jobs

   (4) Manufacturing Overhead Control   129,500

           Salaries Payable or AP Control   20,000

           Accounts Payable Control   9,500

           Accumulated Amortization Control   30,000

           Rent Payable Control   70,000

Source Document: Amortization Schedule, Rent Schedule, Maintenance wages due, Invoices for miscellaneous factory overhead items

Subsidiary Ledger: Manufacturing Overhead Records

   (5) Work-in-Process Control   200,000

           Manufacturing Overhead Allocated   200,000

                        ($80,000 \times $2.50)

Source Document: Labour Time Records, Job Cost Record

Subsidiary Ledger: Work-in-Process Inventory Records by Jobs

   (6) Finished Goods Control [b]   387,000

           Work-in-Process Control   387,000

Source Document: Job Cost Record, Completed Job Cost Record

Subsidiary Ledger: Work-in-Process Inventory Records by Jobs, Finished Goods Inventory Records by Jobs

4-28 (cont'd)

vii.	Cost of Goods Sold [c]	432,000	
	Finished Goods Control		432,000

Source Document: Sales Invoice, Completed Job Cost Record
Subsidiary Ledger: Finished Goods Inventory Records by Jobs

viii.	Manufacturing Overhead Allocated	200,000	
	Manufacturing Overhead Control		184,000
	Cost of Goods Sold		16,000

Source Document: Prior Journal Entries

ix.	Administrative Expenses	7,000	
	Marketing Expenses	120,000	
	Salaries Payable Control		30,000
	Accounts Payable Control		90,000
	Accumulated Amortization, Office Equipment		7,000

Source Document: Amortization Schedule, Marketing Payroll Request, Invoice for Advertising, Sales Commission Schedule.
Subsidiary Ledger: Employee Salary Records, Administration Cost Records, Marketing Cost Records.

[a] Materials used = Beginning direct materials inventory + Purchases − Ending direct materials inventory
= $9,000 + $124,000 − $11,000 = $122,000

[b] Cost of goods manufactured = Beginning WIP inventory + Manufacturing cost − Ending WIP inventory
= $6,000 + ($122,000 + $80,000 + $200,000) − $21,000
= 387,000

[c] Cost of Goods Sold = Beginning fin. goods inventory + Cost of goods manuf. − Ending fin. goods inventory
= $69,000 + $387,000 − $24,000 = $432,000

4-28 (cont'd)

1. T-accounts

Direct Materials Control

Bal. 1/1/2009	9,000	(2) Materials used	122,000
(1) Purchases	124,000		
Bal. 12/31/2009	11,000		

Work-in-Process Control

Bal. 1/1/2009	6,000	(6) Cost of goods	387,000
(2) Direct materials used	122,000	manufactured	
(3) Direct manuf. labour	80,000		
(5) Manuf. overhead allocated	200,000		
Bal. 12/31/2009	21,000		

Finished Goods Control

Bal. 1/1/2009	69,000	(7) Cost of goods sold	432,000
(6) Cost of goods manuf.	387,000		
Bal. 12/31/2009	24,000		

Cost of Goods Sold

(7) Goods sold	432,000	(8) Adjust for overallocation	16,000
	416,000		

Manufacturing Overhead Control

(3) Indirect labour	54,500	(8) To close	184,000
(4) Supplies	20,000		
(4) Miscellaneous	9,500		
(4) Amortization	30,000		
(4) Rent	70,000		
Bal.	0		

Manufacturing Overhead Allocated

(8) To close	200,000	(5) Manuf. overhead allocated	200,000
		Bal.	0

4-30 (30 min.) **Proration of overhead.**

1.

$$\text{Budgeted manufacturing overhead rate} = \frac{\text{Budgeted manufacturing overhead cost}}{\text{Budgeted direct manufacturing labour cost}}$$

$$= \frac{\$100,000}{\$200,000} = 50\% \text{ of direct manufacturing labour cost}$$

2. Overhead allocated = 50% × Actual direct manufacturing labour cost
= 50% × $220,000 = $110,000

Overallocated plant overhead = Actual plant overhead costs – Allocated plant overhead costs

= $106,000 – $110,000 = –$4,000

Overallocated plant overhead = $4,000

3a. All overallocated plant overhead is written off to cost of goods sold.
Both work in process (WIP) and finished goods inventory remain unchanged.

Account	Dec. 31 Balance (Before Proration) (1)	Proration of $4,000 Overallocated Manuf. Overhead (2)	Dec. 31, 2009 Balance (After Proration) (3) = (1) – (2)
WIP	$ 50,000	$ 0	$ 50,000
Finished Goods	240,000	0	240,000
Cost of Goods Sold	560,000	4,000	556,000
Total	$850,000	$4,000	$846,000

3b. Overallocated plant overhead prorated based on ending balances:

Account	Dec. 31 Balance (Before Proration) (1)	Balance as a Percent of Total (2) = (1) ÷ $850,000	Proration of $4,000 Overallocated Manuf. Overhead (3) = (2) × $4,000	Dec. 31, 2009 Balance (After Proration) (4) = (1) – (3)
WIP	$50,000	0.0588	0.0588 × $4,000 = $ 235	$49,765
Finished Goods	240,000	0.2824	0.2824 × $4,000 = 1,130	238,870
Cost of Goods Sold	560,000	0.6588	0.6588 × $4,000 = 2,635	557,365
Total	$850,000	1.0000	$4,000	$846,000

4-30 (cont'd)

3c. Overallocated plant overhead prorated based on 2009 overhead in ending balances:

Account	Dec. 31, 2009 Balance (Before Proration) (1)	Allocated MOH in Dec. 31, Balance (2)	Allocated MOH in Dec. 31 Balance as a % of Total (3) = (2) ÷ $110,000	Proration of $4,000 Overallocated Manuf. Overhead (4) = (3) × $4,000	Dec. 31, Balance (After Proration) (5) = (1) – (4)
WIP	$50,000	$10,000[a]	0.0909	0.0909 × $4,000= $ 364	$ 49,636
Finished Goods	240,000	30,000[b]	0.2727	0.2727 × $4,000= $1,091	238,909
Cost of Goods Sold	560,000	70,000[c]	0.6364	0.6364 × $4,000= $2,545	557,455
Total	$850,000	$110,000	1.0000	$4,000	$846,000

[a,b,c] Overhead allocated = Direct manuf. labour cost × 50% = $20,000; 60,000; 140,000 × 50%

4. Writing off all of the overallocated plant overhead to Cost of Goods Sold (CGS) is usually warranted when CGS is large relative to Work-in-Process and Finished Goods Inventory and the overallocated plant overhead is immaterial. Both these conditions apply in this case. ROW should write off the $4,000 overallocated plant overhead to Cost of Goods Sold Account.

4-32 (20–25 min.) **Proration of overhead.**

1. Calculation of Over- or Underallocated Manufacturing Overhead
   Under- or Overallocated MOH = Actual MOH – Allocated MOH
   Under- or Overallocated MOH = $337,000 - $302,000
      = $35,000 UNDERallocated

2. Proration Schedule

	Unadjusted Balance	Calculation	%	Underallocated Overhead	Prorated Amount
WIP	$26,000	[26/150]	17.3%	$35,000	$6,067
Finished Goods	$37,625	[37.625/150]	25.1%	$35,000	$8,779
CGS	$86,375	[86.375/150]	57.6%	$35,000	$20,154
Total	$150,000		100.0%		$35,000

4-32 (cont'd)

Journal Entry if written off to CGS:

Dr. CGS $35,000

Dr. MOH Allocated $302,000

   Cr. MOH Control $337,000

Journal Entry if prorated

Dr. Cost of Goods Sold $ 20,154

Dr. Work in Process Inventory $ 6,067

Dr. Finished Goods Inventory $ 8,779

Dr. MOH Allocated $302,000

   Cr. MOH Control $337,000

3. For this company, the difference between the two methods may be significant because cost of goods sold only represents 57.6% of the unadjusted balances of the three accounts (Work in Process, Finished Goods and Cost of Goods Sold). As a result, the two methods would result in a difference of $14,846 ($35,000 - $20,154) in reported income (income would be higher under proration). Under proration, $14,846 is costed to inventories and appears on the Balance Sheet instead of being written off to the Income Statement as an increase to Cost of Goods Sold.

4-34 (25-30 min.) Job costing with two direct- and two indirect-cost categories, law firm (continuation of 4-33).

1.

	Professional Partner Labour	Professional Manager Labour
Budgeted compensation/professional	$ 200,000	$80,000
Budgeted hours of billable time per professional		
Budgeted direct-cost rate	$\div 1,600$	$\div 1,600$
	$125 per hour*	$50 per hour†

*Can also be calculated as:

$$\frac{\text{Total budgeted partner labour costs}}{\text{Total budgeted partner labour-hours}} = \frac{\$200,000 \times 5}{1,600 \times 5} = \frac{\$1,000,000}{8,000} = \$125$$

†Can also be calculated as

$$\frac{\text{Total budgeted manager labour costs}}{\text{Total budgeted manager labour-hours}} = \frac{\$80,000 \times 20}{1,600 \times 20} = \frac{\$1,600,000}{32,000} = \$50$$

4-34 (cont'd)

2.

	General Support	Administration Support
Budgeted total costs	$1,800,000	$400,000
Divided by budgeted quantity of allocation base	÷ 40,000 hours	÷ 8,000 hours $50 per hour
Budgeted indirect cost rate	$45 per hour	

3.

	Richardson		Punch	
Direct costs:				
Professional partners, $125 × 60; $125 × 30	$7,500		$3,750	
Professional manager, $50 × 40; $50 × 120	2,000		6,000	
Direct costs		$ 9,500		$ 9,750
Indirect costs:				
General support, $45 × 100; $45 × 150	4,500		6,750	
Admin. support, $50 × 60; $50 × 30	3,000		1,500	
Indirect costs		7,500		8,250
Total costs		$17,000		$18,000

4.

	Richardson	Punch
Single direct - Single indirect (from Problem 4–33)	$12,000	$18,000
Multiple direct – Multiple indirect (from requirement 3 of Problem 4-34)	17,000	18,000
Difference	$ 5,000 undercosted	$ 0 no change

The Richardson and Punch jobs differ in their use of resources. The Richardson job has a mix of 60% partners and 40% manager, while Punch has a mix of 20% partners and 80% associates. Thus, the Richardson job is a relatively high user of the more costly partner-related resources (both direct partner costs and indirect partner secretarial support). The refined-costing system increases the reported cost in Problem 4-34 for the Richardson job by 41.7% (from $12,000 to $17,000).

4-36 (20 min.) Normal costing, overhead allocation, working backwards.

1.

$$\text{Manufacturing overhead allocated} \quad = \quad \$5,175,000$$

Manufacturing overhead is allocated at 180% of direct manufacturing labour costs.

$$\text{Manufacturing overhead allocated} \quad = \quad 180\% \times \text{Direct manufacturing labour costs}$$

$$\text{That is,} \quad \$5,175,000 \quad = \quad 1.8 \times \text{Direct manufacturing labour costs}$$

$$\text{Hence,} \quad \text{Direct manufacturing labour costs} \quad = \quad \$5,175,000/1.8 = \$2,875,000$$

2.

Manufacturing Costs Incurred = Direct Materials + Direct Labour + MOH Allocated
$9,732,500   =   DM + $2,875,000 + $5,175,000
Direct Materials   = $1,682,500

3. Note the structure of entries made to the Work-in-Process T-account

Work in Process			
Beginning balance, 1-1-2010	xxx	Costs of goods manufactured	
Manufacturing costs	xxx	(transferred to finished goods)	xxx
Ending balance, 12-31-2010	xxx		

Beg. WIP + Manufacturing Costs – Cost of Goods Manufactured = Ending WIP
$236,000 + $9,732,500 - $9,612,200 =   Ending WIP
Ending WIP   = $356,300

4-38 (40 min.) Disposition of overhead over/underallocation, two indirect-cost pools.

1.

$$\text{Budgeted manufacturing overhead cost rate for the Machining Department} = \frac{\text{Budgeted manufacturing overhead costs in the Machining Department}}{\text{Budgeted machine-hours in the Machining Department}}$$

$$= \$5,850,000/90,000 = \$65 \text{ per machine-hour}$$

$$\text{Budgeted manufacturing overhead cost rate for the Assembly Department} = \frac{\text{Budgeted manufacturing overhead costs in the Assembly Department}}{\text{Budgeted direct manufacturing labour-hours in the Assembly Department}}$$

$$= \$7,812,000/124,000 = \$63 \text{ per direct manufacturing labour-hour}$$

2. **Machining Department**

Total actual machine-hours $= 69,000 + 6,900 + 16,100 = 92,000$ machine-hours

Manufacturing overhead allocated $= 92,000 \times \$65 = \$5,980,000$

$$\text{Over/Underallocated MOH} = \text{Actual manufacturing overhead costs} - \text{Manufacturing overhead allocated}$$

$$= \$5,470,000 - \$5,980,000$$

$$= \$510,000 \text{ OVERALLOCATED}$$

Assembly Department

Total actual direct manufacturing labour-hours $= 83,200 + 12,800 + 32,000 = 128,000$

Manufacturing overhead allocated $= 128,000 \times \$63 = \$8,064,000$

$$\text{Over/Underallocated MOH} = \text{Actual manufacturing overhead costs} - \text{Manufacturing overhead allocated}$$

$$= \$8,234,000 - \$8,064,000$$

$$= \$170,000 \text{ UNDERALLOCATED}$$

4-38 (cont'd)

2. a. Write-off to Cost of Goods Sold leads to

(i) lower Cost of Goods Sold of $510,000 as a result of overallocation of manufacturing overhead in the Machining Department

(ii) higher Cost of Goods Sold of $170,000 as a result of underallocation of manufacturing overhead in the Assembly Department. Hence,

Cost of Goods Sold = $21,600,000 – $510,000 + $170,000 = $21,260,000

b. Proration based on ending balances (before proration) in Work in Process, Finished Goods, and Cost of Goods Sold.

Account balances in each account after proration follows:

Account (1)	Account Balance (2)	Proration of ($510,000) Overallocated Overhead in Machining Dept. (3)	Proration of $170,000 Underallocated Overhead in Assembly Dept. (4)	Account Balance (after Proration) (5) = (2) + (3) + (4)
Work in Process	$7,600,000 (23.75%)	0.2375 × ($510,000) = ($121,125)	0.2375 × $170,000 = $40,375	$ 7,519,250
Finished Goods	2,800,000 (8.75%)	0.0875 × ($510,000) = ($44,625)	0.0875 × $170,000 = $14,875	$ 2,770,250
Cost of Goods Sold	21,600,000 (67.50%)	0.675 × ($510,000) = ($344,250)	0.675 × $170,000 = $114,750	$21,370,500
	$32,000,000 (100.00%)	($510,000)	$170,000	$31,660,000

c. Proration based on the overhead allocated (before proration) in the ending balances of Cost of Goods Sold, Finished Goods, and Work in Process for each Department follows.

Machining Department

Account (1)	Overhead Costs Allocated to Each Account in Machining Department Using Budgeted Machine-Hour Rate × Actual Machine-hours (2)	Proration of ($510,000) Overallocated Overhead (3)
Work in process	$65 ×16,100 = $1,046,500 (17.5%)	0.175 × ($510,000) = ($ 89,250)
Finished goods	$65 × 6,900 = 448,500 (7.5%)	0.075 × ($510,000) = ($ 38,250)
Cost of goods sold	$65 ×69,000 = 4,485,000 (75%)	0.75 × ($510,000) = ($382,500)
	$5,980,000 100%	($510,000)

4-38 (cont'd)

Assembly Department

Account (1)	Overhead Costs Allocated to Each Account in Assembly Department Using Budgeted Direct Manuf. Labour-hour Rate × Actual Direct Manuf. Labour-hours (2)	Proration of $170,000 Underallocated Assembly Overhead (3)
Work in process	$63 × 32,000 = $2,016,000 (25%)	0.25 × $170,000 = $ 42,500
Finished goods	$63 × 12,800 = 806,400 (10%)	0.10 × $170,000 = 17,000
Cost of goods sold	$63 ×83,200 = 5,241,600 (65%)	0.65 × $170,000 = 110,500
	$8,064,000 (100%)	$170,000

Account balances in each account after proration of overallocated Machining Department costs and underallocated Assembly Department costs follow.

Account (1)	Account Balance (before) Proration) (2)	Prorated ($510,000) of Overallocated Machining Department Overhead (calculated earlier) (3)	Prorated $170,000 of Underallocated Assembly Department Overhead (calculated earlier) (4)	Account Balance (after Proration) (5)=(2)+(3)+(4)
Work in process	$7,600,000	($89,250)	$ 42,500	$ 7,553,250
Finished goods	2,800,000	(38,250)	17,000	2,778,750
Cost of goods sold	21,600,000	(382,500)	110,500	21,328,000
	$32,000,000	($510,000)	$170,000	$31,660,000

3. If the purpose is to report the most accurate inventory and cost of goods sold figures, the preferred method is to prorate based on the manufacturing overhead allocated amount in the inventory and cost of goods sold accounts (as in requirement 2c). Note, however, that prorating based on ending balances in Work in Process, Finished Goods, and Cost of Goods Sold (as in requirement 2b) yields a close approximation to the more accurate proration in requirement 2c. Also note that the write-off to Cost of Goods Sold method (as in requirement 2a) results in a difference of only $68,000 ($21,328,000 - $21,260,000) or less than 1% to the balance of Cost of Goods Sold. Furthermore, the Write Off to Cost of Goods Sold method is simpler than the other methods. Depending on the objectives of the disposal of over/underallocation, a manager may prefer any one of the methods over the other two.

4-40 (20 min.) Job costing, contracting, ethics.

1. Direct manufacturing costs:

Direct materials	$40,000	
Direct manufacturing labour	8,400	$48,400
Indirect manufacturing costs,		
175% × $8,400		14,700
Total manufacturing costs		$63,100

    Aerospace bills the Armed Forces $82,030 ($63,100 × 130%) for 100 X7 seats or $820.30 ($82,030 ÷ 100) per X7 seat.

2. Direct manufacturing costs:

Direct materials	$40,000	
Direct manufacturing labour[a]	5,800	$45,800
Indirect manufacturing costs,		
175% × $5,800		10,150
Total manufacturing costs		$55,950

    [a]$8,400 – ($50 × 16) setup – ($120 × 15) design
    $8,400 - $800 - $1,800

    Aerospace should have billed the Armed Forces $72,735 ($55,950 × 130%) for 100 X7 seats or $727.35 ($72,735 ÷ 100) per X7 seat.

3. The problems the letter highlights (assuming it is correct) include:
    a. Costs included that should be excluded (design costs),
    b. Costs double-counted (setup included both as a direct cost and in an indirect cost pool), and
    c. Possible conflict of interest in Aerospace Comfort purchasing materials from a family-related company.

    Steps the Armed Forces could undertake include:
    (i)   Use only contractors with a reputation for ethical behaviour as well as quality products or services.
    (ii)   Issue guidelines detailing acceptable and unacceptable billing practices by contractors. For example, prohibit the use of double-counting cost allocation methods by contractors.
    (iii) Issue guidelines detailing acceptable and unacceptable procurement practices by contractors. For example, if a contractor purchases from a family-related company, require that the contractor obtain quotes from at least two other bidders.
    (iv)   Employ auditors who aggressively monitor the bills submitted by contractors.

4-42 (35 min.) General ledger relationships, under- and overallocation.

A summary of the T-accounts for Northley Company before adjusting for under- or overallocation of overhead follows.

Direct Materials Control

Beg	32,000	Material used	
Purchases	431,000	for manufac-	
		turing	403,000
End.	60,000		

Work-in-Process Control

Beg	18,000	Transferred	
Direct		to finished	
materials	403,000	goods	1,307,250
Direct			
manuf.			
labour	380,000		
Manuf.			
overhead			
allocated	593,750		
End	87,500		

Finished Goods Control

1-1-2007	12,250	Cost of	
Transf-		goods	
erred in		sold	1,280,000
from WIP	1,307,250		
12-31-2007	39,500		

Cost of Goods Sold

Finished			
goods			
sold	1,280,000		

Manufacturing Overhead Control

Manufac-		
turing		
overhead		
costs	543,000	

Manufacturing Overhead Allocated

Manufac-		
turing		
overhead		
allocated		
to work		
in process		593,750

1. From the credit entry to Direct Materials T-account,
   Direct materials issued to manufacturing = $403,000.

2. Direct manufacturing labour-hours = $\dfrac{\text{Direct manufacturing labour costs}}{\text{Direct manufacturing wage rate per hour}}$

   = $380,000/$16 = 23,750 hours

   $\dfrac{\text{Manufacturing overhead}}{\text{allocated}}$ = $\dfrac{\text{Direct manufacturing}}{\text{labour-hours}} \times \dfrac{\text{Manufacturing overhead}}{\text{rate}}$

   = 23,750 hours × $25 = $593,750

4-42 (cont'd)

3. From the debit entry to Finished Goods T-account,
   Cost of jobs completed and transferred from WIP = $1,280,000

4. From Work-in-Process T-account,

   Ending Work in Process = $18,000 + $403,000 + $380,000 + $593,750 – $1,307,250

   = $87,500

5. From the credit entry to Finished Goods Control T-account,

   Cost of goods sold (before proration) = $1,280,000

6.

   $$\text{Manufacturing overhead overallocated} = \text{Debits to Manufacturing Overhead Control} - \text{Credit to Manufacturing Overhead Allocated}$$

   = $543,000 – $593,750

   = $50,750 overallocated

7. a. Write-off to Cost of Goods Sold will decrease (credit) Cost of Goods Sold by $50,750. Hence, Cost of Goods Sold = $1,280,000 – $50,750 = $1,229,250.

   b. Proration based on ending balances (before proration) in Work in Process, Finished Goods, and Cost of Goods Sold.

   Account balances in each account after proration follows.

Account (1)	Account Balance (2)		Proration of $50,750 Overallocated Manufacturing Overhead (3)		Balance (after Proration) (4)=(2)-(3)
Work in Process	$87,500	(6.22%)	6.22% × $50,750 =	$3,156	$ 84,344
Finished Goods	39,500	(2.81%)	2.81% × $50,750 =	1,425	38,075
Cost of Goods Sold	1,280,000	(90.97%)	90.97% × $50,750 =	46,169	1,233,831
Total	$1,407,000	(100.00%)		$50,750	$1,356,250

4-42 (cont'd)

8. Operating income under the write-off to Cost of Goods Sold and Proration based on ending balances (before proration) follows:

	Write-off to Cost of Goods Sold	Proration Based on Ending Balances
Revenues	$1,664,000	$1,664,000
Cost of goods sold	1,229,250	1,233,831
Gross margin	434,750	430,169
Marketing and distribution costs	199,750	199,700
Operating income	$ 235,000	$ 230,469

9. If the purpose is to report the most accurate inventory and cost of goods sold figures, the preferred method is to prorate based on the manufacturing overhead allocated component in the Work in Process, Finished Goods, and Cost of Goods Sold accounts. Proration based on the balances in Work in Process, Finished Goods, and Cost of Goods Sold will equal the proration based on the manufacturing overhead allocated component if the proportions of direct costs to manufacturing overhead costs are constant in the Work in Process, Finished Goods, and Cost of Goods Sold accounts. Even if this is not the case, the proration based on Work in Process, Finished Goods, and Cost of Goods Sold balances will better approximate the results if actual cost rates had been used than the write-off to Cost of Goods Sold method.

However, materiality is always a consideration in how to dispose of under/over allocated manufacturing overhead. In this case, because over 90% of the product has been sold, the overallocated overhead is almost totally adjusted to Cost of Goods Sold under the proration method. The income difference is only $4,531 ($235,000-$230,469) and as a percentage of sales is insignificant at less than 1% ($4,531/$1,664,000). The main merit of the write-off to cost of goods sold method is its simplicity. Accuracy and the effect on operating income favour the proration approach when amounts are material. However the simpler approach is preferred when amounts are immaterial.

4-44 (30 min.) Allocation and proration of overhead.

1. Budgeted overhead rate = Budgeted overhead costs ÷ Budgeted labour costs
   = £1,500 ÷ £2,000 = 75% of labour cost

2. Ending work in process

	Job 1	Job 2	Total
Direct material costs	£25	£15	£ 40
Direct labour costs	20	32	52
Overhead (0.75 × Direct labour costs)	15	24	39
Total costs	£60	£71	£131

Cost of goods sold = Beginning WIP + Manufacturing costs – Ending WIP
= £0 + (£900 + £1,800 + £1,800 × 0.75) – £131 = £3,919

3. Overhead allocated = 0.75 × £1,800 = £1,350

Overallocated overhead = Actual overhead – Allocated overhead
= £1,250 – £1,350 = £100 overallocated

4.a. All overallocated overhead is written off to cost of goods sold.

WIP inventory remains unchanged.

Account (1)	Dec. 31 Account Balance (Before Proration) (2)	Write-off of £100 Overallocated Overhead (3)	Dec. 31 Account Balance (After Proration) (4) = (2) + (3)
Work in Process	£ 131	£ 0	£ 131
Cost of Goods Sold	3,919	(100)	3,819
	£4,050	£(100)	£3,950

4b. Overallocated overhead prorated based on ending balances

Account (1)	Dec. 31, Balance (Before Proration) (2)	Balance as a Percent of Total (3) = (2) ÷ £4,050	Proration of £100 Overallocated Overhead (4) = (3) × £100	Dec. 31 Balance (After Proration) (5) = (2) + (4)
WIP	£ 131	0.03	£ (3)	£ 128
CGS	3,919	0.97	(97)	3,822
	£4,050	1.00	£(100)	£3,950

4-44 (cont'd)

5. Writing off all of the overallocated overhead to Cost of Goods Sold (COGS) is warranted when COGS is large relative to Work-in-Process Inventory and Finished Goods Inventory and the overallocated overhead is immaterial. Both these conditions apply in this case. Franklin & Son Printing should write off the £100 overallocated overhead to Cost of Goods Sold account.

CHAPTER 5
ACTIVITY-BASED COSTING AND ACTIVITY-BASED MANAGEMENT

5-2 Overcosting may result in competitors entering a market and taking market share for products that a company erroneously believes are low-margin or even unprofitable.

Undercosting may result in companies selling products on which they are in fact losing money, when they erroneously believe them to be profitable.

5-4 An activity-based approach refines a costing system by focusing on individual activities as the fundamental cost objects. It uses the cost of these activities as the basis for assigning costs to other cost objects such as products or services.

5-6 It is important to classify costs into a cost hierarchy because costs in different cost pools relate to different cost-allocation bases and not all cost-allocation bases are unit-level. For example, an allocation base like setup hours is a batch-level allocation base, and design hours is a product-sustaining base, both insensitive to the number of units in a batch or the number of units of product produced. If costs were not classified into a cost hierarchy, the alternative would be to consider all costs as unit-level costs, leading to misallocation of those costs that are not unit-level costs.

5-8 Four decisions for which ABC information is useful are
1. pricing and product mix decisions,
2. cost reduction and process improvement decisions,
3. product design decisions, and
4. decisions for planning and managing activities.

5-10 "Tell-tale" signs that indicate when ABC systems are likely to provide the most benefits are as follows:
1. Significant amounts of indirect costs are allocated using only one or two cost pools.
2. All or most indirect costs are identified as output-unit-level costs (i.e., few indirect costs are described as batch-level, product-sustaining, or facility-sustaining costs).
3. Products make diverse demands on resources because of differences in volume, process steps, batch size, or complexity.
4. Products that a company is well suited to make and sell show small profits, whereas products that a company is less suited to produce and sell show large profits.
5. Operations staff has significant disagreements with the accounting staff about the costs of manufacturing and marketing products and services.

5-12 No, ABC systems apply equally well to service companies such as banks, railroads, hospitals, and accounting firms, as well as merchandising companies such as retailers and distributors.

5-14 Increasing the number of indirect-cost pools does NOT guarantee increased accuracy of product or service costs. If the existing cost pool is already homogeneous, increasing the number of cost pools will not increase accuracy. If the existing cost pool is not homogeneous, accuracy will increase only if the increased cost pools themselves increase in homogeneity vis-à-vis the single cost pool.

5-16 (20 min.) **Cost hierarchy.**

1. a. Indirect manufacturing labour costs of $1,200,000 support direct manufacturing labour and are output unit-level costs. Direct manufacturing labour generally increases with output units, and so will the indirect costs to support it.
   b. Batch-level costs are costs of activities that are related to a group of units of a product rather than each individual unit of a product. Purchase order-related costs (including costs of receiving materials and paying suppliers) of $600,000 relate to a group of units of product and are batch-level costs.
   c. Cost of indirect materials of $350,000 generally changes with labour-hours or machine-hours which are unit-level costs. Therefore, indirect material costs are output unit-level costs.
   d. Setup costs of $700,000 are batch-level costs because they relate to a group of units of product produced after the machines are set up.
   e. Costs of designing processes, drawing process charts, and making engineering changes for individual products, $900,000, are product-sustaining because they relate to the costs of activities undertaken to support individual products regardless of the number of units or batches in which the product is produced.
   f. Machine-related overhead costs (amortization and maintenance) of $1,200,000 are output unit-level costs because they change with the number of units produced.
   g. Plant management, plant rent, and insurance costs of $950,000 are facility-sustaining costs because the costs of these activities cannot be traced to individual products or services but support the organization as a whole.

2. The complex boom box made in many batches will use significantly more batch-level overhead resources compared to the simple boom box that is made in a few batches. In addition, the complex boom box will use more product-sustaining overhead resources because it is complex. Because each boom box requires the same amount of machine-hours, both the simple and the complex boom box will be allocated the same amount of overhead costs per boom box if Teledor uses only machine-hours to allocate overhead costs to boom boxes. As a result, the complex boom box will be undercosted (it consumes a relatively high level of resources but is reported to have a relatively low cost) and the simple boom box will be overcosted (it consumes a relatively low level of resources but is reported to have a relatively high cost).

5-16 (cont'd)

3.   Using the cost hierarchy to calculate activity-based costs can help Teledor to identify both the costs of individual activities and the cost of activities demanded by individual products. Teledor can use this information to manage its business in several ways:

   a. Teledor can improve pricing and product mix decisions. Knowing the resources needed to manufacture and sell different types of boom boxes can help Teledor to price the different boom boxes and also identify which boom boxes are more profitable. It can then emphasize its more profitable products.

   b. Teledor can use information about the costs of different activities to improve processes and reduce costs of the different activities. Teledor could have a target of reducing costs of activities (setups, order processing, etc.) by, say, 3% and constantly seek to eliminate activities and costs (such as engineering changes) that its customers perceive as not adding value.

   c. Teledor management can identify and evaluate new designs to improve performance by analyzing how product and process designs affect activities and costs.

   d. Teledor can use its ABC systems and cost hierarchy information to plan and manage activities. What activities should be performed in the period and at what cost?

5-18 (20 min.) Plantwide indirect cost rates.

1.

Actual plant-wide variable MOH rate based on machine-hours, $308,600 ÷ 4,000	$77.15 per machine-hour

	United Motors	Holden Motors	Leland Vehicle	Total
Variable manufacturing overhead, allocated based on machine-hours ($77.15 × 120; $77.15 × 2,800; $77.15 × 1,080)	$9,258	$216,020	$83,322	$308,600

2.

Department	Variable MOH in 2009	Total Driver Units	Rate	
Design	$39,000	390	$100	per CAD-design hour
Engineering	29,600	370	$ 80	per engineering hour
Production	240,000	4,000	$ 60	per machine-hour

	United Motors	Holden Motors	Leland Vehicle	Total
Design-related overhead, allocated on CAD-design hours (110 × $100; 200 × $100; 80 × $100)	$11,000	$ 20,000	$ 8,000	$ 39,000
Production-related overhead, allocated on engineering hours (70 × $80; 60 × $80; 240 × $80)	5,600	4,800	19,200	29,600
Engineering-related overhead, allocated on machine-hours (120 × $60; 2,800 × $60; 1,080 × $60)	7,200	168,000	64,800	240,000
Total	$23,800	$192,800	$92,000	$308,600

3.

	United Motors	Holden Motors	Leland Vehicle
a. Department rates (Requirement 2)	$23,800	$192,800	$92,000
b. Plantwide rate (Requirement 1)	$ 9,258	$216,020	$83,322
Ratio of (a) ÷ (b)	2.57	0.89	1.10

5-18 (cont'd)

The variable manufacturing overhead allocated to United Motors increases by 157% under the department rates, the overhead allocated to Holden decreases by about 11% and the overhead allocated to Leland increases by about 10%.

The three contracts differ sizably in the way they use the resources of the three departments. The percentage of total driver units in each department used by the companies is:

Department	Cost Driver	United Motors	Holden Motors	Leland Vehicle
Design	CAD-design hours	28%	51%	21%
Engineering	Engineering hours	19	16	65
Production	Machine-hours	3	70	27

The United Motors contract uses only 3% of total machine-hours in 2009, yet uses 28% of CAD design-hours and 19% of engineering hours. The result is that the plantwide rate, based on machine-hours, will greatly underestimate the cost of resources used on the United Motors contract. This explains the 157% increase in indirect costs assigned to the United Motors contract when department rates are used.

In contrast, the Holden Motors contract uses less of design (51%) and engineering (16%) than of machine-hours (70%). Hence, the use of department rates will report lower indirect costs for Holden Motors than does a plantwide rate.

Holden Motors was probably complaining under the use of the simple system because its contract was being overcosted relative to its consumption of MOH resources. United, on the other hand, was having its contract undercosted and underpriced by the simple system. Assuming that AP is an efficient and competitive supplier, if the new department-based rates are used to price contracts, United will be unhappy. AP should explain to United how the calculation was done, and point out United's high use of design and engineering resources relative to production machine-hours. Discuss ways of reducing the consumption of those resources, if possible, and show willingness to partner with them to do so. If the price increase is going to be steep, perhaps offer to phase in the new prices.

4. Other than for pricing, AP can also use the information from the department-based system to examine and streamline its own operations so that there is maximum value added from all indirect resources. It might set targets over time to reduce both the consumption of each indirect resource and the unit costs of the resources. The department-based system gives AP more opportunities for targeted cost management.

5. It would not be worthwhile to further refine the cost system into an ABC system if there wasn't much variation among contracts in the consumption of activities within a department. If, for example, most activities within the design department were, in fact, driven by CAD-design hours, then the more refined system would be more costly and no more accurate than the department-based cost system. Even if there were sufficient variation, considering the relative sizes of the 3 department cost pools, it may only be cost-effective to further analyze the engineering cost pool, which consumes 78% ($240,000 \div $308,600) of the manufacturing overhead.

5-20 (25 min.) Allocation of costs to activities, unused capacity.

1.

Indirect Resources	Percentage of Costs Used by Each Activity				2009 Expenditures
	Academic Instruction	Administration	Sports Training	Community Relationships	
Teachers' salaries and benefits	60%	20%	8%	12%	$4,000,000
Principals' salaries and benefits	10%	60%	5%	25%	400,000
Facilities cost	35%	15%	45%	5%	2,600,000
Office staff salaries and benefits	5%	60%	10%	25%	300,000
Sports program staff salaries and benefits	35%	10%	45%	10%	500,000
					$7,800,000

Indirect Resources	Actual Resource Cost Used by Each Activity				2009 Expenditures
	Academic Instruction	Administration	Sports Training	Community Relationships	
Teachers' salaries and benefits	$2,400,000	$ 800,000	$ 320,000	$480,000	$4,000,000
Principals' salaries and benefits	40,000	240,000	20,000	100,000	400,000
Facilities cost	910,000	390,000	1,170,000	130,000	2,600,000
Office staff salaries and benefits	15,000	180,000	30,000	75,000	300,000
Sports program staff salaries and benefits	175,000	50,000	225,000	50,000	500,000
Total	$3,540,000	$1,660,000	$1,765,000	$835,000	$7,800,000
No. of students	500	500	500	500	500
Cost per student	$7,080	$ 3,320	$3,530	$1,670	$15,600
Percent of total cost by activity	45%	21%	23%	11%	100%

The overall cost of educating each student is $15,600. Of this, $7,080 (or 45%) is spent on academic instruction and $3,320 (or 21%) is spent on administration.

2. Cost of ice hockey program = $300,000
   Total cost of activities w/o ice hockey program = $7,800,000 – $300,000 = $7,500,000
   Per student cost of educational program w/o hockey = $7,500,000 ÷ 500 = $15,000

3. Net cost of ice hockey program with $1,000 fee = $300,000 – (30 × $1,000) = $270,000
   Total cost of activities with ice hockey program fee = $7,500,000 + $270,000 = $7,770,000
   Per student cost of educational program with hockey fee = $7,770,000 ÷ 500 = $15,540

Charging a fee helps a bit but the net cost of the ice hockey program is still high and significantly increases the cost of educating each student.

5-20 (cont'd)

4.

Academic instruction capacity	600	students
Cost of academic instruction activity (from requirement 1 calculations)	$3,540,000	
Cost of academic instruction per student at full utilization = $3,540,000 ÷ 600	$5,900	
Academic instruction resource costs used by current student population = 500 × $5,900	$2,950,000	
Cost of excess academic instruction capacity = $3,540,000 – $2,950,000	$590,000	

Most of the costs at Harmon school are fixed in the short run. So, Smith must try to recruit more students to the school. If, in the long run, it seems like the student population is going to be stable at around 500, he should plan how some of the excess capacity can be cut back so that the fixed school capacity is better utilized; that is, he should work to reduce the cost of excess capacity. One problem with that plan is that "cutting excess academic instruction capacity" may eventually mean reducing the number of sections in each grade and letting teachers go, and if this involves the loss of experienced teachers, that could cause long-term damage to the school.

Unrelated to the excess capacity issue, but with the aim of improving the school's economics, he should consider doing away with expensive activities like the ice hockey program which raises the cost per student substantially, even after a large fee is charged from students who choose to play the sport.

5-22 (30 min.) Make versus buy, activity-based costing.

1. The expected manufacturing cost per unit of CMCBs in 2009 is as follows:

	Total Manufacturing Costs of CMCB (1)	Manufacturing Cost per Unit (2) = (1) ÷ 15,000
Direct materials $194 × 15,000	$2,910,000	$194.00
Direct manufacturing labour $72 × 15,000	$1,080,000	72.00
Variable batch manufacturing costs $1,740 × 125	217,500	14.50
Fixed manufacturing costs		
Avoidable fixed manufacturing costs	360,000	24.00
Unavoidable fixed manufacturing costs	900,000	60.00
Total manufacturing costs	$5,467,500	$364.50

2. The following table identifies the incremental costs in 2009 if Svenson (a) made CMCBs and (b) purchased CMCBs from Minton.

	Total Incremental Costs		Per-Unit Incremental Costs	
Incremental Items	Make	Buy	Make	Buy
Cost of purchasing CMCBs from Minton $340 × 15,000				$340
Direct materials	$2,910,000	$5,100,000	$194.00	
Direct manufacturing labour	1,080,000		72.00	
Variable batch manufacturing costs	217,500		14.50	
Avoidable fixed manufacturing costs	360,000		24.00	
Total incremental costs	$4,567,500	$5,100,000	$304.50	$340
Difference in favour of making	↑ $532,500 ↑		↑ $35.50 ↑	

Note that the opportunity cost of using capacity to make CMCBs is zero since Svenson would keep this capacity idle if it purchases CMCBs from Minton.

Svenson should continue to manufacture the CMCBs internally, since the incremental costs to manufacture are $304.50 per unit compared with the $340 per unit that Minton has quoted. Note that the unavoidable fixed manufacturing costs of $900,000 ($60 per unit) will continue to be incurred whether Svenson makes or buys CMCBs. These are not incremental costs under either the make or the buy alternative and are hence irrelevant.

5-22 (cont'd)

3. Svenson should continue to make CMCBs. The simplest way to solve this problem is to recognize that Svenson would prefer to keep any excess capacity idle rather than use it to make CB3s. Why? Because expected incremental future revenues from CB3s ($2,418,000) are <u>less</u> than expected incremental future costs ($2,504,000). If Svenson keeps its capacity idle, we know from requirement 2 that it should make CMCBs rather than buy them.

     An important point to note is that, because Svenson forgoes no contribution by not being able to make and sell CB3s, the opportunity cost of using its facilities to make CMCBs is zero. It is therefore not forgoing any profits by using the capacity to manufacture CMCBs. If it does not manufacture CMCBs, rather than lose money on CB3s, Svenson will keep the capacity idle.

     A longer and more detailed approach is to use the total alternatives or opportunity cost analyses shown in the chapter.

TOTAL-ALTERNATIVES APPROACH TO MAKE-OR-BUY DECISIONS

	Choices for Svenson		
Relevant Items	**Make CMCBs and Do Not Make CB3s**	**Buy CMCBs and Do Not Make CB3s**	**Buy CMCBs and Make CB3s**
Total incremental costs of making/buying CMCBs (from requirement 2)	$4,567,500	$5,100,000	$5,100,000
Excess of future costs over future revenues from CB3s	0	0	86,000
Total relevant costs	$4,567,500	$5,100,000	$5,186,000

Svenson will minimize manufacturing costs by making CMCBs.

OPPORTUNITY COST APPROACH TO MAKE/BUY DECISIONS

	Choices for Svenson	
Incremental Items	**Make CMCB**	**Buy CMCB**
Total incremental costs of making/buying CMCBs (from requirement 2)	$4,567,500	$5,100,000
Opportunity cost: profit contribution forgone because capacity cannot be used to make CB3s	0*	0
Total relevant costs	$4,567,500	$5,100,000
Difference in favour of making CMCBs	↥ $532,500 ↥	

*Opportunity cost is 0 because Svenson does not give up anything by manufacturing CMCBs. Had it not manufactured CMCBs, it would be best off leaving the capacity idle (rather than manufacturing and selling CB3s).

5-24 (15–20 min.) ABC, wholesale, customer profitability.

	Chain			
	1	2	3	4
Gross sales	$50,000	$30,000	$100,000	$70,000
Sales returns	10,000	5,000	7,000	6,000
Net sales	40,000	25,000	93,000	64,000
Cost of goods sold (80%)	32,000	20,000	74,400	51,200
Gross margin	8,000	5,000	18,600	12,800
Customer-related costs:				
Regular orders				
$20 × 40; 150; 50; 70	800	3,000	1,000	1,400
Rush orders				
$100 × 10; 50; 10; 30	1,000	5,000	1,000	3,000
Returned items				
$10 × 100; 26; 60; 40	1,000	260	600	400
Catalogues and customer				
support	1,000	1,000	1,000	1,000
Customer related costs	3,800	9,260	3,600	5,800
Contribution (loss) margin	$ 4,200	$ (4,260)	$ 15,000	$ 7,000
Contribution (loss) margin as				
percentage of gross sales	8.4%	(14.2%)	15.0%	10.0%

The analysis indicates that customers' profitability (loss) contribution varies widely from (14.2%) to 15.0%. Immediate attention to Chain 2 is required which is currently showing a contribution loss. The chain has a disproportionate number of both regular orders and rush orders. Villeagas should work with the management of Chain 2 to find ways to reduce the number of orders, while maintaining or increasing the sales volume. If this is not possible, Villeagas should consider dropping Chain 2, if it can save the customer-related costs.

Chain 1 has a disproportionate number of sale returns. The causes of these should be investigated so that the profitability contribution of Chain 1 could be improved.

5-26 (30 min.) ABC, product costing at banks, cross-subsidization.

1.

	Robinson	Skerrett	Farrel	Total
Revenues				
Spread revenue on annual basis (2.5% ×; $2,600, $1,200, $40,000)	$ 65.00	$ 30.00	$1,000.00	$ 1,095.00
Monthly fee charges ($35×; 0, 12, 0)	0.00	420.00	0.00	420.00
Total revenues	65.00	450.00	1,000.00	1,515.00
Costs				
Deposit/withdrawal with teller $4.00 × 45; 55; 10	180.00	220.00	40.00	440.00
Deposit/withdrawal with ATM $1.20× 12; 24; 18	14.40	28.80	21.60	64.80
Deposit/withdrawal prearranged monthly: $0.80 × 0; 15; 60	0	12.00	48.00	60.00
Bank cheques written $11.25× 10; 5; 4	112.50	56.25	45.00	213.75
Foreign currency drafts $12.50 × 4; 1; 7	50.00	12.50	87.50	150.00
Inquiries $2.50 × 12; 20; 11	30.00	50.00	27.50	107.50
Total costs	386.90	379.55	269.60	$1,036.05
Operating income	$(321.90)	$ 70.45	$730.40	$ 478.95

The assumption that the Robinson and Farrel accounts exceed $2,500 every month and the Skerrett account is less than $2,500 each month means the monthly charges apply only to Skerrett.

One student with a banking background noted that in this solution 100% of the spread is attributed to the "borrowing side of the bank." He noted that often the spread is divided between the "borrowing side" and the "lending side" of the bank.

2. Cross-subsidization across individual Premier Accounts occurs when profits made on some accounts are offset by losses on other accounts. The aggregate profitability on the three customers is $478.95. The Farrel account is highly profitable ($730.40), while the Robinson account is sizably unprofitable.

FIB should be very concerned about the cross-subsidization. Competition likely would "understand" that high-balance low-activity type accounts (such as Farrel) are highly profitable. Offering free services to these customers is not likely to retain these accounts if other banks offer higher interest rates. Competition likely will reduce the interest rate spread FIB can earn on the high-balance low-activity accounts they are able to retain.

5-26 (cont'd)

3.   Possible changes FIB could make are:

a.   Offer higher interest rates on high-balance accounts to increase FIB's competitiveness in attracting and retaining these accounts.

b.   Introduce charges for individual services. The ABC study reports the cost of each service. FIB has to decide if it wants to price each service at cost, below cost, or above cost. If it prices above cost, it may use advertising and other means to encourage additional use of those services by customers.

c.   Increase the minimum balance for unlimited use of services.

5-28 (20-30 min.)   Job costing with single direct-cost category, single indirect-cost pool, law firm.

1.   Pricing decisions at Wigan Associates are heavily influenced by reported cost numbers. Suppose Wigan is bidding against another firm for a client with a job similar to that of Widnes Coal. If the costing system overstates the costs of these jobs, Wigan may bid too high and fail to land the client. If the costing system understates the costs of these jobs, Wigan may bid low, land the client, and then lose money in handling the case.

2.

	Widnes Coal	St. Helen's Glass	Total
Direct professional labour, $70 × 104; $70 × 96	$ 7,280	$ 6,720	$14,000
Indirect costs allocated, $105 × 104; $105 × 96	10,920	10,080	21,000
Total costs to be billed	$18,200	$16,800	$35,000

5-30 (30 min.) **Job costing with multiple direct-cost categories, multiple indirect-cost pools, law firm (continuation of 5-28 and 5-29).**

1.

	Widnes Coal	St. Helen's Glass	Total
Direct costs:			
Partner professional labour,			
$100 × 24; $100 × 56	$ 2,400	$ 5,600	$ 8,000
Associate professional labour,			
$50 × 80; $50 × 40	4,000	2,000	6,000
Research support labour	1,600	3,400	5,000
Computer time	500	1,300	1,800
Travel and allowances	600	4,400	5,000
Telephones/faxes	200	1,000	1,200
Photocopying	250	750	1,000
Total direct costs	9,550	18,450	28,000
Indirect costs allocated:			
Indirect costs for partners,			
$57.50 × 24; $57.50 × 56	1,380	3,220	4,600
Indirect costs for associates,			
$20 × 80; $20 × 40	1,600	800	2,400
Total indirect costs	2,980	4,020	7,000
Total costs to be billed	$12,530	$22,470	$35,000

Comparison	Widnes Coal	St. Helen's Glass	Total
Single direct cost/			
Single indirect cost pool	$18,200	$16,800	$35,000
Multiple direct costs/			
Single indirect cost pool	$14,070	$20,930	$35,000
Multiple direct costs/			
Multiple indirect cost pools	$12,530	$22,470	$35,000

The higher the percentage of costs directly traced to each case, and the greater the number of homogeneous indirect cost pools linked to the cost drivers of indirect costs, the more accurate the product cost of each individual case.

5-30 (cont'd)

The Widnes and St. Helen's cases differ in how they use "resource areas" of Wigan Associates:

	Widnes Coal	St. Helen's Glass
Partner professional labour	30.0%	70.0%
Associate professional labour	66.7	33.3
Research support labour	32.0	68.0
Computer time	27.8	72.2
Travel and allowances	12.0	88.0
Telephones/faxes	16.7	83.3
Photocopying	25.0	75.0

The Widnes Coal case makes relatively low use of the higher-cost partners but relatively higher use of the lower-cost associates than does St. Helen's Glass. As a result, it also uses less of the higher indirect costs required to support partners compared to associates. The Widnes Coal case also makes relatively lower use of the support labour, computer time, travel, phones/faxes, and photocopying resource areas than does the St. Helen's Glass case.

2. The specific areas where the multiple direct/multiple indirect (MD/MI) approach can provide better information for decisions at Wigan Associates include:

Pricing and product (case) emphasis decisions. In a bidding situation using single direct/single indirect (SD/SI) or multiple direct/single indirect (MD/SI) data, Wigan may win bids for legal cases on which it will subsequently lose money. It may also not win bids on which it would make money with a lower-priced bid.

From a strategic viewpoint, SD/SI or MD/SI exposes Wigan Associates to cherry-picking by competitors. Other law firms may focus exclusively on Widnes Coal-type cases and take sizable amounts of "profitable" business from Wigan Associates. MD/MI reduces the likelihood of Wigan Associates losing cases on which it would have made money.

Client relationships. MD/MI provides a better "road map" for clients to understand how costs are accumulated at Wigan Associates. Wigan can use this road map when meeting with clients to plan the work to be done on a case *before* it commences. Clients can negotiate ways to get a lower-cost case from Wigan, given the information in MD/MI—for example, (a) use a higher proportion of associate labour time and a lower proportion of partner time, and (b) use fax machines more and air travel less. If clients are informed in advance about how costs will be accumulated, there is less likelihood of disputes about bills submitted to them *after* the work is done.

5-30 (cont'd)

Cost control. The MD/MI approach better highlights the individual cost areas at Wigan Associates than does the SD/SI or MD/SI approaches:

	MD/MI	SD/SI	MD/SI
Number of direct cost categories	7	1	7
Number of indirect cost categories	2	1	1
Total	9	2	8

MD/MI is likely to promote better cost-control practices than SD/SI or MD/SI, as the nine cost categories in MD/MI give Wigan a better handle on how to effectively manage different categories of both direct and indirect costs.

5-32 (30 min.)   Plantwide versus department overhead cost rates.
1.

	Amounts (in thousands)			
	Moulding	Component	Assembly	Total
Manufacturing department overhead	$30,000	$24,000	$29,000	$83,000
Service departments:				
Power				36,000
Maintenance				12,800
Total estimated plantwide overhead				$131,800

Estimated direct manufacturing labour-hours (DMLH):	
Moulding	600
Component	3,000
Assembly	1,400
Total estimated DMLH	5,000

Plantwide overhead rate $= \dfrac{\text{Estimated plantwide overhead}}{\text{Estimated DMLH}}$

$= \$131,800/5,000 = \$26.36$ per DMLH

2.   The department overhead cost rates are shown in Solution Exhibit 5-33.

3.   Merrick Corporation should use department rates to allocate plant overhead to its products. A plantwide rate is appropriate when all products pass through the same processes, and all departments are similar. Departmental rates are appropriate when the converse is true. Merrick's departments are dissimilar in that the Moulding Department is machine-intensive and the other two departments are labour-intensive. Department rates better capture cause-and-effect relationships at Merrick than does a plantwide rate.

5-32 (cont'd)

SOLUTION EXHIBIT 5-33

a.

	Service		Department (in thousands)	Manufacturing	
	Power	Maintenance	Moulding	Component	Assembly
Departmental overhead costs	$36,000	$ 12,800	$30,000	$24,000	$29,000
Allocation of maintenance costs (direct method) $12,800 × 100/150, 30/150, 20/150*		(12,800)	8,533	2,560	1,707
Allocation of power costs $36,000× 400/900, 380/900, 120/900†	(36,000)		16,000	15,200	4,800
Total budgeted overhead of manufacturing departments	$ 0	$ 0	$54,533	$41,760	$35,507

b.

	Power	Maintenance	Moulding	Component	Assembly
Allocation Base			800 MH	3,000 DMLH	1,400 DMLH
Budgeted Overhead Rate (Budgeted overhead ÷ Base)			$68.17/MH	$13.92/DMLH	$25.36/DMLH

*Labour-hours for maintenance costs: 100 + 30 + 20 = 150

†Kilowatt-hours for power usage: 400 + 380 + 120 = 900

95

5-34 (40-50 min.) **ABC, product cross-subsidization.**

1. Total indirect costs are $715,800
    [$140,000+$48,000+$50,000+$60,000+$35,000+$96,000+$13,800+$148,000+$50,000+$75,000]
    Budgeted manufacturing plantwide overhead rate:

Plantwide rate:	=	$715,800/[30,000+30,000]
	=	$11.93 per direct labour-hour

To produce 15,000 units of Jordan, the company has budgeted 30,000 hours; therefore, each unit takes 2 hours. To manufacture 5,000 units of Shenandoah, the company has budgeted 30,000 labour-hours, so each unit requires 6 hours.

Per Unit Cost	Jordan	Shenandoah
Direct material	$100.00	$200.00
Direct labour @ $20/hour	$40.00	$120.00
Allocated OH at $11.93/DL hour	$23.86	$71.58
Total	$163.86	$391.58

Parts 2 & 3:

Students have some discretion in forming cost pools. Certain choices are more obvious than others. Since we have information on orders processed, number of setups, number of requisitions, percentage of units inspected, maintenance hours, and design and support hours, it would make sense to use this information in the creation of cost pools. Therefore it is expected most students would calculate the following rates:

Activity	Cost Driver	Budgeted Cost	Activity Base	Pool Rate
Purchasing materials	# of requisitions	$50,000	160 [50+110]	$312.50
Receiving goods	Orders processed	$35,000	800 [150+650]	$43.75
Setting up	# of setups	$13,800	115 [15+100]	$120.00
Inspection	Units inspected	$148,000	2,500*	$59.20
Design & support	Hours	$125,000	500 [100+400]	$250.00
Maintenance	Maintenance hours	$140,000	1,400 [450+950]	$100.00

* [10%*15,000] + [20%*5,000] = 1,500 + 1,000 = 2,500

This leaves us with 3 activities to classify:

> Utilities, Factory Rental, and Indirect Materials.

A good cost driver for utilities is likely machine-hours. Since we are told that facility costs (i.e. factory rental) are allocated on the basis of machine-hours, we can group utilities and factory rental into the same pool.

Pool Rate:	=	[$48,000 + $96,000]/[2,000+2,000]
	=	$144,000/4,000 = $36.00 per machine-hour

Indirect materials will likely cause the most variation. Possible drivers may be number of units produced, machine-hours, or possibly cost of direct materials.

5-34 (cont'd)

The following solutions show two possible classifications:
- Separate cost pool allocated on the basis of number of units produced
- Classification with facility costs under the assumption machine-hours would be the cost driver

Assumption A: Indirect materials allocated on the basis of number of units produced:
Indirect materials pool rate: $60,000/[15,000+5,000] = $3.00 per unit

Allocation of Overhead using ABC:

	Jordan	Shenandoah
Purchasing @ $312.50 [50/110]	$15,625.00	$34,375.00
Receiving @ $43.75 [150/650]	$6,562.50	$28,437.50
Setting up @ $120.00 [15/100]	$1,800.00	$12,000.00
Inspection @ $59.20 [1,500/1,000]	$88,800.00	$59,200.00
Design & support @ $250 [100/400]	$25,000.00	$100,000.00
Maintenance @ $100 [450/950]	$45,000.00	$95,000.00
Subtotal	$182,787.50	$329,012.50
Indirect materials @ $3.00 [15,000/5,000]	$45,000.00	$15,000.00
Facility @ $36 [2,000/2,000]	$72,000.00	$72,000.00
Total allocated overhead	$299,787.50	$416,012.50
Number of units produced	15,000	5,000
Per unit cost of overhead	$19.986	$83.203

Assumption B: Indirect materials allocated on the basis of machine-hours.
Pool rate   =   [$48,000+$96,000+$60,000]/[2,000+2,000]
                 = $204,000/4,000 = $51.00 per machine-hour

	Jordan	Shenandoah
Purchasing @ $312.50 [50/110]	$15,625.00	$34,375.00
Receiving @ $43.75 [150/650]	$6,562.50	$28,437.50
Setting up @ $120.00 [15/100]	$1,800.00	$12,000.00
Inspection @ $59.20 [1,500/1,000]	$88,800.00	$59,200.00
Design & support @ $250 [100/400]	$25,000.00	$100,000.00
Maintenance @ $100 [450/950]	$45,000.00	$95,000.00
Subtotal	$182,787.50	$329,012.50
Facility @ $51 [2,000/2,000]	$102,000.00	$102,000.00
Total allocated overhead	$284,787.50	$431,012.50
Number of units produced	15,000	5,000
Per unit cost of overhead	$18.986	$86.203

5-34 (cont'd)

Parts 3 & 4.
Assumption A:

	Jordan	Shenandoah
Per unit cost of overhead – using ABC	$19.99	$83.20
Add: Direct materials	$100.00	$200.00
Add: Direct labour	$40.00	$120.00
Total unit cost – ABC	$159.99	$403.20
Unit cost – plantwide rate	$163.86	$391.58
Dollar difference (decrease)/increase	($3.87)	$11.62
Percentage difference	(2.4%)	3.0%

Assumption B:

	Jordan	Shenandoah
Per unit cost of overhead – using ABC	$18.99	$86.20
Add: Direct materials	$100.00	$200.00
Add: Direct labour	$40.00	$120.00
Total unit cost – ABC	$158.99	$406.20
Unit cost – plantwide rate	$163.86	$391.58
Dollar difference (decrease)/increase	($4.87)	$14.62
Percentage difference	(3.0%)	3.7%

The activity based costing system does not result in large differences between the costs, but in a competitive market these differences could be important.

5-36 (35-40 min.) Activity-based costing, product cross-subsidization.

1. Plantwide overhead rate $=$ $\dfrac{\text{Total Budgeted Overhead}}{\text{Total Budgeted Direct Labour-Hours}}$

$=$ $\dfrac{[\$7,200 + \$9,800 + \$3,230 + \$1,820]}{[\$39,200/\$28]}$

$=$ $\$22,050/1,400$

$=$ $\$15.75$ per direct labour-hour

2. Total and unit manufacturing cost of each product:

Direct labour is split equally between the two models, therefore each model has $39,200/2 or $19,600 of direct labour costs.

Since both products have equal direct labour cost and a similar average wage rate, then manufacturing overhead would be equally allocated, $22,050/2 = $11,025 per product.

Per unit DL costs for Diagnostic = $19,600/600 = $32.66, 1.167 hours ($32.66/$28)

Per unit DL costs for Profiler = $19,600/350 = $56.00, 2 hours/unit($56/$28)

Per unit MOH costs for Diagnostic = 1.167*$15.75 = $18.38

Per unit MOH costs for Profiler = 2 * $15.75 = $31.50

	Diagnostic	**Profiler**
Unit Cost:		
Direct materials	$5.50	$26.50
Direct labour	$32.66	$56.00
MOH allocated	$18.38	$31.50
Total per unit cost	$56.54	$114.00
Total Costs:		
Direct materials	$3,300	$9,275
Direct labour	$19,600	$19,600
Manufacturing overhead	$11,025	$11,025
Total Costs	$33,925	$39,900

3. Activity rates for each pool:

Activity	Budgeted Cost	Budgeted Activity	Pool Rate
Setups	$7,200	15 [5+10]	$480 per setup
Machining	$9,800	700 [210+490]	$14 per machine-hour
Assembly	$3,230	950 [600+350]	$3.40 per unit
Quality testing	$1,820	65*	$28 per unit tested

*Company inspects 5% of Diagnostic Model and 10% of Profiler

= [5%*600] + [10%*350] = 30+35 = 65 units

5-36 (cont'd)

4.   Total and unit manufacturing cost of each product under ABC:

	Diagnostic	Profiler
Setups @ $480 [5/10]	$2,400	$4,800
Machining @ $14 [210/490]	$2,940	$6,860
Assembly @ $3.40 [600/350]	$2,040	$1,190
Quality testing @ $28 [30/35]	$840	$980
Total MOH allocated	$8,220	$13,830
Direct materials	$3,300	$9,275
Direct labour	$19,600	$19,600
Total manufacturing costs	$31,120	$42,705
# of units produced	600	350
Cost per unit – ABC	$51.87	$122.01

5. Comparison:

	Diagnostic	Profiler
Cost per unit –plantwide rate	$56.54	$114.00
Cost per unit – ABC	$51.87	$122.01
Difference	Reduction of $4.67	Increase of $8.01
Percentage change	8.3% cost decrease	7.0% cost increase

The company should consider switching to ABC, because the cost differences are material and may affect selling prices as well as volumes.

5-38 (30 min.) Make/buy, activity-based costing, opportunity costs.

1. Relevant costs under buy alternative:

Purchases, 10,000 × $12.20	$122,000

Relevant costs under make alternative:

Direct materials	$60,000
Direct manufacturing labour	30,000
Variable manufacturing overhead	20,000
Inspection, setup, materials handling	2,500
Machine rent	3,500
Total relevant costs under make alternative	$116,000

The allocated fixed plant administration and insurance will not change whether Ace makes or buys the chains. Hence these costs are irrelevant to the make/buy decision. The analysis indicates that Ace should not buy the chains from the outside supplier.

2. Relevant costs under the make alternative:

Relevant costs (as computed in requirement 1)	$116,000

Relevant costs under the buy alternative:

Costs of purchases (10,000 × $12.20)	$122,000
Additional fixed costs	18,500
Additional contribution margin from using the space where the chains were made to upgrade the bicycles by adding mud flaps and reflector bars, 10,000 × ($25 – $20.50)	(45,000)
	$ 95,500

Ace should now buy the chains from the outside vendor and use its own capacity to upgrade its own bicycles.

3. (a) Since mud flaps and reflectors are added anyway and yield an additional contribution of $45,000, minus additional fixed costs of $18,500, they are irrelevant to the analysis.

   (b) Cost of manufacturing chains:

Variable costs ($6.00 + $3.00 + $2.00 = $11.00) × 6,400	=	$70,400
Batch costs, $250/batch × 8 batches	=	2,000
Machine rent	=	3,500
		$75,900

Cost of buying chains, $12.20 × 6,400	$78,080

In this case, Ace should manufacture the chains.

CHAPTER 6
MASTER BUDGET AND RESPONSIBILITY ACCOUNTING

6-2 A *master budget* is a single comprehensive income statement that combines information from many individual budgeted income statements. The term "master" refers to it being a comprehensive organization-wide set of budgets that coordinates all financial projections for a set period of time, for the entire organization.

6-4 Strategy, plans, and budgets are interrelated and affect one another. Strategy is a broad term that usually means selection of overall objectives. Strategic analysis underlies both long-run and short-run planning. In turn, these plans lead to the formulation of budgets. Budgets provide feedback to managers about the likely effects of their strategic plans. Managers use this feedback to revise their strategic plans.

6-6 A company that shares its own internal budget information with other companies can gain multiple benefits. One benefit is better coordination with suppliers, which can reduce the likelihood of supply shortages. Better coordination with customers can result in increased sales as demand by customers is less likely to exceed supply. Better coordination across the whole supply chain can also help a company reduce inventories and thus reduce the costs of holding inventories. Suppliers and customers become "partners in profit." Here satisfied customers sell the final product to new customers.

6-8 The steps in preparing an operating budget are:

1. Prepare the revenue budget
2. Prepare the production budget (in units)
3. Prepare the direct materials usage budget and direct materials purchases budget
4. Prepare the direct manufacturing labour budget
5. Prepare the manufacturing overhead budget
6. Prepare the ending inventories budget
7. Prepare the cost of goods sold budget
8. Prepare the nonproduction costs budget
9. Prepare the budgeted income statement

6-10 Sensitivity analysis adds an extra dimension to budgeting. It enables managers to examine how budgeted amounts change with changes in the underlying assumptions. This helps managers to monitor those assumptions that are most critical to a company attaining its budget and to make timely adjustments to plans when appropriate.

6-12 Non-output-based cost drivers can be incorporated into budgeting by the use of activity-based budgeting (ABB). ABB focuses on the budgeted cost of activities necessary to produce and sell products and services. Non-output-based cost drivers, such as the number of part numbers, number of batches, and number of new products, can be used with ABB.

6-14 Equal or across-the-board reductions is a strategy that penalizes honest business functions and rewards those that pad the budgets. The strategy produces a perverse incentive, rewarding the overstatement of budgeted costs and the understatement of budgeted revenues.

6-16 (20 min.) Budgeting and behaviour.

1. (a) Gain additional insight into the strategy of an organization. Exhibit 6-1 shows arrows pointing both ways between strategy analysis and long-term planning and short-term planning. Detailed analysis for budgeting can sometimes highlight strategy assumptions (such as cost levels and demand levels) that are not likely to hold.
   (b) Anticipate resource demands in a timely way. Budgeting can highlight working capital shortages, cash shortages, personnel shortages, and so on. Early warning signals can enable a company to take action to avoid having small problems become large problems.
   (c) Improve the communication level in an organization. The budgeting process itself can assist in having diverse groups gain a better understanding of how other groups affect their performance. Sharing budgets across organizations in a supply chain can help a company better meet end-point customer demand. Communication with suppliers can reduce parts shortages.

2. Factors to consider when preparing sales forecasts include:

   (a) Any constraining variables on sales. For example, if demand outstrips available productive capacity or a key component is in short supply, the sales forecast should be based on the maximum units that can be produced.
   (b) Information from customers about their new product developments and advertising plans. Proactive not reactive.
   (c) Feedback from customers about satisfaction with a company's products vis-à-vis satisfaction levels for the products of competitors. This is customer conformance feedback telling managers how well the actual output conformed to the customer's expectations.
   (d) Likely new product releases by competitors or new entrants into a market. Again this is proactive not reactive.

6-18 (15 min.) Sales budget, service setting.

1.

McGrath & Sons	2009 Volume	At 2009 Selling Prices	Expected 2010 Change in Volume	Expected 2010 Volume
Radon Tests	11,000	$250	+5%	11,550
Lead Tests	15,200	$200	-10%	13,680

McGrath & Sons Sales Budget
For the Year Ended December 31, 2010

	Selling Price	Units Sold	Total Revenues
Radon Tests	$250	11,550	$2,887,500
Lead Tests	$200	13,680	2,736,000
			$5,623,500

2.

McGrath & Sons	2009 Volume	Planned 2010 Selling Prices	Expected 2010 Change in Volume	Expected 2010 Volume
Radon Tests	11,000	$250	+5%	11,550
Lead Tests	15,200	$190	-5%	14,440

McGrath & Sons Sales Budget
For the Year Ended December 31, 2010

	Selling Price	Units Sold	Total Revenues
Radon Tests	$250	11,550	$2,887,500
Lead Tests	$190	14,440	2,743,600
			$5,631,100

Expected revenues at the new 2010 prices are $5,631,100, which are greater than the expected 2010 revenues of $5,623,500 if the prices are unchanged. So, if the goal is to maximize sales revenue and if Jim McGrath's forecasts are reliable, the company should lower its price for a lead test in 2010.

6-20 (5 min.) Direct materials budget.

Direct materials to be used in production (bottles)	2,100,000
Add target ending direct materials inventory (bottles)	55,000
Total requirements (bottles)	2,155,000
Deduct beginning direct materials inventory (bottles)	23,700
Direct materials to be purchased (bottles)	2,131,300

6-22 (30 min.) Sales and production budget.

1.

	Selling Price	Units Sold	Total Revenues
l-litre bottles	$0.50	6,240,000[a]	$ 3,120,000
16-litre units	7.00	2,220,000[b]	15,540,000
			$18,660,000

[a]520,000 × 12 months = 6,240,000
[b]185,000 × 12 months = 2,220,000

2.

Budgeted unit sales (1-litre bottles)	6,240,000
Add target ending finished goods inventory	976,000
Total requirements	7,216,000
Deduct beginning finished goods inventory	1,275,000
Units to be produced	5,941,000

3.
$$\text{Beginning inventory} = \text{Budgeted sales} + \text{Target ending inventory} - \text{Budgeted production}$$
$$= 2,220,000 + 265,000 - 2,090,000$$
$$= 395,000 \text{ 16-litre units}$$

6-24 (15-20 min.) Revenue, production, and purchases budget.

1. 985,000 motorcycles × 505,000 yen = 497,425,000,000 yen

2.

Budgeted sales (units)	985,000
Add target ending finished goods inventory	115,000
Total requirements	1,100,000
Deduct beginning finished goods inventory	152,000
Units to be produced	948,000

3.

Direct materials to be used in production, 948,000 × 2	1,896,000
Add target ending direct materials inventory	28,000
Total requirements	1,924,000
Deduct beginning direct materials inventory	19,000
Direct materials to be purchased	1,905,000
Cost per wheel in yen	21,300
Direct materials purchase cost in yen	40,576,500,000

Note the relatively small inventory of wheels. In Japan, suppliers tend to be located very close to the major manufacturer. Inventories are controlled by just-in-time (JIT) and similar systems. Indeed, some direct materials inventories are almost nonexistent.

6-26 (30 min.)   Cash flow analysis.

1.   The cash that TabComp Inc. can expect to collect during April 2008 is calculated below:

April cash receipts:	
April cash sales ($400,000 × .25)	$100,000
April credit card sales ($400,000 × .30 × .96)	115,200
Collections on account:	
March ($480,000 × .45 × .70)	151,200
February ($500,000 × .45 × .28)	63,000
January (uncollectable–not relevant)	0
Total collections	$429,400

2.   (a)   The projected number of the MZB-33 computer hardware units that TabComp Inc. will order on January 25, 2008, is calculated as follows.

	MZB-33 Units
March sales	110
Plus: Ending inventory[a]	27
Total needed	137
Less: Beginning inventory[b]	33
Projected purchases in units	104

[a]0.30 × 90 unit sales in April

[b]0.30 × 110 unit sales in March

(b)

Selling price = $2,025,000 ÷ 675 units, or for March, $330,000 ÷110 units	
= $3,000 per unit	
Purchase price per unit, 60% × $3,000	$ 1,800
Projected unit purchases	X 104
Total MZB-33 purchases, $1,800 × 104	$187,200

3.   Monthly cash budgets are prepared by companies such as TabComp Inc. in order to plan for their cash needs. This means identifying when both excess cash and cash shortages may occur. A company needs to know when cash shortages will occur so that prior arrangements can be made with lending institutions in order to have cash available for borrowing when the company needs it. At the same time, a company should be aware of when there will be excess cash available for investment or for repaying loans.

6-28 (20-30 min.) Kaizen approach to activity-based budgeting (continuation of 6-27).

1.

Activity	Cost Hierarchy	Budgeted Cost-Driver Rates		
		January	February	March
Ordering	Batch-level	$90.00	$89.82	$89.64
Delivery	Batch-level	82.00	81.84	81.67
Shelf-stocking	Output-unit-level	21.00	20.96	20.92
Customer support	Output-unit-level	0.18	0.18	0.18

The March 2009 rates can be used to compute the total budgeted cost for each activity area in March 2009:

Activity	Cost Hierarchy	Soft Drinks	Fresh Produce	Packaged Food	Total
Ordering $89.64 × 14; 24; 14	Batch-level	$1,255	$2,151	$1,255	$4,661
Delivery $81.67 × 12; 62; 19	Batch-level	980	5,064	1,552	7,596
Shelf-stocking $20.92 × 16; 172; 94	Output-unit-level	335	3,598	1,966	5,899
Customer support $0.179 × 4,600; 34,200; 10,750	Output-unit-level	823	6,122	1,924	8,869
Total		$3,393	$16,935	$6,697	$27,025

2. A kaizen budgeting approach signals management's commitment to systematic cost reduction. Compare the budgeted costs from Question 6-27 and 6-28.

	Ordering	Delivery	Shelf-Stocking	Customer Support
Question 6-27	$4,680	$7,626	$5,922	$8,919
Question 6-28 (Kaizen)	4,661	7,596	5,899	8,869

The kaizen budget number will show unfavorable variances for managers whose activities do not meet the required monthly cost reductions. This likely will put more pressure on managers to creatively seek out cost reductions by working "smarter" within FS or by having "better" interactions with suppliers or customers.

One limitation of kaizen budgeting, as illustrated in this question, is that it assumes small incremental improvements each month. It is possible that some cost improvements arise from large discontinuous changes in operating processes, supplier networks, or customer interactions. Companies need to highlight the importance of seeking these large discontinuous improvements as well as the small incremental improvements.

6-30 (30 min.) Budgeted income statement.

Easecom Company
Budgeted Income Statement for 2011
(in thousands)

Revenues
  Equipment ($6,000 × 1.06 × 1.10) $6,996
  Maintenance contracts ($1,800 × 1.06)   1,908
      Total revenues $8,904
Cost of goods sold ($4,600 × 1.03 × 1.06)   5,022
Gross margin   3,882
Operating costs:
  Marketing costs ($600 + $250)   850
  Distribution costs ($150 × 1.06)   159
  Customer maintenance costs ($1,000 + $130) 1,130
  Administrative costs   900
      Total operating costs   3,039
Operating income $ 843

6-32 (40 min.) Cash budgeting for distributor.

1. The pro forma cash budget for Montrose for the second quarter of 2010 is presented below. Supporting calculations are presented on the next page.

Montrose Inc.
Cash Budget
For the Second Quarter 2010

	April	May	June
Beginning balance	$ 600,000	$ 600,000	$ 1,476,000
Collections[1]			
February sales	4,800,000		
March sales	6,480,000	4,320,000	
April sales		8,280,000	5,520,000
May sales			9,000,000
Total receipts	11,280,000	12,600,000	14,520,000
Total cash available	11,880,000	13,200,000	15,996,000
Disbursements			
Accounts payable[5]	4,986,000	5,682,000	6,342,000
Hourly wages[2]	4,140,000	4,500,000	5,040,000
General & administrative[3]	1,080,000	1,080,000	1,080,000
Property taxes			408,000
Income taxes[4]	1,536,000		
Total disbursements	11,742,000	11,262,000	12,870,000
Cash balance	138,000	1,938,000	3,126,000
Cash borrowed	462,000		
Cash repaid		(462,000)	
Ending balance	$ 600,000	$1,476,000	$ 3,126,000

[1] 60% of sales in first month; 40% of sales in second month
[2] 30% of current month sales
[3] (Total less property taxes and amortization) ÷ 12
[4] 40% × $3,840,000
[5] See schedule on next page.

6-32 (cont'd)

Supporting Calculations

Accounts payable—parts received:

Month	40% of Revenues	Timing	February	March	April	May	June
February	$4,800,000	.30	$1,440,000				
March	4,320,000	.70	3,024,000				
March	4,320,000	.30		$1,296,000			
April	5,520,000	.70		3,864,000			
April	5,520,000	.30			$1,656,000		
May	6,000,000	.70			4,200,000		
May	6,000,000	.30				$1,800,000	
June	6,720,000	.70				4,704,000	
			$4,464,000	$5,160,000	$5,856,000	$6,504,000	
Payment							
February	$4,464,000	.25			$1,116,000		
March	5,160,000	.75			3,870,000		
March	5,160,000	.25				$1,290,000	
April	5,856,000	.75				4,392,000	
April	5,856,000	.25					$1,464,000
May	6,504,000	.75					4,878,000
			$ 0	$ 0	$4,986,000	$5,682,000	$6,342,000

2. Cash budgeting is important for Montrose because as sales grow so will expenditures for input factors. Since these expenditures generally precede cash receipts, the company must plan for possible financing to cover the gap between payments and receipts. The cash budget shows the probable cash position at certain points in time, allowing the company to plan for borrowing, as Mon Montroseose must do in April.

   Cash budgeting also facilitates the control of excess cash. The company may be losing investment opportunities, if excess cash is left idle in a chequing account. The cash budget alerts management to periods when there will be excess cash available for investment, thus facilitating financial planning and cash control.

6-34 (45 min.) Sensitivity analysis, changing budget assumptions, and Kaizen approach.

1.

	Chippo	Choco	Total
Revenues			
Chippo, $3.60 × 600,000	$2,160,000		$2,160,000
Choco, $3.60 × 600,000		$2,160,000	2,160,000
	$2,160,000	$2,160,000	$4,320,000
Cost of goods sold			
Chocolate chips			
($2.40 × 300,000[a]; $2.40 × 150,000[b])	720,000	360,000	1,080,000
Cookie dough			
($1.20 × 300,000[a]; $1.20 × 450,000[b])	360,000	540,000	900,000
Direct manufacturing labour			
($24 × 2,400; $24 × 3,600)	57,600	86,400	144,000
Indirect manufacturing costs			
(50% × $192,000; 50% × $192,000)	96,000	96,000	192,000
Cost of goods sold	1,233,600	1,082,400	2,316,000
Gross margin	$ 926,400	$1,077,600	$2,004,000

[a]Chippo: 600,000 × 0.50 = 300,000 kilograms chocolate chips; 600,000 × 0.50 = 300,000 kilograms cookie dough
[b]Choco: 600,000 × 0.25 = 150,000 kilograms chocolate chips; 600,000 × 0.75 = 450,000 kilograms cookie dough

2.

	Chippo	Choco	Total
Revenues			
Chippo $3.60 × 600,000	$2,160,000		$2,160,000
Choco $3.60 × 600,000		$2,160,000	2,160,000
	$2,160,000	$2,160,000	$4,320,000
Cost of goods sold			
Chocolate chips			
($2.33 × 300,000; $2.33 × 150,000)	699,000	349,500	1,048,500
Cookie dough			
($1.16 × 300,000; $1.16 × 450,000)	348,000	522,000	870,000
Direct manufacturing labour			
($24 × 2,400; $24 × 3,600)	57,600	86,400	144,000
Indirect manufacturing costs			
(50% × $192,000; 50% × $192,000)	96,000	96,000	192,000
	1,200,600	1,053,900	2,254,500
Gross margin	$ 959,400	$1,106,100	$2,065,500

6-34 (cont'd)

3.

	Chippo	Choco	Total
Revenues			
Chippo $3.60 × 600,000	$2,160,000		$2,160,000
Choco $3.60 × 600,000		$2,160,000	2,160,000
	$2,160,000	$2,160,000	$4,320,000
Cost of goods sold			
Chocolate chips			
($2.33 × 300,000; $2.33 × 150,000)	699,000	349,500	1,048,500
Cookie dough			
($1.16 × 300,000; $1.16 × 450,000)	348,000	522,000	870,000
Direct manufacturing labour			
($24 × 2,376[c]; $24 × 3,564[d])	57,024	85,536	142,560
Indirect manufacturing costs			
(50% × $188,160[e]; 50% × $188,160[e])	94,080	94,080	188,160
	1,198,104	1,051,116	2,249,220
Gross margin	$ 961,896	$1,108,884	$2,070,780

[c]2,400 (1 – 0.01)
[d]3,600 (1 – 0.01)
[e]192,000 (1 – 0.02)

6-36 (60 min.) Comprehensive problem with ABC costing.

1.

Revenue Budget
For the Month of April

	Units	Selling Price	Total Revenues
Cat-allac	500	$160	$ 80,000
Dog-eriffic	300	250	75,000
Total			$155,000

2.

Production Budget
For the Month of April

	Product	
	Cat-allac	Dog-eriffic
Budgeted unit sales	500	300
Add target ending finished goods inventory	35	15
Total required units	535	315
Deduct beginning finished goods inventory	15	30
Units of finished goods to be produced	520	285

6-36 (cont'd)

3a.

Direct Material Usage Budget in Quantity and Dollars
For the Month of April

	Plastic	Metal	Total
	Material		
Physical Units Budget			
Direct materials required for			
Cat-allac (520 units × 4 kgs. and 0.5 kg.)	2,080 kgs.	260 kgs.	
Dog-errific (285 units × 6 kgs. and 1 kg.)	1,710 kgs.	285 kgs.	
Total quantity of direct material to be used	3,790 kgs.	545 kgs.	
Cost Budget			
Available from beginning direct materials inventory			
(under a FIFO cost-flow assumption)			
Plastic: 250 kgs. × $3.80 per kg.	$ 950		
Metal: 60 kgs. × $3 per kg.		$ 180	
To be purchased this period			
Plastic: (3,790 – 250) kgs. × $4 per kg.	14,160		
Metal: (545 – 60) kgs. × $3 per kg.		1,455	
Direct materials to be used this period	$15,110	$ 1,635	$16,745

Direct Material Purchases Budget
For the Month of April

	Plastic	Metal	Total
	Material		
Physical Units Budget			
To be used in production (requirement 3)	3,790 kgs.	545 kgs.	
Add target ending inventory	380 kgs.	55 kgs.	
Total requirements	4,170 kgs.	600 kgs.	
Deduct beginning inventory	250 kgs.	60 kgs.	
Purchases to be made	3,920 kgs.	540 kgs.	
Cost Budget			
Plastic: 3,920 kgs. × $4	$15,680		
Metal: 540 kgs. × $3		$ 1,620	
Purchases	$15,680	$ 1,620	$ 17,300

6-36 (cont'd)

4.

Direct Manufacturing Labour Costs Budget
For the Month of April

	Output Units Produced (requirement 2)	DMLH per Unit	Total Hours	Hourly Wage Rate	Total
Cat-allac	520	3	1,560	$10	$15,600
Dog-errific	285	5	1,425	10	14,250
Total					$29,850

5. Machine Setup Overhead

	Cat-allac	Dog-errific	Total
Units to be produced	520	285	
Units per batch	÷ 20	÷15	
Number of batches	26	19	
Setup time per batch	× 1.5 hrs.	× 1.75 hrs.	
Total setup time	39 hrs.	33.25 hrs.	72.25 hrs.

Budgeted machine setup costs = $100 per setup hour × 72.25 hours
= $7,225

Processing Overhead
Budgeted machine-hours (MH) = (10 MH per unit × 520 units) + (18 MH per unit × 285 units)
= 5,200 MH + 5,130 MH = 10,330 MH
Budgeted processing costs = $5 per MH × 10,330 MH
= $51,650

Inspection Overhead
Budgeted inspection hours = (0.5 × 26 batches) + (0.6 × 19 batches)
= 13 + 11.4 = 24.4 inspection hrs.
Budgeted inspection costs = $16 per inspection hr. × 24.4 inspection hours
= $390.40

Manufacturing Overhead Budget
For the Month of April

Machine setup costs	$ 7,225
Processing costs	51,650
Inspection costs	390
Total costs	$59,265

115

6-36 (cont'd)

6.

Unit Costs of Ending Finished Goods Inventory
April 30, 20xx

		Product			
		Cat-allac		Dog-errific	
	Cost per Unit of Input	Input per Unit of Output	Total	Input per Unit of Output	Total
Plastic	$ 4	4 kgs.	$ 16.00	6 kgs.	$ 24.00
Metal	3	0.5 kgs.	1.50	1 kg.	3.00
Direct manufacturing labour	10	3 hrs.	30.00	5 hrs.	50.00
Machine setup	100	0.075 hrs. [1]	7.50	0.1167 hr[1]	11.67
Processing	5	10 MH	50.00	18 MH	90.00
Inspection	16	0.025 hr[2]	0.40	0.04 hr.[2]	0.64
Total			$105.40		$179.31

[1] 39 setup hours ÷ 520 units = 0.075 hours per unit; 33.25 setup hours ÷ 285 units = 0.1167 hours per unit
[2] 13 inspection hours ÷ 520 units = 0.025 hours per unit; 11.4 inspection hours ÷ 285 units = 0.04 hours per unit

Ending Inventories Budget
April 30, 20xx

	Quantity	Cost per Unit	Total	
Direct Materials				
Plastic	380	$4	$1,520	
Metals	55	3	165	$1,685
Finished goods				
Cat-allac	35	$105.40	$3,689	
Dog-errific	15	179.31	2,690	6,379
Total ending inventory				$8,064

6-36 (cont'd)

7.

Cost of Goods Sold Budget
For the Month of April, 20xx

Beginning finished goods inventory, April, 1 ($1,500 + $5,580)		$ 7,080
Direct materials used (requirement 3)	$16,745	
Direct manufacturing labour (requirement 4)	29,850	
Manufacturing overhead (requirement 5)	59,265	
Cost of goods manufactured		105,860
Cost of goods available for sale		112,940
Deduct: Ending finished goods inventory, April 30 (reqmt. 6)		6,379
Cost of goods sold		$106,561

8.

Nonmanufacturing Costs Budget
For the Month of April, 20xx

Salaries ($36,000 ÷ 2 **Error! Objects cannot be created from editing field codes.** 1.05)	$18,900
Other fixed costs ($36,000 ÷ 2)	18,000
Sales commissions ($155,000 **Error! Objects cannot be created from editing field codes.** 1%)	1,550
Total nonmanufacturing costs	$38,450

9.

Budgeted Income Statement
For the Month of April, 20xx

Revenues	$155,000
Cost of goods sold	106,561
Gross margin	48,439
Operating (nonmanufacturing) costs	38,450
Operating income	$ 9,989

6-38 (15 min.) Responsibility and Controllability.

The time lost in the plant should be charged to the purchasing department. Certainly, the plant manager could not be asked to underwrite a loss which is due to failure of delivery over which he had no supervision. Although the purchasing agent may feel that he has done everything he possibly could, he must realize that, in the whole organization, he is *the one* who is in the best position to evaluate the situation. He receives an assignment. He may accept it or reject it. But if he accepts, he must perform. If he fails, the damage is evaluated. Everybody makes mistakes. The important point is to avoid making too many mistakes and also to understand fully that the extensive control reflected in "responsibility accounting" is the necessary balance to the great freedom of action that individual executives are given.

Discussions of this problem have again and again revealed a tendency among students (and among accountants and managers) to "fix the blame" — as if the variances arising from a responsibility accounting system should pinpoint misbehaviour and provide answers. The point is that no accounting system or variances can provide answers. However, variances can lead to questions. In this case, in deciding where the penalty should be assigned, the student might inquire *who should be asked — not who should be blamed.*

Classroom discussions have also raised the following diverse points:

(a) Is the railway company liable? Yes, and they have liability insurance.

(b) Costs of idle time are usually routinely charged to the production department. Should the information system be fine-tuned to reallocate such costs to the purchasing department? Both purchasing and the plant manager answer to either a business manager or an operations manager. The buck stops here. Some companies have the purchasing department answer directly to the plant manager, which would be a probable result of the above mistake. Give accountability to the plant manager as his/her authority warrants it.

(c) How will the purchasing managers behave in the future regarding willingness to take risks?

The text emphasizes the following: Beware of overemphasis on controllability. For example, a time-honoured theme of management is that responsibility should not be given without accompanying authority. Such a guide is a useful first step, but responsibility accounting is more far-reaching. The basic focus should be on *information* or *knowledge*, not on control. The key question is: "Who is the best informed?" Put another way, "Who is the person who can tell us the most about the specific item, regardless of ability to exert personal control?"

CHAPTER 7
FLEXIBLE BUDGETS, VARIANCES, AND
MANAGEMENT CONTROL: I

7-2   A *favourable variance* – denoted F– is a variance that increases operating income relative to the budgeted amount. An *unfavourable variance* – denoted U – is a variance that decreases operating income relative to the budgeted amount.

7-4   The master-budget schedules (illustrated in Chapter 6) that are relevant to the development of a flexible budget are the revenue budget, direct materials usage budget, direct manufacturing labour budget, manufacturing overhead budget, nonproduction costs budget, and a schedule of quantities used in cost allocation bases as well as budgeted cost allocation rates (or cost drivers and cost driver rates if ABC budgeting is used).

7-6   The dollar value of a variance will catch attention but the value is in explaining what caused the variance. There are often multiple causes of a single variance.

7-8   Possible causes of a favourable materials price variance are:
- purchasing officer negotiated more skillfully than was planned in the budget,
- purchasing manager bought in larger lot sizes than budgeted, thus obtaining quantity discounts,
- materials prices decreased unexpectedly due to, say, industry oversupply,
- budgeted purchase prices were set without careful analysis of the market, and
- purchasing manager received unfavourable terms on nonpurchase price factors (such as lower quality materials).

7-10   The arithmetic signals a variance exists but does not explain why. Anyone can do the arithmetic but managers familiar with the process must explain what caused an efficiency or a price variance.

7-12   An individual business function, such as production, is interdependent with other business functions. Factors outside of production can explain why variances arise in the production area. For example:
- purchasing of lower quality materials that creates excess waste
- poor design of products or processes can lead to a sizable number of defects, and
- marketing personnel making promises for delivery times that require a large number of rush orders that create production-scheduling difficulties.

7-14   Variances can be calculated at the activity level as well as at the company level. For example, a price variance and an efficiency variance can be computed for an activity area.

7-16 (15 min.) Flexible budget.

The existing performance report is a Level 1 analysis, based on a static budget. It makes no adjustment for changes in output levels. The budgeted output level is 10,000 units—direct materials of $460,000 in the static budget ÷ budgeted direct materials cost per attaché case of $46.

The following is a Level 2 analysis that presents a flexible-budget variance and a sales-volume variance of each direct cost category:

	Actual Results (1)	Flexible-Budget Variances (2)=(1)–(3)	Flexible Budget (3)	Sales-Volume Variances (4)=(3)–(5)	Static Budget (5)
Output units	9,050	0	9,050	950 U	10,000
Direct materials	$436,800	$20,500 U	$416,300 [1]	$43,700 F	$460,000
Direct manufacturing labour	93,600	520 F	94,120 [2]	9,880 F	104,000
Direct marketing labour	132,000	3,490 U	128,510 [3]	13,490 F	142,000
Total direct costs	$662,400	$23,470 U	$638,930	$67,070 F	$706,000

$23,470 U $67,070 F

Flexible-budget variance   Sales-volume variance

$43,600 F

Static-budget variance

The Level 1 analysis shows total direct costs have a $43,600 favourable variance. However, the Level 2 analysis reveals that this favourable variance is due to the reduction in output of 950 units from the budgeted 10,000 units. Once this reduction in output is taken into account (via a flexible budget), the flexible-budget variance shows each direct cost category but one to have an unfavourable variance indicating less efficient use of each direct cost item than was budgeted.

Each direct cost category has an actual unit variable cost that exceeds its budgeted unit cost except for direct manufacturing labour:

	Actual	Budgeted
Units	9,050	10,000
Direct materials	$48.27	$46.00
Direct manufacturing labour	$10.34	$ 10.40
Direct marketing labour	$14.59	$14.20

Analysis of price and efficiency variances for each cost category could assist in further identifying the causes of these more aggregated (Level 2) variances.

1) flexible budget = cost based on budgeted unit cost times the actual quantity. ($46 × 9,050 = $416,300)

2) $10.40 × 9,050 = $94,120

3) $14.20 × 9,050 = $128,510

7-18 (10 min.) Benchmarking.

1. The managers at S&S need further information to interpret these variances. Based only on the dollar amounts, the direct labour variance appears to be most critical followed in order by the direct labour price variance, the direct materials efficiency variance, and the direct materials price variance. The other information needed is a guideline about what "normal" variance values are. All the unfavourable variances would be extremely small in a multi-million dollar company but perhaps very large in a privately owned and managed $100,000 per year operating profit company.

    If these variances are beyond the acceptable or normal range, then the managers should begin with the largest unfavourable variance, direct labour efficiency variance, because this poses the largest threat to operating income. It may, however, be the case that the added labour hours arose because of poor quality materials purchased at lower prices. There are many factors that interact to cause variances.

2. A standard is not an ideal. A benchmark is the best that can currently be achieved by any competitor in an industry. A standard does not imply excellence, whereas a benchmark implies a strategy of continuous improvement to meet or exceed the benchmark. Cost benchmarks indicate a company has adopted an overall strategy of cost leadership.

7-20 (20-30 min.) Price and efficiency variances.

1. The key information items are:

	Actual	Budgeted
Output units (scones)	60,800	60,000
Input units	17,000	16,000
Cost per input unit	$0.99	$1.11

Peterson budgets to obtain 3.75 (60,000 ÷ 16,000) pumpkin scones from each kilogram of pumpkin. The flexible-budget variance is $1,167 F.

	Actual Results (1)	Flexible-Budget Variance (2)=(1)-(3)	Flexible Budget (3)	Sales-Volume Variance (4)=(3)-(5)	Static Budget (5)
Pumpkin costs	16,830 [a]	$1,167 F	$17,997 [b]	$237 U	$17,760 [c]

[a]17,000 × $0.99 = $16,830
[b]60,800 ÷ 3.75 × $1.11 = $17,997
[c]60,000 ÷ 3.75 × $1.11 = $17,750

7-20 (cont'd)

2.

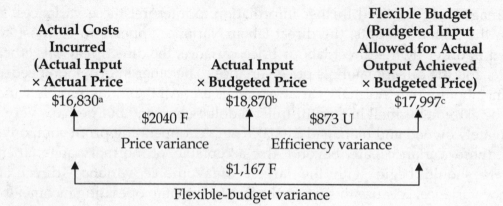

Actual Costs Incurred (Actual Input × Actual Price		Actual Input × Budgeted Price		Flexible Budget (Budgeted Input Allowed for Actual Output Achieved × Budgeted Price)
$16,830ᵃ		$18,870ᵇ		$17,997ᶜ
	$2040 F		$873 U	
	Price variance		Efficiency variance	
		$1,167 F		
		Flexible-budget variance		

ᵃ17,000 × $0.99 = $16,830
ᵇ17,000 × $1.11 = $18,870 (no inventory involved)
ᶜ60,800 ÷ 3.75 × $1.11 = $17,997

3. The favourable flexible-budget variance of $1,167 has two offsetting components:

   (a) favourable price variance of $2,040—reflects the $0.99 actual purchase cost being lower than the $1.11 budgeted purchase cost per kilogram.

   (b) unfavourable efficiency variance of $873—reflects the actual materials yield of 3.58 scones per kilogram of pumpkin (60,800 ÷ 17,000 = 3.58) being less than the budgeted yield of 3.75 (60,000 ÷ 16,000 = 3.75)

One explanation is that Peterson purchased lower-quality pumpkins at a lower cost per kilogram.

7-22 (25 min.) Comprehensive variance analysis.

1. Variance Analysis for Sol Electronics for the second quarter of 2009

	Second-Quarter 2009 Actuals (1)	Flexible Budget Variance (2) = (1) – (3)		Flexible Budget for Second Quarter (3)	Sales Volume Variance (4) = (3) – (5)		Static Budget (5)
Units	4,800	0		4,800	800	F	4,000
Selling price	$ 71.50			$ 70.00			$ 70.00
Sales	$343,200	$7,200	F	$336,000	$56,000	F	$280,000
Variable costs							
Direct materials	57,600	2,592	F	60,192 [a]	10,032	U	50,160
Direct manuf. labour	30,240	1,440	U	28,800 [b]	4,800	U	24,000
Other variable costs	47,280	720	F	48,000 [c]	8,000	U	40,000
Total variable costs	135,120	1,872	F	136,992	22,832	U	114,160
Contribution margin	208,080	9,072	F	199,008	33,168	F	165,840
Fixed costs	68,400	400	U	68,000	0		68,000
Operating income	$139,680	$8,672	F	$131,008	$33,168	F	$97,840

[a] 4,800 units $\times$ 2.2 kg per unit $\times$ $5.70 per kg = $60,192
[b] 4,800 units $\times$ 0.5 hrs. per unit $\times$ $12 per hr. = $28,800
[c] 4,800 units $\times$ $10 per unit = $48,000

	Second-Quarter 2009 Actuals	Price Variance		Actual Input Qty. $\times$ Budgeted Price	Efficiency Variance		Flexible Budget for Second Quarter
Direct materials	$57,600	$2,880	U	$54,720 [a]	$5,472	F	$60,192
Direct manuf. labour (DML)	30,240	4,320	U	25,920 [b]	2,880	F	28,800

[a] 4,800 units $\times$ 2 kg per unit $\times$ $5.70 per kg = $54,720
[b] 4,800 units $\times$ 0.45 DMLH per unit $\times$ $12 per DMLH = $25,920

7-22 (cont'd)

2.   The following details, revealed in the variance analysis, should be used to rebut the union if it focuses on the favourable operating income variance:

   *   Most of the static budget operating income variance of $41,840F ($139,680 – $97,840) comes from a favourable sales volume variance, which only arose because Sol sold more units than planned.
   *   Of the $8,672 F flexible-budget variance in operating income, most of it comes from the $7,200F flexible-budget variance in sales.
   *   The net flexible-budget variance in total variable costs of $1,872 F is small, and it arises from direct materials and other variable costs, not from labour. Direct manufacturing labour flexible-budget variance is $1,440 U.
   *   The direct manufacturing labour price variance, $4,320U, which is large and unfavourable, is indeed partially offset by direct manufacturing labour's favourable efficiency variance—but the efficiency variance is driven by the fact that Sol is using new, more expensive materials. Shaw may have to "prove" this to the union, which will insist that it's because workers are working smarter. Even if workers are working smarter, the favourable direct manufacturing labour efficiency variance of $2,880 does not fully offset the unfavourable direct manufacturing labour price variance of $4,320.

3.   Changing the standards may make them more realistic, making it easier to negotiate with the union. But the union will resist any tightening of labour standards, and it may be too early (is one quarter's experience sufficient?); a change of standards at this point may be viewed as opportunistic by the union. Perhaps a continuous improvement program to change the standards will be more palatable to the union and will achieve the same result over a somewhat longer period of time.

7-24 (30 min.) Direct materials and direct manufacturing labour variances.

1.

May 2009	Actual Results (1)	Price Variance (2) = (1)–(3)		Actual Quantity × Budgeted Price (3)	Efficiency Variance (4) = (3) – (5)		Flexible Budget (5)
Units	550						550
Direct materials	$12,705.00	$1,815.00	U	$10,890.00ᵃ	$990.00	U	$9,900.00ᵇ
Direct labour	$ 8,464.50	$ 104.50	U	$ 8,360.00ᶜ	$440.00	F	$8,800.00ᵈ
Total price variance		$1,919.50	U				
Total efficiency variance					$550.00	U	

ᵃ 7,260 m × $1.50 per m = $10,890
ᵇ 550 lots × 12 m per lot × $1.50 per m = $9,900
ᶜ 1,045 hours × $8.00 per hour = $8,360
ᵈ 550 lots × 2 hours per lot × $8 per hour = $8,800

Total flexible-budget variance for both inputs = $1,919.50U + $550U = $2,469.50U

Total flexible-budget cost of direct materials and direct labour = $9,900 + $8,800 = $18,700

Total flexible-budget variance as % of total flexible-budget costs = $2,469.50 ÷ $18,700 = 13.21%

7-24 (cont'd)

2.

May 2010	Actual Results (1)	Price Variance (2) = (1) – (3)		Actual Quantity × Budgeted Price (3)	Efficiency Variance (4) = (3) – (5)		Flexible Budget (5)
Units	550						550
Direct materials	$11,828.36a	$1,156.16	U	$10,672.20b	$772.20	U	$9,900.00c
Direct manuf. labour	$ 8,295.21d	$ 102.41	U	$ 8,192.80e	$607.20	F	$8,800.00c
Total price variance		$1,258.57	U				
Total efficiency variance					$165.00	U	

a Actual dir. mat. cost, May 2010 = Actual dir. mat. cost, May 2009 × 0.98 × 0.95 = $12,705 × 0.98 × 0.95
$$= \$11.828.36$$

Alternatively, actual dir. mat. cost, May 2010

$$= (\text{Actual dir. mat. quantity used in May 2009} \times 0.98) \times (\text{Actual dir. mat. price in May 2009} \times 0.95)$$

$$= (7,260 \text{ m} \times 0.98) \times (\$1.75/\text{m} \times 0.95)$$

$$= 7,114.80 \times \$1.6625 = \$11,828.36$$

b $(7,260 \text{ m} \times 0.98) \times \$1.50 \text{ per m} = \$10,672.20$

c Unchanged from 2009.

d Actual dir. labour cost, May 2010 = Actual dir. manuf. cost May 2009 × 0.98 = $8,464.50 × 0.98 = $8,295.21

Alternatively, actual dir. labour cost, May 2010

$$= (\text{Actual dir. manuf. labour quantity used in May 2009} \times 0.98) \times \text{Actual dir. labour price in 2009}$$

$$= (1,045 \text{ hours} \times 0.98) \times \$8.10 \text{ per hour}$$

$$= 1,024.10 \text{ hours} \times \$8.10 \text{ per hour} = \$8,295.21$$

e $(1,045 \text{ hours} \times 0.98) \times \$8.00 \text{ per hour} = \$8,192.80$

Total flexible-budget variance for both inputs = $1,258.57U + $165U = $1,423.57U

Total flexible-budget cost of direct materials and direct labour = $9,900 + $8,800 = $18,700

Total flexible-budget variance as % of total flexible-budget costs = $1,423.57 ÷ $18,700 = 7.61%

7-24 (cont'd)

3. Efficiencies have improved in the direction indicated by the production manager—but it is unclear whether they are a trend or a one-time occurrence. Also, overall, variances are still 7.6% of flexible input budget. GloriaDee should continue to use the new material, especially in light of its superior quality and feel, but it may want to keep the following points in mind:

    - The new material costs substantially more than the old ($1.75 in 2009 and $1.6625 in 2010 vs. $1.50 per metre). Its price is unlikely to come down within the coming year. Standard material price should be re-examined and possibly changed.
    - GloriaDee should continue to work to reduce direct materials and direct manufacturing labour content. The reductions from May 2009 to May 2010 are a good development and should be encouraged.

7-26 (30 min.) Flexible budget, working backward.

1.

	Actual Results (1)	Flexible-Budget Variances (2)=(1)-(3)	Flexible Budget (3)	Sales-Volume Variances (4)=(3)-(5)	Static Budget (5)
Units sold	650,000	0	650,000	50,000 F	600,000
Revenues	$4,290,000	$1,560,000 F	$2,730,000ᵃ	$210,000 F	$2,520,000
Variable costs	3,090,000	1,530,000 U	1,560,000ᵇ	120,000 U	1,440,000
Contribution margin	1,200,000	30,000 F	1,170,000	90,000 F	1,080,000
Fixed costs	840,000	120,000 U	720,000	0	720,000
Operating income	$ 360,000	$90,000 U	$ 450,000	$90,000 F	$ 360,000
		$90,000 U		$90,000 F	
		Total flexible-budget variance		Total sales-volume variance	
			$0		
			Total static-budget variance		

ᵃ650,000 × $4.20 = $2,730,000
ᵇ650,000 × $2.40 = $1,560,000

2.

Actual selling price:	$4,290,000 ÷ 650,000	=	$6.60
Budgeted selling price:	2,520,000 ÷ 600,000	=	4.20
Actual variable cost per unit:	3,090,000 ÷ 650,000	=	4.75
Budgeted variable cost per unit:	1,440,000 ÷ 600,000	=	2.40

7-26 (cont'd)

3. The CEO's reaction was inappropriate. A nil total static-budget variance is due to offsetting total flexible-budget and total sales-volume variances. In this case, these two variances exactly offset each other:

Total flexible-budget variance	$90,000 Unfavourable
Total sales-volume variance	$90,000 Favourable

A closer look at the variance components reveals some major deviations from plan. Actual variable costs increased from $2.40 to $4.75, causing an unfavourable flexible-budget variable cost variance of $1,530,000. Such an increase could be a result of, for example, a jump in platinum prices. Specialty Bearings was able to pass most of the increase in costs on to their customers—average selling price went up about 57%, bringing about an offsetting favourable flexible-budget variance in the amount of $1,560,000. An increase in the actual number of units sold also contributed to more favourable results. Although such an increase in quantity in the face of a price increase may appear counterintuitive, customers may have forecast higher future platinum prices and therefore decided to stock up.

The most important lesson learned here is that a superficial examination of summary level data (Levels 0 and 1) may be insufficient. It is imperative to scrutinize data at a more detailed level (Level 2). Had Specialty Bearings not been able to pass costs on to customers, losses would have been considerable.

7-28 (20 min.) Finance function activities, benchmarking (continuation of 7-27).

1. The key new insight is how Bouquets.com compares with "world-class" organizations. At face value, there is much room for improvement. The per unit cost differences are dramatic:

	Bouquets.com		
	2010 Budgeted	2010 Actual	"World-Class" Cost Performance
Receivables	$0.767	$0.90	$0.12 per remittance
Payables	$3.48	$3.36	$0.85 per invoice
Travel	$9.12	$8.88	$1.90 per travel claim

7-28 (cont'd)

2. For any meaningful comparison, the figures being compared must be comparable. Weber should first determine whether there is an "apples to apples" comparison with these figures. Are costs of the finance department activities measured the same across Bouquets.com and the company with "world-class" cost performance? Suppose, for example, that Bouquets.com allocates other costs into the finance area (such as the President's salary), while the $1.90 per travel claim figure is for finance department costs only.

Weber should consider whether the benchmark company also obtains information on why the large cost differences occur. For example, is it because the "world-class" performer is using new technologies in the finance area? If this is the case, then is Weber willing to invest in new technologies in the same way that "world-class" finance function organizations do? If not, then the $1.90 benchmark could be unattainable, no matter how hard and smart the travel claim-processing group performs.

In addition, Weber should consider whether the benchmark company provides a valid comparison point. The benchmark company is a world-class retail company that has traditional retail and Internet-based retail functions. Bouquets.com is an Internet company. Costs and activities of Internet companies are going to differ from those of traditional retailers.

7-30 (30 min.) Journal entries and T-accounts (continuation of 7-29).

For requirement 1 from Exercise 7-29:

a.	Direct Materials Control	18,500	
	Direct Materials Price Variance	370	
	Accounts Payable Control		18,870
	To record purchase of direct materials.		
b.	Work-in-Process Control	20,000	
	Direct Materials Efficiency Variance		1,500
	Direct Materials Control		18,500
	To record direct materials used.		
c.	Work-in-Process Control	10,000	
	Direct Manufacturing Labour Price Variance		180
	Direct Manufacturing Labour Efficiency Variance		1,000
	Wages Payable Control		8,820
	To record liability for and allocation of direct labour costs.		

7-30 (cont'd)

Direct Materials Control		Direct Materials Price Variance		Direct Materials Efficiency Variance	
(a) 18,500	(b) 18,500	(a) 370			(b) 1,500

Work-in-Process Control		Direct Manufacturing Labour Price Variance		Direct Manuf. Labour Efficiency Variance	
(b) 20,000			(c) 180		(c) 1,000
(c) 10,000					

Wages Payable Control		Accounts Payable Control	
	(c) 8,820		(a) 18,870

For requirement 2 from Exercise 7-29:

The following journal entries pertain to the measurement of price and efficiency variances when 6,000 sq. m of direct materials are purchased:

a1. Direct Materials Control   30,000
     Direct Materials Price Variance   600
          Accounts Payable Control   30,600
     To record direct materials purchased.

a2. Work-in-Process Control   20,000
     Direct Materials Control   18,500
     Direct Materials Efficiency Variance   1,500
     To record direct materials used.

Direct Materials Control		Direct Materials Price Variance	
(a1) 30,000	(a2) 18,500	(a1) 600	

Accounts Payable Control		Work-in-Process Control	
	(a1) 30,600	(a2) 20,000	

7-30 (cont'd)

Direct Materials
Efficiency Variance

	(a2) 1,500

The T-account entries related to direct manufacturing labour are the same as in requirement 1. The difference between standard costing and normal costing for direct cost items is:

	Standard Costs	**Normal Costs**
Direct Costs	Standard price(s) × Standard input allowed for actual outputs achieved	Actual price(s) × Actual input

These journal entries differ from the *normal costing* entries because Work-in-Process Control is no longer carried at "actual" costs. Furthermore, Direct Materials Control is carried at standard unit prices rather than actual unit prices. Finally, variances appear for direct materials and direct manufacturing labour under *standard costing* but not under *normal costing*.

7-32 (45–50 min.) Activity-based costing, flexible-budget variances for finance-function activities.

1. *Receivables*

   Receivables is an output unit level activity. Its flexible-budget variance can be calculated as follows:

$$\text{Flexible-budget variance} = \text{Actual costs} - \text{Flexible-budget costs}$$

$$= (\$0.80 \times 945,000) - (\$0.639 \times 945,000)$$
$$= \$756,000 - \$603,855$$
$$= \$152,145 \text{ U}$$

   Payables
   Payables is a batch level activity.

		Static-Budget Amounts	**Actual Amounts**
a.	Number of deliveries	1,000,000	945,000
b.	Batch size (units per batch)	5	4.468
c.	Number of batches (a ÷ b)	200,000	211,504
d.	Cost per batch	$2.90	$2.85

131

7-32 (cont'd)

e. Total payables activity cost (c × d) $580,000 $602,786

Step 1: The number of batches in which payables should have been processed
= 945,000 actual units ÷ 5 budgeted units per batch
= 189,000 batches

Step 2: The flexible-budget amount for payables
= 189,000 batches × $2.90 budgeted cost per batch
= $548,100

The flexible-budget variance can be computed as follows:

Flexible-budget variance = Actual costs − Flexible-budget costs
= (211,504 × $2.85) − (189,000 × $2.90)
= $602,786 − $548,100 = $54,686 U

Travel expenses
Travel expenses is a batch level activity.

		Static-Budget Amounts	Actual Amounts
a.	Number of deliveries	1,000,000	945,000
b.	Batch size (units per batch)	500	501.587
c.	Number of batches (a ÷ b)	2,000	1,884
d.	Cost per batch	$7.60	$7.45
e.	Total travel expenses activity cost (c × d)	$15,200	$14,036

Step 1: The number of batches in which the travel expense should have been processed
= 945,000 actual units ÷ 500 budgeted units per batch
= 1,890 batches

Step 2: The flexible-budget amount for travel expenses
= 1,890 batches × $7.60 budgeted cost per batch
= $14,364

The flexible budget variance can be calculated as follows:
Flexible budget variance = Actual costs − Flexible-budget costs
= (1,884 × $7.45) − (1,890 × $7.60)
= $14,036 − $14,364 = $328 F

7-32 (cont'd)

2. The flexible budget variances can be subdivided into price and efficiency variances.

$$\text{Price variance} = \left[\begin{array}{cc} \text{Actual price} & \text{Budgeted price} \\ \text{of input} & \text{of input} \end{array} \right] \times \begin{array}{c} \text{Actual quantity} \\ \text{of input} \end{array}$$

$$\text{Efficiency variance} = \left[\begin{array}{cc} \text{Actual quantity} & \text{Budgeted quantity of} \\ \text{of input used} & \text{input allowed for} \\ & \text{actual output} \end{array} \right] \times \begin{array}{c} \text{Budgeted price} \\ \text{of input} \end{array}$$

Receivables

Price Variance	=	($0.800 – $0.639) × 945,000
	=	$152,145 U
Efficiency variance	=	(945,000 – 945,000) × $0.639
	=	$0

Payables

Price variance	=	($2.85 – $2.90) × 211,504
	=	$10,575 F
Efficiency variance	=	(211,504 – 189,000) × $2.90
	=	$65,262 U

Travel expenses

Price variance	=	($7.45 – $7.60) × 1,884
	=	$283 F
Efficiency variance	=	(1,884-1,890) × $7.60
	=	$46 F

7-34 (30-40 min.) Direct materials variances, long-term agreement with supplier.

1.

Month (1)	Total Actual Direct Materials Usage in Dollars (2)	Average Actual Direct Materials Purchase Price per Kilogram of Metal (3)	Total Actual Quantity of Direct Materials in Kilograms (4) = (2) ÷ (3)	Number of Machining Systems Produced (5)	Actual Direct Materials Input in Kilograms per Machining System (6) = (4) ÷ (5)
January	$290,880	$144	2,020	10	202
February	343,872	144	2,388	12	199
March	530,712	151.2	3,510	18	195
April	474,317	153.6	3,088	16	193
May	304,128	144	2,112	11	192

Materials Price Variance

Month (1)	Actual Costs Incurred: Actual Input × Actual Price (2)	Actual Input (3)	Budgeted Price per Unit of Input (4)	Actual Input × Budgeted Price (5) = (3) × (4)	Direct Materials Price Variance (6) = (2) − (5)
January	$290,880	2,020	$144	$290,880	$ 0
February	343,872	2,388	144	343,872	0
March	530,712	3,510	144	505,440	25,272 U
April	474,317	3,088	144	444,672	29,645 U
May	304,128	2,112	144	304,128	0

Materials Efficiency Variance

Month (1)	Actual Input × Budgeted Price (2)	Budgeted Input per Unit of Output (3)	Actual Output Achieved (4)	Budgeted Price per Unit of Input (5)	Flexible Budget (Budgeted Input Allowed for Actual Output Achieved × Budgeted Price) (6) = (3) × (4) × (5)	Direct Materials Efficiency Variance (7) = (2) − (6)
January	$290,880	198	10	$144	$285,120	$ 5,760 U
February	343,872	198	12	144	342,144	1,728 U
March	505,440	198	18	144	513,216	7,776 F
April	444,672	198	16	144	456,192	11,520 F
May	304,128	198	11	144	313,632	9,504 F

7-34 (cont'd)

2. The unfavourable materials price variances in March and April imply that Metalmoulder paid more than $144 per kilogram above the 2,400 kilogram contract amount.

Month (1)	Total Actual Costs Incurred (2)	Contract Amount for 2,400 kg: 2,400 × $144 (3)	Cost for Purchases Above 2,400 kg (4) = (2) – (3)	Quantity of Purchases Above 2,400 kg (5)	Actual Price per Kilogram of Purchases Above 2,400 kg (6) = (4) ÷ (5)
March	$530,712	$345,600	$185,112	1,110	$166.77
April	474,317	345,600	128,717	688	187.09

The percentage price increases for the additional purchases above 2,400 kilograms are:

	Actual Price	Standard Price	% Increase
March	$166.77	$144	15.8
April	187.09	144	29.9

With a long-term agreement that has a fixed purchase-price clause for a set minimum quantity, no price variance will arise when the purchase amount is below the minimum quantity (assuming the budgeted price per unit is the contract price per unit). A price variance will occur only when the purchased amount exceeds the set minimum quantity. A price variance signals that the purchased amount exceeds this set minimum quantity (2,400 kilograms per month).

It is likely that the supplier will charge a higher price (above $144) for purchases above the 2,400 base. If a lower price were charged, the purchaser might apply pressure to renegotiate the contract purchase price for the base amount. If the purchasing officer is able to negotiate only a small price increase for additional purchases above the base amount, the purchasing performance may well be "favourable" despite the materials price variance being labelled "unfavourable."

Metalmoulder may see the advantage of a long-term contract in factors other than purchase price (for example, a higher quality of materials, a lower required level of inventories because of more frequent deliveries, and a guaranteed availability of materials). In general, the existence of a long-term agreement reduces the importance of materials price variances when evaluating the month-to-month performance of a purchasing officer.

7-36 (30 min.) Direct manufacturing labour and direct materials variances, missing data.

1.

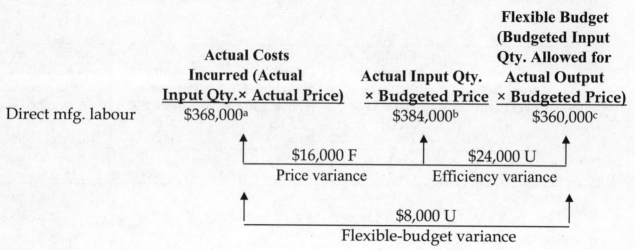

	Actual Costs Incurred (Actual Input Qty.× Actual Price)	Actual Input Qty. × Budgeted Price	Flexible Budget (Budgeted Input Qty. Allowed for Actual Output × Budgeted Price)
Direct mfg. labour	$368,000[a]	$384,000[b]	$360,000[c]

$16,000 F
Price variance

$24,000 U
Efficiency variance

$8,000 U
Flexible-budget variance

[a] Given (or 32,000 hours × $11.50/hour)
[b] 32,000 hours × $12/hour = $384,000
[c] 6,000 units × 5 hours/unit × $12/hour = $360,000

2.   Unfavourable direct materials efficiency variance of $12,500 indicates that more pounds of direct materials were actually used than the budgeted quantity allowed for actual output.

$$= \frac{\$12,500 \text{ efficiency variance}}{\$2 \text{ per pound budgeted price}}$$

$$= 6,250 \text{ pounds}$$

Budgeted pounds allowed for the output achieved = 6,000 × 20 = 120,000 pounds
Actual pounds of direct materials used = 120,000 + 6,250 = 126,250 pounds

3. Actual price paid per pound $= \dfrac{\$292,500}{150,000}$

$$= \$1.95 \text{ per pound}$$

7-36 (cont'd)

4.

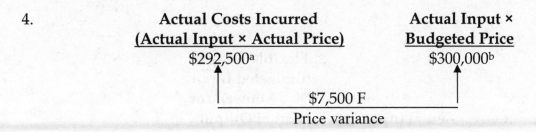

Actual Costs Incurred (Actual Input × Actual Price)	Actual Input × Budgeted Price
$292,500ᵃ	$300,000ᵇ

$7,500 F
Price variance

ᵃ Given
ᵇ 150,000 pounds × $2/pound = $300,000

7-38 (20 min.) Direct materials and manufacturing labour variances, journal entries.

1.
Direct Materials:

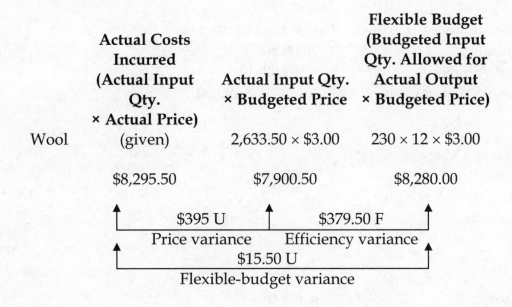

	Actual Costs Incurred (Actual Input Qty. × Actual Price)	Actual Input Qty. × Budgeted Price	Flexible Budget (Budgeted Input Qty. Allowed for Actual Output × Budgeted Price)
Wool	(given)	2,633.50 × $3.00	230 × 12 × $3.00
	$8,295.50	$7,900.50	$8,280.00

$395 U $379.50 F
Price variance   Efficiency variance
$15.50 U
Flexible-budget variance

137

7-38 (cont'd)

Direct Manufacturing Labour:

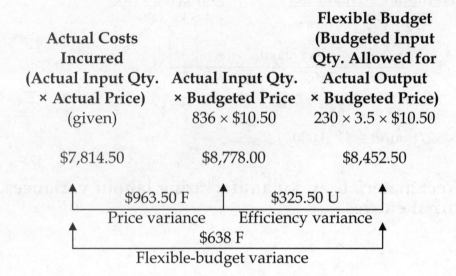

	Actual Costs Incurred (Actual Input Qty. × Actual Price) (given)	Actual Input Qty. × Budgeted Price	Flexible Budget (Budgeted Input Qty. Allowed for Actual Output × Budgeted Price)
		836 × $10.50	230 × 3.5 × $10.50
	$7,814.50	$8,778.00	$8,452.50

$963.50 F $325.50 U

Price variance   Efficiency variance

$638 F

Flexible-budget variance

2.

Direct Materials Price Variance (time of purchase = time of use):

Direct Materials Control	7,900.50	
Direct Materials Price Variance	395.00	
Accounts Payable Control or Cash		8,295.50

Direct Materials Efficiency Variance:

Work-in-Process Control	8,280.00	
Direct Materials Efficiency Variance		379.50
Direct Materials Control		7,900.50

Direct Manufacturing Labour Variances:

Work-in-Process Control	8,452.50	
Direct Mfg. Labour Efficiency Variance	325.50	
Direct Mfg. Labour Price Variance		963.50
Wages Payable or Cash		7,814.50

7-38 (cont'd)

3.   Plausible explanations for the above variances include:

Shayna paid a little bit extra for the wool, but the wool was thicker and allowed the workers to use less of it. Shayna used more inexperienced workers in April than she usually does. This resulted in payment of lower wages per hour, but the new workers were more inefficient and took more hours than normal. Overall though, the lower wage rates resulted in Shayna's total wage bill being significantly lower than expected.

7-40 (60 min.) Comprehensive variance analysis, responsibility issues.

1a.   Actual selling price = \$82.00
Budgeted selling price = \$80.00
Actual sales volume = 7,275 units
Selling price variance
= (Actual sales price – Budgeted sales price) × Actual sales volume
= (\$82 – \$80) × 7,275 = \$14,550 Favourable

1b.   Development of Flexible Budget

		Budgeted Unit Amounts	Actual Volume	Flexible Budget Amount
Revenues		\$80.00	7,275	\$582,000
Variable costs				
DM–Frames	\$2.20/g × 3.00 g	6.60[a]	7,275	48,015
DM–Lenses	\$3.10/g × 6.00 g	18.60[b]	7,275	135,315
Direct manuf. labour	\$15.00/hr. × 1.20 hrs.	18.00[c]	7,275	130,950
Total variable manufacturing costs				314,280
Fixed manufacturing costs				112,500
Total manufacturing costs				426,780
Gross margin				\$155,220

[a]\$49,500 ÷ 7,500 units; [b]\$139,500 ÷ 7,500 units; [c]\$135,000 ÷ 7,500 units

7-40 (cont'd)

	Actual Results (1)	Flexible-Budget Variances (2)=(1)-(3)	Flexible Budget (3)	Sales - Volume Variance (4)=(3)-(5)	Static Budget (5)
Units sold	7,275		7,275		7,500
Revenues	$596,550	$ 14,550 F	$582,000	$ 18,000 U	$600,000
Variable costs					
DM–Frames	55,872	7,857 U	48,015	1,485 F	49,500
DM–Lenses	150,738	15,423 U	135,315	4,185 F	139,500
Direct manuf. labour	145,355	14,405 U	130,950	4,050F	135,000
Total variable costs	351,965	37,685 U	314,280	9,720 F	324,000
Fixed manuf. costs	108,398	4,102 F	112,500	0	112,500
Total costs	460,363	33,583 U	426,780	9,720 F	436,500
Gross margin	$ 136,187	$19,033 U	$155,220	$ 8,280 U	$163,500

Level 2 $19,033 U $ 8,280 U

   Flexible-budget variance   Sales-volume variance

Level 1 $27,313 U

      Static-budget variance

1c. Price and Efficiency Variances

DM–Frames–Actual grams used = 3.20 per unit × 7,275 units = 23,280 g
  Price per gram = $55,872 ÷ 23,280 = $2.40
DM–Lenses–Actual grams used = 7.00 per unit × 7,275 units = 50,925 g
  Price per gram = $150,738 ÷ 50,925 = $2.96
Direct Labour–Actual labour hours = $145,355 ÷ 14.80 = 9,821.3 hours
Labour hours per unit = 9,821.3 ÷ 7,275 units = 1.35 hours per unit

7-40 (cont'd)

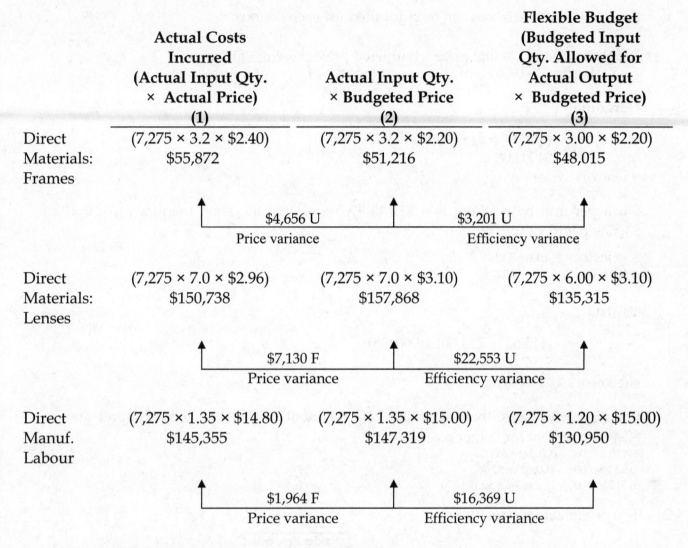

	Actual Costs Incurred (Actual Input Qty. × Actual Price) (1)	Actual Input Qty. × Budgeted Price (2)	Flexible Budget (Budgeted Input Qty. Allowed for Actual Output × Budgeted Price) (3)
Direct Materials: Frames	(7,275 × 3.2 × $2.40) $55,872	(7,275 × 3.2 × $2.20) $51,216	(7,275 × 3.00 × $2.20) $48,015
	↑ $4,656 U Price variance	↑ $3,201 U Efficiency variance	↑
Direct Materials: Lenses	(7,275 × 7.0 × $2.96) $150,738	(7,275 × 7.0 × $3.10) $157,868	(7,275 × 6.00 × $3.10) $135,315
	↑ $7,130 F Price variance	↑ $22,553 U Efficiency variance	↑
Direct Manuf. Labour	(7,275 × 1.35 × $14.80) $145,355	(7,275 × 1.35 × $15.00) $147,319	(7,275 × 1.20 × $15.00) $130,950
	↑ $1,964 F Price variance	↑ $16,369 U Efficiency variance	↑

2. Possible explanations for the price variances are:
    (a) Unexpected outcomes from purchasing and labour negotiations during the year.
    (b) Higher quality of frames and/or lower quality of lenses purchased.
    (c) Standards set incorrectly at the start of the year.

Possible explanations for the uniformly unfavourable efficiency variances are:
    (a) Substantially higher usage of lenses due to poor quality lenses purchased at lower price.
    (b) Lesser trained workers hired at lower rates result in higher materials usage (for both frames and lenses), as well as lower levels of labour efficiency.
    (c) Standards set incorrectly at the start of the year.

7-42 (30-40 min.) **Procurement costs, variance analysis, governance.**

1. Purchase price variances can be computed for each country.

$$\text{Purchase price variance} = \left(\begin{array}{c}\text{Actual price} \\ \text{of input}\end{array} - \begin{array}{c}\text{Budgeted price} \\ \text{of input}\end{array}\right) \times \begin{array}{c}\text{Actual quantity} \\ \text{of input}\end{array}$$

Hergonia

$$= (\$15.60^* - \$14.00) \times 250{,}000$$
$$= \$400{,}000 \text{ U}$$

*$3,900,000 ÷ 250,000 = $15.60

On a per-unit basis, there is a $12.43[1] payment to the shoe manufacturer and a $3.17[2] payment for "other costs."

(1) $3,108,000 ÷ 250,000 = $12.43
(2) $792,000 ÷ 250,000 = $3.17

Tanista

$$= (\$13.67^* - \$14.00) \times 900{,}000$$
$$= \$297{,}000 \text{ F}$$

*$12,300,000 ÷ 900,000 = $13.67

On a per-unit basis, there is an $11.26[3] payment to the shoe manufacturer and a $2.40[4] payment for "other costs."

(3) $10,136,000 ÷ 900,000 = $11.26
(4) $2,164,000[5] ÷ 900,000 = $2.40
(5) $12,300,000 − 10,136,000 = $2,164,000

2. The organization structure is:

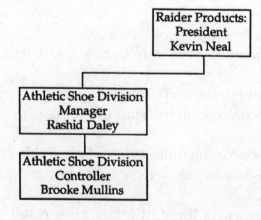

7-42 (cont'd)

Daley and Mullins face many ethical issues:

(a) Reliability of cost information to be presented to the board of directors. There are minimal or questionable receipts for $792,000 in Hergonia and $2,164,000 in Tanista.

(b) Potential existence of kickback payments in both Hergonia and Tanista.

(c) Employment of young children (many of them under 15 years).

Should Daley and Mullins be forthright and present all their concerns on (a), (b), and (c)?

Both Daley and Mullins face the dilemma that any discussion of (a), (b), or (c) will raise questions about their own behaviour at the time the acquisitions were made. Board members may ask "When did you first know about (a), (b), and (c)?" and "If it is only recently, why did you not undertake examination of these issues at the time you supported the acquisitions?"

3. Mullins has very high standards of ethical conduct to meet — see Exhibit 1-5 of the text. She should not make presentations to the Board based on information she has strong doubts about. If she decides to make the presentation, all her concerns and caveats should be presented.

She should require detailed documentation for all payments. No future payments should be made without adequate documentation.

Investigation of kickback allegations should be made, however difficult that may be. Mullins should be able to show she made a good-faith effort to ensure kickback payments are not an ongoing practice in Hergonia or Tanista.

CHAPTER 8
FLEXIBLE BUDGETS, VARIANCES,
AND MANAGEMENT CONTROL: II

8-2 Budgeted overhead cost rates may be set internally while standard overhead cost rates are set using some external engineering or competitor data. Benchmark overhead cost rates are the lowest possible rates achieved.

8-4 Sales volume variance arises when the actual volume sold differs from the pro forma amount in the static budget. The sum of the variable overhead spending and efficiency variances will reconcile to the flexible budget variance but not to the static budget because the volumes differ.

8-6 Reasons for a $30,000 favourable variable-overhead efficiency variance are:
- Workers more skillful in using machines than budgeted.
- Production scheduler was able to schedule jobs better than budgeted, resulting in lower-than-budgeted machine-hours.
- Machines operated with fewer slowdowns than budgeted.
- Machine time standards set with padding built in by machine-workers.

8-8 Choosing to write off or prorate underallocated or overallocated overhead will affect the inventory values and cost of goods sold. Deliberately choosing to write off a material overallocation or underallocation will either understate or overstate net income. Only non-material values should be written off.

8-10 For planning and control purposes, fixed overhead costs are a lump sum amount that is not controlled on a per-unit basis. In contrast, for inventory costing purposes, fixed overhead costs are allocated to products on a per-unit basis. See Exhibit 8-3 in the text.

8-12 All companies must satisfy their customers to remain in business. Non-financial measures of customer satisfaction are therefore relevant information for managers making both short-term operating and long-term strategic decisions.

8-14 Non-manufacturing firms also allocate costs that cannot be traced economically to a cost object. These costs include those of acquiring prospective customers, customer account maintenance (contract and billing, collections), and general technical and legal support. Knowing the actual consumption of homogeneous resources in the cost allocation bases of these cost pools for the budgeted quantity of customers compared to pro forma amounts is relevant. This information will affect the actual overhead rates compared to budgeted and is an attention-getting financial performance measure.

8-16 (20 min.) Variable manufacturing overhead, variance analysis.

1. Variable Manufacturing Overhead Variance Analysis for Esquire Clothing for June 2010

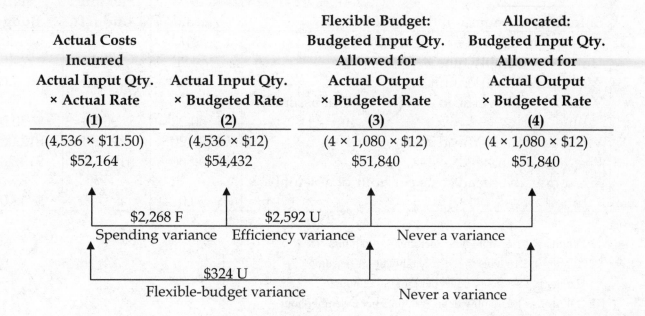

2. Esquire had a favourable spending variance of $2,268 because the actual variable overhead rate was $11.50 per DMLH versus $12 budgeted. It had an unfavourable efficiency variance of $2,592 U because each suit averaged 4.2 labour-hours (4,536 hours ÷ 1,080 suits) versus 4.0 budgeted labour-hours.

8-18 (30–40 min.) **Manufacturing overhead, variance analysis.**

1. The summary information is:

Solutions Corporation (June 2009)	Actual	Flexible Budget	Static Budget
Output units (number of assembled units)	216	216	200
Hours of assembly time	411	432[c]	400[a]
Assembly hours per unit	1.90[b]	2.00	2.00
Variable mfg. overhead cost per hour of assembly time	$ 30.22[d]	$ 30.00	$ 30.00
Variable mfg. overhead costs	$12,420	$12,960[e]	$12,000[f]
Fixed mfg. overhead costs	$20,560	$19,200	$19,200
Fixed mfg. overhead costs per hour of assembly time	$ 50.02[g]		$ 48.00[h]

[a] 200 units × 2 assembly hours per unit = 400 hours

[b] 411 hours ÷ 216 units = 1.90 assembly hours per unit

[c] 216 units × 2 assembly hours per unit = 432 hours

[d] $12,420 ÷ 411 assembly hours = $30.22 per assembly hour

[e] 432 assembly hours × $30 per assembly hour = $12,960

[f] 400 assembly hours × $30 per assembly hour = $12,000

[g] $20,560 ÷ 411 assembly hours = $50.02 per assembly hour

[h] $19,200 ÷ 400 assembly hours = $48 per assembly hour

8-18 (cont'd)

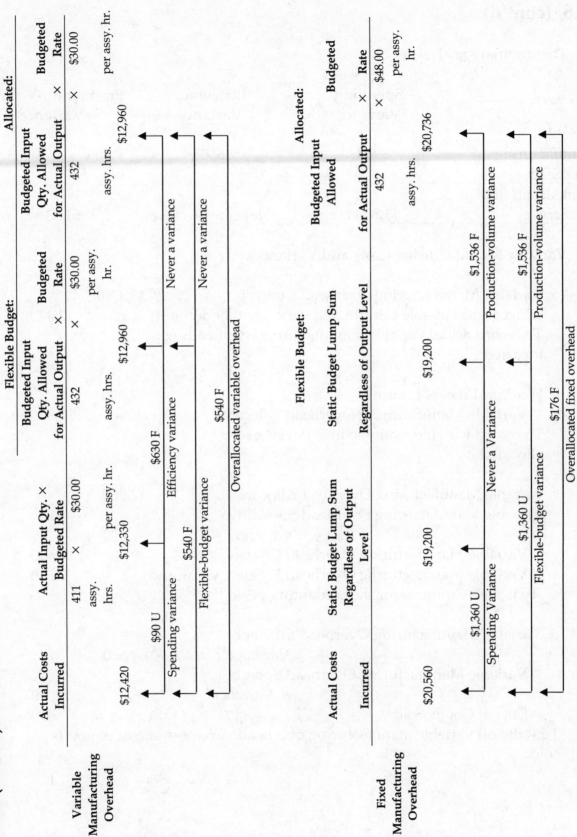

Variable Manufacturing Overhead

	Actual Costs Incurred	Actual Input Qty. × Budgeted Rate	Flexible Budget: Budgeted Input Qty. Allowed for Actual Output × Budgeted Rate	Allocated: Budgeted Input Qty. Allowed for Actual Output × Budgeted Rate
	$12,420	411 assy. hrs. × $30.00 per assy. hr. $12,330	432 assy. hrs. × $30.00 per assy. hr. $12,960	432 assy. hrs. × $30.00 per assy. hr. $12,960

$90 U Spending variance $630 F Efficiency variance   Never a variance

$540 F Flexible-budget variance   Never a variance

$540 F Overallocated variable overhead

Fixed Manufacturing Overhead

	Actual Costs Incurred	Flexible Budget: Static Budget Lump Sum Regardless of Output Level	Static Budget Lump Sum Regardless of Output Level	Allocated: Budgeted Input Allowed for Actual Output × Budgeted Rate
	$20,560	$19,200	$19,200	432 assy. hrs. × $48.00 per assy. hr. $20,736

$1,360 U Spending Variance   Never a Variance $1,536 F Production-volume variance

$1,360 U Flexible-budget variance $1,536 F Production-volume variance

$176 F Overallocated fixed overhead

8-18 (cont'd)

The summary analysis is:

	Spending Variance	Efficiency Variance	Production-Volume Variance
Variable Manufacturing Overhead	$90 U	$630 F	Never a variance
Fixed Manufacturing Overhead	$1,360 U	Never a variance	$1,536 F

2. **Variable Manufacturing Costs and Variances**

   a. Variable Manufacturing Overhead Control   12,420
      Accounts Payable Control and various other accounts   12,420
   To record actual variable manufacturing overhead costs incurred.

   b. Work-in-Process Control   12,960
      Variable Manufacturing Overhead Allocated   12,960
   To record variable manufacturing overhead allocated.

   c. Variable Manufacturing Overhead Allocated   12,960
      Variable Manufacturing Overhead Spending Variance   90
      Variable Manufacturing Overhead Control   12,420
      Variable Manufacturing Overhead Efficiency Variance   630
   To isolate variances for the accounting period.

   d. Variable Manufacturing Overhead Efficiency Variance   630
      Variable Manufacturing Overhead Spending Variance   90
      Cost of Goods Sold   540
   To write off variable manufacturing overhead variances to cost of goods sold.

8-18 (cont'd)

Fixed Manufacturing Costs and Variances

a. Fixed Manufacturing Overhead Control   20,560

   Salaries Payable, Acc. Amortization, various other

                                        accounts   20,560

  To record actual fixed manufacturing overhead costs incurred.

b. Work-in-Process Control   20,736

   Fixed Manufacturing Overhead Allocated   20,736

  To record fixed manufacturing overhead allocated.

c. Fixed Manufacturing Overhead Allocated   20,736

   Fixed Manufacturing Overhead Spending Variance   1,360

     Fixed Manufacturing Overhead Production-Volume Variance   1,536

     Fixed Manufacturing Overhead Control   20,560

  To isolate variances for the accounting period.

d. Fixed Manufacturing Overhead Production-Volume

                             Variance   1,536

   Fixed Manufacturing Overhead Spending Variance   1,360

   Cost of Goods Sold   176

To write off fixed manufacturing overhead variances to cost of goods
sold.

3. Planning and control of *variable* manufacturing overhead costs has both a long-run and a short-run focus. It involves Solutions planning to undertake only value-added overhead activities (a long-run view) and then managing the cost drivers of those activities in the most efficient way (a short-run view). Planning and control of *fixed* manufacturing overhead costs at Solutions have primarily a long-run focus. It involves undertaking only value-added fixed-overhead activities for a budgeted level of output. Solutions makes most of the key decisions that determine the level of fixed-overhead costs at the start of the accounting period.

8-20 (20-25 min.) Spending and efficiency overhead variances, service sector.

1. $$\text{Budgeted variable overhead rate} = \text{\$2 per hour of home delivery time}$$

Budgeted fixed overhead rate:

$$= \frac{\$28,800}{9,600 \times 0.80} = \frac{28,800}{7,680}$$

$$= \$3.75 \text{ per hour of home delivery time}$$

A detailed comparison of actual and flexible budgeted amounts is:

	Actual	Flexible Budget	Static Budget
Output units (deliveries)	8,952	8,952	9,600
Allocation base (hours)	6,714	7,162[a]	7,680[b]
Allocation base per output unit	0.75[c]	0.80	0.80
Variable MOH	$17,008	$14,323[d]	–
Variable MOH per hour	$2.53[e]	$2.00	$2.00
Fixed MOH	$33,120	$28,800	$28,800
Fixed MOH per hour	$4.93[f]	–	$3.75[g]

[a] 8,952 × 0.80 = 7,162
[b] 9,600 × 0.80 = 7,680
[c] 6,714 ÷ 8,952 = 0.75
[d] 8,952 × 0.80 × $2.00 = $14,323
[e] $17,008 ÷ 6,714 = $2.53
[f] $33,120 ÷ 6,714 = $4.93
[g] $28,800 ÷ 7,680 = $3.75

The required variances are:

	Spending Variance	Efficiency Variance
Variable overhead	$3,580 U	$895 F
Fixed overhead	$4,320 U	–

8-20 (cont'd)

These variances are computed as follows:

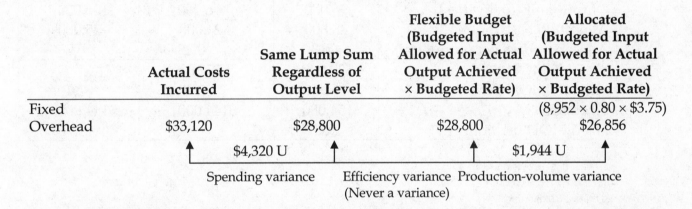

The spending variances for variable and fixed overhead are both unfavourable. This means that TS had increases in either or both the cost of individual items (such as telephone calls and gasoline) in the overhead cost pools, or higher-than-budgeted usage of these individual items per unit of the allocation base (delivery time). The favourable efficiency variance for variable overhead costs results from more efficient use of the cost allocation base. Each delivery takes 0.75 hours versus a budgeted 0.80 hours.

2. TS best manages its fixed overhead costs by long-term planning of capacity rather than day-to-day decisions. This involves planning to undertake only value-added fixed-overhead activities and then determining the appropriate level for those activities. Most fixed overhead costs are committed well before they are incurred. In contrast, for variable overhead, a mix of long-run planning and daily monitoring of the use of individual items is required to manage costs efficiently. TS plans to undertake only value-added variable-overhead activities (a long-run focus) and then manage the cost drivers of those activities in the most efficient way (a short-run focus).

8-22 (20-25 min.) Spending and efficiency overhead variances, distribution.

1. Budgeted variable overhead rate = $2.40 per hour of delivery time

   Budgeted fixed overhead rate = $\dfrac{\$144,000}{100,000 \times 0.25} = \dfrac{\$144,000}{25,000}$

   = $5.76 per hour of delivery time

A detailed comparison of actual and flexible budgeted amounts is:

	Actual	**Flexible Budget**	**Static Budget**
Output units (deliveries)	96,000	96,000	100,000
Allocation base (hours)	28,800	24,000[a]	25,000[b]
Allocation base per output unit	0.30[c]	0.25	0.25
Variable MOH	$72,000	$57,600[d]	—
Variable MOH per hour	$2.50[e]	$2.40	$2.40
Fixed MOH	$154,080	$144,000	$144,000
Fixed MOH per hour	$5.35[f]	—	$5.76[g]

[a]96,000 × 0.25 = 24,000
[b]100,000 × 0.25 = 25,000
[c]28,800 ÷ 96,000 = 0.30
[d]96,000 × 0.25 × $2.40 = $57,600
[e]$72,000 ÷ 28,800 = $2.50
[f]$154,080 ÷ 28,800 = $5.35
[g]$144,000 ÷ 25,000 = $5.76

The required variances are:

	Spending Variance	**Efficiency Variance**	**Production-Volume Variance**
Variable overhead	$2,880 U	$11,520 U	—
Fixed overhead	$10,080 U	—	$5,760 U

8-22 (cont'd)

These variances are computed as follows:

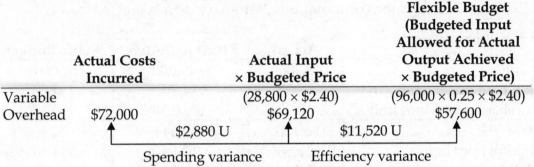

	Actual Costs Incurred	Actual Input × Budgeted Price	Flexible Budget (Budgeted Input Allowed for Actual Output Achieved × Budgeted Price)
Variable Overhead	$72,000	(28,800 × $2.40) $69,120	(96,000 × 0.25 × $2.40) $57,600

$2,880 U ← Spending variance

$11,520 U ← Efficiency variance

	Actual Costs Incurred	Same Lump Sum Regardless of Output Level	Same Lump Sum Regardless of Output Level	Allocated (Budgeted Input Allowed for Actual Output Achieved × Budgeted Rate)
Fixed Overhead	$154,080	$144,000	$144,000	(96,000 × 0.25 × $5.76) $138,240

$10,080 U ← Spending variance

← Efficiency variance (Never a variance)

$5,760 U ← Production-volume variance

The spending variances for variable and fixed overhead are both unfavourable. This means that SDS had increases in either or both the cost of individual items (such as gasoline and truck maintenance) or higher-than-budgeted usage of these individual items per unit of the allocation base (delivery time). The unfavourable efficiency variance for variable overhead results from less efficient use of the cost allocation base—each delivery takes 0.30 hours versus a budgeted 0.25 hours.

2. The single direct cost category is delivery driver payments. The major problem in managing these costs is to restrain the rate of increase in the rate paid to drivers per delivery. SDS faces the challenge of having a low-cost delivery infrastructure. For example, purchasing delivery trucks with low fuel consumption will help reduce variable overhead costs. Purchasing vehicles with low annual maintenance will help reduce fixed overhead costs. Variable overhead costs are controlled by both cost planning, well before their incurrence, and day-to-day decisions. In contrast, most fixed overhead cost items are controlled by planning decisions made prior to the start of the year.

8-24 (30-40 min.) Straightforward coverage of manufacturing overhead, standard-cost system.

1. Solution Exhibit 8-24 shows the computations. Summary details are:

	Actual	Flexible Budget	Static Budget
Output units	49,200	49,200	52,000[a]
Allocation base (machine-hours)	15,960	14,760[b]	15,600
Allocation base per output unit	0.32[c]	0.30	0.30
Variable MOH	$186,120	$212,544[d]	—
Variable MOH per hour	$11.66[e]	$14.40	$14.40
Fixed MOH	$481,200	$468,000	$468,000
Fixed MOH per hour	$30.15[f]	—	$30.00[g]

[a]15,600 ÷ 0.30 = 52,000   [e]$186,120 ÷ 15,960 = $11.66
[b]49,200 × 0.30 = 14,760   [f]$481,200 ÷ 15,960 = $30.15
[c]15,960 ÷ 49,200 = 0.32   [g]$468,000 ÷ 15,600 = $30.00
[d]49,200 × 0.30 × $14.40 = $212,544

Four-Variance Analysis	Spending Variance	Efficiency Variance	Production Volume Variance
Variable Manufacturing Overhead	$43,704 F	$17,280 U	Never a variance
Fixed Manufacturing Overhead	$13,200 U	Never a variance	$25,200 U

2. 1. Variable Manuf. Overhead Control $186,120
       Accounts Payable Control and other accounts $186,120

   2. Work in Process Control $212,544[1d]
       Variable Manuf. Overhead Allocated $212,544[1d]

   3. Fixed Manuf. Overhead Control $481,200
       Wages Payable Control, Accumulated
          Amortization Control, etc. $481,200

   4. Work in Process Control $442,800
       Fixed Manuf. Overhead Allocated $442,800

8-24 (cont'd)

3. The control of variable manufacturing overhead requires the identification of the cost drivers for such items as energy, supplies, and repairs. Control often entails monitoring nonfinancial measures that affect each cost item, one by one. Examples are kilowatts used, quantities of lubricants used, and repair parts and hours used. The most convincing way to discover why overhead performance did not agree with a budget is to investigate possible causes, line item by line item.

    Individual fixed manufacturing overhead items are not usually affected very much by day-to-day control. Instead, they are controlled periodically through planning decisions and budgeting procedures that may sometimes have horizons covering six months or a year (for example, management salaries) and sometimes covering many years (for example, long-term leases and amortization on plant and equipment).

SOLUTION EXHIBIT 8-24

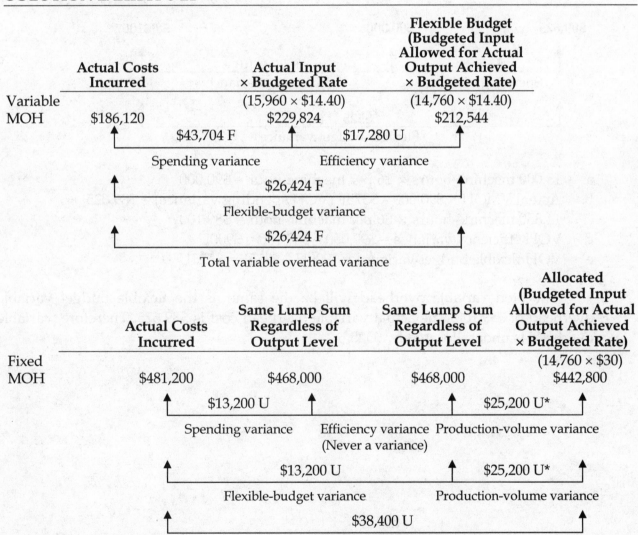

	Actual Costs Incurred	Actual Input × Budgeted Rate	Flexible Budget (Budgeted Input Allowed for Actual Output Achieved × Budgeted Rate)
Variable MOH	$186,120	(15,960 × $14.40) $229,824	(14,760 × $14.40) $212,544

$43,704 F $17,280 U

Spending variance   Efficiency variance

$26,424 F

Flexible-budget variance

$26,424 F

Total variable overhead variance

	Actual Costs Incurred	Same Lump Sum Regardless of Output Level	Same Lump Sum Regardless of Output Level	Allocated (Budgeted Input Allowed for Actual Output Achieved × Budgeted Rate)
Fixed MOH	$481,200	$468,000	$468,000	(14,760 × $30) $442,800

$13,200 U $25,200 U*

Spending variance   Efficiency variance   Production-volume variance
(Never a variance)

$13,200 U $25,200 U*

Flexible-budget variance   Production-volume variance

$38,400 U

Total fixed overhead variance

*Alternative computation:
15,600 denominator hours – 14,760 budgeted hours allowed = 840 hours; 840 × $30 = $25,200 U

8-26 (30 min.) Overhead variances, missing information.

1. In the columnar presentation of variable overhead variance analysis, all numbers shown in bold are calculated from the given information, in the order (a)–(e).

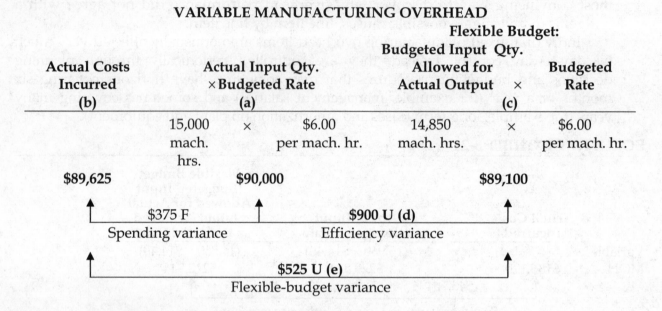

VARIABLE MANUFACTURING OVERHEAD

a. 15,000 machine-hours × $6 per machine-hour = $90,000
b. Actual VMOH = $90,000 – $375F (VOH spending variance) = $89,625
c. 14,850 machine-hours × $6 per machine-hour = $89,100
d. VOH efficiency variance = $90,000 – $89,100 = $900U
e. VOH flexible budget variance = $900U – $375F = $525U

Allocated variable overhead will be the same as the flexible budget variable overhead of $89,100. The actual variable overhead cost is $89,625. Therefore, variable overhead is underallocated by $525.

8-26 (cont'd)

2. In the columnar presentation of fixed overhead variance analysis, all numbers shown in bold are calculated from the given information, in the order (a) – (e).

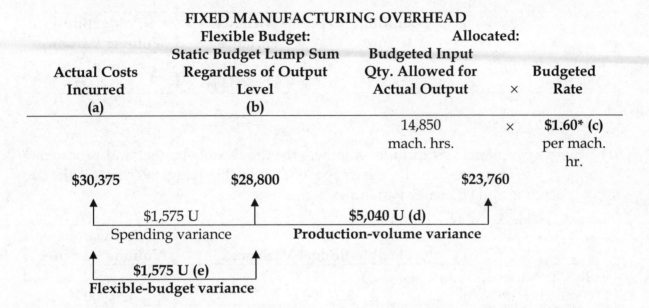

FIXED MANUFACTURING OVERHEAD

a. Actual FOH costs = $120,000 total overhead costs – $89,625 VOH costs = $30,375
b. Static budget FOH lump sum = $30,375 – $1,575 spending variance = $28,800
c. *FOH allocation rate = $28,800 FOH static-budget lump sum **Error! Objects cannot be created from editing field codes.**18,000 static-

$$\text{budget machine-hours}$$
$$= \$1.60 \text{ per machine-hour}$$

Allocated FOH   = 14,850 machine-hours × $1.60 per machine-hour = $23,760
d. PVV = $28,800 – $23,760 = $5,040U
e. FOH flexible budget variance = FOH spending variance = $1,575 U

Allocated fixed overhead is $23,760. The actual fixed overhead cost is $30,375. Therefore, fixed overhead is underallocated by $6,615.

8-28 (30 min.) Four-variance analysis, working backwards.

1. To arrive at the three-variance analysis amounts, simply sum the values in each column of the table provided in the question:

	Spending Variance	Efficiency Variance	Production-Volume Variance
Total Operating Overhead	$27,600 F	$28,800 F	$20,400 U

Two-Variance Analysis

The two-variance analysis includes numbers for the flexible-budget and production-volume (PVV) variances. The PVV is as above. The flexible-budget variance is the sum of the spending and efficiency variances:

	Flexible-Budget Variance	Production-Volume Variance
Total Operating Overhead	$56,400 F	$20,400 U

One-Variance Analysis

The total overhead variance is simply the sum of the flexible-budget and the production-volume variances:

	Total Overhead Variance
Total Operating Overhead	$36,000 F

2. The total overhead variance is $36,000 F. The total overhead variance is equal to the difference between the total actual operating overhead incurred and the operating overhead allocated to the actual output units. Therefore, if the actual operating overhead was $420,000, this must be $36,000 less than budgeted for, i.e., the operating overhead allocated to actual output units provided is $456,000.

3. Flexible-budget variance for fixed overhead is equal to the spending variance since the flexible-budget variance is equal to the sum of the spending and efficiency variances, and there is never an efficiency variance for fixed overhead. Therefore fixed operating overhead flexible budget variance is $16,800 U. The PVV is $20,400 U. The under- or overallocation of fixed operating overhead is determined as the sum of the flexible-budget variance and the PVV. So, summing $16,800 U and $20,400 U, the total fixed overhead variance is $37,200 U—actual fixed operating overhead was higher than budgeted for, i.e., fixed operating overhead was underallocated.

8-28 (cont'd)

4. Variances in the four-variance analysis are not necessarily independent. The cause of one variance may affect another. For example, consider the case where Lookmeup.com acquires less expensive Internet access for its servers. This may give rise to a favourable spending variance. However, cheaper Internet access may be of lower quality and require longer connection times and congestion, and may even result in down time, resulting in an unfavourable efficiency variance.

8-30 (40 min.) Comprehensive review of Chapters 7 and 8, flexible budget.

1. A summary of the variances for the four categories of cost is:

<u>Static-Budget Variances</u>

Direct materials	$53,568 U
Direct labour	6,134 U
Variable indirect	4,723 U
Fixed indirect	8,400 U

<u>Flexible-Budget Variances</u>		<u>Sales-Volume Variances</u>	
Direct materials	$39,168 U[e]	Direct materials	$14,400 U
Direct labour	2,534 U[f]	Direct labour	3,600 U
Variable indirect	77 F	Variable indirect	4,800 U
Fixed indirect	8,400 U	Fixed indirect	–

<u>Price-Spending Variances</u>		<u>Efficiency Variances</u>	
Direct materials	$20,736 U	Direct materials	$18,432 U
Direct labour	2,074 F	Direct labour	4,608 U
Variable indirect	6,221 F	Variable indirect	6,144 U
Fixed indirect	8,400 U	Fixed indirect	–

8-30 (cont'd)

a. <u>Direct Cost Variances</u>

The key items for computing the sales-volume, price, and efficiency for direct cost items are:

Unit	Actual Quantity of Inputs (1)	Actual Unit Cost of Inputs (2)	Actual Cost of Inputs (3) = (1) × (2)	Budgeted Unit Cost of Inputs (4)	Actual Quantity of Inputs × Budgeted Cost of Inputs (5) = (1) × (4)
Direct materials	17,280,000* pages	$0.0156[a]	$269,568*	$0.0144[c]	$248,832
Direct labour costs	1,728[b] hours	$34.80*	$60,134*	$36.00[d]	$62,208

[a]$269,568 ÷ 17,280,000 = $0.0156 per page
[b]$60,134 ÷ $34.80 = 1,728 hours
[c]$216,000 ÷ 15,000,000 = $0.0144 per page
[d]$54,000 ÷ $\frac{15,000,000}{10,000}$ = $36.00 per hour

[e]$53,568 U – $14,400 U = $39,168 U or $20,736 U + $18,432 U = $39,168 U
[f]$6,134 U – $3,600 U = $2,534 U or $2,074 F + $4,608 U = $2,534 U
*Given

	Budgeted Input Allowed per Output Unit (1)	Actual Output Achieved (2)	Budgeted Unit Cost of Inputs (3)	Flexible Budget (5) = (1) × (2) × (3)
Direct materials	50	320,000	$0.0144	$230,400
Direct labour costs	0.005[a]	320,000	$36.00	57,600

[a]Budgeted 10,000 pages produced per labour-hour yields budgeted output of 200 newspapers (50 pages each) per hour. Thus each output unit is budgeted to require 0.005 units of a direct labour-hour.

The sales-volume variances for direct materials and direct labour are:

$$\text{Sales-volume variance} = \left(\begin{array}{c}\text{Flexible-budget}\\\text{amount}\end{array}\right) - \left(\begin{array}{c}\text{Static-budget}\\\text{amount}\end{array}\right)$$

Direct materials
= (320,000 × 50 × $0.0144) – ($216,000)
= $230,400 – $216,000
= $14,400 U

Direct labour
= $\left(\dfrac{320,000 \times 50}{10,000} \times \$36\right) - (\$54,000)$
= $57,600 – $54,000
= $3,600 U

8-30 (cont'd)

The price and efficiency variances for direct materials and direct labour are:

	Actual Costs Incurred (Actual Input × Actual Price)	Price Variance	Actual Input × Budgeted Prices	Efficiency Variance	Flexible Budget (Budgeted Input Allowed for Actual Output Achieved × Budgeted Price)
Direct materials	$269,568	$20,736 U	$248,832	$18,432 U	$230,400
Direct labour costs	60,134	2,074 F	$62,208	$4,608 U	57,600

b. Indirect Cost Variances

A summary of the information is:

	Actual	Flexible Budget	Static Budget
Output units (papers)	320,000	320,000	300,000
Allocation base (print page)	17,280,000	16,000,000[b]	15,000,000
Allocation base per output unit	54[c]	50	50
Variable MOH	$76,723*	$76,800[d]	$72,000
Variable MOH per print page	$0.0044[e]	$0.0048[a]	$0.0048[a]
Fixed MOH	$116,400*	$108,000	$108,000
Fixed MOH per print page	$0.0067[g]	—	$0.0072[f]

[a]$72,000 ÷ 15,000,000 = $0.0048 per printed page   [e]$76,723 ÷ 17,280,000 = $0.00444 rounded to 0.0044
[b]320,000 × 50 = 16,000,000 pages   [f]$108,000 ÷ 15,000,000 = $0.0072 per printed page
[c]$17,280,000 ÷ 320,000 = 54   [g]$116,400 ÷ 17,280,000 = $0.0067 per printed page
[d]$320,000 × 50 × $0.0048 = $76,800

The flexible-budget and sales-volume variances for variable indirect costs are:

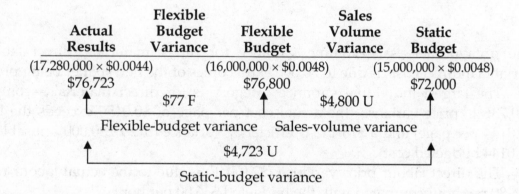

Actual Results	Flexible Budget Variance	Flexible Budget	Sales Volume Variance	Static Budget
(17,280,000 × $0.0044)		(16,000,000 × $0.0048)		(15,000,000 × $0.0048)
$76,723	$77 F	$76,800	$4,800 U	$72,000

Flexible-budget variance   Sales-volume variance

$4,723 U

Static-budget variance

8-30 (cont'd)

The spending and efficiency variances for variable indirect costs are:

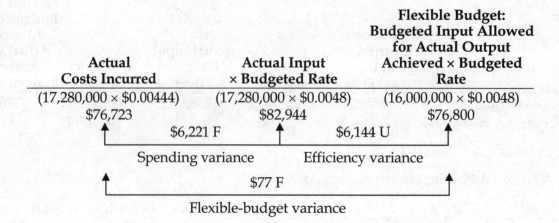

	Actual Costs Incurred	Actual Input × Budgeted Rate	Flexible Budget: Budgeted Input Allowed for Actual Output Achieved × Budgeted Rate
	(17,280,000 × $0.00444)	(17,280,000 × $0.0048)	(16,000,000 × $0.0048)
	$76,723	$82,944	$76,800

$6,221 F → Spending variance

$6,144 U → Efficiency variance

$77 F → Flexible-budget variance

The spending and production-volume variances for fixed indirect costs are:

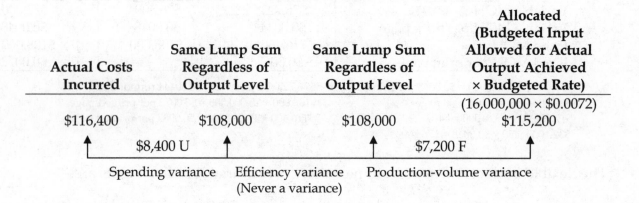

	Actual Costs Incurred	Same Lump Sum Regardless of Output Level	Same Lump Sum Regardless of Output Level	Allocated (Budgeted Input Allowed for Actual Output Achieved × Budgeted Rate)
				(16,000,000 × $0.0072)
	$116,400	$108,000	$108,000	$115,200

$8,400 U → Spending variance

Efficiency variance (Never a variance)

$7,200 F → Production-volume variance

2. The unfavourable sales-volume variance for direct materials, direct labour, and variable indirect costs is due to 20,000 extra copies of the newspaper being produced.

   The largest individual variance category is for direct materials—comprising a $20,736 U price variance (the actual cost per page of $0.0156 exceeds the budgeted $0.0144 per page) and a $18,432 U efficiency variance (the 1,280,000 unusable pages × $0.0144 budgeted cost).

   The direct labour price variance ($2,074 F) is due to the actual labour rate being $34.80 per hour compared with the budgeted $36.00 per hour.

   The unfavourable variable indirect costs efficiency variance of $6,144 U is due to 1,280,000 extra pages being used (the cost allocation base) over the quantity budgeted.

   The spending variance for fixed indirect costs is due to actual costs being $8,400 above the budgeted $108,000. An analysis of the line items in this budget would help assist in determining the causes of this variance.

8-32 (60 min.) Journal entries (continuation of 8–31).

1. Key information underlying the computation of variances is:

	Actual Results	Flexible-Budget Amount	Static-Budget Amount
1. Output units (food processors)	960	960	888
2. Machine-hours	1,824	1,920	1,776
3. Machine-hours per output unit	1.90	2.00	2.00
4. Variable MOH costs	$76,608	$76,800	$71,040
5. Variable MOH costs per machine-hour (Row 4 ÷ Row 2)	$42.00	$40.00	$40.00
6. Variable MOH costs per unit (Row 4 ÷ Row 1)	$79.80	$80.00	$80.00
7. Fixed MOH costs	$350,208	$348,096	$348,096
8. Fixed MOH costs per machine-hour (Row 7 ÷ Row 2)	$192.00	$181.30	$196.00
9. Fixed MOH costs per unit (7 ÷ 1)	$364.80	$362.60	$392.00

Solution Exhibit 8-32 shows the computation of the variances.

Journal entries for variable MOH, year ended December 31, 2010:

Variable MOH Control	76,608	
Accounts Payable Control and Other Accounts		76,608
Work-in-Process Control	76,800	
Variable MOH Allocated		76,800
Variable MOH Allocated	76,800	
Variable MOH Spending Variance	3,648	
Variable MOH Control		76,608
Variable MOH Efficiency Variance		3,840

8-32 (cont'd)

Journal entries for fixed MOH, year ended December 31, 2010:

Fixed MOH Control	350,208	
Wages Payable, Accumulated Amortization, etc.		350,208
Work-in-Process Control	376,320	
Fixed MOH Allocated		376,320
Fixed MOH Allocated	376,320	
Fixed MOH Spending Variance	2,112	
Fixed MOH Control		350,208
Fixed MOH Production-Volume Variance		28,224

2. Adjustment of COGS

Variable MOH Efficiency Variance	3,840	
Fixed MOH Production-Volume Variance	28,224	
Variable MOH Spending Variance		3,648
Fixed MOH Spending Variance		2,112
Cost of Goods Sold		26,304

SOLUTION EXHIBIT 8-32

Variable Manufacturing Overhead

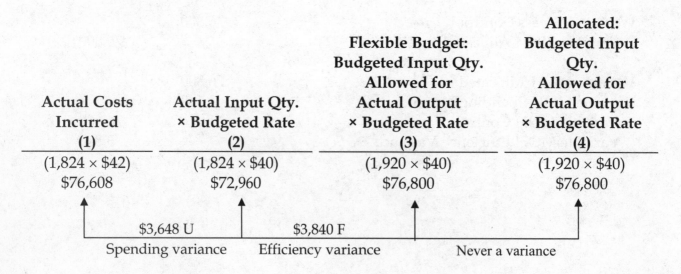

Actual Costs Incurred (1)	Actual Input Qty. × Budgeted Rate (2)	Flexible Budget: Budgeted Input Qty. Allowed for Actual Output × Budgeted Rate (3)	Allocated: Budgeted Input Qty. Allowed for Actual Output × Budgeted Rate (4)
(1,824 × $42)	(1,824 × $40)	(1,920 × $40)	(1,920 × $40)
$76,608	$72,960	$76,800	$76,800

$3,648 U $3,840 F

Spending variance   Efficiency variance   Never a variance

8-32 (cont'd)

Fixed Manufacturing Overhead

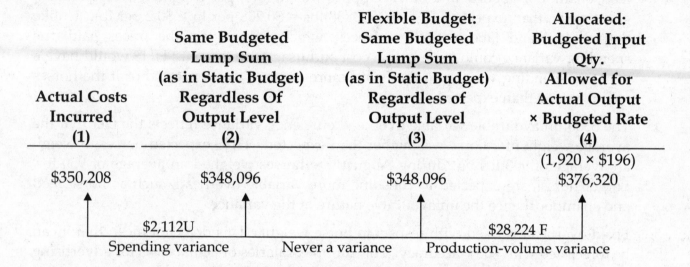

Actual Costs Incurred (1)	Same Budgeted Lump Sum (as in Static Budget) Regardless Of Output Level (2)	Flexible Budget: Same Budgeted Lump Sum (as in Static Budget) Regardless of Output Level (3)	Allocated: Budgeted Input Qty. Allowed for Actual Output × Budgeted Rate (4)
			(1,920 × $196)
$350,208	$348,096	$348,096	$376,320

$2,112U — Spending variance

Never a variance

$28,224 F — Production-volume variance

8-34 (30–40 min.) Graphs and overhead variances.

1. Variable Overhead Variance Analysis for Heather's Horse Spa for August 2009

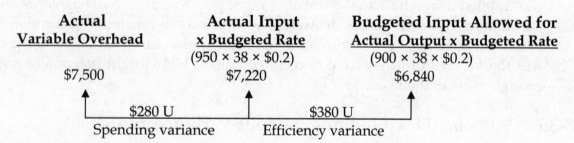

Actual Variable Overhead	Actual Input x Budgeted Rate (950 × 38 × $0.2)	Budgeted Input Allowed for Actual Output x Budgeted Rate (900 × 38 × $0.2)
$7,500	$7,220	$6,840

$280 U — Spending variance

$380 U — Efficiency variance

2. Fixed Overhead Variance Analysis for Heather's Horse Spa for August 2009

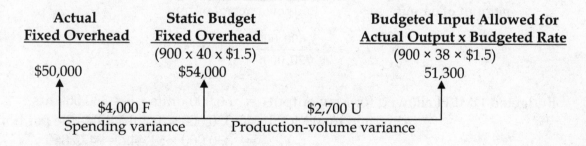

Actual Fixed Overhead	Static Budget Fixed Overhead (900 x 40 x $1.5)	Budgeted Input Allowed for Actual Output x Budgeted Rate (900 × 38 × $1.5)
$50,000	$54,000	51,300

$4,000 F — Spending variance

$2,700 U — Production-volume variance

8-34 (cont'd)

3. The variable overhead spending variance arises from the fact that the cost of horse feed, shampoo, ribbons, and other supplies was higher, per weighted average horse-guest week, than expected ($7,500/(950×38)lbs = $0.208 per lb > $0.2 per lb). Unlike the material and labour price variances, which only reflect the prices paid, the spending variance could have both a cost and usage component. HHS would have a negative spending variance if they paid more for feed than expected or if the horses ate more feed than expected.

4. The $380 unfavourable variable overhead efficiency variance reflects the fact that the average weight of a horse was higher than expected. HHS expected horses to weigh an average of 900 lbs but during August, the horses weighed an average of 950 lbs. Larger horses are expected to consume more variable overhead, such as horse feed and shampoo, hence the unfavourable nature of the variance.

5. Fixed overhead is fixed with respect to horse weight. This does not mean that it can be forecasted with 100% accuracy. For example, salaries or actual costs for advertising may have been higher than expected, leading to the $4,000 favourable variance.

6. The production-volume variance of $2,700 exists because the fixed overhead rate was based on the forecasted number of horse guest-weeks, 40, while the fixed overhead was applied using the actual number of horse guest-weeks, 38. The overestimation of the number of horse guests in August would lead to an under-absorption of fixed overhead, resulting in the unfavourable production-volume variance. If the estimate was too far off from the actual number of horses, HHS might potentially not charge enough to cover their costs.

8-36 (15-25 min.) Flexible budgets, four-variance analysis.

1.
$$\text{Budgeted hours allowed per unit of output} = \frac{\text{Budgeted DLH}}{\text{Budgeted actual output}}$$

$$= \frac{3,600,000}{720,000} = 5 \text{ hours}$$

Budgeted DMLH allowed for May output = 66,000 units × 5 = 330,000 hrs.

Allocated total MOH = 330,000 × Total MOH rate per hour

= 330,000 × $1.442 = $475,860

Allocated fixed MOH = 330,000 × $0.732 = $241,560

Flexible budget for VMOH = 330,000 × $0.71 = $234,300

8-36 (cont'd)

2,3,4,5. See Solution Exhibit 8-36.

Variable overhead rate per DMLH= $0.30 + $0.41 = $0.71
Fixed overhead rate per DMLH = $0.216 + $0.18 + $0.336 = $0.732
Fixed overhead budget for May = ($777,600 + $648,000 + $1,209,600) ÷ 12
= $2,635,200 ÷ 12 = $219,600

Using the format of Exhibit 8-12 for variable overhead and then fixed overhead:

Actual variable overhead: $90,000 + $133,000 = $223,000
Actual fixed overhead: $61,200 + $64,800 + $84,000 = $210,000

An overview of the four-variance analysis using the block format of the text is:

Four-Variance Analysis	Spending Variance	Efficiency Variance	Production Volume Variance
Variable Manufacturing Overhead	$650 F	$10,650 F	Never a variance
Fixed Manufacturing Overhead	$9,600 F	Never a variance	$21,960 F

8-36 (cont'd)

SOLUTION EXHIBIT 8-36

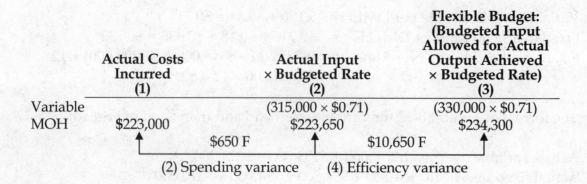

	Actual Costs Incurred (1)	Actual Input × Budgeted Rate (2)	Flexible Budget: (Budgeted Input Allowed for Actual Output Achieved × Budgeted Rate) (3)
Variable MOH	$223,000	(315,000 × $0.71) $223,650	(330,000 × $0.71) $234,300

$650 F ← (2) Spending variance

$10,650 F ← (4) Efficiency variance

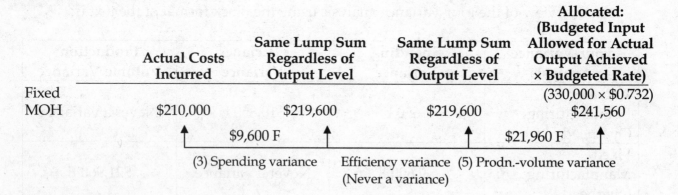

	Actual Costs Incurred	Same Lump Sum Regardless of Output Level	Same Lump Sum Regardless of Output Level	Allocated: (Budgeted Input Allowed for Actual Output Achieved × Budgeted Rate)
Fixed MOH	$210,000	$219,600	$219,600	(330,000 × $0.732) $241,560

$9,600 F ← (3) Spending variance

Efficiency variance (Never a variance)

$21,960 F ← (5) Prodn.-volume variance

Alternative computation of the production-volume variance:

$$= \left[\begin{pmatrix} \text{Budgeted hours} \\ \text{allowed for actual} \\ \text{output achieved} \end{pmatrix} - \begin{pmatrix} \text{Denominator} \\ \text{hours} \end{pmatrix} \right] \times \begin{bmatrix} \text{Budgeted} \\ \text{fixed} \\ \text{overhead} \\ \text{rate} \end{bmatrix}$$

$$= \left[(330,000) - \left(\frac{3,600,000}{12} \right) \right] \times \$0.732$$

$$= (330,000 - 300,000) \times \$0.732 = \$21,960 \text{ F}$$

8-38 (30 min.) Activity-based costing, batch-level variance analysis.

1. Static budget number of setups
   = Budgeted books produced/ Budgeted books per setup
   = 200,000 ÷ 500 = 400 setups

2. Flexible budget number of setups
   = Actual books produced / Budgeted books per setup
   = 216,000 ÷ 500 = 432 setups

3. Actual number of setups
   = Actual books produced / Actual books per setup
   = 216,000/480 = 450 setups

4. Static budget number of hours
   = Static budget # of setups × Budgeted hours per setup
   = 400 × 6 = 2,400 hours

   Fixed overhead rate
   = Static budget fixed overhead / Static budget number of hours
   = 72,000/2,400 = $30 per hour

5. Budgeted variable overhead cost of a setup
   = Budgeted variable cost per setup-hour × Budgeted number of setup-hours
   = $100 × 6 = $600.

   Budgeted total overhead cost of a setup
   = Budgeted variable overhead cost + Fixed overhead rate × Budgeted number of
                                                                  setup hours
   = $600 + $30 × 6 = 780.

The charge of $700 covers the budgeted incremental (i.e., variable overhead) cost of a setup, but not the budgeted full cost.

8-38 (cont'd)

6. Variable Setup Overhead Variance Analysis for Jo Nathan Publishing Company for 2009

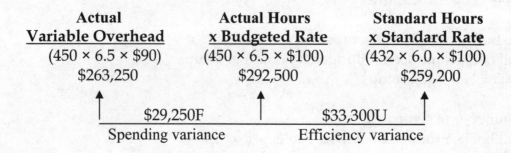

Actual	**Actual Hours**	**Standard Hours**
Variable Overhead	**x Budgeted Rate**	**x Standard Rate**
(450 × 6.5 × $90)	(450 × 6.5 × $100)	(432 × 6.0 × $100)
$263,250	$292,500	$259,200

$29,250F — Spending variance $33,300U — Efficiency variance

7. Fixed Setup Overhead Variance Analysis for Jo Nathan Publishing Company for 2009

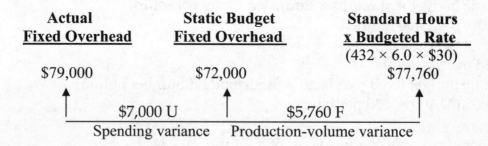

Actual	**Static Budget**	**Standard Hours**
Fixed Overhead	**Fixed Overhead**	**x Budgeted Rate**
		(432 × 6.0 × $30)
$79,000	$72,000	$77,760

$7,000 U — Spending variance $5,760 F — Production-volume variance

8. Rejecting an order may have implications for future orders (i.e., professors would be reluctant to order books from this publisher again). Jo Nathan should consider factors such as prior history with the customer and potential future sales.

   If a book is relatively new, Jo Nathan might consider running a full batch and holding the extra books in case of a second special order or just hold the extra books until next semester.

   If the special order comes at a heavy volume time, Jo should look at the opportunity cost of filling it, i.e., accepting the order may interfere with or delay the printing of other books.

8-40 (30–40 min.) Comprehensive review of Chapters 7 and 8, working backward from given variances.

1. Solution Exhibit 8-40 outlines the Chapter 7 and 8 framework underlying this solution.

    a. Kilograms of direct materials purchased = $176,000 ÷ $1.10 = 160,000 kilograms
    b. Kilograms of excess direct materials used = $69,000 ÷ $11.50 = 6,000 kilograms
    c. Variable manufacturing overhead spending variance = $10,350 – $18,000 = $7,650 F
    d. Standard direct manufacturing labour rate = $800,000 ÷ 40,000 hours = $20 per hour

        Actual direct manufacturing labour rate = $20 + $0.50 = $20.50
        Actual direct manufacturing labour-hours = $522,750 ÷ $20.50 = 25,500 hours
    e. Standard variable manufacturing overhead rate = $480,000 ÷ 40,000
        = $12 per direct manuf. labour-hour

        Variable manuf. overhead efficiency variance of $18,000 ÷ $12 = 1,500 excess hours

        Actual hours – Excess hours = Standard hours allowed for units produced
        25,500 – 1,500 = 24,000 hours
    f. Budgeted fixed manufacturing overhead rate = $640,000 ÷ 40,000 hours
        = $16 per direct manuf. labour-hour

        Fixed manufacturing overhead allocated = $16 × 24,000 hours = $384,000
        Production-volume variance = $640,000 – $384,000 = $256,000 U

2. The control of variable manufacturing overhead requires the identification of the cost drivers for such items as energy, supplies, and repairs. Control often entails monitoring nonfinancial measures that affect each cost item, one by one. Examples are kilowatts used, quantities of lubricants used, and repair parts and hours used. The most convincing way to discover why overhead performance did not agree with a budget is to investigate possible causes, line item by line item.

    Individual fixed overhead items are not usually affected very much by day-to-day control. Instead, they are controlled periodically through planning decisions and budgeting procedures that may sometimes have planning horizons covering six months or a year (for example, management salaries) and sometimes covering many years (for example, long-term leases and depreciation on plant and equipment).

8-40 (cont'd)
Solution Exhibit 8-40

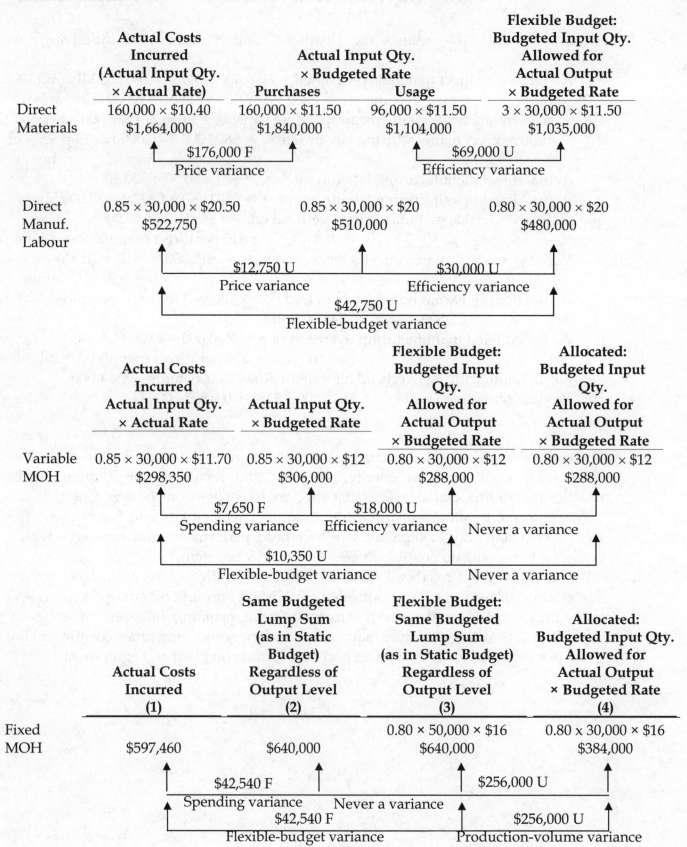

8-42 (20 minutes) Non-financial performance measures

1. The cost of the ball bearings would be indirect materials if it is either not possible to trace the costs to individual products, or if the cost is so small relative to other costs that it is impractical to do so. Since Department B makes a fairly constant number of finished products (400 units) each day, it would be easy to trace the cost of bearings to the wheels completed daily. However, the fact that Rollie measures ball bearings by weight and discards leftover bearings at the end of each day suggests that they are a relatively inexpensive item and not worth the effort to restock or track in inventory. As such, it could be argued that ball bearings should be classified as overhead (e.g., indirect materials).

2. Non-financial performance measures for Department B might include:
   - Number or proportion of wheels sent back for rework and/or amount or proportion of time spent on rework;
   - Number of wheels thrown away, ratio of wheels thrown away to wheels reworked, and/or ratio of bad to good wheels;
   - Amount of down time for broken machines during the day;
   - Weight of ball bearings discarded, or ratio of weights used and discarded.

3. If the number of wheels thrown away is significant relative to the number of reworked wheels, then it is not efficient to rework them and so Rollie should re-examine the rework process or even just throw away all the bad wheels without rework.

   If the amount of rework is significant, then the original process is not turning out quality goods in a timely manner. Rollie might slow down the process in Department B so it takes a little longer to make each good wheel, but the number of good wheels will be higher and may even save time overall if rework time drops considerably. They might also need to service the machines more often than just after the total daily production run, in which case they will trade off intentional down time for more efficient processing.

   If the amount of unintentional down time is significant they might bring in the mechanics during the day to fix a machine that goes down during a production run.

   Finally, Rollie might consider determining a better measure of ball bearings to requisition each day so that fewer are discarded, and might also keep any leftover ball bearings for use the next day.

CHAPTER 9
INCOME EFFECTS OF DENOMINATOR LEVEL ON INVENTORY VALUATION

9-2 The term *direct costing* is a misnomer for variable costing for two reasons:

a. Variable costing does not include all direct costs as inventoriable costs. Only variable direct manufacturing costs are included. Any fixed direct manufacturing costs and any direct nonmanufacturing costs (either variable or fixed) are excluded from inventoriable costs.

b. Variable costing includes as inventoriable costs not only direct manufacturing costs but also some indirect costs (variable indirect manufacturing costs).

9-4 The main issue between variable costing and absorption costing is the proper timing of the release of fixed manufacturing costs as costs of the period:

a. at the time of incurrence, or

b. at the time the finished units to which the fixed overhead relates are sold. Variable costing uses (a) and absorption costing uses (b).

9-6 Variable costing does not view fixed costs as unimportant or irrelevant, but it maintains that the distinction between behaviours of different costs is crucial for certain decisions. The planning and management of fixed costs is critical, irrespective of what inventory costing method is used.

9-8 (a) The factors that affect the breakeven point under variable costing are:
1. Fixed (manufacturing and operating) costs.
2. Contribution margin per unit.

(b) The factors that affect the breakeven point under absorption costing are:
1. Fixed (manufacturing and operating) costs.
2. Contribution margin per unit.
3. Production level in units in excess of breakeven sales in units.
4. Denominator level chosen to set the fixed manufacturing cost rate.

9-10 Examples of dysfunctional decisions managers may make to increase reported operating income are:

a. Plant managers may switch production to those orders that absorb the highest amount of manufacturing overhead, irrespective of the demand by customers.

b. Plant managers may accept a particular order to increase production even though another plant in the same company is better suited to handle that order.

c. Plant managers may defer maintenance beyond the current period to free up more time for production.

9-12 The *downward demand spiral* is the continuing reduction in demand for a company's product that occurs when the prices of competitors' products are not met and (as demand drops further), higher and higher unit costs result in more and more reluctance to meet competitors' prices. Pricing decisions need to consider competitors and customers as well as costs.

9-14 The *theoretical capacity* and *practical capacity* denominator-level concepts emphasize what a plant can supply. The *normal capacity utilization* and *master-budget capacity utilization* concepts emphasize what customers demand in products produced by a plant.

9-16 (30 min.) Variable and absorption costing, explaining operating income differences.

1. Key inputs for income statement computations are:

	April	May
Beginning inventory	0	150
Production	500	400
Goods available for sale	500	550
Units sold	350	520
Ending inventory	150	30

The unit fixed and total manufacturing costs per unit under absorption costing are:

		April	May
(a)	Fixed manufacturing costs	$2,000,000	$2,000,000
(b)	Units produced	500	400
(c)=(a)÷(b)	Unit fixed manufacturing costs	$4,000	$5,000
(d)	Unit variable manufacturing costs	$10,000	$10,000
(e)=(c)+(d)	Unit total manufacturing costs	$14,000	$14,000

9-16 (cont'd)

(a) Variable costing

	April 2010		May 2010	
Revenues[a]		$8,400,000		$12,480,000
Variable costs				
Beginning inventory	$ 0		$1,500,000	
Variable cost of goods manufactured[b]	5,000,000		4,000,000	
Cost of goods available for sale	5,000,000		5,500,000	
Ending inventory[c]	1,500,000		300,000	
Variable manufacturing cost of goods sold	3,500,000		5,200,000	
Variable marketing costs[d]	1,050,000		1,560,000	
Total variable costs		4,550,000		6,760,000
Contribution margin		3,850,000		5,720,000
Fixed costs				
Fixed manufacturing costs	2,000,000		2,000,000	
Fixed marketing costs	600,000		600,000	
Total fixed costs		2,600,000		2,600,000
Operating income		$1,250,000		$ 3,120,000

[a]$24,000 × 350; 520
[b]$10,000 × 500; 400
[c]$10,000 × 150; 30
[d]$3,000 × 350; 520

9-16 (cont'd)

(b) Absorption costing

	April 2010		May 2010	
Revenues[a]		$8,400,000		$12,480,000
Cost of goods sold				
Beginning inventory	$ 0		$2,100,000	
Variable manufacturing costs[b]	5,000,000		4,000,000	
Fixed manufacturing costs[c]	2,000,000		1,600,000	
Cost of goods available for sale	7,000,000		7,700,000	
Ending inventory[d]	2,100,000		420,000	
Adjustment for production-volume variance[e]	0		400,000 U	
Cost of goods sold		4,900,000		7,680,000
Gross margin		3,500,000		4,800,000
Marketing costs				
Variable marketing costs[f]	1,050,000		1,560,000	
Fixed marketing costs	600,000		600,000	
Total marketing costs		1,650,000		2,160,000
Operating income		$1,850,000		$ 2,640,000

[a]$24,000 × 350; 520
[b]$10,000 × 500; 400
[c]($4,000 × 500); ($4,000 × 400)
[d]($14,000 × 150; $14,000 × 30)   April's Production – Sales = Ending inventory: May's beginning inventory plus production minus sales =
                                                                    May's ending inventory (30)
[e]$2,000,000 – $2,000,000; $2,000,000 - $1,600,000
[e]($3,000 × 350; $3,000 × 520)

177

9-16 (cont'd)

2.

$$\begin{pmatrix} \text{Absorption-costing} \\ \text{operating income} \end{pmatrix} - \begin{pmatrix} \text{Variable-costing} \\ \text{operating income} \end{pmatrix} = \begin{pmatrix} \text{Fixed manufacturing} \\ \text{costs in} \\ \text{ending inventory} \end{pmatrix} - \begin{pmatrix} \text{Fixed manufacturing} \\ \text{costs in} \\ \text{beginning inventory} \end{pmatrix}$$

April:

$$\$1,850,000 - \$1,250,000 \quad = \quad (\$4,000 \times 150) - (\$0)$$
$$\$600,000 \quad = \quad \$600,000$$

May:

$$\$2,640,000 - \$3,120,000 \quad = \quad (\$4,000 \times 30) - (\$4,000 \times 150)$$
$$-\$480,000 \quad = \quad \$120,000 - \$600,000$$
$$-\$480,000 \quad = \quad -\$480,000$$

The difference between absorption and variable costing is due solely to moving fixed manufacturing costs into inventories as inventories increase (as in April) and out of inventories as they decrease (as in May).

Therefore:

when inventories ↑: absorption costing > variable costing

and when inventories ↓: absorption costing < variable costing

9-18 (40 min.) Variable and absorption costing, explaining operating-income differences.

1. Key inputs for income statement computations are:

	January	February	March
Beginning inventory	0	300	300
Production	1,000	800	1,250
Goods available for sale	1,000	1,100	1,550
Units sold	700	800	1,500
Ending inventory	300	300	50

The budgeted fixed manufacturing cost per unit and budgeted total manufacturing cost per unit under absorption costing are:

		January	February	March
(a)	Budgeted fixed manufacturing costs	$400,000	$400,000	$400,000
(b)	Budgeted production	1,000	1,000	1,000
(c)=(a)÷(b)	Budgeted fixed manufacturing cost per unit	$400	$400	$400
(d)	Budgeted variable manufacturing cost per unit	$900	$900	$900
(e)=(c)+(d)	Budgeted total manufacturing cost per unit	$1,300	$1,300	$1,300

9-18 (cont'd)

(a) Variable Costing

	January 2009	February 2009	March 2009
Revenues[a]	$2,100,000	$2,400,000	$4,500,000
Variable costs			
Beginning inventory[b]	$ 0	$270,000	$ 270,000
Variable manufacturing costs[c]	900,000	720,000	1,125,000
Cost of goods available for sale	900,000	990,000	1,395,000
Deduct ending inventory[d]	(270,000)	(270,000)	(45,000)
Variable cost of goods sold	630,000	720,000	1,350,000
Variable operating costs[e]	420,000	480,000	900,000
Total variable costs	1,050,000	1,200,000	2,250,000
Contribution margin	1,050,000	1,200,000	2,250,000
Fixed costs			
Fixed manufacturing costs	400,000	400,000	400,000
Fixed operating costs	140,000	140,000	140,000
Total fixed costs	540,000	540,000	540,000
Operating income	$ 510,000	$ 660,000	$1,710,000

a $3,000 × 700; $3,000 × 800; $3,000 × 1,500
b $? × 0; $900 × 300; $900 × 300
c $900 × 1,000; $900 × 800; $900 × 1,250
d $900 × 300; $900 × 300; $900 × 50
e $600 × 700; $600 × 800; $600 × 1,500

9-18 (cont'd)

(b) Absorption Costing

	January 2009	February 2009	March 2009
Revenues[a]	$2,100,000	$2,400,000	$4,500,000
Cost of goods sold			
Beginning inventory[b]	$ 0	$ 390,000	$ 390,000
Variable manufacturing costs[c]	900,000	720,000	1,125,000
Allocated fixed manufacturing costs[d]	400,000	320,000	500,000
Cost of goods available for sale	1,300,000	1,430,000	2,015,000
Deduct ending inventory[e]	(390,000)	(390,000)	(65,000)
Adjustment for prod. vol. var.[f]	0	80,000 U	(100,000) F
Cost of goods sold	910,000	1,120,000	1,850,000
Gross margin	1,190,000	1,280,000	2,650,000
Operating costs			
Variable operating costs[g]	420,000	480,000	900,000
Fixed operating costs	140,000	140,000	140,000
Total operating costs	560,000	620,000	1,040,000
Operating income	$ 630,000	$ 660,000	$1,610,000

[a] $3,000 × 700; $3,000 × 800; $3,000 × 1,500
[b] $?× 0; $1,300 × 300; $1,300 × 300
[c] $900 × 1,000; $900 × 800; $900 × 1,250
[d] $400 × 1,000; $400 × 800; $400 × 1,250
[e] $1,300 × 300; $1,300 × 300; $1,300 × 50
[f] $400,000 – $400,000; $400,000 – $320,000; $400,000 – $500,000
[g] $600 × 700; $600 × 800; $600 × 1,500

9-18 (cont'd)

2. $$\left(\begin{array}{c}\text{Absorption-costing}\\\text{operating income}\end{array}\right) - \left(\begin{array}{c}\text{Variable costing}\\\text{operating income}\end{array}\right) = \left(\begin{array}{c}\text{Fixed manufacturing}\\\text{costs in}\\\text{ending inventory}\end{array}\right) - \left(\begin{array}{c}\text{Fixed manufacturing}\\\text{costs in}\\\text{beginning inventory}\end{array}\right)$$

January: $630,000 – $510,000 = ($400 × 300) – $0
$120,000 = $120,000

February: $660,000 – $660,000 = ($400 × 300) – ($400 × 300)
$0 = $0

March: $1,610,000 – $1,710,000 = ($400 × 50) – ($400 × 300)
– $100,000 = – $100,000

The difference between absorption and variable costing is due solely to moving fixed manufacturing costs into inventories as inventories increase (as in January) and out of inventories as they decrease (as in March).

9-20 (10 min.) Absorption and variable costing.

The answers are 1(a) and 2(c). Computations:

1. **Absorption Costing**:

Revenues[a]		$4,800,000
Cost of goods sold:		
Variable manufacturing costs[b]	$2,400,000	
Allocated fixed manufacturing costs[c]	360,000	2,760,000
Gross margin		2,040,000
Operating costs:		
Variable operating[d]	1,200,000	
Fixed operating	400,000	1,600,000
Operating income		$ 440,000

[a] $40 × 120,000
[b] $20 × 120,000
[c] Fixed manufacturing rate = $600,000 ÷ 200,000 = $3 per output unit
Fixed manufacturing costs = $3 × 120,000
[d] $10 × 120,000

9-20 (cont'd)

2. Variable Costing:

Revenues[a]		$4,800,000
Variable costs:		
Variable manufacturing cost of goods sold[b]	$2,400,000	
Variable operating costs[c]	1,200,000	3,600,000
Contribution margin		1,200,000
Fixed costs:		
Fixed manufacturing costs	600,000	
Fixed operating costs	400,000	1,000,000
Operating income		$ 200,000

[a] $40 × 120,000
[b] $20 × 120,000
[c] $10 × 120,000

9-22 (40 min) Absorption versus variable costing.

1. The variable manufacturing cost per unit is $55 + $45 + $120 = $220.

2009 Variable-Costing-Based Operating Income Statement

Revenues (8,960 × $1,200 per unit)		$10,752,000
Variable costs		
Beginning inventory	$ 0	
Variable manufacturing costs (10,000 units × $220 per unit)	2,200,000	
Cost of goods available for sale	2,200,000	
Deduct: Ending inventory (1,040[a] units × $220 per unit)	(228,800)	
Variable cost of goods sold	1,971,200	
Variable marketing costs (8,960 units × $75 per unit)	672,000	
Total variable costs		2,643,200
Contribution margin		8,108,800
Fixed costs		
Fixed manufacturing costs	1,471,680	
Fixed R&D	981,120	
Fixed marketing	3,124,480	
Total fixed costs		5,577,280
Operating income		$2,531,520

[a] Beginning Inventory 0 + Production 10,000 – Sales 8,960 = Ending Inventory 1,040 units

9-22 (cont'd)

2.

2009 Absorption-Costing-Based Operating Income Statement

Revenues (8,960 units × $1,200 per unit)		$10,752,000
Cost of goods sold		
Beginning inventory	$ 0	
Variable manufacturing costs (10,000 units × $220 per unit)	2,200,000	
Allocated fixed manufacturing costs (10,000 units × $165 per unit)	1,650,000	
Cost of goods available for sale	3,850,000	
Deduct ending inventory (1,040 units × ($220 + $165) per unit)	(400,400)	
Deduct favourable production volume variance	(178,320)[a] F	
Cost of goods sold		3,271,280
Gross margin		7,480,720
Operating costs		
Variable marketing costs (8,960 units × $75 per unit)	672,000	
Fixed R&D	981,120	
Fixed marketing	3,124,480	
Total operating costs		4,777,600
Operating income		$2,703,120

[a] PVV = Allocated $1,650,000 ($165 × 10,000) – Actual $1,471,680 = $178,320

3. 2009 operating income under absorption costing is greater than the operating income under variable costing because in 2009 inventories increased by 1,040 units, and under absorption costing fixed overhead remained in the ending inventory, and resulted in a lower cost of goods sold (relative to variable costing). As shown below, the difference in the two operating incomes is exactly the same as the difference in the fixed manufacturing costs included in ending vs. beginning inventory (under absorption costing).

Operating income under absorption costing	$2,703,120
Operating income under variable costing	2,531,520
Difference in operating income under absorption vs. variable costing	$ 171,600
Under absorption costing:	
Fixed mfg. costs in ending inventory (1,040 units × $165 per unit)	$ 171,600
Fixed mfg. costs in beginning inventory (0 units × $165 per unit)	0
Change in fixed mfg. costs between ending and beginning inventory	$ 171,600

9-22 (cont'd)

4. Relative to the obvious alternative of using contribution margin (from variable costing), the absorption-costing-based gross margin has some pros and cons as a performance measure for Electron's supervisors. It takes into account both variable costs and fixed costs—costs that the supervisors should be able to control in the long-run—and therefore it is a more complete measure than contribution margin which ignores fixed costs (and may cause the supervisors to pay less attention to fixed costs). The downside of using absorption-costing-based gross margin is the supervisor's temptation to use inventory levels to control the gross margin—in particular, to shore up a sagging gross margin by building up inventories. This can be offset by specifying, or limiting, the inventory build-up that can occur, charging the supervisor a carrying cost for holding inventory, and using nonfinancial performance measures such as the ratio of ending to beginning inventory.

9-24 (30-40 min.) Income statements.

1.

Mass Company
Income Statements
For the Year 2010
(in thousands)

(a) **Variable Costing:**

Revenues (25,000 × $48)		$1,200.00
Variable costs:		
Beginning inventory (2,000 × $26.10)	$ 52.20	
Variable cost of goods manufactured (29,000[1] × $26.10)	756.90	
Cost of goods available for sale	809.10	
Ending inventory (6,000 × $26.10)	156.60	
Variable manufacturing cost of goods sold	652.50	
Variable marketing and administrative costs		
(25,000 × $1.20)	30.00	
Variable costs		$ 682.50
Contribution margin		$ 517.50
Fixed costs:		
Fixed manufacturing overhead costs	120.00	
Fixed marketing and admin. costs	190.00	
Fixed costs		310.00
Operating income		$ 207.50

[1] Production = Sales – Beginning inventory + Ending inventory
= 25,000 – 2,000 + 6,000 = 29,000

9-24 (cont'd)

(b) Absorption Costing:

Revenues (25,000 × $48)		$1,200.00
Cost of goods sold:		
Beginning inventory (2,000 × $30.90[2])	$ 61.80	
Variable manufacturing costs (29,000 × $26.10)	756.90	
Fixed manufacturing costs (given)	120.00	
Cost of goods available for sale	938.70	
Ending inventory (6,000 × $30.24)[3]	181.44	
Cost of goods sold		757.26
Gross margin		442.74
Marketing and administrative costs:		
Variable marketing and admin. costs (25,000×$1.20)	30.00	
Fixed marketing and admin. costs	190.00	
Marketing and admin. costs		220.00
Operating income		$ 222.74

[2] Production 2009 = Sales – Beginning inventory + Ending inventory
      = 25,000 – 2,000 + 2,000 = 25,000
∴ Fixed Manufacturing O/H per unit = $120,000 ÷ 25,000 = $4.80
∴ Standard Variable cost per unit plus fixed manufacturing O/H per unit = $26.10 + 4.80 = $30.90

[3] Production 2010 = 29,000 units
∴ Fixed Manufacturing O/H per unit = $120,000 ÷ 29,000 = $4.14
∴ Standard Variable cost per unit plus fixed manufacturing O/H per unit = $26.10 + 4.14 = $30.24

2.

$$\begin{pmatrix} \text{Absorption} & \text{Variable} \\ \text{costing} & \text{costing} \\ \text{operating} - \text{operating} \\ \text{income} & \text{income} \end{pmatrix} = \begin{pmatrix} \text{Fixed} & \text{Fixed} \\ \text{manuf. costs} & \text{manuf. costs} \\ \text{in ending} - \text{in beginning} \\ \text{inventory} & \text{inventory} \end{pmatrix}$$

$$\$222,740 - \$207,500 = [(6,000 \times \$4.14) - (2,000 \times \$4.80)]$$
$$\$15,240 = \$24,840 - \$9,600$$
$$\$15,240 = \$15,240$$

The operating income figures differ because the amount of fixed manufacturing costs in the ending inventory differs from that in the beginning inventory.

9-24 (cont'd)

3. Advantages:
   (a) The fixed costs are reported as period costs (and not allocated to inventory), thus increasing the likelihood of better control of these costs.
   (b) Operating income is directly influenced by changes in unit sales (and not influenced by build-up of inventory).
   (c) The impact of fixed costs on operating income is emphasized.
   (d) The income statements are in the same form as used for cost-volume-profit analysis.
   (e) Product line, territory, etc. contribution margins are emphasized and more readily ascertainable.

   Disadvantages:
   (a) Total costs may be overlooked when considering operating problems.
   (b) Distinction between fixed and variable costs is arbitrary for many costs.
   (c) Emphasis on variable costs may cause some managers to ignore fixed costs.
   (d) A new variable-costing system may be too costly to install unless top managers think that operating decisions will be improved collectively.

9-26 (35 min.) Absorption costing and production volume variance — alternative capacity bases

1. Inventoriable cost per unit = Variable production cost + Fixed manufacturing overhead/Capacity

Capacity Type	Capacity Level	Fixed Mfg. Overhead	Fixed Mfg. Overhead Rate	Variable Production Cost	Inventoriable Cost per Unit
Theoretical	800,000	$1,000,000	$1.25	$2.50	$3.75
Practical	500,000	$1,000,000	$2.00	$2.50	$4.50
Normal	250,000	$1,000,000	$4.00	$2.50	$6.50
Master Budget	200,000	$1,000,000	$5.00	$2.50	$7.50

9-26 (cont'd)

2. ELF's actual production level is 220,000 bulbs. We can compute the production-volume variance as:

Production Volume Variance = Budgeted Fixed Mfg. Overhead
     – (Fixed Mfg. Overhead Rate × Actual Production Level)

Capacity Type	Capacity Level	Fixed Mfg. Overhead	Fixed Mfg. Overhead Rate	Fixed Mfg. Overhead Rate × Actual Production	Production Volume Variance
Theoretical	800,000	$1,000,000	$1.25	$ 275,000	$725,000 U
Practical	500,000	$1,000,000	$2.00	$ 440,000	$560,000 U
Normal	250,000	$1,000,000	$4.00	$ 880,000	$120,000 U
Master Budget	200,000	$1,000,000	$5.00	$1,100,000	$100,000 F

3. Operating income for ELF given production of 220,000 bulbs and sales of 200,000 bulbs @ $9 apiece:

	Theoretical	Practical	Normal	Master Budget
Revenue	$1,800,000	$1,800,000	$1,800,000	$1,800,000
Less: Cost of goods sold [a]	750,000	900,000	1,300,000	1,500,000
Production-volume variance	725,000 U	560,000 U	120,000 U	(100,000)F
Gross margin	325,000	340,000	380,000	400,000
Variable selling [b]	50,000	50,000	50,000	50,000
Fixed selling	250,000	250,000	250,000	250,000
Operating income	$ 25,000	$ 40,000	$ 80,000	$ 100,000

[a]200,000 × 3.75, × 4.50, × 6.50, × 7.50
[b]200,000 × 0.25

9-28 (40 min.) Variable costing versus absorption costing.

1. **Absorption Costing:**

Proteus Company
Income Statement
For the Year 2010

Revenues (540,000 × $6.00)		$3,240,000
Cost of goods sold:		
Beginning inventory (30,000 × $4.30[a])	$ 129,000	
Variable manufacturing costs (550,000[b] × $3.60)	1,980,000	
Fixed manuf. overhead costs (550,000 × $0.70)	385,000	
Cost of goods available for sale	2,494,000	
Ending inventory (40,000 × $4.30)	172,000	
Cost of goods sold (at standard costs)		2,322,000
Gross margin (at standard costs)		918,000
Adjustment for variances (50,000[c] × $0.70)		35,000
Gross margin		883,000
Marketing and administrative costs:		
Variable marketing and admin. costs (540,000 × $1)	540,000	
Fixed marketing and admin. costs	120,000	
Adjustment for variances	0	
Marketing and administrative costs		660,000
Operating income		$ 223,000

[a]$3.60 + ($7.00 ÷ 10) = $3.60 + $0.70 = $4.30
[b] Production = Sales – Beginning inventory + Ending inventory
        = 540,000 – 30,000 + 40,000
        = 550,000
[c][(10 × 60,000) – 550,000)] = 50,000 units

9-28 (cont'd)

2.   Variable Costing:

Proteus Company
Income Statements for the Year 2010

Revenues		$3,240,000
Variable costs:		
Beginning inventory (30,000 × $3.60)	$ 108,000	
Variable cost of goods manufactured		
(550,000 × $3.60)	1,980,000	
Cost of goods available for sale	2,088,000	
Ending inventory (40,000 × $3.60)	144,000	
Variable manufacturing cost of goods sold	1,944,000	
Variable marketing and administrative costs	540,000	
Total variable costs (at standard cost)	2,484,000	
Adjustment for variances	0	
Total variable costs		2,484,000
Contribution margin		756,000
Fixed costs:		
Fixed manufacturing overhead costs	420,000	
Fixed marketing and administrative costs	120,000	
Adjustment for variances	0	
Total fixed costs		540,000
Operating income		$216,000

The difference in operating income between the two costing methods is:

$$
\begin{pmatrix}
\text{Absorption} \\ \text{costing} \\ \text{operating} \\ \text{income}
\end{pmatrix}
-
\begin{pmatrix}
\text{Variable} \\ \text{costing} \\ \text{operating} \\ \text{income}
\end{pmatrix}
=
\begin{pmatrix}
\text{Fixed} \\ \text{manuf. costs} \\ \text{in ending} \\ \text{inventory}
\end{pmatrix}
-
\begin{pmatrix}
\text{Fixed} \\ \text{manuf. costs} \\ \text{in beginning} \\ \text{inventory}
\end{pmatrix}
$$

$$\$223,000 - \$216,000 = [(40,000 \times \$0.70) - (30,000 \times \$0.70)]$$
$$\$7,000 = \$28,000 - \$21,000$$
$$\$7,000 = \$7,000$$

The absorption-costing operating income exceeds the variable-costing figure by $7,000 because of the increase of $7,000, during 2010, in the amount of fixed manufacturing costs in ending inventory vis-à-vis beginning inventory.

9-28 (cont'd)

3.

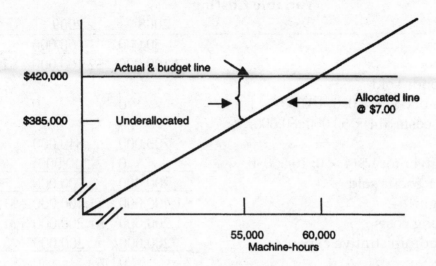

9-30 (40 min.) **Variable and absorption costing, sales, and operating-income changes.**

1. Headsmart's annual fixed manufacturing costs are $1,200,000. It allocates $24 of fixed manufacturing costs to each unit produced. Therefore, it must be using $1,200,000 ÷ $24 = 50,000 units (annually) as the denominator level to allocate fixed manufacturing costs to the units produced.

We can see from Headsmart's income statements that it disposes of any production volume variance against cost of goods sold. In 2009, 60,000 units were produced instead of the budgeted 50,000 units. This resulted in a favourable production volume variance of $240,000 F ((60,000 – 50,000) units × $24 per unit), which, when written off against cost of goods sold, increased gross margin by that amount.

The breakeven calculation, same for each year, is shown below:

Calculation of breakeven volume	2008	2009	2010
Selling price ($2,100,000 ÷ 50,000; $2,100,000 ÷ 50,000; $2,520,000 ÷ 60,000)	$42	$42	$42
Variable cost per unit (all manufacturing)	14	14	14
Contribution margin per unit	$28	$28	$28
Total fixed costs (fixed mfg. costs + fixed selling & admin. costs)	$1,400,000	$1,400,000	$1,400,000
Breakeven quantity = Total fixed costs ÷ contribution margin per unit	50,000	50,000	50,000

9-30 (cont'd)

3.

Variable Costing

	2008	2009	2010
Sales (units)	50,000	50,000	60,000
Revenues	$2,100,000	$2,100,000	$2,520,000
Variable cost of goods sold			
Beginning inventory $14 × 0; 0; 10,000	0	0	140,000
Variable manuf. costs $14 × 50,000; 60,000; 50,000	700,000	840,000	700,000
Deduct ending inventory $14 × 0; 10,000; 0	0	(140,000)	0
Variable cost of goods sold	700,000	700,000	840,000
Contribution margin	$1,400,000	$1,400,000	$1,680,000
Fixed manufacturing costs	$1,200,000	$1,200,000	$1,200,000
Fixed selling and administrative expenses	200,000	200,000	200,000
Operating income	$ 0	$ 0	$ 280,000

Explaining variable costing operating income

	2008	2009	2010
Contribution margin ($28 contribution margin per unit × sales units)	$1,400,000	$1,400,000	$1,680,000
Total fixed costs	1,400,000	1,400,000	1,400,000
Operating income	$ 0	$ 0	$ 280,000

4.

Reconciliation of absorption/variable costing

operating incomes	2008	2009	2010
(1) Absorption costing operating income (ACOI)	$0	$240,000	$ 40,000
(2) Variable costing operating income (VCOI)	0	0	280,000
(3) Difference (ACOI – VCOI)	$0	$240,000	$(240,000)
(4) Fixed mfg. costs in ending inventory under absorption costing (ending inventory in units × $24 per unit)	$0	$240,000	$ 0
(5) Fixed mfg. costs in beginning inventory under absorption costing (beginning inventory in units × $24 per unit)	0	0	240,000
(6) Difference = (4) – (5)	$0	$240,000	$(240,000)

9-30 (cont'd)

In the table above, row (3) shows the difference between the operating income under absorption costing and the operating income under variable costing, for each of the three years. In 2008, the difference is $0; in 2009, absorption costing income is greater by $240,000; and in 2010, it is less by $240,000. Row (6) above shows the difference between the fixed costs in ending inventory and the fixed costs in beginning inventory under absorption costing, which is $0 in 2008, $240,000 in 2009 and –$240,000 in 2010. Row (3) and row (6) explain and reconcile the operating income differences between absorption costing and variable costing.

Stuart Weil is surprised at the non-zero, positive net income (reported under absorption costing) in 2009, when sales were at the 'breakeven volume' of 50,000; further, he is concerned about the drop in operating income in 2010, when, in fact, sales increased to 60,000 units. In 2009, starting with zero inventories, 60,000 units were produced and 50,000 were sold, i.e., at the end of the year, 10,000 units remained in inventory. These 10,000 units had each absorbed $24 of fixed costs (total of $240,000), which would remain as assets on Headsmart's balance sheet until they were sold. Cost of goods sold, representing only the costs of the 50,000 units sold in 2009, was accordingly reduced by $240,000, the production volume variance, resulting in a positive operating income even though sales were at breakeven levels. The following year, in 2010, production was 50,000 units and sales were 60,000 units, i.e., all of the fixed costs that were included in 2009 ending inventory flowed through COGS in 2010. Contribution margin in 2010 was $1,680,000 (60,000 units × $28), but, in absorption costing, COGS also contains the allocated fixed manufacturing costs of the units sold, which were $1,440,000 (60,000 units × $24), resulting in an operating income of $40,000 = 1,680,000 – $1,440,000 – $200,000 (fixed sales and admin.) Hence the drop in operating income under absorption costing, even though sales were greater than the computed breakeven volume: inventory levels decreased sufficiently in 2010 to cause 2010's operating income to be lower than 2009 operating income.

Note that beginning and ending with zero inventories during the 2008–2010 period, under both costing methods, Headsmart's total operating income was $280,000.

9-32 (30 min.) Cost allocation, downward demand spiral.

SOLUTION EXHIBIT 9-32

	2009 Master Budget (1)	Practical Capacity (2)	2010 Master Budget (3)
Budgeted fixed costs	$1,533,000	$1,533,000	$1,533,000
Denominator level	1,022,000	1,460,000	876,000
Budgeted fixed cost per meal			
Budgeted fixed costs ÷ Denominator level ($1,533,000÷1,022,000; $1,533,000÷1,460,000; $1,533,000÷876,000)	$ 1.50	$ 1.05	$ 1.75
Budgeted variable cost per meal	4.50	4.50	4.50
Total budgeted cost per meal	$ 6.00	$ 5.55	$ 6.25

1. The 2009 budgeted fixed costs are $1,533,000. Deliman budgets for 1,022,000 meals in 2009, and this is used as the denominator level to calculate the fixed cost per meal. $1,533,000÷1,022,000 = $1.50 fixed cost per meal. (see column (1) in Solution Exhibit 9-32).

2. In 2010, three retirement homes have dropped out of the purchasing group and the master budget is 876,000 meals. If this is used as the denominator level, fixed cost per meal = $1,533,000 ÷ 876,000 = $1.75 per meal, and the total budgeted cost per meal would be $6.25 (see column (3) in Solution Exhibit 9-32). If the retirement homes have already been complaining about quality and cost and are allowed to purchase from outside, they will not accept this higher price. More retirement homes may begin to purchase meals from outside the system, leading to a downward demand spiral, possibly putting Deliman out of business.

3. The basic problem is that Deliman has excess capacity and the associated excess fixed costs. If Smith uses the practical capacity of 1,460,000 meals as the denominator level, the fixed cost per meal will be $1.05 (see column (2) in Solution Exhibit 9-32), and the total budgeted cost per meal would be $5.55, probably a more acceptable price to the customers (it may even draw back the three retirement homes that have chosen to buy outside). This denominator level will also isolate the cost of unused capacity and not allocate it to the meals produced. To make the $5.55 price per meal profitable in the long run, Smith will have to find ways to either use the extra capacity or reduce Deliman's practical capacity and the related fixed costs.

9-34 (40 min.) Variable costing and absorption costing, The All-Fixed Company.

This problem always generates active classroom discussion.

1. The treatment of fixed manufacturing overhead in absorption costing is affected primarily by what denominator level is selected as a base for allocating fixed manufacturing costs to units produced. In this case, is 10,000 tonnes per year, 20,000 tonnes, or some other denominator level the most appropriate base?

    We usually place the following possibilities on the board or overhead projector and then ask the students to indicate by vote how many used one denominator level versus another. Incidentally, discussion tends to move more clearly if variable-costing income statements are discussed first, because there is little disagreement as to computations under variable costing.

    (a) Variable-Costing Income Statements:

		2009	2010	Together
Revenues (and contribution margin)		$300,000	$300,000	$600,000
Fixed costs:				
Manufacturing costs	$280,000			
Marketing and administrative cost	40,000	320,000	320,000	640,000
Operating income		$ (20,000)	$ (20,000)	$ (40,000)

    (b) Absorption-Costing Income Statements:
    The ambiguity about the 10,000- or 20,000-tonne denominator level is intentional. If you wish, the ambiguity may be avoided by giving the students a specific denominator level in advance.

    Alternative 1. Use 20,000 tonnes as a denominator; fixed manufacturing overhead per unit is $280,000 ÷ 20,000 = $14.

	2009	2010	Together
Revenues	$300,000	$300,000	$600,000
Manufacturing costs @ $14	280,000	—	280,000
Deduct ending inventory	140,000	—	—
Cost of goods sold	140,000	140,000*	280,000
Underallocated manuf. overhead —			
output level variance	—	280,000	280,000
Marketing and administrative costs	40,000	40,000	80,000
Total costs	180,000	460,000	640,000
Operating income	$120,000	$(160,000)	$ (40,000)

*Inventory carried forward from 2009 and sold in 2010.

9-34 (cont'd)

Alternative 2. Use 10,000 tonnes as a denominator; fixed manufacturing overhead per unit is $280,000 ÷ 10,000 = $28.

	2009	2010	Together
Revenues	$300,000	$300,000	$600,000
Manufacturing costs @ $28	560,000	–	560,000
Deduct ending inventory	280,000	–	–
Cost of goods sold	280,000	280,000*	560,000
Underallocated manuf. overhead— output level variance	–	280,000	–
Overallocated manuf. overhead— output level variance	(280,000)	–	–
Marketing and administrative costs	40,000	40,000	80,000
Total costs	40,000	600,000	640,000
Operating income	$260,000	$(300,000)	$ (40,000)

*Inventory carried forward from 2009 and sold in 2010.

Note that operating income under variable costing follows sales and is not affected by inventory changes.

Note also that students will understand the variable-costing presentation much more easily than the alternatives presented under absorption costing.

2.   Breakeven point $= \dfrac{\text{Fixed costs}}{\text{Contribution margin per tonne}} = \dfrac{\$320,000}{\$30}$

   = 10,667 (rounded) tonnes per year or 21,334 for two years.

If the company could sell 667 more tons per year at $30 each, it could get the extra $20,000 contribution margin needed to break even.

Most students will say that the breakeven point is 10,667 tonnes per year under both absorption costing and variable costing. The logical question to ask a student who answers 10,667 tonnes for variable costing is: "What operating income do you show for 2009 under absorption costing?" If a student answers $120,000 (alternative 1 above), or $260,000 (alternative 2 above), ask: "But you say your breakeven point is 10,667 tonnes. How can you show an operating income of ≥ $120,000 on only 10,667 tonnes sold during 2009?"

The answer to the above dilemma lies in the fact that operating income is affected by both sales and production under absorption costing.

9-34 (cont'd)

<u>Optional:</u> Given that sales would be 10,000 tonnes in 2009, solve for the production level that will provide a breakeven level of zero operating income. Using the formula in the chapter, sales of 10,000 units, and a fixed manufacturing overhead rate of $14 (based on $280,000 ÷ 20,000 tonnes denominator level = $14):

Let P = Production level

$$\begin{array}{c}\text{Breakeven} \\ \text{sales} \\ \text{in units}\end{array} = \frac{\left(\begin{array}{c}\text{Total fixed} \\ \text{costs}\end{array}\right) + \left[\left(\begin{array}{c}\text{Fixed manuf.} \\ \text{overhead} \\ \text{rate}\end{array}\right) \times \left(\begin{array}{c}\text{Breakeven} \\ \text{sales in} \\ \text{units}\end{array} - \begin{array}{c}\text{Units} \\ \text{produced}\end{array}\right)\right]}{\text{Unit contribution margin}}$$

10,000 tonnes	=	$\dfrac{\$320{,}000 + \$14(10{,}000 - P)}{\$30}$
$300,000	=	$320,000 + $140,000 − $14P
$14P	=	$160,000
P	=	11,429 tonnes (rounded)

Proof:

Gross margin, 10,000 × ($30 − $14)		$160,000
Output level variance,		
(20,000 − 11,429) × $14	$119,994	
Marketing and administrative costs	40,000	159,994
Operating income (due to rounding)		$ 6

Given that production would be 20,000 tonnes in 2009, solve for the breakeven unit sales level. Using the formula in the chapter and a fixed manufacturing overhead rate of $14 (based on a denominator level of 20,000 units):

Let N	=	Breakeven sales in units
N	=	$\dfrac{\left(\begin{array}{c}\text{Total fixed} \\ \text{costs}\end{array}\right) + \left[\left(\begin{array}{c}\text{Fixed manuf.} \\ \text{overhead} \\ \text{rate}\end{array}\right) \times \left(N - \begin{array}{c}\text{Units} \\ \text{produced}\end{array}\right)\right]}{\text{Unit contribution margin}}$
N	=	$\dfrac{\$320{,}000 + \$14(N - 20{,}000)}{\$30}$
$30N	=	$320,000 + $14N − $280,000
$16N	=	$40,000
N	=	2,500 units

9-34 (cont'd)

Proof:

Gross margin, 2,500 × ($30 – $14)		$40,000
Output level MOH variance	$ 0	
Marketing and administrative costs	40,000	40,000
Operating income		$ 0

We find it helpful to put the following comparisons on the board:

Variable costing breakeven	=	fn(sales)
	=	10,667 tonnes
Absorption-costing breakeven	=	fn(sales and production)
	=	fn(10,000 and 11,429)
	=	fn(2,500 and 20,000)

3. Absorption costing inventory cost: Either $140,000 or $280,000 at the end of 2009, and zero at the end of 2010.

    Variable costing: Zero at all times. This is a major criticism of variable costing and focuses on the issue of the definition of an asset.

4. Operating income is affected by both production <u>and</u> sales under absorption costing. Hence, most managers would prefer absorption costing because their performance in any given reporting period, at least in the short run, is influenced by how much production is scheduled near the end of a period.

9-36 (25-35 min.) Comparison of variable costing and absorption costing.

1. Operating income is a function of both sales and production under absorption costing, whereas it is a function only of sales under variable costing. Therefore, inventory changes can have dramatic effects on operating income under absorption costing. In this case, the severe decline in inventory has resulted in enormous fixed costs from beginning inventory being charged against 2010 operations.

2. The income statement deliberately contains an ambiguity about whether the fixed manufacturing overhead of $1,200,000 is the budgeted or actual amount. Of course, it must be the budgeted amount, because the spending variance and the output level variance are shown separately. Therefore:

$$\frac{\text{Production volume}}{\text{Manuf. costs variance}} = \frac{\text{Budgeted fixed}}{\text{manufacturing overhead}} - \frac{\text{Fixed manufacturing}}{\text{overhead allocated}}$$

$$\$480,000 = \$1,200,000 - \text{Allocated}$$

$$\text{Allocated} = \$720,000, \text{ which is } 60\% \text{ of denominator level}$$

3. Note that the answer to (3) is independent of (2). The difference in operating income of $378,000 ($720,000 – $342,000) is explained by the release of $378,000 of fixed manufacturing costs when the inventories were decreased during 2010:

	Absorption Costing	Variable Costing	Fixed Manuf. Overhead in Inventory
Inventories:			
December 31, 2009	$1,980,000	$1,584,000	$396,000
December 31, 2010	90,000	72,000	18,000
Release of fixed manuf. costs			$378,000

The above schedule in this requirement is a formal presentation of the equation:

$$\begin{pmatrix} \text{Absorption} \\ \text{costing} \\ \text{operating} \\ \text{income} \end{pmatrix} - \begin{pmatrix} \text{Variable} \\ \text{costing} \\ \text{operating} \\ \text{income} \end{pmatrix} = \begin{pmatrix} \text{Fixed} \\ \text{manuf. costs} \\ \text{in ending} \\ \text{inventory} \end{pmatrix} - \begin{pmatrix} \text{Fixed} \\ \text{manuf. costs} \\ \text{in beginning} \\ \text{inventory} \end{pmatrix}$$

$$(\$342,000 - \$720,000) = (\$18,000 - \$396,000)$$
$$-\$378,000 = -\$378,000$$

9-36 (cont'd)

Alternatively, the presence of fixed manufacturing overhead costs in each income statement can be analyzed:

Absorption costing,	
Fixed manuf. costs in cost of goods sold	
($5,490,000 – $4,392,000)	$1,098,000
Production volume MOH variance	480,000
	$1,578,000
Variable costing, fixed manufacturing costs	1,200,000
charged to expense	
Difference in operating income explained	$ 378,000

Although it is not required, the following supplementary analysis may clarify the relationships:

	Absorption Costing	Variable Costing
Inventory, December 31, 2009	$1,980,000	$1,584,000
Cost of goods manufactured*	3,600,000	2,880,000
Available for sale	5,580,000	4,464,000
Inventory, December 31, 2010	90,000	72,000
Cost of goods sold	$5,490,000	$4,392,000

*Computed from the other data, which are given.

4.   a.   Absorption costing is more likely than variable costing to lead to inventory buildups. Under absorption costing, operating income in a given accounting period is increased because some fixed manufacturing overhead is accounted for as an asset (inventory) instead of an expense (fixed cost written off during the current period).

b.   Although variable costing will counteract undesirable inventory buildups, other measures can be used without abandoning absorption costing. Examples include budget targets and nonfinancial measures of performance such as maintaining specific inventory levels, inventory turnovers, delivery schedules, and equipment maintenance schedules.

9-38 (30-40 min.) Some additional requirements for Problem 9-37; absorption costing and production-volume variances.

1.

Revenues (1,070 × $1,200)		$1,284,000
Cost of goods sold:		
Beginning inventory (50 × $960)	$ 48,000	
Variable manufacturing costs (1,180 × $240[a])	283,200	
Fixed manufacturing costs (1,180 × $720)	849,600	
Cost of goods available for sale	1,180,800	
Ending inventory (160 × $960)	153,600	
Cost of goods sold (at std. costs)		1,027,200
Gross margin (at standard costs)		256,800
Adjustment for variances[b]		14,400
Gross margin		242,400
Marketing and administrative costs:		
Variable marketing, distribution and customer service costs (1,070 × $60)	64,200	
Fixed marketing, distribution and customer service costs (12 × $12,000)	144,000	
Adjustment for variances	0	
Marketing and admin. costs		208,200
Operating income		$ 34,200

[a]960 – 720 = 240
[b]Unfavourable production-volume variance = 20 × $720 = $14,400

The decrease in operating income from $48,000 for Jan.–Nov. 2010 to $34,200 for Jan.–Dec. 2010 arises because:

Operating income through November 30, 2010			$48,000
Additional revenues		$84,000	
Additional cost of goods sold	$67,200		
Additional other variable costs	4,200	71,400	12,600
			60,600
Production-volume variance		14,400	
Additional other fixed costs		12,000	26,400
Operating income for 2010			$34,200

2. Fixed manufacturing overhead rate:

Total fixed manufacturing overhead (1,200 units × $720)	$864,000
Divide by practical capacity (125 units × 12 months)	1,500
Equals fixed manufacturing overhead rate	$576 per unit
Units produced during 2010	1,180
Production-volume variance:	
(1,500 – 1,180 units) × $576 = 320 units × $576=	$184,320 U

9-40 (55 min.) Variable and absorption costing and breakeven points.

1. a.

2009 Variable-Costing-Based Operating Income Statement

Revenues (800 cat trees x $300 per tree)		$240,000
Variable costs		
Beginning inventory	$ 0	
Variable manufacturing costs (1,000 trees × $75 per tree.)	75,000	
Cost of goods available for sale	75,000	
Deduct: Ending inventory (200 trees × $75 per tree)	(15,000)	
Variable cost of goods sold	60,000	
Variable shipping costs (800 trees × $25 per tree)	20,000	
Total variable costs		80,000
Contribution margin		160,000
Fixed costs		
Fixed manufacturing costs	100,000	
Fixed selling and administrative	50,000	
Total fixed costs		150,000
Operating income		$ 10,000

1. b.

2009 Absorption-Costing-Based Operating Income Statement

Revenues (800 cat trees x $300 per tree)		$240,000
Cost of goods sold		
Beginning inventory	$ 0	
Variable manufacturing costs (1,000 trees. × $75 per tree)	75,000	
Allocated fixed manufacturing costs (1,000 trees × $100* per tree)	100,000	
Cost of goods available for sale	175,000	
Deduct ending inventory (200 trees × ($75 + $100) per tree)	(35,000)	
Cost of goods sold		140,000
Gross margin		100,000
Operating costs		
Variable marketing costs (800 trees × $25 per pkg.)	20,000	
Fixed selling and administrative	50,000	
Total operating costs		70,000
Operating income		$ 30,000

*Fixed manufacturing rate = Fixed manufacturing cost/production
= $100,000/1000 trees
= $100 per tree

9-40 (cont'd)

2. Breakeven point in units:

a. Variable Costing:

$$QT = \frac{\text{Total Fixed Costs} + \text{Target Operating Income}}{\text{Contribution Margin Per Unit}}$$

$$QT = \frac{(\$100,000 + \$50,000) + \$0}{\$300 - (\$75 + \$25)}$$

$$QT = \frac{\$150,000}{\$200}$$

$$QT = 750 \text{ cat trees}$$

b. Absorption costing:

Fixed manufacturing cost rate = $100,000 ÷ 1,000 = $100 per cat tree

$$QT = \frac{\text{Total Fixed Cost} + \text{Target OI} + \left[\text{Fixed Manuf. Cost Rate} \times \left(\text{Breakeven Sales in Units} - \text{Units Produced} \right) \right]}{\text{Contribution Margin Per Unit}}$$

$$QT = \frac{\$150,000 + [\$100\,(QT - 1,000)]}{\$200}$$

$$QT = \frac{\$150,000 + \$100\,QT - \$100,000}{\$200}$$

$$\$200\,QT - \$100\,QT = \$150,000 - \$100,000$$

$$\$100\,QT = \$50,000$$

$$QT = 500 \text{ cat trees}$$

203

9-40 (cont'd)

3.   Breakeven point in units:

a.   Variable Costing:

$$QT = \frac{\text{Total Fixed Costs} + \text{Target Operating Income}}{\text{Contribution Margin Per Unit}}$$

$$QT = \frac{(\$100{,}000 + \$50{,}000) + \$0}{\$300 - (\$100 + \$25)}$$

$$QT = \frac{\$150{,}000}{\$175}$$

$$QT = 857.14 \text{ cat trees}$$

b.   Absorption costing:

Fixed manufacturing cost rate = $\$100{,}000 \div 1{,}000 = \$100$ per cat tree

$$QT = \frac{\begin{array}{c}\text{Total Fixed} \\ \text{Cost}\end{array} + \begin{array}{c}\text{Target} \\ \text{OI}\end{array} + \left[\begin{array}{c}\text{Fixed Manuf.} \\ \text{Cost Rate}\end{array} \times \left(\begin{array}{c}\text{Breakeven} \\ \text{Sales in Units}\end{array} - \begin{array}{c}\text{Units} \\ \text{Produced}\end{array}\right)\right]}{\text{Contribution Margin Per Unit}}$$

$$QT = \frac{\$150{,}000 + \left[\$100\,(QT - 1{,}000)\right]}{\$175}$$

$$QT = \frac{\$150{,}000 + \$100\,QT - \$100{,}000}{\$175}$$

$\$175\,QT - \$100\,QT = \$150{,}000 - \$100{,}000$

$\$75\,QT = \$50{,}000$

$QT = 666.66$ cat trees

9-40 (cont'd)

4. Units needed to achieve target operating income:

a. Variable Costing:

$$QT = \frac{\text{Total Fixed Costs} + \text{Target Operating Income}}{\text{Contribution Margin Per Unit}}$$

$$QT = \frac{(\$100{,}000 + \$50{,}000) + \$10{,}000}{\$300 - (\$75 + \$25)}$$

$$QT = \frac{\$160{,}000}{\$200}$$

$$QT = 800 \text{ cat trees}$$

b. Absorption costing:

Fixed manufacturing cost rate = $\$100{,}000 \div 1{,}000 = \$100$ per cat tree

$$QT = \frac{\begin{array}{c}\text{Total Fixed} \\ \text{Cost}\end{array} + \begin{array}{c}\text{Target} \\ \text{OI}\end{array} + \left[\begin{array}{c}\text{Fixed Manuf.} \\ \text{Cost Rate}\end{array} \times \left(\begin{array}{c}\text{Breakeven} \\ \text{Sales in Units}\end{array} - \begin{array}{c}\text{Units} \\ \text{Produced}\end{array}\right)\right]}{\text{Contribution Margin Per Unit}}$$

$$QT = \frac{\$150{,}000 + \$30{,}000 + \left[\$100\,(QT - 1{,}000)\right]}{\$200}$$

$$QT = \frac{\$180{,}000 + \$100\,QT - \$100{,}000}{\$200}$$

$$\$200\,QT - \$100\,QT = \$180{,}000 - \$100{,}000$$

$$\$100\,QT = \$80{,}000$$

$$QT = 800 \text{ cat trees}$$

9-42 (20 min.) **Absorption costing, governance (continuation of 9-41).**

1. Behaviours that might suggest problems for AEC with the existing bonus plan and accounting system include:
   a. Plant managers switching production orders at year-end to those orders that absorb the highest amount of manufacturing overhead, irrespective of the demand by customers of AEC.
   b. Plant managers at one division of AEC accepting orders that they know another plant of AEC is better suited to handle.
   c. Plant managers deferring maintenance beyond the normal maintenance period.

2. Possible changes include:
   a. Change the incentive scheme so that there are not the major discontinuities at 15% and 10%.
   b. Change the operating income measure to variable costing rather than absorption costing.
   c. Add other performance measures (such as inventory turnover) that explicitly penalize "building for inventory."
   d. Emphasize the importance of managers considering AEC total benefits and costs of their decisions. This could be done via persuasion or by an incentive system based on AEC operating income rather than 100% of each division's operating income.

CHAPTER 10
QUANTITATIVE ANALYSES OF COST FUNCTIONS

10-2 OLS linear regression is a standardized set of arithmetic manipulations of two sets of data points to identify and assess the strength of a proposed linear relationship. The results are presented as a graph, coefficients defining the regression line, and benchmark statistical indicators of reliability. The regression line is estimated so as to minimize the sum of squared differences between the actual data points (X,Y) and the data points on the regression line (X,y).

The goal of OLS linear regression is to provide the management accountant with reliable, objective justification that by controlling the quantity of a common input consumed, the size of the indirect cost pool will be controlled in a predictable way.

10-4 The first assumption is that the predictor variable or common input has an economic effect on the outcome variable or size of the indirect cost pool. If true then controlling the size of the predictor variable will control the size of the outcome variable to some extent. The second assumption is that the relationship between the predictor and outcome variables can reasonably be modelled as a continuous straight line. The third assumption is that the differences between the estimated regression line and actual data points are distributed normally around each estimated data point. The last is that the error terms do not systematically change either with values of the predictor variable or other error terms.

The data available, especially in smaller companies, is often mismatched, inaccurately measured, or inaccurately recorded. While most companies have good financial data collection systems to support their financial reporting, non-financial data collection systems are not as sophisticated. For financial data, timely as well as accurate recording may be a problem, especially if the records are not kept on an accrual basis. Cash basis accounting will create a timing mismatch for common input and indirect cost data. Common inputs are measured in non-financial quantities and if they are not critical inputs there may be no measures at all or it may be very expensive to extract the relevant data from existing purchasing and inventory control records. Unitized fixed costs may be mistaken for unit costs especially when an indirect cost pool includes a very wide variety of costs.

10-6 A linear cost function is described by a mathematical equation $Y = a + bx$ where a and b are called coefficients. The intercept, a, is the value of Y when X=0 and the slope b is the predicted value of y obtained by multiplying X by b. Once the two coefficient values are known, any point on the line can be calculated or predicted if either X or y are also known.

10-6 (cont'd)

Three alternative linear cost functions are

1. Variable cost function—a cost function in which total costs change in proportion to the changes in the level of activity in the relevant range.
2. Fixed cost function—a cost function in which total costs do not change with changes in the level of activity in the relevant range.
3. Mixed cost function—a cost function that has both variable and fixed elements. Total costs change but not in proportion to the changes in the level of activity in the relevant range.

10-8 Causality in a cost function runs from the cost driver to the dependent variable. Thus, choosing the highest observation and the lowest observation of the cost driver is appropriate in the high-low method. (There are no tests of reliability for a line constructed in this way as there are for a regression line. Reliability and explanatory power depend entirely upon the internal expertise of those participating in the analysis.)

10-10 The residual value u, or error term, is the difference between the value of the actual data points (X,Y) and the estimated data points (X,y) on the linear-regression line.

10-12 Three criteria important when choosing among alternative cost functions are

1. Economic plausibility.
2. Goodness of fit.
3. Slope of the regression line.

10-14 A discontinuous linear cost function appears as a series of straight lines with different slopes within a continuous relevant range and no gaps between the lines, or as a series of straight lines with gaps or discontinuities between them within a relevant range. Examples of a discontinuous linear cost function are either step-variable or fixed-cost functions.

Companies may hire external work measurement consultants to conduct industrial engineering studies to clarify the relationships between common inputs and various cost pools. Companies may also decide to work with their own internal expertise using either the conference or account analysis method. If no formal financial accounting information system has been created, then the conference method would be a better choice. Once data are collected and outliers removed, the data points for quantities of input and sizes of indirect cost pools can be plotted.

10-16 (10 min.) OLS linear regression.

1.   Comparing the calculated values of t for the coefficients a, and b, you note that the critical value for $d.f.$ = 25 and a confidence level of 95% of 2.704 is higher than the calculated t value of 1.006 for the intercept coefficient a but lower than the calculated t value for the slope coefficient b of 3.865. You can be confident there is only a very small chance, about 7 in 10,000, or .0007, that the slope is a random value—but there is an unacceptably high probability of over 3 in 10 that the value of the intercept is a random value.

2.   Specification analysis or checking the quality of the data input is the first step a managerial accountant should take BEFORE doing any analyses. These data may not represent a plausible economic causal relationship, the data may not be linear, the residuals may not be normally distributed, and the residuals may not display a uniform or constant variance. The first step is to undertake a specification analysis by plotting the sets of data individually.

10-18 (10 min.) Estimating a cost function.

1.   Slope coefficient $= \dfrac{\text{Difference in costs}}{\text{Difference in machine-hours}}$

$$= \frac{\$5,400 - \$4,000}{10,000 - 6,000}$$

$$= \frac{\$1,400}{4,000} = \$0.35 \text{ per machine-hour}$$

Constant = Total cost – (Slope coefficient × Quantity of cost driver)

$$= \$5,400 - (\$0.35 \times 10,000) = \$1,900$$

$$= \$4,000 - (\$0.35 \times 6,000) = \$1,900$$

The cost function based on the two observations is
Maintenance costs = \$1,900 + \$0.35 × Machine-hours

2.   The cost function in requirement 1 is an estimate of how costs behave within the relevant range, not at cost levels outside the relevant range. If there are no months with zero machine-hours represented in the maintenance account, data in that account cannot be used to estimate the fixed costs at the zero machine-hours level. Rather, the constant component of the cost function provides the best available starting point for a straight line that approximates how a cost behaves within the relevant range.

10-20 (20 min.) **Discontinuous linear cost functions.**

1. K
2. B
3. G
4. J   Note that A is incorrect because, although the cost per kilogram eventually equals a constant at $9.20, the total dollars of cost increases linearly from that point onward.
5. I   The total costs will be the same regardless of the volume level.
6. L
7. F   This is a classic step-function cost.
8. K
9. C

10-22 (10 min.) **Interpreting results of regression analysis**.

1. Management accountants should compare the graph of the residuals, and there is no systematic change in the residuals for either DMH or DMLH. Next examine the two regression line graphs and the r^2 to help justify a recommendation. For DMH, the r^2 indicates that a change in quantity of DMH explains slightly more than 52% of a change in the indirect cost pool, whereas for DMLH the r^2 is almost 17%, which is below the benchmark 30% for reliability. The high value of the intercept a, and the low value of the slope b for DMLH, reinforce the low explanatory power revealed by the r^2. Practically speaking, managers changing the quantity of DMLH consumed could not expect to see any change in the indirect manufacturing labour cost pool. Those changing the quantity of DMH consumed could expect to see a change in the size of the indirect manufacturing labour cost pool. If these were the only two alternatives, the statistical results justify DMH as the cost-allocation base.

2. The least costly alternative may be to collect more data points. Less than 31 data points means that the r^2 needs to be quite high and although DMH does exceed the benchmark value of 30%, the managers would have to decide how much they would pay to improve on that and possibly obtain a statistically significant value of *a* as well as *b*. The other possibility is to add a predictor variable, which is part of an ABC project. Adding a predictor variable could require creating a process to collect the data because the reason DMH and DMLH were chosen is that the data were readily and economically available. The improvement to indirect cost pool control needs to be balanced against the cost of that improvement.

10-24 (30–40 min.) Linear cost approximation.

1. Slope coefficient (b) $= \dfrac{\text{Difference in cost}}{\text{Difference in labor-hours}} = \dfrac{\$529,000 - \$400,000}{7,000 - 4,000} = \$43.00$

Constant (a) $= \$529,000 - (\$43.00 \times 7,000)$

$= \$228,000$

Cost function $= \$228,000 + \$43.00 \times \text{professional labour-hours}$

The linear cost function is plotted in Solution Exhibit 10-24.

No, the constant component of the cost function does not represent the fixed overhead cost of the Calgary Group. The relevant range of professional labour-hours is from 3,000 to 8,000. The constant component provides the best available starting point for a straight line that approximates how a cost behaves within the 3,000 to 8,000 relevant range.

2. A comparison at various levels of professional labour-hours follows. The linear cost function is based on the formula of $228,000 per month plus $43.00 per professional labour-hour.

Total overhead cost behaviour:

	Month 1	Month 2	Month 3	Month 4	Month 5	Month 6
Professional labour-hours	3,000	4,000	5,000	6,000	7,000	8,000
Actual total overhead costs	$340,000	$400,000	$435,000	$477,000	$529,000	$587,000
Linear approximation	357,000	400,000	443,000	486,000	529,000	572,000
Actual minus linear approximation	$(17,000)	$ 0	$ (8,000)	$ (9,000)	$ 0	$ 15,000

The data are shown in Solution Exhibit 10-24. The linear cost function overstates costs by $8,000 at the 5,000-hour level and understates costs by $15,000 at the 8,000-hour level.

3.

	Based on Actual	Based on Linear Cost Function
Contribution before deducting incremental overhead	$38,000	$38,000
Incremental overhead	35,000	43,000
Contribution after incremental overhead	$ 3,000	$ (5,000)

The total contribution margin actually forgone is $3,000.

10-24   (cont'd)

SOLUTION EXHIBIT 10-24
Linear Cost Function Plot of Professional Labour-Hours
on Total Overhead Costs for Calgary Consulting Group

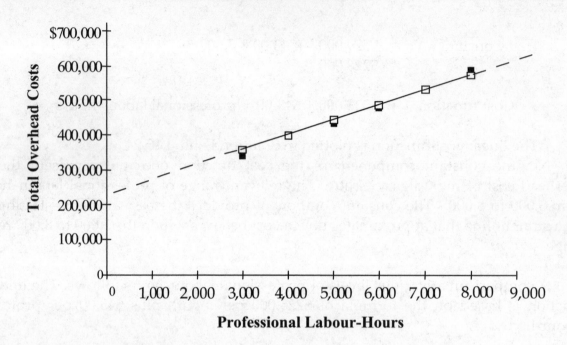

10-26 (30-40 min.) **Regression analysis, activity-based costing, choosing cost drivers.**

1. a. Solution Exhibit 10-26A presents the plots and regression line of number of packaged units moved on distribution costs.

SOLUTION EXHIBIT 10-26A
Plots and Regression Line of Number of Packaged Units Moved on Distribution Costs

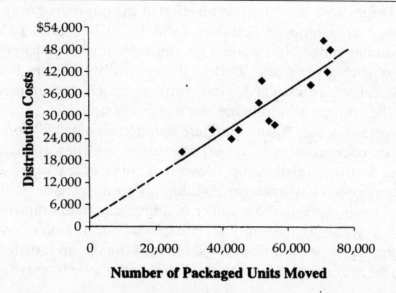

b. Solution Exhibit 10-26B presents the plots and regression line of number of shipments made on distribution costs.

SOLUTION EXHIBIT 10-26B
Plots and Regression Line of Number of Shipments Made on Distribution Costs

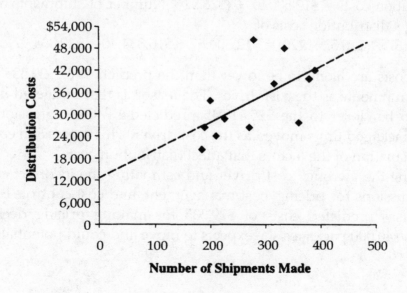

10-26 (cont'd)

Number of packaged units moved appears to be a better cost driver of distribution costs for the following reasons:

(i) *Economic plausibility.* Both number of packaged units moved and number of shipments are economically plausible cost drivers. Because the product is heavy, however, costs of freight are likely to be a sizable component of distribution costs. Thus, number of packaged units moved will affect distribution costs significantly because freight costs are largely a function of the number of units transported.

(ii) *Goodness of fit.* Compare Solution Exhibits 10-26A and 10-26B. Number of packaged units moved has a better goodness of fit with distribution costs than do number of shipments made. That is, the vertical differences between actual and predicted values are smaller for the number of packaged units moved regression than for the number of shipments made regression.

(iii) *Slope of regression line.* Again, compare Solution Exhibits 10-26A and 10-26B. The number of packaged units moved regression line has a relatively steep slope indicating a strong relationship between number of packaged units moved and distribution costs. On average, distribution costs increase with the number of packaged units moved. The number of shipments made regression line is flatter and has a wider scatter of observations about the line, indicating a weak relationship between number of shipments made and distribution costs. On average, the number of shipments made has a smaller effect on distribution costs.

2. Using the preferred cost function,
   Distribution costs = $1,618.45 + ($0.595 × Number of packaged units moved), Goldstein would budget distribution costs of
   $1,618.45 + ($0.595 × 40,000) = $1,618.45 + 23,800 = $25,418.45

3. Using the "other" cost function
   Distribution costs = $12,500.57 + ($76.52 × Number of shipments made), Goldstein would budget distribution costs of
   $12,500.57 + ($76.52 × 220) = $12,500.57 + $16,834.40 = $29,334.97

The actual costs are likely to be lower than the prediction of $29,335 made using the number of shipments as the cost driver. The reason is that budgeted distribution costs are likely to be closer to the $25,418.45 predicted by the regression equation with number of packaged units moved as the cost driver. This regression equation provides a better explanation of the factors that affect distribution costs.

Choosing the "wrong" cost driver and estimating the incorrect cost function can have repercussions for pricing, cost management, and cost control. To the extent that Goldstein uses predicted costs of $29,335 for making pricing decisions, she may overprice the 40,000 packages she expects to move and could potentially lose business.

10-26 (cont'd)

Question 10 - 26 X1	
Regression Statistics	
Multiple R	0.88671984
R Square	0.78627207
Adjusted R Square	**0.76489928**
Standard Error	4732.36378
Observations	12

Here the R squared value is good at 0.76. This means that only 76% of the variation in 'distribution costs' is explained by variation in the X1 variable, '# of packaged units moved'.
The model fit is good however with a Significance F of 0.00012.
The intercept coefficient is poor with a 0.77 p-value. This means that the intercept value is only significant at 33% confidence level or a level of significance of 77 %.
The coefficient for the X1 variable '# of packaged units moved' is highly significant with p-value of 0.00012 or a confidence level of > 99.99%.
X1 or the # of packaged units moved is a much better cost driver than the # of shipments made (X2 ..next pg) as the R sq. value is far superior ie a better correlation between variances.

ANOVA

	df	SS	MS	F	Significance F	
Regression	1	823887330.2	823887330.2	36.788458	**0.000121119**	0.999878881
Residual	10	223952669.8	22395266.98			
Total	11	1047840000				

	Coefficients	Standard Error	t Stat	P-value	Lower 95%	Upper 95%	
Intercept	**1618.45074**	5478.852297	0.295399593	**0.7737311**	-10589.19288	13826.0944	0.226268873
X1; packaged units	**0.59503635**	0.098104224	6.065348927	**0.0001211**	0.376446518	0.81362618	0.999878881

Distribution Costs =   1618.451 + 0.595036*(# of packaged units moved)

RESIDUAL OUTPUT

Observation	Predicted Y	Residuals	month	Y distribution costs	X1 # of packaged units moved
1	31965.3046	1634.695412	January	33600	51000
2	27205.0138	-3205.013788	February	24000	43000
3	18279.4685	2120.531462	March	20400	28000
4	41485.8862	-3085.886187	April	38400	67000
5	45056.1043	2943.895713	May	48000	73000
6	33750.4136	-4950.413638	June	28800	54000
7	23634.7957	2765.204312	July	26400	37000
8	44461.0679	-2461.067937	August	42000	72000
9	43866.0316	6533.968413	september	50400	71000
10	34940.4863	-7340.486337	October	27600	56000
11	32560.3409	7039.659062	November	39600	52000
12	28395.0865	-1995.086488	December	26400	45000
			sum	405600	649000

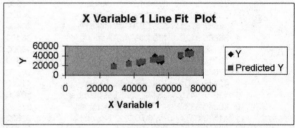

215

10-26 (cont'd)

Question 10 - 26

X2

Regression Statistics

Multiple R	0.59930534
R Square	0.3591669
Adjusted R Square	**0.29508359**
Standard Error	8194.45276
Observations	12

ANOVA

	df	SS	MS	F	Significance F	
Regression	1	376349439.8	376349439.8	5.604687	**0.039450435**	0.960549565
Residual	10	671490560.2	67149056.02			
Total	11	1047840000				

	Coefficients	Standard Error	t Stat	P-value	Lower 95%	Upper 95%	
Intercept	**12500.5705**	9302.673759	1.343761037	**0.20872**	-8227.078202	33228.219	0.791279945
X2 shipments	**76.5248963**	32.32414665	2.367422011	**0.03945**	4.502209565	148.54758	0.960549565

Distribution Costs = 12500.5705 + 76.5248963*(# of shipments)

RESIDUAL OUTPUT

				Y distribution costs	X2 # of shipments made
Observation	**Predicted Y**	**Residuals**	**month**		
1	27805.5498	5794.450207	January	33600	200
2	28570.7988	-4570.798755	February	24000	210
3	26657.6763	-6257.676349	March	20400	185
4	36605.9129	1794.087137	April	38400	315
5	38136.4108	9863.589212	May	48000	335
6	29718.6722	-918.6721992	June	28800	225
7	27040.3008	-640.3008299	July	26400	190
8	42345.2801	-345.280083	August	42000	390
9	33927.5415	16472.45851	september	50400	280
10	40049.5332	-12449.5332	October	27600	360
11	41580.0311	-1980.03112	November	39600	380
12	33162.2925	-6762.292531	December	26400	270
				405600	3340

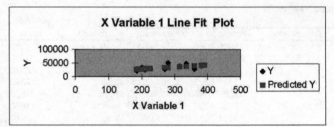

X Variable 1 Line Fit Plot

Data for Q 10 - 26

month	distribution costs	# of packaged units moved	# of shipments made
January	33600	51000	200
February	24000	43000	210
March	20400	28000	185
April	38400	67000	315
May	48000	73000	335
June	28800	54000	225
July	26400	37000	190
August	42000	72000	390
september	50400	71000	280
October	27600	56000	360
November	39600	52000	380
December	26400	45000	270
	405600	649000	3340 sums
	Y	X1	X2

To see the problems in cost management, suppose Waterloo Corporation moves 40,000 units in 220 shipments in the next month while incurring actual costs of $28,200. Compared with the budget of $29,335, management would consider this a good performance and seek ways to replicate it. In fact, on the basis of the preferred cost driver, the number of packaged units moved, actual distribution costs of $28,200 are higher than what they should be ($25,418)—a performance that management should seek to correct and improve rather than replicate.

10-28 (20 min.) Learning curve, incremental unit-time learning model.

1. The direct manufacturing labour-hours (DMLH) required to produce the first 2, 3, and 4 units, given the assumption of an incremental unit-time learning curve of 90%, are as follows:

Cumulative Number of Units (X) (1)	90% Learning Curve Individual Unit Time for Xth Unit (y): Labour-hours (2)	Cumulative Total Time: Labour-Hours (3)
1	3,000	3,000
2	2,700 = (3,000 × 0.90)	5,700
3	2,539	8,239
4	2,430 = (2,700 × 0.90)	10,669

Values in column (2) are calculated using the formula $y = aX^b$ where a = 3,000, X = 2, 3, or 4, and b = – 0.152004, which gives
when $X = 2$, $y = 3,000 \times 2^{-0.152004} = 2,700$
when $X = 3$, $y = 3,000 \times 3^{-0.152004} = 2,539$
when $X = 4$, $y = 3,000 \times 4^{-0.152004} = 2,430$

	Variable Costs of Producing		
	2 Units	3 Units	4 Units
Direct materials $80,000 × 2; 3; 4	$160,000	$240,000	$ 320,000
Direct manufacturing labour $25 × 5,700; 8,239; 10,669	142,500	205,975	266,725
Variable manufacturing overhead $15 × 5,700; 8,239; 10,669	85,500	123,585	160,035
Total variable costs	$388,000	$569,560	$746,760

2.

	Variable Costs of Producing	
	2 Units	4 Units
Incremental unit-time learning model (from requirement 1)	$388,000	$746,760
Cumulative average-time learning model (from Exercise 10-27)	376,000	708,800
Difference	$ 12,000	$ 37,960

10-28 (cont'd)

Total variable costs for manufacturing 2 and 4 units are lower under the cumulative average-time learning curve relative to the incremental unit-time learning curve. Direct manufacturing labour-hours required to make additional units decline more slowly in the incremental unit-time learning curve relative to the cumulative average-time learning curve when the same 90% factor is used for both curves. The reason is that, in the incremental unit-time learning curve, as the number of units double only the last unit produced has a cost of 90% of the initial cost. In the cumulative average-time learning model, doubling the number of units causes the average cost of *all* the additional units produced (not just the last unit) to be 90% of the initial cost.

10-30   (30-40 min.) **High-low versus regression method.**

1.   The first step is the specification analysis to assure the quality of the input data sets. The plot of the residuals does not illustrate any pattern and this means the residual values are random and normally distributed. The OLS regression line provides evidence that the relationship between advertising expense and revenue is linear and it is economically plausible that increased advertising expense would stimulate purchases/sales of the product. The r^2 of 0.643 assures the managerial accountant that in fact change in advertising expense explains slightly over 64% of the change in revenue. The critical value of the t statistic for 99% confidence level and d.f. of 9 is 3.250. The calculated t values for both the intercept a of 6.831 and slope coefficient b of 8.723 both exceed the critical value, therefore the managerial accountant can be confident that these are not random values. The p-statistic tells the managerial accountant that there is a probability of 0.0001 or 1 in 10,000 that it is incorrect to reject the null hypothesis H_0 for the intercept a, and probability of 0.005 or 5 in 1,000 it is incorrect to reject the null hypothesis H_0 for the slope coefficient b. These results not only meet the criteria of the specification analysis but provide strong evidence that by controlling advertising expense, managers can control revenue.

10-30   (cont'd)

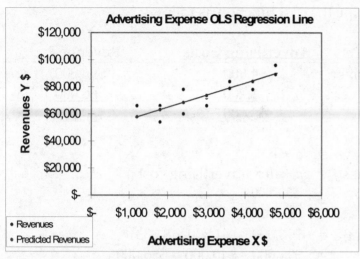

Regression Statistics			
R Square	0.642728316	Intercept a	47401.87
Adjusted R Square	0.598069356	t Stat	6.831096
Standard Error	7816.230418	P-value	0.000134
Observations	10		
		Slope coefficient b	8.722741
		t Stat	3.793669
		P-value	0.005284

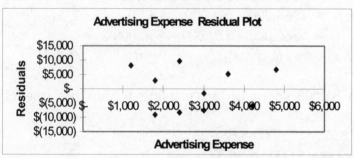

The exhibit above also shows the regression line of advertising costs on revenues. We evaluate the estimated regression equation using the criteria of economic plausibility, goodness of fit, and slope of the regression line.

Economic plausibility. Advertising costs appears to be a plausible cost driver of revenues. Restaurants frequently use newspaper advertising to promote their restaurants and increase their patronage.

Goodness of fit. The vertical differences between actual and predicted revenues appear to be reasonably small. This indicates that advertising costs are related to restaurant revenues.

Slope of regression line. The slope of the regression line appears to be relatively steep. This indicates that, on average, restaurant revenues increase with newspaper advertising.

10-30 (cont'd)

2. The high-low method would estimate the cost function as follows:

	X **Advertising Costs**	Y **Revenues**
Highest observation of cost driver	$4,800	$96,000
Lowest observation of cost driver	1,200	66,000
Difference	$3,600	$30,000

$$y = a + bx$$
$$\text{Revenues} = a + (b \times \text{advertising costs})$$
$$\text{Slope coefficient } (b) = \frac{\$30,000}{\$3,600} = 8.333$$
$$\text{Constant } (a) = \$96,000 - (\$4,800 \times 8.333)$$
$$= \$96,000 - \$40,000 = \$56,000$$

or
$$\text{Constant } (a) = \$66,000 - (\$1,200 \times 8.333)$$
$$= \$66,000 - \$10,000 = \$56,000$$

$$\text{Revenues} = \$56,000 + (8.333 \times \text{Advertising costs})$$

3. The increase in revenues for each $1,000 spent on advertising within the relevant range is
   a. Using the regression equation, 8.723 × $1,000 = $8,723
   b. Using the high-low equation, 8.333 × $1,000 = $8,333

4. The high-low equation does fairly well in estimating the relationship between advertising costs and revenues. However, Martinez and Brown should use the regression equation. The reason is that the regression equation uses information from all observations, whereas the high-low method relies only on the observations that have the highest and lowest values of the cost driver. These observations are generally not representative of all the data.

10-30 (cont'd)

Q 10 - 30

Regression Statistics	
Multiple R	0.801703384
R Square	0.642728316
Adjusted R Square	**0.598069356**
Standard Error	7816.230418
Observations	10

The model fit re Significance F is not bad with a confidence level > 99%.
However the R squared value of 0.598, means only 60% of the variation in the dependent variable Revenue (Y) is explained by variation in the independent variable Advertising Expense or X.
the level of significance is good for both the intercept coefficient and the coefficient for Advertising Expense (< 0.0001 or < 0.01% and < 0.01 or < 1%...this corresponds to confidence levels of > 99.99 % and > 99% respectively)

ANOVA

	df	SS	MS	F	Significance F
Regression	1	879252336.4	879252336.4	14.39192	**0.005284118**
Residual	8	488747663.6	61093457.94		
Total	9	1368000000			

	Coefficients	Standard Error	t Stat	P-value	Lower 95%	Upper 95%	ower 95.0%	Upper 95.0%
Intercept	**47401.86916**	6939.131186	6.831095693	**0.000134**	31400.20396	63403.53	31400.2	63403.53
Advertising Expen:	**8.722741433**	2.299289135	3.793668792	**0.005284**	3.420571185	14.02491	3.420571	14.02491

Y = 47,401.869 + 8.7227*X

RESIDUAL OUTPUT

Observation	Predicted Revenue	Residuals
1	68336.4486	-8336.448598
2	78803.73832	5196.261682
3	63102.80374	2897.196262
4	84037.38318	-6037.383178
5	57869.15888	8130.841121
6	68336.4486	9663.551402
7	63102.80374	-9102.803738
8	89271.02804	6728.971963
9	73570.09346	-7570.093458
10	73570.09346	-1570.093458

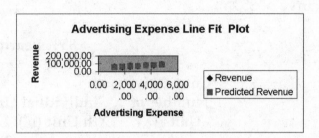

Data for Q 10 - 30

Month	Y Revenue	X Advertising Expense
March	60,000.00	2,400.00
April	84,000.00	3,600.00
May	66,000.00	1,800.00
June	78,000.00	4,200.00
July	66,000.00	1,200.00
August	78,000.00	2,400.00
September	54,000.00	1,800.00
October	96,000.00	4,800.00
November	66,000.00	3,000.00
December	72,000.00	3,000.00
sums	720,000.00	28,200.00

10-32 (20–30 min.) Cost estimation, incremental unit-time learning model.

1. Cost to produce the 2nd through the 8th boats:

Direct materials, 7 × $100,000	$ 700,000
Direct manufacturing labour (DML), 49,358[1] × $30	1,480,740
Variable manufacturing overhead, 49,358 × $20	987,160
Other manufacturing overhead, 25% of DML costs	370,185
Total costs	$3,538,085

[1]The direct labour-hours to produce the second through the eighth boats can be calculated via a table format, given the assumption of an incremental unit-time learning curve of 85%:

85% Learning Curve

Cumulative Number of Units (X) (1)	Individual Unit Time for Xth Unit (y^*): Labour-Hours (2)		Cumulative Total Time: Labour-Hours (3)
1	10,000		10,000
2	8,500	= (10,000 × 0.85)	18,500
3	7,729		26,229
4	7,225	= (8,500 × 0.85)	33,454
5	6,857		40,311
6	6,570		46,881
7	6,337		53,217
8	6,141	= (7,225 × 0.85)	59,358

*Calculated as $y = pX^q$ where $p = 10,000$, $q = -0.234465$, and $X = 1, 2, 3, \ldots 8$.

The direct manufacturing labour-hours to produce the second through the eighth boat is 59,358 – 10,000 = 49,358 hours.

2. Difference in total costs to manufacture the second through the eighth boat under the incremental unit-time learning model and the cumulative average-time learning model is $3,538,085 (calculated in requirement 1 of this problem) – $2,949,975 (from requirement 1 of Problem 10-36) = $588,110, i.e., the total costs are higher for the incremental unit-time model.

10-32 (cont'd)

The incremental unit-time learning curve has a slower rate of decline in the time required to produce successive units than does the cumulative average-time learning curve (see Problem 10-31, requirement 1). Assuming the same 85% factor is used for both curves:

Cumulative Number of Units	Estimated Cumulative Direct Manufacturing Labour-Hours	
	Cumulative Average-Time Learning Model	Incremental Unit-Time Learning Model
1	10,000	10,000
2	17,000	18,500
4	28,900	33,454
8	49,130	59,358

The reason is that, in the incremental unit-time learning model, as the number of units double, only the last unit produced has a cost of 85% of the initial cost. In the cumulative average-time learning model, doubling the number of units causes the average cost of *all* the additional units produced (not just the last unit) to be 85% of the initial cost.

Nautilus should examine its own internal records on past jobs and seek information from engineers, plant managers, and workers when deciding which learning curve better describes the behaviour of direct manufacturing labour-hours on the production of the PT109 boats.

10-34 (40-50 min.)   Appendix: Regression; choosing among models

1. Solution Exhibit 10-34A presents the regression output for (a) setup costs and number of setups and (b) setup costs and number of setup hours.

SOLUTION EXHIBIT 10-34A
Regression Output for (a) Setup Costs and Number of Setups and (b) Setup Costs and Number of Setup Hours

Number of Setups

Regression Statistics	
Multiple R	0.5807364
R Square	0.3372548
Adjusted R Square	0.2425769
Standard Error	28720.995
Observations	9

ANOVA

	df	SS	MS	F	Significance F
Regression	1	2938383589	2938383589	3.562128	0.101066787
Residual	7	5774269011	824895573		
Total	8	8712652600			

	Coefficients	Standard Error	t Stat	P-value	Lower 95%	Upper 95%	Lower 95.0%	Upper 95.0%
Intercept	3905.3482	41439.10166	0.09424307	0.927557	-94082.55656	101893.25	-94082.5566	101893.2529
Number of Setups	410.09094	217.2828325	1.887360052	0.1010668	-103.701317	923.88319	-103.701317	923.883193

Number of Setups

Regression Statistics	
Multiple R	0.923210231
R Square	0.85231713
Adjusted R Square	0.831219577
Standard Error	13557.86298
Observations	9

ANOVA

	df	SS	MS	F	Significance F
Regression	1	7425943061	7425943061	40.39886224	0.00038302
Residual	7	1286709539	183815648.5		
Total	8	8712652600			

	Coefficients	Standard Error	t Stat	P-value	Lower 95%	Upper 95%	Lower 95.0%	Upper 95.0%
Intercept	3348.71803	12878.63428	0.260021207	0.80232966	-27104.41289	33801.849	-27104.41289	33801.84896
Number of Setup Hours	56.2692934	8.85292724	6.35600993	0.00038302	35.33544701	77.20314	35.33544701	77.20313989

10-34 (cont'd)

2. Solution Exhibit 10-34B presents the plots and regression lines for (a) number of setups versus setup costs and (b) number of setup hours versus setup costs.

SOLUTION EXHIBIT 10-34B

Plots and Regression Lines for (a) Number of Setups versus Setup Costs and (b) Number of Setup Hours versus Setup Costs

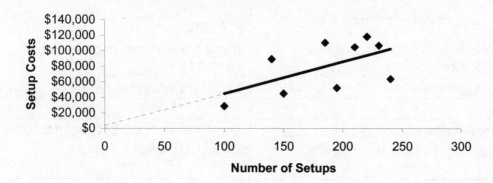

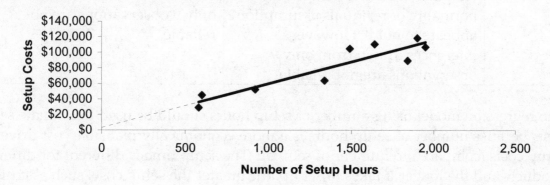

10-34 (cont'd)

3.

	Number of Setups	**Number of Setup Hours**
Economic plausibility	A positive relationship between setup costs and the number of setups is economically plausible.	A positive relationship between setup costs and the number of setup hours is also economically plausible, especially since setup time is not uniform, and the longer it takes to set up, the greater the setup costs, such as costs of setup labour and setup equipment.
Goodness of fit	$r^2 = 34\%$ standard error of regression $=\$28,721$ Poor goodness of fit.	$r^2 = 85\%$ standard error of regression $=\$13,558$ Excellent goodness of fit.
Significance of independent variables	The *t*-value of 1.89 is not significant at the 0.05 level.	The *t*-value of 6.36 is significant at the 0.05 level.
Specification analysis of estimation assumptions	Based on a plot of the data, the linearity assumption holds, but the constant variance assumption may be violated. The Durbin-Watson statistic of 1.12 suggests the residuals are independent. The normality of residuals assumption appears to hold. However, inferences drawn from only 9 observations are not reliable.	Based on a plot of the data, the assumptions of linearity, constant variance, independence of residuals (Durbin-Watson = 1.50), and normality of residuals hold. However, inferences drawn from only 9 observations are not reliable.

4. The regression model using number of setup hours should be used to estimate setup costs because number of setup hours is a more economically plausible cost driver of setup costs (compared to number of setups). The setup time is different for different products and the longer it takes to set up, the greater the setup costs such as costs of setup labour and setup equipment. The regression of number of setup hours and setup costs also has a better fit, a significant independent variable, and better satisfies the assumptions of the estimation technique.

10-36 (30-40 min.) **Appendix: Purchasing department cost drivers, multiple regression analysis (continuation of Problem 10-35).**

The problem reports the exact t-values from the computer runs of the data. Because the coefficients and standard errors given in the problem are rounded to three decimal places, dividing the coefficient by the standard error may yield slightly different t-values.

1. Regression 4 is a well-specified regression model:

Economic plausibility: Both independent variables are plausible and are supported by the findings of the Couture Fabrics study.

Goodness of fit: The r^2 of 0.63 indicates an excellent goodness of fit.

Significance of independent variables: The t-value on number of POs is 2.14 while the t-value on number of Ss is 2.00. These t-values are either significant or border on significance.

Specification analysis: Results are available to examine the independence of residuals assumptions. The Durbin-Watson statistic of 1.90 indicates that the assumption of independence is not rejected.

Regression 4 is consistent with the findings in Problem 10-35 that both the number of purchase orders and the number of suppliers are drivers of purchasing department costs. Regressions 2, 3, and 4 all satisfy the four criteria outlined in the text. Regression 4 has the best goodness of fit (0.63 for Regression 4 compared to 0.42 and 0.39 for Regressions 2 and 3, respectively). Most importantly, it is economically plausible that both the number of purchase orders and the number of suppliers drive purchasing department costs. We would recommend that Jones use Regression 4 over Regressions 2 and 3.

2. Regression 5 adds an additional independent variable (MP\$) to the two independent variables in Regression 4. This additional variable (MP\$) has a t-value of –0.07, implying its slope coefficient is insignificantly different from zero. The r^2 in Regression 5 (0.63) is the same as that in Regression 4 (0.63), implying the addition of this third independent variable adds close to zero explanatory power. In summary, Regression 5 adds very little to Regression 4. We would recommend that Jones use Regression 4 over Regression 5.

3. Budgeted purchasing department costs for the Saskatoon store next year are

$$\$485{,}384 + (\$123.22 \times 3{,}900) + (\$2{,}952 \times 110) = \$1{,}290{,}662$$

10-36 (cont'd)

4. Multicollinearity is a frequently encountered problem in cost accounting; it does not arise in simple regression because there is only one independent variable in a simple regression. One consequence of multicollinearity is an increase in the standard errors of the coefficients of the individual variables. This frequently shows up in reduced t-values for the independent variables in the multiple regression relative to their t-values in the simple regression:

Variables	t-value in Multiple Regression	t-value from Simple Regressions in Problem 10-39
Regression 4:		
# of POs	2.14	2.43
# of Ss	2.00	2.28
Regression 5:		
# of POs	1.95	2.43
# of Ss	1.84	2.28
MP$	–0.07	0.84

The decline in the t-values in the multiple regressions is consistent with some (but not very high) collinearity among the independent variables. Pairwise correlations between the independent variables are:

Correlation	
# of POs ÷ # of Ss	0.29
# of POs ÷ MP$	0.27
# of Ss ÷ MP$	0.34

There is no evidence of difficulties due to multicollinearity in Regressions 4 and 5.

5. Decisions in which the regression results in Problems 10-35 and 10-36 could be useful are:

- *Cost management decisions:* Flashy Fashion could restructure relationships with the suppliers so that fewer separate purchase orders are made. Alternatively, it may aggressively reduce the number of existing suppliers.

10-36 (cont'd)

- *Purchasing policy decisions:* Flashy Fashion could set up an internal charge system for individual retail departments within each store. Separate charges to each department could be made for each purchase order and each new supplier added to the existing ones. These internal charges would signal to each department ways in which their own decisions affect the total costs of Flashy Fashion.

- *Accounting system design decisions:* Flashy Fashion may want to discontinue allocating purchasing department costs on the basis of the dollar value of merchandise purchased. Allocation bases better capturing cause-and-effect relations at Flashy Fashion are the number of purchase orders and the number of suppliers.

10-38 (30min.) High-low method and regression analysis.

1.   See Solution Exhibit 10-38.

SOLUTION EXHIBIT 10-38
Plot, High-Low Line, and Regression Line for Number of Customers per Week versus Weekly Total Costs for Happy Business College Restaurant

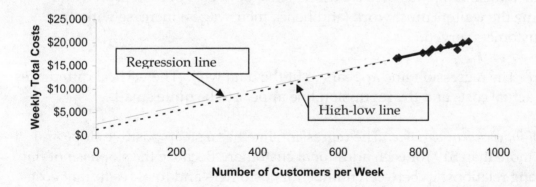

10-38 (cont'd)

2.

	Number of Customers per week	Weekly Total Costs
Highest observation of cost driver (Week 9)	925	$20,305
Lowest observation of cost driver (Week 2)	745	16,597
Difference	180	$ 3,708

Weekly total costs = $a + b$ (number of customers per week)

$$\text{Slope coefficient } (b) \quad = \quad \frac{\$3,708}{180} = \$20.60 \text{ per customer}$$

$$\text{Constant } (a) \quad = \$20,305 - (\$20.60 \times 925) = \$1,250$$
$$= \$16,597 - (\$20.60 \times 745) = \$1,250$$

$$\text{Weekly total costs} \quad = \$1,250 + \$20.60 \text{ (number of customers per week)}$$

See high-low line in Solution Exhibit 10-38.

3. Solution Exhibit 10-38 presents the regression line.

Economic Plausibility. The cost function shows a positive economically plausible relationship between number of customers per week and weekly total restaurant costs. Number of customers is a plausible cost driver since both cost of food served and amount of time the waiters must work (and hence their wages) increase with the number of customers served.

Goodness of fit. The regression line appears to fit the data well. The vertical differences between the actual costs and the regression line appear to be quite small.

Significance of independent variable. The regression line has a steep positive slope and increases by more than $19 for each additional customer. Because the slope is not flat, there is a strong relationship between number of customers and total restaurant costs.

The regression line is the more accurate estimate of the relationship between number of customers and total restaurant costs because it uses all available data points, while the high-low method relies only on two data points and may therefore miss some information contained in the other data points. Nevertheless, the graphs of the two lines are fairly close to each other, so the cost function estimated using the high-low method appears to be a good approximation of the cost function estimated using the regression method.

10-38 (cont'd)

4. The cost estimate by the two methods will be equal where the two lines intersect. You can find the number of customers by setting the two equations to be equal and solving for x. That is,

$$\$1{,}250 + \$20.60x = \$2{,}453 + \$19.04x$$
$$\$20.60\,x - \$19.04\,x = \$2{,}453 - \$1{,}250$$
$$1.56\,x = 1{,}203$$
$$x = 771.15 \text{ or} \approx 771 \text{ customers.}$$

CHAPTER 11
DECISION MAKING AND RELEVANT INFORMATION

11-2 *Relevant costs* are those expected future costs that differ among alternative courses of action. Historical costs are irrelevant because they are past costs and therefore cannot differ among alternative future courses of action.

11-4 *Quantitative factors* are outcomes that are measured in numerical terms. Some quantitative factors are financial—that is, they can be easily expressed in financial terms. Direct materials is an example of a quantitative financial factor. *Qualitative factors* are factors that are not measured in numerical terms. An example is employee morale.

11-6 Variable costs are irrelevant if they do not differ between alternatives under consideration.

11-8 *Opportunity cost* is the contribution to income that is forgone (rejected) by not using a limited resource in its next-best alternative use.

11-10 No. Managers should aim to get the highest contribution margin per unit of the constraining (that is, scarce, limiting, or critical) factor. The constraining factor is what restricts or limits the production or sale of a given product (for example, availability of machine-hours).

11-12 No. Cost written off as amortization is irrelevant when it pertains to a past cost. But the purchase cost of new equipment to be acquired in the future that will then be written off as amortization is often relevant.

11-14 The three steps in solving a linear programming problem are:
(a) Determine the objective.
(b) Specify the constraints.
(c) Compute the optimal solution.

11-16 (20 min.) Relevant and irrelevant costs.

1.

	Make	Buy
Relevant costs		
Variable costs	$180	
Avoidable fixed costs	20	
Purchase price		$210
Unit relevant cost	$200	$210

Dalton Computers should reject Peach's offer. The $30 of fixed costs are irrelevant because they will be incurred regardless of this decision. When comparing relevant costs between the choices, Peach's offer price is higher than the cost to continue to produce.

2.

	Keep	Replace	Difference
Cash operating costs (4 years)	$80,000	$48,000	$32,000
Current disposal value of old machine		(2,500)	2,500
Cost of new machine		8,000	(8,000)
Total relevant costs	$80,000	$53,500	$26,500

AP Manufacturing should replace the old machine. The cost savings are far greater than the cost to purchase the new machine.
Note this question instructs the student to ignore the time value of money.

11-18 (30 min.) Equipment upgrade versus replacement.

1. Based on the analysis in the table below, TechMech will be better off by $180,000 over three years if it replaces the current equipment.

	Over 3 years		Difference
Comparing Relevant Costs of Upgrade and Replace Alternatives	Upgrade (1)	Replace (2)	in Favour of Replace (3) = (1) – (2)
Cash operating costs			
$140; $80 per desk × 6,000 desks per yr. × 3 yrs.	$2,520,000	$1,440,000	$1,080,000
Current disposal price		(600,000)	600,000
One time capital costs, written off periodically as amortization	2,700,000	4,200,000	(1,500,000)
Total relevant costs	$5,220,000	$5,040,000	$ 180,000

11-18 (cont'd)

Note that the book value of the current machine ($1,500,000 – $600,000 = $900,000) would either be written off as depreciation over three years under the upgrade option, or all at once in the current year under the replace option. Its net effect would be the same in both alternatives: to increase costs by $900,000 over three years; hence, it is irrelevant in this analysis.

2.   Suppose the capital expenditure to replace the equipment is $X. From requirement 1, column (2), substituting for the one-time capital cost of replacement, the relevant cost of replacing is $1,440,000 – $600,000 + $X. From column (1), the relevant cost of upgrading is $5,220,000. We want to find X such that
$1,440,000 – $600,000 + $X < $5,220,000 (i.e., TechMech will favour replacing)
Solving the above inequality gives us X < $5,220,000 – $840,000 = $4,380,000.

TechMech would prefer to replace, rather than upgrade, if the replacement cost of the new equipment does not exceed $4,380,000. Note that this result can also be obtained by taking the original replacement cost of $4,200,000 and adding to it the $180,000 difference in favour of replacement calculated in requirement 1.

3.   Suppose the units produced and sold over 3 years equal y. Using data from requirement 1, column (1), the relevant cost of upgrade would be $140y + $2,700,000, and from column (2), the relevant cost of replacing the equipment would be $80y – $600,000 + $4,200,000. TechMech would want to upgrade if

$$\$140y + \$2,700,000 < \$80y - \$600,000 + \$4,200,000$$
$$\$60y < \$900,000$$
$$y < \$900,000 \div \$60 = 15,000 \text{ units}$$

or upgrade when y < 15,000 units (or 5,000 per year for 3 years) and replace when y > 15,000 units over 3 years.

When production and sales volume is low (less than 5,000 per year), the higher operating costs under the upgrade option are more than offset by the savings in capital costs from upgrading. When production and sales volume is high, the higher capital costs of replacement are more than offset by the savings in operating costs in the replace option.

11-18 (cont'd)

4. Operating incomes for the first year under each alternative are shown below:

| | Year 1 | |
	Upgrade (1)	Replace (2)
Revenues (6,000 × $500)	$3,000,000	$3,000,000
Cash operating costs		
$140; $80 per desk × 6,000 desks per year	840,000	480,000
Depreciation ($900,000[a] + $2,700,000) ÷ 3; $4,200,000 ÷ 3	1,200,000	1,400,000
Loss on disposal of old equipment (0; $900,000 – $600,000)	0	300,000
Total costs	2,040,000	2,180,000
Operating Income	$ 960,000	$ 820,000

[a]The book value of the current production equipment is $1,500,000 × 3 ÷ 5 = $900,000; it has a remaining useful life of 3 years.

First-year operating income is higher by $140,000 under the upgrade alternative, and Dan Doria, with his one-year horizon and operating income-based bonus, will choose the upgrade alternative, even though, as seen in requirement 1, the replace alternative is better in the long run for TechMech. This exercise illustrates the possible conflict between the decision model and the performance evaluation model.

11-20 (25-30 min.) Closing and opening stores.

1. Solution Exhibit 11-20, Column 1, presents the relevant loss in revenues and the relevant savings in costs from closing the Surrey store. Lopez is correct that Sundry Corporation's operating income would increase by $7,000 if it closes down the Surrey store. Closing down the Surrey store results in a loss of revenues of $860,000 but cost savings of $867,000 (from cost of goods sold, rent, labour, utilities, and corporate costs). Note that by closing down the Surrey store, Sundry Corporation will save none of the equipment-related costs because this is a past cost. Also note that the relevant corporate overhead costs are the actual corporate overhead costs of $44,000 that Sundry expects to save by closing the Surrey store. The corporate overhead of $40,000 allocated to the Surrey store is irrelevant to the analysis.

11-20 (cont'd)

2.　　Solution Exhibit 11-20, Column 2, presents the relevant revenues and relevant costs of opening another store like the Surrey store. Lopez is correct that opening such a store would increase Sundry Corporation's operating income by $11,000. Incremental revenues of $860,000 exceed the incremental costs of $849,000 (from higher cost of goods sold, rent, labour, utilities, and some additional corporate costs). Note that the cost of equipment written off as amortization is relevant because it is an expected future cost that Sundry will incur only if it opens the new store. Also note that the relevant corporate overhead costs are the $4,000 of actual corporate overhead costs that Sundry expects to incur as a result of opening the new store. Sundry may, in fact, allocate more than $4,000 of corporate overhead to the new store but this allocation is irrelevant to the analysis.

　　　The key reason that Sundry's operating income increases either if it closes down the Surrey store or if it opens another store like it is the behaviour of corporate overhead costs. By closing down the Surrey store, Sundry can significantly reduce corporate overhead costs presumably by reducing the corporate staff that oversees the Surrey operation. On the other hand, adding another store like Surrey does not increase actual corporate costs by much, presumably because the existing corporate staff will be able to oversee the new store as well.

SOLUTION EXHIBIT 11-20

Relevant-Revenue and Relevant-Cost Analysis of Closing Surrey Store and Opening Another Store Like It.

	(Loss in Revenues) and Savings in Costs from Closing Surrey Store (1)	Incremental Revenues and (Incremental Costs) of Opening New Store Like Surrey Store (2)
Revenues	$(860,000)	$ 860,000
Cost of goods sold	660,000	(660,000)
Lease rent	75,000	(75,000)
Labour costs	42,000	(42,000)
Amortization of equipment	0	(22,000)
Utilities (electricity, heating)	46,000	(46,000)
Corporate overhead costs	44,000	(4,000)
Total costs	867,000	(849,000)
Effect on operating income (loss)	$ 7,000	$ 11,000

11-22 (30 min.) Product mix, constrained resource.

1.

	Units (1)	Machine-Hours Per Unit (2) = Var. Mach. Cost/Unit ÷ $200/Hour	Machine-Hours Demanded (3) = (1) × (2)
Nealy	1,800	$600 ÷ $200 = 3	5,400
Tersa	4,500	$500 ÷ $200 = 2.5	11,250
Pelta	39,000	$200 ÷ $200 = 1	39,000
Total			55,650

2.

	Nealy	Tersa	Pelta
Selling price	$3,000	$2,100	$800
Variable costs:			
Direct materials	750	500	100
Variable machining	600	500	200
Sales commissions (5%, 5%, 10%)	150	105	80
Total variable costs	1,500	1,105	380
Contribution margin per unit	$1,500	$ 995	$420

3. Total machine-hours needed to satisfy demand exceed the machine-hours available (55,650 needed > 50,000 available). Consequently Marion Taylor needs to evaluate these products based on the contribution margin per machine-hour.

	Nealy	Tersa	Pelta
Unit contribution margin	$1,500	$995	$420
Machine-hours (MH) per unit	÷3 MH	÷2.5 MH	÷1 MH
Unit contribution margin per MH	$ 500	$398	$420

Based on this analysis, Marion Taylor should produce to meet the demand for products with the highest unit contribution margin per machine-hour, first Nealy, then Pelta, and finally Tersa. The optimal product mix will be as follows:

Nealy	1,800 units	=	5,400 MH
Pelta	39,000 units	=	39,000 MH
Tersa	2,240 units (5,600 MH ÷ 2.5 MH/unit)	=	5,600 MH (50,000 – 5,400 – 39,000)
Total			50,000 MH

11-22 (cont'd)

4. The optimal product mix in Part 3 satisfies the demand for Nealy and Pelta and leaves only 2,260 units (4,500 – 2,240) of Tersa unfilled. These remaining units of Tersa require 5,650 machine-hours (2,260 units × 2.5 MH per unit). The maximum price Marion Taylor is willing to pay for extra machine-hours is $398 per machine-hour, which is the unit contribution per machine-hour for additional units of Tersa, or $2,248,700 ($395 × 5,560) in total. That is, total cost per machine-hour for these units will be $398 + $200 (variable cost per machine-hour) = $598 per machine-hour.

11-24   (20 min.) Special Order.

1.

Revenues from special order ($11×10,000 racquets)	$110,000
Variable manufacturing costs ($9[1]×10,000 racquets)	(90,000)
Increase in operating income if Lanny order accepted	$ 20,000

[1] Direct materials + Direct manufacturing labour + Variable manufacturing overhead = $6 + $2 + $1 = $9

Swat should accept Lanny's special order because it increases operating income by $20,000. Since no variable selling costs will be incurred on this order, this cost is irrelevant. Similarly, fixed costs are irrelevant because they will be incurred regardless of the decision.

2a.

Revenues from special order ($11 × 10,000 racquets)	$110,000
Variable manufacturing costs ($9 × 10,000 racquets)	(90,000)
Contribution margin foregone ([$16 – $10[1]] ×10,000 racquets)	(60,000)
Decrease in operating income if Lanny order accepted	$ (40,000)

[1] Direct mat'ls + Direct manuf. labour + Variable manuf. overhead + Variable selling exp. = $6 + $2 + $1 + $1 = $10

Based strictly on financial considerations, Swat should reject Lanny's special order because it results in a $40,000 reduction in operating income.

2b. Swat will be indifferent between the special order and continuing to sell to regular customers if the special order price is $15. At this price, Swat recoups the variable manufacturing costs of $90,000 and the contribution margin given up from regular customers of $60,000 ([$90,000 + $60,000] ÷ 10,000 units = $15). Looked at a different way, Swat expects the full price of $16 less the $1 saved on variable selling costs.

11-24 (cont'd)

2c. Swat may be willing to accept a loss on this special order if the possibility of future long-term sales seem likely. However, Swat should also consider the effect on customer relationships by refusing sales from existing customers. Also, Swat cannot afford to adopt the special order price long-term or other customers may ask for price concessions.

11-26 (25 min.) Product mix, constrained resource.

1.

	A110	B382	C657
Selling price	$84	$ 56	$70
Variable costs:			
Direct materials (DM)	24	15	9
Other variable costs	28	27	40
Total variable costs	52	42	49
Contribution margin	$32	$ 14	$21
Kilograms of DM per unit[1]	÷8kg	÷5kg	÷3kg
Contribution margin per lb.	$ 4 per kg	$2.80 per kg	$ 7 per kg

> [1]A110: Direct material cost per unit/Cost per kg of Bistide= $24/$3 = 8 kg per unit
> B382: Direct material cost per unit/Cost per kg of Bistide = $15/$3 = 5 kg per unit
> C657: Direct material cost per unit/Cost per kg of Bistide = $9/$3 = 3 kg per unit

First, satisfy minimum requirements.

	A110	B382	C657	Total
Minimum units	200	200	200	
Times kilograms per unit	×8	×5	×3	
Kg needed for minimum units	1,600	1,000	600	3,200 kg

The remaining 1,800 kilograms (5,000 – 3,200) should be devoted to C657 because it has the highest contribution margin per kg of direct material. Since each unit of C657 requires 3 kgs of Bistide, the remaining 1,800 kg can be used to produce another 600 units of C657. The following combination yields the highest contribution margin given the 5,000 kg constraint on availability of Bistide.

    A110: 200 units

    B382: 200 units

    C657: 800 units (200 minimum + 600 extra)

11-26 (cont'd)

2. The demand for Westford's products exceeds the materials available. Assuming that fixed costs are covered by the original product mix, Westford should be willing to pay up to an additional $7 per kg (the contribution margin per kg of C657) for another 1,000 kg of Bistide. That is, Westford should be willing to pay $3 + $7 = $10 per kg of Bistide[1]. This cost assumes that sufficient demand exists to sell another 333 units (1000 kg ÷ 3 kg per unit) of C657. If not, then the maximum price falls to an additional $4 per kg (the contribution margin per pound of A110) so that Westford can produce up to 125 more units of A110 (1,000 kg ÷ 8 kg per unit). In this case, Westford would be willing to pay $3 + $4 = $7 per kg. If there is insufficient demand to sell another 125 units of A110, then the maximum price Westford would be willing to pay falls to an additional $2.80 per kg (the contribution margin per kg of B382). Westford would be willing to pay $2.80 + $3 = $5.80 per kg of Bistide.

[1]An alternative calculation focuses on column 3 for C657 of the table in requirement 1.

Selling price	$70
Other variable costs (excluding direct materials)	40
Contribution margin	$30
Divided by kg of direct material per unit	÷3
Direct material cost per kg that Westford can pay without contribution margin becoming negative	$10

11-28 (25 min.)   Closing down divisions.

1.

	Division A	Division D
Sales	$550,000	$460,000
Variable costs of goods sold ($490,000×0.85; $390,000×0.96)	416,500	374,400
Variable S,G, & A ($140,000×0.64; $120,000×0.78)	89,600	93,600
Total variable costs	506,100	468,000
Contribution margin	$ 43,900	$(8,000)

11-28 (cont'd)

2.

	Division A	Division D
Fixed costs of goods sold ($490,000 – $416,500; $390,000 – $374,400)	$ 73,500	$15,600
Fixed S,G, & A ($140,000 – $89,600; $120,000 – $93,600)	50,400	26,400
Total fixed costs	$123,900	$42,000
Fixed costs savings if shut down ($123,900×0.50; $42,000×0.50)	$61,950	$21,000

Division A's contribution margin of $43,900 does not cover its avoidable fixed costs of $61,950. In other words, the fixed costs that can be avoided of $61,950 are greater than its contribution margin of $43,900. By closing Division A, the remaining divisions will need to generate sufficient profits to cover the entire $61,950 unavoidable fixed costs of Division A.

Division D earns a negative contribution margin, which means its revenues are less than its variable costs. Division D also generates $21,000 of avoidable fixed costs. Based strictly on financial considerations, Division D should be closed because the company will save $29,000 ($21,000 + $8,000).

An alternative set of calculations is as follows:

	Division A	Division D
Total variable costs	$506,100	$468,000
Avoidable fixed costs if shut down	61,950	21,000
Total cost savings if shut down	568,050	489,000
Loss of revenues if shut down	550,000	460,000
Cost savings minus loss of revenues	$ 18,050	$ 29,000

Division A and Division D should be shut down because cost savings from shutting down each Division exceeds loss of revenues.

11-28 (cont'd)

3. Before deciding to close Division A and Division D, management should consider the role that each Division's product line plays relative to other product lines. For instance, if the product manufactured by Division D attracts customers to the company, then dropping Division D may have a detrimental effect on the revenues of the remaining divisions. Management may also want to consider the impact on the morale of the remaining employees if Division A and Division D are closed. Talented employees may become fearful of losing their jobs and seek employment elsewhere.

11-30 (15 min.) Make or buy (continuation of 11-29).

The maximum price Class Company should be willing to pay is $4.974 per unit.

| | | Proposed | | |
		Make New Product	Old Product	Total
	Present			
Sales	$2,250,000	$1,537,500	$2,250,000	$3,787,500
Variable (or purchase) costs:				
Manufacturing	1,110,000	870,000	1,492,200 *	2,362,200
Marketing and other	516,000	270,000	412,800	682,800
Total variable costs	1,626,000	1,140,000	1,905,000	3,045,000
Contribution margin	624,000	397,500	345,000	742,500
Fixed costs:				
Manufacturing	225,000	225,000	—	225,000
Marketing and other	330,000	112,500	330,000	442,500
Total fixed costs	555,000	337,500	330,000	667,500
Operating income	$ 69,000	$ 60,000	$ 15,000	$ 75,000

*This is an example of opportunity costs, whereby subcontracting at a price well above the $4.45 current manufacturing (absorption) cost is still desirable because the old product will be displaced in manufacturing by a new product that is more profitable.

Because the new product promises an operating income of $60,000 (ignoring the irrelevant problems of how fixed marketing costs may be newly reallocated between products), the old product must generate $15,000 to accomplish management's overall objectives. Maximum costs that can be incurred on the old product to earn a $15,000 profit are $2,235,000 ($2,250,000 – $15,000). From the $2,235,000, the fixed costs of $330,000 must be covered, leaving $1,905,000 of total variable costs. Maximum purchase cost: $1,905,000 – $412,800 = $1,492,200. Maximum purchase cost per unit: $1,492,200 ÷ 300,000 units = $4.974 per unit.

11-30 (cont'd)

Alternative Computation

Operating income is $10.25 – $9.85 = $0.40 per unit		
for 150,000 new units	$60,000	
Target operating income	75,000	
Profit required on old product	$15,000	

Sales price of old product		$7.500
Profit required ($15,000/300,000)		0.050
Total costs allowed per unit		$7.450
Continuing costs for old product other than purchase cost:		
Fixed manufacturing costs—all transferred to		
new product	$ —	
Variable marketing costs ($1.72 × 80%)	1.376	
Fixed marketing costs	1.100	2.476
Maximum purchase cost per unit		$4.974

11-32 (20 min.) Opportunity cost.

1. The opportunity cost to Wolverine of producing the 2,000 units of Orangebo is the contribution margin lost on the 2,000 units of Rosebo that would have to be forgone, as computed below:

Selling price		$20
Variable costs per unit:		
Direct materials	$ 2	
Direct manufacturing labour	3	
Variable manufacturing overhead	2	
Variable marketing costs	4	11
Contribution margin per unit		$ 9
Contribution margin for 2,000 units		$ 18,000

      The opportunity cost is $18,000. Opportunity cost is the maximum contribution to operating income that is forgone (rejected) by not using a limited resource in its next-best alternative use.

11-32 (cont'd)

2. Contribution margin from manufacturing 2,000 units of Orangebo and purchasing 2,000 units of Rosebo from Buckeye is $16,000, as follows:

	Manufacture Orangebo	Purchase Rosebo	Total
Selling price	$15	$20	
Variable costs per unit:			
Purchase costs	–	14	
Direct materials	2		
Direct manufacturing labour	3		
Variable manufacturing costs	2		
Variable marketing overhead	2	4	
Variable costs per unit	9	18	
Contribution margin per unit	$ 6	$ 2	
Contribution margin from manufacturing 2,000 units of Orangebo and purchasing 2,000 units of Rosebo	$12,000	$4,000	$16,000

As calculated in requirement 1, Wolverine's contribution margin from continuing to manufacture 2,000 units of Rosebo is $18,000. Accepting the Miami Company and Buckeye offer will cost Wolverine $2,000 ($16,000 – $18,000). Hence, Wolverine should refuse the Miami Company and Buckeye Corporation's offers.

3. The minimum price would be $9, the sum of the incremental costs as computed in requirement 2. This follows because, if Wolverine has surplus capacity, the opportunity cost = $0. For the short-run decision of whether to accept Orangebo's offer, fixed costs of Wolverine are irrelevant. Only the incremental costs need to be covered for it to be worthwhile for Wolverine to accept the Orangebo offer.

11-34   (30–40 min.) **Optimal product mix.**

1.   Let D represent the batches of Della's Delight made and sold.
        Let B represent the batches of Bonny's Bourbon made and sold.
        The contribution margin per batch of Della's Delight is $300.
        The contribution margin per batch of Bonny's Bourbon is $250.

        The LP formulation for the decision is:

        Maximize $300D + $250 B

        Subject to   30D + 15B ≤ 660 (Mixing Department constraint)
                     15B   ≤ 270 (Filling Department constraint)
                     10D + 15B ≤ 300 (Baking Department constraint)

2.   Solution Exhibit 11-34 presents a graphical summary of the relationships. The optimal corner is the point (18, 8); i.e., 18 batches of Della's Delights and 8 of Bonny's Bourbons.

SOLUTION EXHIBIT 11-34
Graphic Solution to Find Optimal Mix, Della Simpson, Inc.

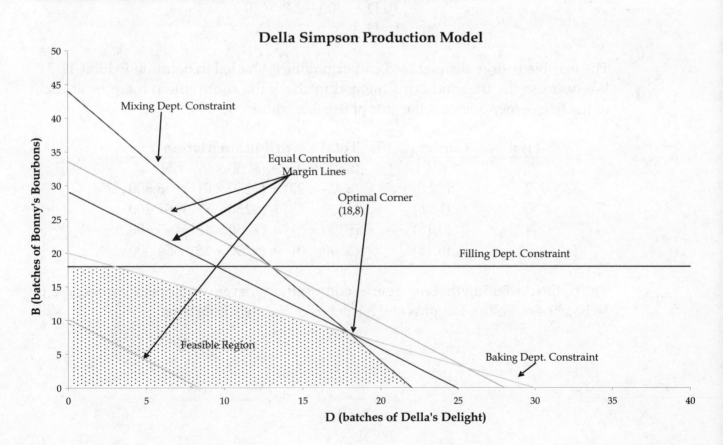

11-34 (cont'd)

We next calculate the optimal production mix using the trial-and-error method. The corner point where the Mixing Dept. and Baking Dept. constraints intersect can be calculated as (18, 8) by solving:

$$30D + 15B = 660 \text{ (1) Mixing Dept. constraint}$$
$$10D + 15B = 300 \text{ (2) Baking Dept. constraint}$$

Subtracting (2) from (1), we have
$$20D = 360$$
$$\text{or } D = 18$$

Substituting in (2)
$$(10 \times 18) + 15B = 300$$
$$\text{that is, } 15B = 300 - 180 = 120$$
$$\text{or } B = 8$$

The corner point where the Filling and Baking Department constraints intersect can be calculated as (3,18) by substituting B = 18 (Filling Department constraint) into the Baking Department constraint:
$$10D + (15 \times 18) = 300$$
$$10D = 300 - 270 = 30$$
$$D = 3$$

The feasible region, defined by 5 corner points, is shaded in Solution Exhibit 11-34. We next use the trial-and-error method to check the contribution margins at each of the five corner points of the area of feasible solutions.

Trial	Corner (D,B)	Total Contribution Margin
1	(0,0)	($300 × 0) + ($250 × 0) = $0
2	(22,0)	($300 × 22) + ($250 × 0) = $6,600
3	(18,8)	($300 × 18) + ($250 × 8) = $7,400
4	(3,18)	($300 × 3) + ($250 × 18) = $5,400
5	(0,18)	($300 × 0) + ($250 × 18) = $4,500

The optimal solution that maximizes contribution margin and operating income is 18 batches of Della's Delights and 8 batches of Bonny's Bourbons.

11-36 (30 min.) Make versus buy, governance.

1. An analysis of relevant costs that shows whether or not Paibec Corporation should make MTR-85 or purchase it from Marley Company for 2011 follows:

	Total Costs for 35,000 Units
Cost to purchase MTR-85 from Marley	
Bid price from Marley, $22.20 × 35,000	$777,000
Equipment lease penalty	8,500
Total incremental cost to purchase	785,500
Cost for Paibec to make MTR-85 in 2011	
Direct materials ($243,200/32,000) * 1.06 * 35,000	281,960
Direct labour ($152,000/32,000) * 1.08 * 35,000	179,550
Plant space rental	98,000
Equipment leasing costs	45,000
Variable manufacturing overhead ($320,000× 60%)/32,000 $6/unit * 35,000	210,000
Fixed manufacturing overhead (not relevant)	–
Total incremental cost to make MTR-85	814,510
Savings if purchased from Marley	$ 29,010

2. Based solely on the financial results, the 35,000 units of MTR-85 for 2011 should be purchased from Marley. The total cost to purchase from Marley would be $785,500, or $29,010 less than if the units were made by Paibec.

   At least three other factors that Paibec Corporation should consider before agreeing to purchase MTR-85 from Marley Company are the following:

   - The quality of the Marley component should be equal to, or better than, the quality of the internally made component, or else the quality of the final product might be compromised and Paibec's reputation affected.
   - Marley's reliability as an on-time supplier is important, since late deliveries could hamper Paibec's production schedule and delivery dates for the final product.
   - Layoffs may result if the component is outsourced to Marley. This could impact Paibec's other employees and cause labour problems or affect the company's position in the community. In addition, there may be termination costs which have not been factored into the analysis.

11-36 (cont'd)

3. Lynn Hardt would consider the request of John Porter to be unethical for the following reasons, based on the CMA Code of Ethics standard:

    *   Prepare complete and clear reports and recommendations after appropriate analysis of relevant and reliable information. Adjusting cost is unethical.
    *   Refrain from either actively or passively subverting the attainment of the organization's legitimate and ethical objectives. Paibec has a legitimate objective of trying to obtain the component at the lowest cost possible, regardless of whether it is manufactured by Paibec or outsourced to Marley.
    *   Communicate unfavourable as well as favourable information and professional judgments or opinions. Hardt needs to communicate the proper and accurate results of the analysis, regardless of whether or not it is favourable to Paibec.
    *   Refrain from engaging in or supporting any activity that would discredit the profession. Falsifying the analysis would discredit Hardt and the profession.
    *   Communicate information fairly and objectively. Hardt needs to perform an objective make/buy analysis and communicate the results fairly.
    *   Disclose fully all relevant information that could reasonably be expected to influence an intended user's understanding of the reports, comments, and recommendations presented. Hardt needs to disclose fully the analysis and the expected cost increases.

    Hardt should indicate to Porter that the costs derived under the make alternative are correct. If Porter still insists on making the changes to lower the costs of making MTR-85 internally, Hardt should raise the matter with Porter's superior, after informing Porter of her plans. If, after taking all these steps, there is continued pressure to understate the costs, Hardt should consider resigning from the company, rather than engage in unethical conduct.

11-38 (30 min) Optimal production plan, computer manufacturer.

1. Let X = Units of printers
   and Y = Units of desktop computers

   Objective: Maximize total contribution margin of $250X + $140Y
   Constraints:

For production line 1:	$7.2X + 4.8Y \leq 28.8$	equation 1)
For production line 2:	$12X \leq 24$	equation 2)
Sales of X and Y:	$X - Y \leq 0$	equation 3)
Negative production impossible:	$X \geq 0$	equation 4)
	$Y \geq 0$	equation 5)

2. Solution Exhibit 11-38 presents a graphical summary of the relationships. The sales-mix constraint here is somewhat unusual. The X – Y = 0 line is the one going upward at a 45° angle from the origin. Using the trial-and-error method:

   Using equations 1) and 2):
   $$7.2X + 4.8Y = 28.8$$
   $$12X = 24$$
   $$X = 2$$

   $$(7.2 \times 2) + 4.8Y = 28.8$$
   $$4.8Y = 14.4$$
   $$Y = 3$$

   Using equations 3) and 2):
   $$X - Y = 0$$
   $$12X = 24$$
   $$X = 2$$
   $$2 - Y = 0$$
   $$Y = 2$$

   Using equations 1) and 4):
   $$7.2X + 4.8Y = 28.8$$
   $$X = 0$$
   $$0 + 4.8Y = 28.8$$
   $$Y = 6$$

   Using equations 1) and 5):
   $$7.2X + 4.8Y = 28.8$$
   $$Y = 0$$
   $$7.2X + 0 = 28.8$$
   $$X = 4$$

   Using equations 4) and 5):
   $$X = 0$$
   $$Y = 0$$

11-38 (cont'd)

The 4 corners of the area of feasible solutions are:
(0,0), (2,2), (2,3), and (0,6)

Trial	Corner (X,Y)	Total Contribution Margin
1	(0, 0)	$250(0) + $140(0) = $ 0
2	(2, 2)	250(2) + 140(2) = 780
3	(2, 3)*	250(2) + 140(3) = 920
4	(0;,6)	250(0) + 140(6) = 840

*The optimal solution that maximizes operating income is 2 printers and 3 computers.

SOLUTION EXHIBIT 11-38
Graphic Solution to Find Optimal Mix, Information Technology, Inc.

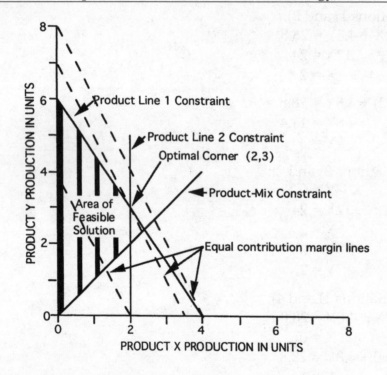

11-40 (40 min.) Optimal product mix.

In order to maximize OmniSport's profitability, OmniSport should manufacture 12,000 snowboard bindings, manufacture 1,000 pairs of skates, and purchase 6,000 pairs of skates from Colcott Inc. This combination of manufactured and purchased goods maximizes the contribution per available machine-hour, which is the limiting resource, as shown below.

Because snowboards have a higher contribution per machine-hour than skates, OmniSport should manufacture the maximum number of snowboards. Because the contribution per manufactured pair of skates is higher than the contribution from a purchased pair of skates, total contribution will be maximized by using the remaining manufacturing capacity to produce skates and then purchasing the remaining required skates. This optimal combination is calculated as presented on the next page.

	Purchased Skates 6,000 pairs		Manufactured Skates 1,000 pairs		Manufactured Snowboard Bindings 12,000		Total
	Per Unit	Total	Per Unit	Total	Per Unit	Total	Total
Selling price	$145.00	$870,000	$145.00	$145,000	$80.00	$960,000	$1,975,000
Variable costs							
Direct & other materials	105.00	630,000	24.00	24,000	26.00	312,000	966,000
Machine operating costs	—	—	36.80	36,000	12.00	144,000	180,000
Manufacturing overhead costs[1]	—	—	22.80	22,800	4.00	48,000	70,800
Selling & administrative costs	6.00[2]	36,000	12.00[3]	12,000	10.00[4]	120,000	168,000
Variable costs	111.00	666,000	94.80	94,800	52.00	624,000	1,384,800
Contribution margin	$ 34.00	$204,000	$50.20	$50,200	$28.00	$336,000	590,200
Fixed costs							
Manufacturing overhead							36,000
Marketing & administrative costs							72,000[5]
Fixed costs							108,000
Operating income							$ 482,200
Machine-hours per unit	—		1.5		0.5		
Contribution per machine-hour ($39.60 ÷ 1.5; $24 ÷ 0.5)	—		$26.40		$48.00		

[1]Supporting calculations:

Manufacturing overhead:
  Manufactured skates

Machine-hours	=	$36.00 per pair/$24.00 per hour = 1.5 hours per pair
Manufacturing capacity	=	5,000 pairs × 1.5 hours per pair = 7,500 hours
Overhead per machine-hour	=	$30.00 per pair/1.5 hours per pair = $20.00 per hour
Total overhead	=	7,500 hours × $20.00 per hour = $150,000
Total variable overhead	=	$180,000 (total) – $36,000 (fixed) = $114,000 (variable)
Variable overhead per machine-hour	=	$114,000/7,500 hours = $15.20 per hour
Fixed overhead per machine-hour	=	$36,000 fixed overhead/7,500 hours = $4.80 per hour
Variable overhead per pair of skates	=	1.5 hours × $15.20 per hour = $22.80 per pair
Fixed overhead per pair of skates	=	1.5 hours × $4.80 per hour = $7.20 per pair

  Snowboard bindings

Machine-hours	=	$12.00 per board/$24.00 per hour = 0.5 hour per board
Variable overhead per snowboard	=	$12.00 per hour × 1/3 hour per board = $4.00 per board
Fixed overhead per snowboard	=	$12.00 per hour × 1/3 hour per board = $4.00 per board

11-40 (cont'd)

2) $14.00 − $8.00 = $6.00
3) $20.00 − $8.00 = $12.00
4) $18.00 − $8.00 = $10.00
5) $12.00 × 6,000 = $72,000

The task is to maximize contribution margin per machine-hour, not per unit of product, given that the constraint is machine-hours of capacity.

The variable cost for manufacturing a pair of skates = $94.80

The contribution margin per hour = $50.20 ÷ 1.5 hours per pair = $33.47/hour = A

The cost to manufacture for snowboards = $52

The variable contribution margin per snowboard = $28 ÷ 0.5 hours per board = $56 = B

The cost to purchase a pair of skates (no machining required) = $111/pair

Maximize subject to the machine capacity constraint of 7,500 hours:

$1.5A + 0.5B = 7,500$ (1)

$A \leq 8,000$ (2)

$B \leq 12,000$ (3)

To solve, substitute (2) into (1): $1.5(8,000) + 0.5B = 7,500$

$0.5B = 7,500 − 12,000$

$B = (4,500) ÷ 0.5 \therefore B = (9,000)$, an impossible solution (extraneous root).

Now substitute (3) into (1): $1.5A + 0.5(12,000) = 7,500$

$1.5A + 6,000 = 7,500$

$1.5A = 7,500 − 6,000 = 1,500 \therefore A = 1,000$ a possible solution (good root)

Substitute this solution into (1)

$1.5 × 1,000 + 0.5B = 7,500$

$0.5B = 7,500 − 1,500 = 6,000$

$B = 6,000 ÷ 0.5 \therefore B = 12,000$

To maximize the contribution margin manufacture 12,000 snowboards and purchase 6,000 pairs of skates from Colcott. Notice that purchasing a pair of skates consumes none of the constrained resource (machine-hours).

11-40 (cont'd)

OmniSport Contribution Analysis

	Quantity (1)	Machine-Hours per Unit (2)	Total Machine-Hours Used (3)= (1)×(2)	Machine-Hour Balance (4)	Unit Contribution (5)	Total Product Contribution (6) = (1)×(5)
Machine-hours available				7,500		
Snowboard bindings	12,000	0.5	6,000	1,500	$28.00	$336,000
Skates (pairs)—manufacture	1,000	1.5	1,500	—	30.20	50,200
Skates (pairs)—purchase	6,000	—	—	—	34.00	204,000
Total contribution						590,200
Less original contribution (5,000 pairs of skates × $50.20 per pair)			(251,000)			
Improvement in contribution						$339,200

11-42 (30-40 min.) Optimal sales mix for a retailer, sensitivity analysis.

1. Let G = floor space of grocery products carried
   D = floor space of dairy products carried

   The LP formula for the decision is:

   Maximize: $12G + $3.60D
   Subject to: G + D ≤ 48,000
                  G   ≥ 12,000
                  D   ≥ 9,600

2. Always Open may wish to maintain its reputation as a full-service food store carrying both grocery and dairy products. Customers may not be attracted if Always Open carries only the product line with the highest unit contribution margins. (Marketing and economics courses examine this issue under the label of interdependencies in the demand for products.)

3. Solution Exhibit 11-42 presents the graphic solution. The optimal solution is 38,400 square metres of grocery products and 9,600 square metres of dairy products.

   The trial-and-error solution approach is:

Trial	Corner (G; D)	TCM = 12G + 3.6D		
1	(12,000; 9,600)	$12(12,000) + $3.60(9,600)	=	$178,560
2	(12,000; 36,000)	12(12,000) + 3.60(36,000)	=	273,600
3	(38,400; 9,600)	12(38,400) + 3.60(9,600)	=	495,360*

   *Optimal solution is G = 38,400 and D = 9,600.

11-42 (cont'd)

4.   The optimal mix determined in requirement 3 will not change if the contribution margins per square metre change to grocery products, $9.6, and dairy products, $6.0. To avoid cluttering the graphic solution in Solution Exhibit 11-44, we demonstrate this using the trial-and-error solution approach.

Trial	Corner (G; D)	TCM = $9.6G + 6D		
1	(12,000; 9,600)	$9.60(12,000) + $6 (9,600)	=	$172,800
2	(12,000; 36,000)	9.60(12,000) + 6 (36,000)	=	$331,200
3	(38,400; 9,600)	9.60(38,400) + 6 (9,600)	=	$426,240*

*Optimal solution is still G = 38,400 and D = 9,600.

The student can also verify by drawing lines parallel to the line through G = 9,600 and D = 36,000 so that the furthest point where the equal contribution line intersects the feasible region is the point G = 38,400 and D = 9,600.

Based on part 3 the task is to solve: max 12G + 3.6D, where G is square metres for groceries and D is square metres for dairy products. The following constraints are in place:

$G + D \leq 48,000$ (1)
$G \geq 12,000$ (2)
$D \geq 9,600$ (3)

First corner solution: using (2) and (3), the co-ordinates for the first corner are: 12,000; 9,600.

Second corner solution: subtract (2) from (1): 48,000 – 12,000 = 36,000; and now $D \leq$ 36,000, which, substituted into equation (1), gives: $G + 36,000 \leq 48,000 \therefore$, $G \leq$ 12,000 giving the co-ordinates for the second corner, which are: 12,000; 36,000.

Third corner solution: subtract (3) from (1): $G \leq 48,000 – 9,600 \therefore G \leq 38,400$; and now substitute into equation (1): $38,400 + D \leq 9,600$, giving the coordinates for the third corner, which are: 38,400; 9,600.

11-42 (cont'd)

SOLUTION EXHIBIT 11-42
Graphic Solution to Find Optimal Mix, Always Open Inc.

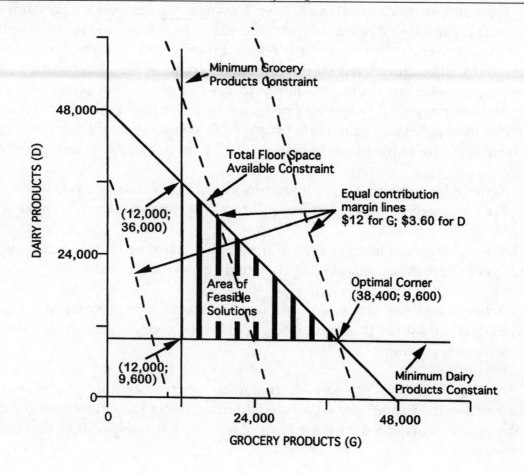

CHAPTER 12
PRICING DECISIONS, PRODUCT PROFITABILITY DECISIONS, AND COST MANAGEMENT

12-2   There are many circumstances when a company might price below full cost, but the key issue is capacity. When a company has idle capacity, pricing to cover outlay costs (normally variable costs but may include relevant fixed costs) will contribute to fixed cost coverage and will be considered by the firm. This could apply in decisions to accept or reject special orders, but could also apply to pricing of existing products. With idle capacity the company might consider pricing a new or struggling product below full cost to penetrate the market and gain market share. The company might also price below full cost to be in line with market-based pricing. It will then work to achieve cost reductions.

12-4   Activity-based costing helps managers in pricing decisions in two ways.
(a) It gives managers more accurate product-cost information for making pricing decisions.
(b) It helps managers to manage costs during value engineering by identifying the cost impact of eliminating, reducing, or changing various activities.

12-6   A target cost per unit is the estimated long-run cost per unit of a product (or service) that, when sold at the target price, enables the company to achieve the targeted operating income per unit.

12-8   A value-added cost is a cost that customers perceive as adding value, or utility, to a product or service. Examples are costs of materials, direct labour, tools, and machinery. Examples of nonvalue-added costs are costs of rework, scrap, expediting, and breakdown maintenance.

12-10 Cost-plus pricing is a pricing approach in which managers add a markup to cost in order to determine price.

12-12 Two examples where the difference in the incremental or outlay costs of two products or services is much smaller than the differences in their prices follow:
1.   The difference in prices charged for a telephone call, hotel room, or car rental during busy versus slack periods is often much greater than the difference in costs to provide these services.
2.   The difference in incremental or outlay costs for an airplane seat sold to a passenger travelling on business or a passenger travelling for pleasure is roughly the same. However, airline companies routinely charge business travellers—those who are likely to start and complete their travel during the same week excluding the weekend—a much higher price than pleasure travellers, who generally stay at their destinations over at least one weekend.

12-14 Three benefits of using a product life-cycle reporting format are:
1. The full set of revenues and costs associated with each product becomes more visible.
2. Differences among products in the percentage of total costs committed at early stages in the life cycle are highlighted.
3. Interrelationships among business function cost categories are highlighted.

12-16 (20-30 min.) Cost-plus target return on investment pricing.

1. Target operating income = target return on investment × invested capital

Target operating income (25% of $1,000,000)	$250,000
Total fixed costs	358,000
Target contribution margin	$608,000

Target contribution per room-night, ($608,000 ÷ 16,000)	$38
Add variable costs per room-night	4
Price to be charged per room-night	$42

Proof

Total room revenues ($42 × 16,000 room-nights)		$672,000
Total costs:		
Variable costs ($4 × 16,000)	$ 64,000	
Fixed costs	358,000	
Total costs		422,000
Operating income		$250,000

The full cost of a room = variable cost per room + fixed cost per room
The full cost of a room = $4 + ($358,000 ÷ 16,000) = $4 + $22.375 = $26.375

Markup per room = Rental price per room – Full cost of a room
= $42 – $26.375 = $15.625
Markup percentage as a fraction of full cost = $15.625 ÷ $26.375 = 59.24%

2. If price is reduced by 10%, the number of rooms Beck could rent would increase by 10%.

The new price per room would be 90% of $42	$37.80
The number of rooms Beck expects to rent is 110% of 16,000	17,600
The contribution margin per room would be $37.80 – $4	$33.80
Contribution margin ($33.80 ×17,600)	$594,880

Because the contribution margin of $594,880 at the reduced price of $37.80 is less than the contribution margin of $608,000 at a price of $42, Beck should not reduce the price of the rooms. Note that the fixed costs of $358,000 will be the same under the $42 and the $37.80 price alternatives and, hence, are irrelevant to the analysis.

12-18 (25 min.) Target costs, effect of product-design changes on product costs.

1. & 2. Indirect cost-allocation rates for 2010 and 2011 are as follows:

| Indirect Cost Category | 2010 | | | 2011 | | |
	Total Costs (1)	Quantity of Cost- Allocation Base (2)	Cost Allocation Rate (3) = (1) ÷ (2)	Total Costs (4)	Quantity of Cost- Allocation Base (5)	Cost Allocation Rate (6) = (4) ÷ (5)
Batch-level costs	$8,858,750	950	$9,325	$9,200,000	1,000	$9,200
Mfg. operations costs	15,255,000	226,000	67.50	16,250,000	250,000	65
Engineering change costs	2,864,160	216	13,260	2,500,000	200	12,500

Manufacturing costs of HJ6 in 2010 and 2011 are as follows:

| | 2010 | | 2011 | |
	Total (1)	Per Unit (2) = (1) ÷ 3,600	Total (3)	Per Unit (4) = (3) ÷ 4,000
Direct materials, $1,500 × 3,600; $1,410 × 4,000	$5,400,000	$1,500.00	$5,640,000	$1,410.00
Batch-level costs, $9,325 × 72; $9,200 × 85	671,400	186.50	782,000	195.50
Mfg. operations costs, $67.5 × 21,600; $65 × 22,440	1,458,000	405.00	1,458,600	364.65
Engineering change costs, $13,260 × 15; $12,500 × 10	198,900	55.25	125,000	31.25
Total	$7,728,300	$2146.75	$8,005,600	$2,001.40

3. Target manufacturing cost   =   Manufactufing cost   ×   88%
   per unit of HJ6 in 2011   per unit in 2010

   = $2,146.75 × 0.88 = $1,889.14

   Budgeted manufacturing cost per unit of HJ6 in 2011 is $2,001.40. Hence, Medical Instruments has not achieved its target manufacturing cost per unit.

4. To reduce the manufacturing cost per unit in 2011, Medical Instruments reduced the cost per unit in each of the four cost categories—direct materials costs, batch-level costs, manufacturing operations costs, and engineering change costs. It achieved this by reducing setup, production order, and materials handling costs per batch, the cost per machine hour, and cost per engineering change, perhaps by becoming more efficient in performing these activities. Efficiency improvements also helped Medical Instruments reduce the quantities of the cost allocation bases used to manufacture HJ6. For example, although production of HJ6 increased by 11.1% [(4,000 – 3,600) ÷ 3,600] between 2010 and 2011, machine-hours worked increased by only 3.9% [(22,440 ÷ 21,600) ÷ 21,600]. Medical Instruments achieved these gains through value engineering activities that retained only those product features that customers wanted while eliminating non-value-added activities and costs.

12-20 (30-40 min.) Life-cycle product costing, product emphasis.

1. A life-cycle income statement traces revenue and costs of each individual software package from its initial research and development to its final customer servicing and support in the marketplace. The two main differences from a fiscal-year-based income statement are:
   (a) Costs incurred in different fiscal periods are included in the same statement.
   (b) Costs and revenue of each package are reported separately rather than aggregated into company-wide categories.

   The benefits of using a product life-cycle report are:
   (a) The full set of revenues and costs associated with each product becomes visible.
   (b) Differences among products in the percentage of total costs committed at early stages in the life cycle are highlighted.
   (c) Interrelationships among business function cost categories are highlighted. What is the effect, for example, of cutting back on R&D and product-design cost categories on customer-service costs in subsequent years?

2.

	Power		Mecha		Solutions	
Revenue ($000s)	$4,578.0		$3,937.5		$2,250.0	
Costs ($000s)						
Research and development	$950.0		$690.0		$430.0	
Design	268.0		167.0		172.0	
Production	456.0		260.0		250.0	
Marketing	679.5		340.0		550.0	
Distribution	95.0		75.0		120.0	
Customer service	450.0	2,898.5	180.0	1,712.0	750.0	2,272.0
Operating income ($000s)		$1,679.5		$ 2,225.5		$ (22.0)

As emphasized in this chapter, the time value of money is not taken into account when summing life-cycle revenue or life-cycle costs. Chapters 21 and 22 discuss this topic in detail.

Rankings of the three packages on profitability (and relative profitability) are:

Operating Income			Operating Income Revenues	
1.	Mecha:	$2,225,000	1. Mecha:	56.52%
2.	Power:	$1,679,500	2. Power:	36.69%
3.	Solutions:	$(22,000)	3. Solutions:	(1.0%)

The Power and Mecha packages should be emphasized, and the Solutions package should be de-emphasized. It is interesting that Solutions had the lowest R&D costs but was the least profitable. But its customer service costs were 417% of the Mecha and 167% of the Power.

12-20 (cont'd)

3.   The cost structures of the three software packages are:

	Power	Mecha	Solutions
Research and development	32.8%	40.3%	18.9%
Design	9.3	9.8	7.6
Production	15.7	15.1	11.0
Marketing	23.4	19.9	24.2
Distribution	3.3	4.4	5.3
Customer service	15.5	10.5	33.0
	100.0%	100.0%	100.0%

The major differences are:

(a)   Power and Mecha have over 40% (42.1% and 50.1% respectively) of their costs in the R&D/product design categories compared to 26.5% for Solutions.

(b)   Solutions has 33.0% of its costs in the customer-service category compared to 15.5% for Power and 10.5% for Mecha.

There are several explanations for these differences:

(a)   Power and Mecha differ sizably from Solutions in their R&D/product design intensity. For example, Power and Mecha may require considerably (a)   more interaction with users, and (b)   more experimentation with software algorithms than does Solutions.

(b)   The software division should have invested more in the R&D/product design categories for Solutions. The high percentage for customer service could reflect the correcting of problems that should have been corrected prior to manufacture. Life-cycle reports highlight possible causal relationships among cost categories. It is stated in the problem that major efforts were made to cut down R&D for the Solutions product. This is most probably reflected in a lower quality product that requires more customer support.

12-22 (20 min.) Life cycle product costing.

1. Variable cost per unit = Production cost per unit + Mktg and distribn. cost per unit
$$= \$50 + \$10 = \$60$$

Total fixed costs over life of Yew = $6,590,000 + $1,450,000 + $19,560,000 + 5,242,000 + $2,900,000
$$= \$35,742,000$$

$$\text{BEP in units} = \frac{\text{Fixed costs}}{\text{Selling price} - \text{Variable cost per unit}} = \frac{\$35,742,000}{\$110 - \$60} = 714,840 \text{ units}$$

2a.

Revenues ($110×1,500,000 units)	$165,000,000
Variable costs ($60×1,500,000 units)	90,000,000
Fixed costs	35,742,000
Operating income	$ 39,258,000

2b.

Revenues	
Year 2 ($240×100,000 units)	$ 24,000,000
Years 3 & 4 ($110×1,200,000 units)	132,000,000
Total revenues	156,000,000
Variable costs ($60×1,300,000 units)	78,000,000
Fixed costs	35,742,000
Operating income	$ 42,258,000

Over the product's life-cycle, Option B results in an overall higher operating income of $3,000,000.

3. Before selecting its pricing strategy, Intentical managers should evaluate whether the same pricing policy will be adopted globally. Different markets may need different pricing. For example, special taxes on imports may mean higher prices in foreign markets. Intentical's pricing strategy must be sensitive to changing customer preferences and reactions of competitors.

12-24 (25 min.) Target rate of return on investment, activity-based costing.

1.

Operating Income Statement, April 2009	
Revenues (12,000 discs × $22 per disc)	$264,000
Materials (12,000 discs × $15 per disc)	180,000
Gross margin	84,000
Ordering (40 vendors × $250 per vendor)	10,000
Cataloguing (20 new titles × $100 per title)	2,000
Delivery and support (400 deliveries × $15 per delivery)	6,000
Billing and collection (300 customers × $50 per customer)	15,000
Operating income	$ 51,000
Rate of return on investment ($51,000 ÷ $300,000)	17.00%

2.   The table below shows that if the selling price of game discs falls to $18 and the cost of each disc falls to $12, monthly gross margin falls to $72,000 (from $84,000 in April), and this results in a return on investment of 13%, which is below EA's target rate of return on investment of 15%. EA will have to cut costs to earn its target rate of return on investment.

Operating Income Statement, May 2009	
Revenues (12,000 discs × $18 per disc)	$216,000
Materials (12,000 discs × $12 per disc)	144,000
Gross margin	72,000
Ordering (40 vendors × $250 per vendor)	10,000
Cataloguing (20 new titles × $100 per title)	2,000
Delivery and support (400 deliveries × $15 per delivery)	6,000
Billing and collection (300 customers × $50 per customer)	15,000
Operating income	$ 39,000
Rate of return on investment ($39,000 ÷ $300,000)	13.00%

12-24 (cont'd)

3.   After EA's workforce has implemented process improvements, its monthly support costs are $31,500, as shown below.

Monthly support costs after process improvements, May 2009	
Ordering (30 vendors × $200 per vendor)	$ 6,000
Cataloguing (15 new titles × $100 per title)	1,500
Delivery and support (450 deliveries × $20 per delivery)	9,000
Billing and collection (300 customers × $50 per customer)	15,000
Total monthly support costs	$31,500

EA now earns $6 ($18 – $12) gross margin per disc. Suppose it needs to sell X game disks to earn at least its 15% target rate of return on investment of $300,000. Then X needs to be such that:

$$\$6\,X - \$31,500 \;\;>= \;\; \$300,000 \times 15\% = \$45,000$$
$$\$6\,X \;\;>= \;\; \$76,500$$
$$X \;\;>= \;\; \$76,500 \div \$6 = 12,750 \text{ game discs}$$

EA must now sell at least 12,750 game discs per month to earn its target rate of return on investment of 15%.

12-26 (30-40 min.) Cost-plus and market-based pricing.

1.   Alberta Temps' full cost per hour of supplying contract labour is

Variable costs	$12
Fixed costs ($240,000 ÷ 80,000 hours)	3
Full cost per hour	$15

Price per hour at full cost plus 20% = $15 × 1.20 = $18 per hour.

2.   Contribution margins for different prices and demand realizations are as follows:

Price per Hour (1)	Variable Cost per Hour (2)	Contribution Margin per Hour (3) = (1) – (2)	Demand in Hours (4)	Total Contribution (5) = (3) × (4)
$16	$12	$4	120,000	$480,000
17	12	5	100,000	500,000
18	12	6	80,000	480,000
19	12	7	70,000	490,000
20	12	8	60,000	480,000

Fixed costs will remain the same regardless of the demand realizations. Fixed costs are, therefore, irrelevant since they do not differ among the alternatives.

The table above indicates that Alberta Temps can maximize contribution margin ($500,000) and operating income by charging a price of $17 per hour.

3.   The cost-plus approach to pricing in requirement 1 does not explicitly consider the effect of prices on demand. The approach in requirement 2 models the interaction between price and demand and determines the optimal level of profitability using concepts of relevant costs. The two different approaches lead to two different prices in requirements 1 and 2. As the chapter describes, pricing decisions should consider both demand or market considerations and supply or cost factors. The approach in requirement 2 is the more balanced approach. In most cases, of course, managers use the cost-plus method of requirement 1 as only a starting point. They then modify the cost-plus price on the basis of market considerations—anticipated customer reaction to alternative price levels and the prices charged by competitors for similar products.

12-28 (25 min.) **Cost-plus, target pricing, working backward.**

1. In the following table, work backwards from operating income to calculate the selling price

Selling price	$ 9.45 (plug)
Less: Variable cost per unit	2.50
Unit contribution margin	$ 6.95
Number of units produced and sold	×500,000 units
Contribution margin	$3,475,000
Less: Fixed costs	3,250,000
Operating income	$ 225,000

a) Total sales revenue = $9.45×500,000 units = $4,725,000

b) Selling price = $9.45 (from above)
Alternatively,

Operating income	$ 225,000
Add fixed costs	3,250,000
Contribution margin	3,475,000
Add variable costs ($2.50 × 500,000 units)	1,250,000
Sales revenue	$4,725,000

$$\text{Selling price} = \frac{\text{Sales revenue}}{\text{Units sold}} = \frac{\$4,725,000}{500,000} = \$9.45$$

c) $$\text{Rate of return on investment} = \frac{\text{Operating income}}{\text{Total investment in assets}} = \frac{\$225,000}{2,500,000} = 9\%$$

d) Markup percent on full cost
Total cost = ($2.50×500,000 units) + $3,250,000 = $4,500,000

$$\text{Unit cost} = \frac{\$4,500,000}{500,000 \text{ units}} = \$9$$

$$\text{Markup \%} = \frac{\$9.45 - \$9}{\$9} = 5\%$$

$$\text{Or} \quad \frac{\$4,725,000 - \$4,500,000}{\$4,500,000} = 5\%$$

12-28 (cont'd)

2.
New fixed costs	= $3,250,000 – $250,000 = $3,000,000
New variable costs	= $2.50 – $0.50 = $2
New total costs	= ($2 × 500,000 units) + $3,000,000 = $4,000,000
New total sales (5% markup)	= $4,000,000 × 1.05 = $4,200,000
New selling price	= $4,200,000 ÷ 500,000 units = $8.40

Alternatively,
New unit cost	= $4,000,000 ÷ 500,000 units = $8
New selling price	= $8 × 1.05 = $8.40

3.   New units sold = 500,000 × 90% = 450,000 units

Revenues ($8.40 × 450,000 units)	$3,780,000
Variable costs ($2.00 × 450,000 units)	900,000
Contribution margin	2,880,000
Fixed costs	3,000,000
Operating income (loss)	$ (120,000)

12-30 (50-60 min.) Target cost, activity-based costing systems (continuation of 12-29).

1. A target cost per unit is the estimated long-run cost per unit of a product (or service) that, when sold at the target price, enables the company to achieve the target operating income per unit. A target cost per unit is the estimated unit long-run cost of a product that will enable a company to enter or to remain in the market and compete profitably against its competitors.

2. The following table presents the manufacturing cost per unit for different cost categories for P-41 REV and P-63 REV.

Cost Categories	P-41 REV	P-63 REV
Direct manufacturing product costs:		
Direct materials	$505.20	$347.62
Indirect manufacturing product costs:		
Materials handling (76 × $1.38; 41 × $1.38)	104.88	56.58
Assembly management (2.9 × $60; 1.5 × $60)	174.00	90.00
Machine insertion of parts (60× $0.80; 30 × $0.80)	48.00	24.00
Manual insertion of parts (15 × $3.20; 8 × $3.20)	48.00	25.60
Quality testing (1.5 × $40; 0.8 × $40)	60.00	32.00
Total indirect manufacturing costs	434.88	228.18
Total manufacturing costs	$940.08	$575.80
Target cost	$975.00	$560.00

P-41 REV is $34.92 below its target cost. However, P-63 REV is $15.80 above its target cost. It appears that Executive Power will have major problems competing with the foreign printer costing $560.

12-30 (cont'd)

3. Total manufacturing costs:

P-41	=	$1,076.80	P-63	=	$646.04
P-41 REV	=	940.08	P-63 REV	=	575.80
Difference	=	$136.72	Difference	=	$ 70.24

The sources of the cost reductions in the redesigned products are:

		P-41	P-63
(a)	Reduction in direct materials costs	$19.80	$27.38
(b)	Changes in design:		
	Reduced materials handling costs because of fewer parts		
	$(90 - 76); (48 - 41) \times \$1.38$	19.32	9.66
	Reduced assembly time		
	$(3.5 - 2.9); (1.8 - 1.5) \times \$60$	36.00	18.00
	Reduced insertion of parts[1]		
	P-41: $(48 - 60) \times \$0.80 + (36 - 15) \times \$3.20$	57.60	
	P-63: $(28 - 30) \times \$0.80 + (12 - 8) \times \$3.20$		11.20
	Reduced quality testing		
	$(1.6 - 1.5); (0.9 - 0.8) \times \$40$	4.00	4.00
		$136.72	$70.24

[1]Note that the reduced costs for insertion of parts comes from two sources: (a) a reduction in total number of parts to be manually inserted, and (b) an increase in the percentage of parts inserted by the lower-cost machine method.

4. The $10.60 reduction in cost per hour of assembly time (from $60 to $49.40) reduces product costs as follows:

P-41 REV: $10.60 × 2.9 hours = $30.74. The new total manufacturing product cost is $909.34 ($940.08 – $30.74)

P-63 REV: $10.60 × 1.5 hours = $15.90. The new total manufacturing product cost is $559.90 ($575.80 – $15.90)

The reduction in the assembly management activity rate further reduces the cost of P-41 REV below the target cost. It also makes it more likely that P-63 REV will achieve its target cost. (The revised cost is now more-or-less equal the target cost.)

12-32 (60 min.)   Cost-plus and market-based pricing.

1. Single pool: OH Allocation Rate = $1,770,000/120,000 hours = $14.75 per testing hour

    Hourly billing rate = $14.75 × 1.40
                         = $20.65 per billing-hour

2.   See Solution Exhibit 12-32.

SOLUTION EXHIBIT 12-32

	HTT	ATT	SST	ACT	AQT	Total
Test pool labour						
(.3, .2, .2, .1, .2)	$186,000	$124,000	$124,000	$62,000	$124,000	$620,000
Supervision						
(.40, .15, .15, .15, .15)	36,000	13,500	13,500	13,500	13,500	90,000
Equip. amortization	63,000	27,000	45,000	33,750	56,250	225,000
Heat						
(.50, .05, .05, .30, .10)	105,000	10,500	10,500	63,000	21,000	210,000
Electricity						
(.30, .10, .10, .40, .10)	45,000	15,000	15,000	60,000	15,000	150,000
Water						
(.00, .00, .20, .20, .60)	0	0	19,600	19,600	58,800	98,000
Setup						
(.25, .10, .30, .15, .20)	18,750	7,500	22,500	11,250	15,000	75,000
Indirect materials						
(.12, .18, .30, .20, .20)	28,800	43,200	72,000	48,000	48,000	240,000
Operating supplies						
(.10, .10, .24, .20, .36)	6,200	6,200	14,880	12,400	22,320	62,000
Total costs	$488,750	$246,900	$336,980	$323,500	$373,870	$1,770,000
Total test-hours	33,600	14,400	31,200	25,200	15,600	
Hourly test-cost	$14.55	$17.15	$10.80	$12.84	$23.97	
Hourly billing rate						
(hourly test-cost × 1.40)	$20.36	$24.00	$15.12	$17.97	$33.55	

3. The new costing method will have the following effects on the pricing structure for each of the five test types given the competitors' hourly billing rates.

	HTT	ATT	SST	ACT	AQT
New hourly billing rate					
(hourly test-cost × 1.40)	$20.36	$24.00	$15.12	$17.97	$33.55
Competitor rate	$20.30	$23.60	$20.00	$18.50	$26.00
New rate over/(under) market	$0.06	$0.40	$(4.88)	$(0.53)	$7.55
Percent over/(under) market	0.3%	1.7%	(24.4)%	(2.9)%	29.0%
Common pool hourly billing rate	$20.65	$20.65	$20.65	$20.65	$20.65
New rate over/(under) market	$0.35	($2.95)	$0.65	$2.15	($5.35)
Percent over/(under) market	1.7%	(12.5)%	3.25%	11.62%	(20.58)%

12-32 (cont'd)

- Best Test will now be pricing all its lab tests more competitively in the market.
- For Heat Testing (HTT), there is minimal variance between the common pool rate, the new separate rate, and the competitors' rates. The HTT rate could either be left at the old rate, or nominally lowered to the competitors' rates or new pool rate without much impact, depending on how Best Test wanted to position the test compared to the competition.
- For Air Turbulence Testing (ATT), the new separate computed billing rate is significantly different from the common pool rate as well as close to the competitors' rates. The same is true of Arctic Condition Testing (ACT). In both cases, Best Test would probably want to adjust billing rates (raise ATT rate and lower ACT rate) to the newly computed rates or competitors' rates to better reflect resources consumed by the tests.
- For Stress Testing (SST), the newly computed rate is dramatically less than both the common pool rate and the competitors' rates. Best Test would want to reduce the price to at least meet the competitors' price or reduce it further to the newly computed price, depending upon how aggressively it wanted to market this test.
- For Aquatic Testing (AQT), the newly computed rate is significantly higher than both the common pool rate and the competitors' rates. Best Test would want to raise the billing rate at least to the competitors' rates to recover its cost plus some contribution towards administrative costs. Its current common billing rate of $20.65 is below the $23.97 cost to perform the AQT test.
- Because the newly computed billing prices for both SST and AQT are significantly different than competitors' prices, the cost assumptions should be further analyzed to verify accuracy and identify opportunities.

4. In general, at least three other internal or external factors that influence pricing structure include:
   - Number and nature of competitors for additional tests and their quality and timeliness of service.
   - Company's overall capacity and its ability to react to volume and mix changes for tests if the demand changes due to the new pricing structure.
   - Number of potential customers, overall demand for the tests, and price elasticity of demand for the tests.
   - Strategic focus, such as desire to gain or defend market share, long-term support for entry into or exit from a market, or stage in the test's product life cycle (introduction, growth, mature, or declining).

12-34 (35-40 min.) Life-cycle product costing, activity-based costing.

1. The budgeted life-cycle operating income for the new watch MX3 is $2,422,500 as shown below.

	Year 1 (1)	Year 2 (2)	Year 3 (3)	Life-Cycle (4)=(1)+(2)+(3)
Revenues $55 × 50,000; $50 × 200,000; $45 × 150,000	$2,750,000	$10,000,000	$6,750,000	$19,500,000
R&D and design costs	1,200,000	150,000	0	1,350,000
Manufacturing costs:				
Variable $20 × 50,000; $18 × 200,000; $18 × 150,000	1,000,000	3,600,000	2,700,000	7,300,000
Batch $860 × 125[1]; $750 × 400[2]; $750 × 300[3]	107,500	300,000	225,000	632,500
Fixed	800,000	800,000	800,000	2,400,000
Marketing costs:				
Variable $4.20 × 50,000; $3.75 × 200,000; $3.50 × 150,000	210,000	750,000	525,000	1,485,000
Fixed	400,000	320,000	320,000	1,040,000
Distribution costs:				
Variable $1.50 × 50,000; $1.50 × 200,000; $1.50 × 150,000	75,000	300,000	225,000	600,000
Batch $160 × 250[4]; $200 × 1,250[5]; $150 × 1,000 [6]	40,000	250,000	150,000	440,000
Fixed	300,000	300,000	300,000	900,000
Customer service costs:				
Variable $3.00 × 50,000; $2.40 × 200,000; $2.00 × 150,000	150,000	480,000	300,000	930,000
Total costs	4,282,500	7,250,000	5,545,000	17,077,500
Operating income	$(1,532,500)	$2,750,000	$ 1,205,000	$ 2,422 500

[1] 50,000 ÷ 400 = 125   [2] 200,000 ÷ 500 = 400   [3] 150,000 ÷ 500 = 300
[4] 50,000 ÷ 200 = 250   [5] 200,000 ÷ 160 = 1,250   [6] 150,000 ÷ 150 = 1,250

2. Budgeted product life-cycle costs for R&D and design $1,350,000
    Total budgeted product life-cycle costs $17,077,500
    Percentage of budgeted product life-cycle costs incurred at the end of the R&D and design stages = $1,350,000/$17,077,500 = 7.91%

3. An analysis reveals that 80% of the total product life-cycle costs of the new watch will be locked in at the end of the R&D and design stages when only 7.91% of the costs have been incurred (requirement 2). The implication is that it will be difficult to alter or reduce the costs of MX3 once Destin finalizes the design of MX3. To reduce and manage total costs, Destin must act to modify the design before costs get locked in.

12-34 (cont'd)

4. The budgeted life-cycle operating income for MX3 if Destin reduces its price by $3.50 is $1,704,500, as shown below. This is less than the operating income of $2,422,500 calculated in requirement 1. Therefore, Destin should not reduce MX3's price by $3.50.

	Year 1 (1)	Year 2 (2)	Year 3 (3)	Life-Cycle (4)=(1)+(2)+(3)
Revenues $51.50 × 55,000; $46.50 × 220,000;				
$41.50 × 165,000 [a],[b]	$2,832,500	$10,320,000	$6,847,500	$19,910,000
R&D and design costs	1,200,000	150,000	0	1,350,000
Manufacturing costs:				
Variable $20 × 55,000; $18 × 220,000;				
$18 × 165,000	1,100,000	3,960,000	2,970,000	8,030,000
Batch $860 × 125[1]; $750 × 440[2];				
$750 × 330[3]	107,500	330,000	247,500	685,000
Fixed	800,000	800,000	800,000	2,400,000
Marketing costs:				
Variable $4.20 × 55,000; $3.75 × 220,000;				
$3.50 × 165,000	231,000	825,000	577,500	1,633,500
Fixed	400,000	320,000	320,000	1,040,000
Distribution costs:				
Variable $1.50 × 55,000; $1.50 × 220,000;				
$1.50 × 165,000	82,500	330,000	247,500	660,000
Batch $160 × 275[4]; $200 × 1,375[5];				
$150 × 1,100[6]	44,000	275,000	165,000	484,000
Fixed	300,000	300,000	300,000	900,000
Customer service costs:				
Variable $3.00 × 55,000; $2.40 × 220,000;				
$2.00 × 165,000	165,000	528,000	330,000	1,023,000
Total costs	4,430,000	7,818,000	5,957,500	18,205,500
Operating income	$(1,597,500)	$2,412,000	$ 890,000	$ 1,704,500

[1]55,000 ÷ 440 = 125   [2]220,000 ÷ 500 = 440   [3]165,000 ÷ 500 = 330
[4]55,000 ÷ 200 = 275   [5]220,000 ÷ 160 = 1,375   [6]165,000 ÷ 150 = 1,100

a) Reduce selling price by 3.50 each year:
   Year 1 $55 – $3.50 = $51.50
   Year 2 $50 – $3.50 = $46.50
   Year 3 $45 – $3.50 = $41.50

b) Increase sales of units 10% each year:
   Year 1   50,000 × 1.1 = 55,000
   Year 2   200,000 × 1.1 = 220,000
   Year 3   150,000 × 1.1 = 165,000

12-36 (25 min.) Cost-plus, target return on investment pricing.

1. Target operating income = Return on capital in dollars = $13,000,000 \times 10\%$ = $1,300,000

2.

Revenues*	$6,000,000
Variable costs [($3.50 + $1.50) \times 500,000 cases	2,500,000
Contribution margin	3,500,000
Fixed costs ($1,000,000 + $700,000 + $500,000)	2,200,000
Operating income (from requirement 1)	$1,300,000

 * solve backwards for revenues

Selling price = $\dfrac{\$6,000,000}{500,000 \text{ cases}} = \$12$ per case.

Markup percent on full cost

 Full cost = $2,500,000 + $2,200,000 = $4,700,000

 Unit cost = $4,700,000 ÷ 500,000 cases = $9.40 per case

 Markup percent on full cost = $\dfrac{\$12 - \$9.40}{\$9.40} = 27.66\%$

3.

Budgeted Operating Income	
Revenues ($14 \times 475,000 cases*)	$6,650,000
Variable costs ($5 \times 475,000 cases)	2,375,000
Contribution margin	4,275,000
Fixed costs	2,200,000
Operating income	$2,075,000

 * New units = 500,000 cases $\times$ 95% = 475,000 cases

Return on investment = $\dfrac{\$2,075,000}{\$13,000,000} = 15.96\%$

Yes, increasing the selling price is a good idea because operating income increases without increasing invested capital, which results in a higher return on investment. The new return on investment exceeds the 10% target return on investment.

CHAPTER 13
STRATEGY, BALANCED SCORECARD, AND STRATEGIC PROFITABILITY ANALYSIS

13-2 Key benefits include a focus on interdependencies within a company as well as the dependence of companies on customers and competition.

13-4 Intellectual capital management is narrowly focused on all the ways in which a company can improve the knowledge available to people at all levels. People must learn something and knowledge is that something they learn either first hand or from what is stored.

13-6 ERM is a strategic approach to risk management, of which one factor is assuring reliable, high quality, timely supply of resources at the lowest cost. Companies that extend their trust to suppliers can co-operate to reduce costs to themselves and the supplier.

13-8 Three key components in doing a strategic analysis of operating income are:
1. The growth component which measures the change in operating income attributable solely to an increase in the quantity of output sold from one year to the next.
2. The price-recovery component which measures the change in operating income attributable solely to changes in the prices of inputs and outputs from one year to the next.
3. The productivity component which measures the change in costs attributable to a change in the quantity of inputs used in the current year relative to the quantity of inputs that would have been used in the previous year to produce current year output.

13-10 Engineered costs result from a cause-and-effect relationship between the cost driver, output, and the (direct or indirect) resources used to produce that output. Discretionary costs arise from periodic (usually) annual decisions regarding the maximum amount to be incurred. There is no measurable cause-and-effect relationship between output and resources used.

13-12 Downsizing (also called rightsizing) is an integrated approach configuring processes, products, and people in order to match costs to the activities that need to be performed for operating effectively and efficiently in the present and future.

13-14 Total factor productivity is the quantity of output produced divided by the costs of all inputs used, where the inputs are costed on the basis of current period prices.

13-16 (15 min.) Balanced scorecard.

1. La Quinta's 2009 strategy is a cost leadership strategy. La Quinta plans to grow by producing high-quality boxes at a low cost delivered to customers in a timely manner. La Quinta's boxes are not differentiated, and there are many other manufacturers who produce similar boxes. To succeed, La Quinta must achieve lower costs relative to competitors through productivity and efficiency improvements.

2. Measures that we would expect to see on La Quinta's balanced scorecard for 2009 are

Financial Perspective
(1) Operating income from productivity gain, (2) operating income from growth, (3) cost reductions in key areas.

These measures evaluate whether La Quinta has successfully reduced costs and generated growth through cost leadership.

Customer Perspective
(1) Market share, (2) new customers, (3) customer satisfaction index, (4) customer retention, (5) time taken to fulfill customer orders.

The logic is that improvements in these customer measures are leading indicators of superior financial performance.

Internal Business Process Perspective
(1) Yield, (2) productivity, (3) order delivery time, (4) on-time delivery.

Improvements in these measures are expected to lead to more satisfied customers and in turn to superior financial performance.

Learning and Growth Perspective
(1) Percentage of employees trained in process and quality management, (2) employee satisfaction, (3) number of major process improvements.

Improvements in these measures have a cause-and-effect relationship with improvements in internal business processes, which in turn lead to customer satisfaction and financial performance.

13-18 (15 min.) **Strategy, balanced scorecard.**

1. Meredith Corporation follows a product differentiation strategy in 2009. Meredith's D4H machine is distinct from its competitors and generally regarded as superior to competitors' products. To succeed, Meredith must continue to differentiate its product and charge a premium price.

2. Balanced scorecard measures for 2009 follow:

Financial Perspective
(1) Increase in operating income from charging higher margins, (2) price premium earned on products.

   These measures indicate whether Meredith has been able to charge premium prices and achieve operating income increases through product differentiation.

Customer Perspective
(1) Market share in high-end special-purpose textile machines, (2) customer satisfaction, (3) new customers.

   Meredith's strategy should result in improvements in these customer measures that help evaluate whether Meredith's product differentiation strategy is succeeding with its customers. These measures are leading indicators of superior financial performance.

Internal Business Process Perspective
(1) Manufacturing quality, (2) new product features added, (3) order delivery time.

   Improvements in these measures are expected to result in more distinctive products delivered to its customers and in turn superior financial performance.

Learning and Growth Perspective
(1) Development time for designing new machines, (2) improvements in manufacturing processes, (3) employee education and skill levels, (4) employee satisfaction.

   Improvements in these measures are likely to improve Meredith's capabilities to produce distinctive products that have a cause-and-effect relationship with improvements in internal business processes, which in turn lead to customer satisfaction and financial performance.

13-20 (20 min.) Analysis of growth, price-recovery, and productivity components (continuation of 13-19).

Effect of the industry market-size factor on operating income

Of the 10-unit increase in sales from 200 to 210 units, 3% or 6 (3% × 200) units are due to growth in market size, and 4 (10 – 6) units are due to an increase in market share. The change in Meredith's operating income from the industry market-size factor rather than from specific strategic actions is:

$280,000 (the growth component in Exercise 13-19) × $\dfrac{6}{10}$ <u>$168,000</u> F

Effect of product differentiation on operating income
The change in operating income due to:
Increase in the selling price of D4H (revenue effect of price recovery) $420,000 F
Increase in price of inputs (cost effect of price recovery)   184,500 U

Growth in market share due to product differentiation

$280,000 (the growth component in Exercise 13-19) × $\dfrac{4}{10}$ <u>112,000</u> F

Change in operating income due to product differentiation   <u>$347,500</u> F

Effect of cost leadership on operating income
The change in operating income from cost leadership is:
Productivity component   <u>$ 92,000</u> F

The change in operating income between 2008 and 2009 can be summarized as follows:

Change due to industry market-size	$168,000 F
Change due to product differentiation	347,500 F
Change due to cost leadership	<u>92,000</u> F
Change in operating income	<u>$607,500</u> F

Meredith has been successful in implementing its product differentiation strategy. More than 57% ($347,500 ÷ $607,500) of the increase in operating income during 2009 was due to product differentiation, i.e., the distinctiveness of its machines. It was able to raise the prices of its machines faster than the costs of its inputs and still grow market share. Meredith's operating income increase in 2009 was also helped by a growth in the overall market and some productivity improvements.

13-22 (20-30 min.) **Balanced scorecard.**

Perspectives	Strategic Objectives	Performance Measures
• Financial	• Increase shareholder value	• Earnings per share • Net income • Return on assets • Return on sales • Return on equity • Product cost per unit • Customer cost per unit
	• Increase profit generated by each salesperson	• Profit per salesperson
• Customer	• Acquire new customers	• Number of new customers
	• Retain customers	• Percentage of customers retained
	• Develop profitable customers	• Customer profitability
• Internal Business Process	• Improve manufacturing quality • Introduce new products • Minimize invoice error rate	• Percentage of defective product units • Percentage of error-free invoices
	• On-time delivery by suppliers	• Percentage of on-time deliveries by suppliers
	• Increase proprietary products	• Number of patents
• Learning and Growth	• Increase information system capabilities	• Percentage of processes with real-time feedback
	• Enhance employee skills	• Average job-related training hours per employee

13-24 (30 min.) Strategic analysis of operating income.

1. Operating income for each year is as follows:

	2008	2009
Revenues ($80,000 × 80; $77,200 × 90)	$6,400,000	$6,948,000
Costs		
Software implementation labour costs		
($80 × 40,000; $82 ×44,000)	3,200,000	3,608,000
Software implementation support costs		
($5,400 × 100; $5,470 × 100)	540,000	547,000
Software development costs		
($155,000 × 4; $160,000 × 4)	620,000	640,000
Total costs	4,360,000	4,795,000
Operating income	$ 2,040,000	$ 2,153,000
Change in operating income	$113,000 F	

2. The Growth Component

$$\text{Revenue effect} \atop \text{of growth} = \left({\text{Actual units of} \atop \text{output sold} \atop \text{in 2009}} - {\text{Actual units of} \atop \text{output sold} \atop \text{in 2008}} \right) \times {\text{Selling} \atop \text{price} \atop \text{in 2008}}$$

$$= (90 - 80) \times \$80,000 = \$800,000 \text{ F}$$

$$\text{Cost effect} \atop \text{of growth for} \atop \text{variable costs} = \left({\text{Units of input} \atop \text{required to produce} \atop \text{2009 output} \atop \text{in 2008}} - {\text{Actual units} \atop \text{of input} \atop \text{used to produce} \atop \text{2008 output}} \right) \times {\text{Input} \atop \text{price} \atop \text{in 2008}}$$

$$\text{Cost effect of} \atop \text{growth for} \atop \text{fixed costs} = \left({\text{Actual units of capacity in} \atop \text{2008 if adequate to produce} \atop \text{2009 output in 2008} \atop \text{OR} \atop \text{If 2008 capacity inadequate} \atop \text{to produce 2009 output in 2008,} \atop \text{units of capacity required} \atop \text{to produce 2009 output in 2008}} - {\text{Actual units} \atop \text{of capacity} \atop \text{in 2008}} \right) \times {\text{Price per} \atop \text{unit of capacity} \atop \text{in 2008}}$$

Software implementation labour costs that would be required in 2009 to produce 90 units instead of the 80 units produced in 2008, assuming the 2008 input-output relationship continued into 2009, equal 45,000 [(40,000/80)× 90] labour-hours. Software implementation support costs would not change since adequate capacity exists in 2008 to support year 2009 output and customers. Software development costs are discretionary costs not directly related to output and, hence, would not change in 2008 even if Snyder had to produce and sell the higher year 2009 output in 2008.

13-24 (cont'd)

The cost effects of growth component are:

Software implementation labour costs	(45,000 – 40,000) ×	$80 =	$400,000	U
Software implementation support costs	(100 – 100) ×	$5,400 =	0	
Software development costs	(4 – 4) ×	$155,000 =	0	
Cost effect of growth			$400,000	U

In summary, the net increase in operating income as a result of the growth component equals:

Revenue effect of growth	$800,000	F
Cost effect of growth	400,000	U
Change in operating income due to growth	$400,000	F

The Price-Recovery Component

$$\text{Revenue effect of price-recovery} = \left(\begin{array}{c}\text{Selling price} \\ \text{in 2009}\end{array} - \begin{array}{c}\text{Selling price} \\ \text{in 2008}\end{array}\right) \times \begin{array}{c}\text{Actual units} \\ \text{of output} \\ \text{sold in 2009}\end{array}$$

$$= (\$77,200 - \$80,000) \times 90 = \$252,000 \text{ U}$$

$$\begin{array}{c}\text{Cost effect of} \\ \text{price-recovery for} \\ \text{variable costs}\end{array} = \left(\begin{array}{c}\text{Input} \\ \text{price in} \\ 2009\end{array} - \begin{array}{c}\text{Input} \\ \text{price in} \\ 2008\end{array}\right) \times \begin{array}{c}\text{Units of input} \\ \text{required to produce} \\ \text{2009 output in 2008}\end{array}$$

$$\begin{array}{c}\text{Cost effect of} \\ \text{price-recovery for} \\ \text{fixed costs}\end{array} = \left(\begin{array}{c}\text{Price per} \\ \text{unit of} \\ \text{capacity} \\ \text{in 2009}\end{array} - \begin{array}{c}\text{Price per} \\ \text{unit of} \\ \text{capacity} \\ \text{in 2008}\end{array}\right) \times \begin{array}{c}\text{Actual units of capacity in} \\ \text{2008, if adequate to produce} \\ \text{2009 output in 2008} \\ \text{OR} \\ \text{If 2008 capacity inadequate to} \\ \text{produce 2009 output in 2008,} \\ \text{units of capacity required to} \\ \text{produce 2009 output in 2008}\end{array}$$

Software implementation labour costs	($82 – $80) ×	45,000 =	$90,000	U
Software implementation support costs	($5,470 – $5,400) ×	100 =	7,000	U
Software development costs	($160,000 – $155,000) ×	4 =	20,000	U
Cost effect of price recovery			$117,000	U

In summary, the net decrease in operating income as a result of the price-recovery component equals:

Revenue effect of price recovery	$252,000	U
Cost effect of price recovery	117,000	U
Change in operating income due to price recovery	$369,000	U

13-24 (cont'd)

The Productivity Component

$$
\begin{matrix}
\text{Cost effect of} \\
\text{productivity for} \\
\text{variable costs}
\end{matrix}
=
\left(
\begin{matrix}
\text{Actual units of} \\
\text{input used to produce} \\
\text{2009 output}
\end{matrix}
-
\begin{matrix}
\text{Units of input} \\
\text{required to produce} \\
\text{2009 output in 2008}
\end{matrix}
\right)
\times
\begin{matrix}
\text{Input} \\
\text{price in} \\
\text{2009}
\end{matrix}
$$

$$
\begin{matrix}
\text{Cost effect of} \\
\text{productivity for} \\
\text{fixed costs}
\end{matrix}
=
\left(
\begin{matrix}
\text{Actual units of} \\
\text{capacity in} \\
\text{2009}
\end{matrix}
-
\begin{matrix}
\text{Actual units of capacity in} \\
\text{2008, if adequate to produce} \\
\text{2009 output in 2008} \\
\text{OR} \\
\text{If 2008 capacity inadequate} \\
\text{to produce 2009 output in 2008,} \\
\text{units of capacity required to} \\
\text{produce 2009 output in 2008}
\end{matrix}
\right)
\times
\begin{matrix}
\text{Price per} \\
\text{unit of} \\
\text{capacity} \\
\text{in 2009}
\end{matrix}
$$

The productivity component of cost changes are:

Software implementation labour costs	$(44{,}000 - 45{,}000) \times$	$82 =	$82,000 F
Software implementation support costs	$(100 - 100) \times$	$5,470 =	0
Software development costs	$(4 - 4) \times \$160{,}000$	=	0
Change in operating income due to productivity			$82,000 F

The change in operating income between 2008 and 2009 can be analyzed as follows:

	Income Statement Amounts in 2008 (1)	Revenue and Cost Effects of Growth Component in 2009 (2)	Revenue and Cost Effects of Price-Recovery Component in 2009 (3)	Cost Effect of Productivity Component in 2009 (4)	Income Statement Amounts in 2009 (5) = (1) + (2) + (3) + (4)
Revenues	$6,400,000	$800,000 F	$252,000 U	—	$6,948,000
Costs	4,360,000	400,000 U	117,000 U	$82,000 F	4,795,000
Operating income	$ 2,040,000	$400,000 F	$369,000 U	$82,000 F	$ 2,153,000
			$113,000 F		

Change in operating income

3. The analysis of operating income indicates that a significant amount of the increase in operating income resulted from Snyder's productivity improvements in 2009. The company had to reduce selling prices while labour costs were increasing, but it was able to increase operating income by improving its productivity. The productivity gains also allowed Snyder to be competitive and grow the business. The unfavourable price recovery component indicates that Snyder could not pass on increases in labour-related wages via price increases to its customers, very likely because its product was not differentiated from competitors' offerings.

281

13-26 (20 min.) Identifying and managing unused capacity (continuation of 13-25).

1. The amount and cost of unused capacity at the beginning of year 2009 based on work performed in year 2009 follows:

	Amount of Unused Capacity	Cost of Unused Capacity
Software implementation support, 100 – 90; (100 – 90) × $5,470	10	$54,700
Software development	Discretionary cost, so cannot determine unused capacity*	Discretionary cost, so cannot be calculated*

*The absence of a cause-and-effect relationship makes identifying unused capacity for discretionary costs difficult. Management cannot determine the software development resources used for the actual output produced to compare against software development capacity.

2. Snyder can reduce capacity by 10 units, for a savings of $54,700 (10 × $5,470 = $54,700). Alternatively, Snyder could consider a reduction of only 5 units in order to accommodate future growth opportunities, etc. If Snyder reduces software implementation support capacity from 100 units to 95 (100 – 5) units, Snyder will save 5 × $5,470 = $27,350. It cannot reduce capacity by more than 10 units because it would then not have enough capacity to perform 90 units of work in 2009 (work that contributes significantly to operating income).

3. Snyder may choose not to downsize because it projects sales increases that would lead to greater demand for and utilization of capacity. Also, maintaining capacity (by retaining employees) boosts employee morale and keeps employees more motivated and productive. It may also save future training costs.

13-28 (20-30 min.) Growth, price-recovery, and productivity components.

1. *The Growth Component*

$$\text{Revenue effect of growth component} = \left(\begin{array}{c} \text{Actual units of} \\ \text{output sold in} \\ 2009 \end{array} - \begin{array}{c} \text{Actual units of} \\ \text{output sold in} \\ 2008 \end{array} \right) \times \begin{array}{c} \text{Output} \\ \text{price in} \\ 2008 \end{array}$$

$$= (31{,}650 - 24{,}580) \times \$20 = 141{,}400 \text{ F}$$

$$\text{Cost effect of growth component} = \left(\begin{array}{c} \text{Actual units of inputs that} \\ \text{would have been used to} \\ \text{produce year 2009 output} \\ \text{assuming the same input--} \\ \text{output relations that} \\ \text{existed in 2008} \end{array} - \begin{array}{c} \text{Actual units of} \\ \text{inputs or capacity} \\ \text{used to produce} \\ \text{year 2008 output} \end{array} \right) \times \begin{array}{c} \text{Input} \\ \text{price in} \\ 2008 \end{array}$$

T-shirts purchased in 2009 when 31,650 units are sold, instead of the 24,580 units sold in 2008, assuming the 2008 input-output relationship continued in 2009, equal 32,191 T-shirts (31,650 ÷ 24,580 × 25,000).

Administrative costs will not change since adequate capacity exists in 2008 to support the number of customers in 2009. The cost effects of growth component are:

Materials costs (32,191 – 25,000) × $13.00	$93,483 U
Administrative costs (40,000 – 40,000) × $2.50	0
Total cost effect of growth component	$93,483 U

In summary, the net increase in operating income as a result of growth component equals:

Revenue effect of growth component	$141,400 F
Cost effect of growth component	93,483 U
Change in operating income due to growth component	$ 47,917 F

13-28 (cont'd)

The Price-Recovery Component

$$
\begin{pmatrix} \text{Revenue effect of} \\ \text{price-recovery} \\ \text{component} \end{pmatrix} = \begin{pmatrix} \text{Output price in} \\ 2009 \end{pmatrix} - \begin{pmatrix} \text{Output price} \\ \text{in 2008} \end{pmatrix} \times \begin{pmatrix} \text{Actual units} \\ \text{of output} \\ \text{sold in 2009} \end{pmatrix}
$$

$$
= \ (\$18.00 - \$20.00) \times 31{,}650 = \$63{,}300 \ U
$$

$$
\begin{pmatrix} \text{Cost effect of} \\ \text{price-recovery} \\ \text{component} \end{pmatrix} = \begin{pmatrix} \text{Input} \\ \text{prices in} \\ 2009 \end{pmatrix} - \begin{pmatrix} \text{Input} \\ \text{prices in} \\ 2008 \end{pmatrix} \times \begin{pmatrix} \text{Actual units of inputs or capacity} \\ \text{that would have been used to} \\ \text{produce year 2009 output} \\ \text{assuming the same input–output} \\ \text{relationship that existed in 2008} \end{pmatrix}
$$

Cost of T-shirts purchased ($11.10 – $13.00) × 32,191	$61,163F
Administrative costs ($2.28 – $2.50) × 40,000	8,800 F
Total cost effect of price-recovery component	$69,963 F

In summary, the net increase in operating income as a result of the price recovery component equals:

Revenue effect of price-recovery component	$63,300 U
Cost effect of price-recovery component	69,963 F
Change in operating income due to price-recovery component	$ 6,663 F

The Productivity Component

$$
\begin{pmatrix} \text{Productivity} \\ \text{component} \end{pmatrix} = \begin{pmatrix} \text{Actual units} \\ \text{of inputs or} \\ \text{capacity used} \\ \text{to produce} \\ 2009 \text{ output} \end{pmatrix} - \begin{pmatrix} \text{Actual units of inputs or} \\ \text{capacity that would have} \\ \text{been used to produce year} \\ 2009 \text{ output assuming the} \\ \text{same input–output} \\ \text{relationship that existed in} \\ 2008 \end{pmatrix} \times \begin{pmatrix} \text{Input price} \\ \text{in 2009} \end{pmatrix}
$$

13-28 (cont'd)

The productivity component of cost changes are:

Cost of T-shirts purchased (32,000 – 32,191) × $11.10	$ 2,120 F
Administrative costs (36,000 – 40,000) × $2.28	9,120 F
Change in operating income due to productivity component	$11,240 F

The strategic analysis of profitability is as follows:

	Income Statement Amounts in 2008 (1)	Revenue and Cost Effects of Growth Component in 2009 (2)	Revenue and Cost Effects of Price-Recovery Component in 2009 (3)	Cost Effect of Productivity Component in 2009 (4)	Income Statement Amounts in 2009 (5)
Revenues	$491,600	$141,400 F	$63,300 U	–	$569,700
Costs	425,000	93,483 U	69,963 F	$11,240 F	437,280
Operating income	$ 66,600	$ 47,917 F	$ 6,663 F	$11,240 F	$ 132,420

2. The analysis indicates that a significant amount of the increase in operating income resulted from Oceano's growth which came from its cost leadership. The company was able to drop its selling price and substantially increase its sales volume. Oceano was also able to earn additional operating income by improving its productivity.

13-30 (35 min.) Balanced scorecard and strategy.

1. Dransfield currently follows a cost leadership strategy, which is reflected in its lower price compared to Yorunt Manufacturing. The electronic component ZP98 is similar to products offered by competitors.

2. In the internal business process perspective, Dransfield needs to set targets for decreasing the percentage of defective products sold and then identify measures that would be leading indicators of achieving this goal. For example, in the learning and growth perspective, Dransfield may want to measure the percentage of employees trained in quality management and the percentage of manufacturing processes with real-time feedback. The logic is that improvements in these measures will drive quality improvements and so reduce the percentage of defective products sold. To achieve its goals, items that Dransfield could include under each perspective of the balanced scorecard follow:

13-30 (cont'd)

Financial Perspective	Operating income from productivity and quality improvement
	Operating income from growth
	Revenue growth
Customer Perspective	Market share in electronic components
	Number of additional customers
	Customer-satisfaction ratings
Internal Business Process Perspective	Percentage of defective products sold
	Order delivery time
	On-time delivery
	Number of major improvements in manufacturing process
Learning and Growth Perspective	Employee-satisfaction ratings
	Percentage of employees trained in quality management
	Percentage of line workers empowered to manage processes
	Percentage of manufacturing processes with real-time feedback

13-32 (20 min.) Analysis of growth, price-recovery, and productivity components (continuation of 13-31)

Effect of the industry market-size factor on operating income

Of the 1,525 increase in sales from 4,500 to 6,025 units, 8% or 360 (8% × 4,500) units are due to growth in market size, and 1,165 (1,525 – 360) units are due to an increase in market share.

The change in Dransfield's operating income from the industry-market size factor rather than from specific strategic actions is:

$$\$58{,}628 \text{ (the growth component in Exercise 13-31)} \times \frac{360}{1{,}525} \qquad \underline{\$13{,}840} \text{ F}$$

Effect of product differentiation on operating income

The change in operating income due to:	
Increase in the selling price of ZP98 (revenue effect of price recovery)	$36,150 F
Increase in price of inputs (cost effect of price recovery)	60,180 U
Change in operating income due to product differentiation	$24,030 U

13-32 (cont'd)

Effect of cost leadership on operating income

The change in operating income from cost leadership is:

Productivity component	$ 2,222 F
Growth in market share due to cost leadership	
$58,628 (the growth component in Exercise 13-31) $\times \dfrac{1,165}{1,525}$	44,788 F
Change in operating income due to cost leadership	$47,010 F

The change in operating income between 2008 and 2009 can be summarized as follows:

Change due to industry market size	$13,840 F
Change due to product differentiation	24,030 U
Change due to cost leadership	47,010 F
Change in operating income	$36,820 F

A thoughtful student might argue that the $24,030 U price-recovery variance could also be thought of as part of the productivity variance. Why? Because a large component of this cost is from conversion costs incurred to improve quality, which is more closely associated with productivity and process improvement rather than product development and product differentiation. Under this assumption, the change in operating income between 2008 and 2009 can be summarized as follows:

Change due to market industry size	$13,840 F
Change due to product differentiation	0
Change due to cost leadership ($47,010 – $24,030)	22,980 F
Change in operating income	$36,820 F

Dransfield has been successful in implementing its cost leadership strategy. The increase in operating income during 2009 was due to quality improvements and sales growth. Dransfield's operating income increase in 2009 was also helped by a growth in the overall market size.

13-34 (20 min.) **Balanced scorecard.**

1. Caltex's strategy is to focus on "service-oriented customers" who are willing to pay a higher price for services. Even though its product is largely a commodity product, gasoline, Caltex wants to differentiate itself through the service it provides at its retailing stations.

    Does the scorecard represent Caltex's strategy? By and large it does. The focus of the scorecard is on measures of process improvement, quality, market share, and financial success from product differentiation. There are some deficiencies that the subsequent assignment questions raise but, abstracting from these concerns for the moment, the scorecard does focus on implementing a product differentiation strategy.

    Having concluded that the scorecard has been reasonably well designed, how has Caltex performed relative to its strategy in 2009? It appears from the scorecard that Caltex was successful in implementing its strategy in 2009. It achieved all targets in the financial, internal business, and learning and growth perspectives. The only target it missed was the market share target in the customer perspective. At this stage, students may raise some questions about whether this is a good scorecard measure. Requirement 3 gets at this issue in more detail. The bottom line is that measuring "market share in the overall gasoline market" rather than in the "service-oriented customer market segment" is not a good scorecard measure, so not achieving this target may not be as big an issue as it may seem at first.

2. Yes, Caltex should include some measure of employee satisfaction and employee training in the learning and growth perspective. Caltex's differentiation strategy and ability to charge a premium price is based on customer service. The key to good, fast, and friendly customer service is well-trained and satisfied employees. Untrained and dissatisfied employees will have poor interactions with customers and cause the strategy to fail. Hence, training and employee satisfaction are very important to Caltex for implementing its strategy. These measures are leading indicators of whether Caltex will be able to successfully implement its strategy and, hence, should be measured on the balanced scorecard.

13-34 (cont'd)

3. Caltex's strategy is to focus on the 60% of gasoline consumers who are service-oriented, not on the 40% price-shopper segment. To evaluate if it has been successful in implementing its strategy, Caltex needs to measure its market share in its targeted market segment, "service-oriented customer," not its market share in the overall market. Given Caltex's strategy, it should not be concerned if its market share in the price-shopper segment declines. In fact, charging premium prices will probably cause its market share in this segment to decline. Caltex should replace "market share in overall gasoline market" with "market share in the service-oriented customer segment" in its balanced scorecard customer measure. Caltex may also want to consider putting a customer satisfaction measure on the scorecard. This measure should capture an overall evaluation of customer reactions to the facility, the convenience store, employee interactions, and quick turnaround. The customer satisfaction measure would serve as a leading indicator of market share in the service-oriented customer segment.

4. Although there is a cause-and-effect link between internal business process measures and customer measures on the current scorecard, Caltex should add more measures to tighten this linkage. In particular, the current scorecard measures focus exclusively on refinery operations and not on gas station operations. Caltex should add measures of gas station performance such as cleanliness of the facility, turnaround time at the gas pumps, the shopping experience at the convenience store, and the service provided by employees. Many companies do random audits of their facilities to evaluate how well their branches and retail outlets are performing. These measures would serve as leading indicators of customer satisfaction and market share in Caltex's targeted segments.

5. Caltex is correct in not measuring changes in operating income from productivity improvements on its scorecard under the financial perspective. Caltex's strategy is to grow by charging premium prices for customer service. The scorecard measures focus on Caltex's success in implementing this strategy. Productivity gains per se are not critical to Caltex's strategy and, hence, should not be measured on the scorecard.

13-36 (25 min.) **Balanced scorecard, governance.**

1. Yes, the Household Product Division (HPD) should include measures of employee satisfaction and customer satisfaction even if these measures are subjective. For a maker of kitchen dishwashers, employee and customer satisfaction are leading indicators of future financial performance. There is a cause-and-effect linkage between these measures and future financial performance. If HPD's strategy is correct and if the scorecard has been properly designed, employee and customer satisfaction information is very important in evaluating the implementation of HPD's strategy.

    HPD should use employee and customer satisfaction measures even though these measures are subjective. One of the pitfalls to avoid when implementing a balanced scorecard is not to use only objective measures in the scorecard. Of course, HPD should guard against inaccuracy and potential for manipulation. Patricia Conley appears to be aware of this. She has tried to understand the reasons for the poor scores and has been able to relate these scores to other objective evidence such as employee dissatisfaction with the new work rules and customer unhappiness with missed delivery dates.

2. Incorrect reporting of employee and customer satisfaction ratings to make division performance look good is unethical. In assessing the situation, a management accountant should consider the following:

    Accuracy is how close you are to the real-world value. Precision is reproductibility and is neither necessary nor sufficient with respect to accuracy.

    Clear reports using relevant and reliable information should be prepared. Preparing reports on the basis of incorrect employee and customer satisfaction ratings in order to make the division's performance look better than it is, is unethical.

    The management accountant has a responsibility to avoid actual or apparent conflicts of interest and advise all appropriate parties of any potential conflict. Conley may be tempted to report better employee and customer satisfaction ratings to please Emburey. The management accountant should communicate favourable as well as unfavourable information.

    A management accountant should require that information be fairly and objectively communicated and that all relevant information should be disclosed.

    Conley should indicate to Emburey that the employee and customer satisfaction ratings are, indeed, appropriate. If Emburey still insists on reporting better employee and customer satisfaction numbers, Conley should raise the matter with one of Emburey's superiors. If, after taking all these steps, there is continued pressure to overstate employee and customer satisfaction ratings, Conley should consider resigning from the company and not engage in unethical behaviour.

13-38 (25 min.) Total factor productivity (continuation of 13-37).

1.

$$\begin{aligned}
\text{Total factor productivity for} \atop \text{2009 using 2009 prices} &= \frac{\text{Quantity of output produced in 2009}}{\text{Costs of inputs used in 2009 based on 2009 prices}} \\[2mm]
&= \frac{2,650,000}{(1,669,500 \times \$4) + (\$8,680,000)} \\[2mm]
&= \frac{2,650,000}{\$6,678,000 + \$8,680,000} = \frac{2,650,000}{\$15,358,000} \\[2mm]
&= 0.1725 \text{ units of output per dollar of input}
\end{aligned}$$

2. By itself, the 2009 TFP of 0.1725 units per dollar of input is not particularly helpful. We need something to compare the 2009 TFP against. We use, as a benchmark, TFP calculated using the inputs that Guble would have used in 2008 to produce 2,650,000 units of output calculated in requirement 1 at 2009 prices. Using the current year's (2009) prices in both calculations controls for input price differences and focuses the analysis on the adjustments the manager made in the quantities of inputs in response to changes in prices.

$$\text{2009 price of capacity} = \frac{\text{Cost of capacity in 2009}}{\text{Capacity in 2009}} = \frac{\$8,680,000}{2,800,000 \text{ units}} = \$3.10 \text{ per unit of capacity}$$

$$\begin{aligned}
\text{Benchmark} \atop \text{TFP} &= \frac{\text{Quantity of output produced in 2009}}{\substack{\text{Costs of inputs that would have been used in 2008} \\ \text{to produce 2009 output at year 2009 input prices}}} \\[2mm]
&= \frac{2,650,000}{(1,987,500 \times \$4) + (3,000,000 \times \$3.10)} \\[2mm]
&= \frac{2,650,000}{\$7,950,000 + \$9,300,000} \\[2mm]
&= \frac{2,650,000}{\$17,250,000} \\[2mm]
&= 0.1536 \text{ units of output per dollar of input}
\end{aligned}$$

* 1,987,600 = 1,875,000 × 2,650,000 ÷ 2,500,000

Using year 2009 prices, total factor productivity increased 12.3% [(0.1725 – 0.1536) ÷ 0.1536] from 2008 to 2009.

13-38 (cont'd)

3. Total factor productivity increased because Guble produced more output per dollar of input in 2009 relative to 2008, measured in both years using 2009 prices. The change in partial productivity of direct materials and conversion costs tells us that Guble used less materials and capacity in 2009, relative to output, than in 2008.

   A major advantage of TFP over partial productivity measures is that TFP combines the productivity of all inputs and so measures gains from using fewer physical inputs *and* substitution among inputs.

   Partial productivities cannot be combined to indicate the overall effect on cost as a result of these individual improvements. The TFP measure allows managers to evaluate the change in overall productivity by simultaneously combining all inputs to measure gains from using fewer physical inputs as well as substitution among inputs.

CHAPTER 14
COST ALLOCATION

14-2 The salary of a plant security guard would be a direct cost when the cost object is the security department or the plant. It would be an indirect cost when the cost object is a product.

14-4 Exhibit 14-2 lists four criteria used to guide cost allocation decisions:
1. Cause and effect.
2. Benefits received.
3. Fairness or equity.
4. Ability to bear.

Either the cause-and-effect criterion or the benefits received criterion is the dominant one when the purpose of the allocation is related to the economic decision purpose or the motivation purpose.

14-6 Cost-benefit considerations can affect costing choices in several ways:
(a) Classifying some immaterial costs as indirect when they could, at high cost, be traced to products, services or customers as direct costs.
(b) Using a small number of indirect cost pools when, at high cost, an increased number of indirect cost pools would provide more homogeneous cost pools.
(c) Using allocation bases that are readily available (or can be collected at low cost) when, at high cost, more appropriate cost allocation bases could be developed.

14-8 Examples of bases used to allocate corporate cost pools to operating divisions are:

Corporate Cost Pools	Possible Allocation Bases
Corporate executive dept.	Sales; assets employed; operating income
Treasury department	Sales; assets employed; estimated time or usage
Legal department	Estimated time or usage; sales; assets employed
Marketing department	Sales; number of sales personnel
Payroll department	Number of employees; payroll dollars
Human resources department	Number of employees; payroll dollars; number of new hires

14-10 Disagree. Allocating costs on "the basis of estimated long-run use by user department managers" means department managers can lower their cost allocations by deliberately underestimating their long-run use.

14-12 The *reciprocal method* is theoretically the most defensible method because it explicitly recognizes the mutual services rendered among all departments, irrespective of whether those departments are operating or support departments.

14-14 The basis for the cost allocation should be clearly defined within the government contract.

14-16 (15-20 min.) Single-rate versus dual-rate cost allocation methods.

1. The total costs in the single-cost pool are fixed ($1,100,000) and variable ($2,200,000) = $3,300,000. The company could use one of two allocation bases (budgeted usage or actual usage) given the information provided.
   - Allocation to Cambridge based on budgeted usage: (60/200) × $3,300,000 = $990,000
   - Allocation to Cambridge based on actual usage: (120/240) × $3,300,000 = $1,650,000

2. Using the dual-rate method (with separate fixed and variable cost pools), several combinations of the budgeted and actual usage allocation bases are possible:

   Fixed Cost Pool: Total costs of $1,100,000:
   - Allocation to Cambridge based on budgeted usage: (60/200) × $1,100,000 = $330,000
   - Allocation to Cambridge based on actual usage: (120/240) × $1,100,000 = $550,000

   Variable Cost Pool: Total costs of $2,200,000:
   - Allocation to Cambridge based on budgeted usage: (60/200) × $2,200,000 = $660,000
   - Allocation to Cambridge based on actual usage: (120/240) × $2,200,000 = $1,100,000

14-16 (cont'd)

The possible combinations are:

Combination	Fixed Cost Pool	Variable Cost Pool	Allocation Function
I	Budgeted Usage	Budgeted Usage	= $330,000 + $660,000 = $990,000
II	Budgeted Usage	Actual Usage	= $330,000 + $1,100,000 = $1,430,000
III	Actual Usage	Budgeted Usage	= $550,000 + $660,000 = $1,210,000
IV	Actual Usage	Actual Usage	= $550,000 + $1,100,000 = $1,650,000

Combinations I and IV give the same cost allocations as in requirement 1. Combination II is a frequently used dual-rate method. The fixed costs are allocated using budgeted usage on the rationale that it better captures the cost of providing capacity. The variable costs are allocated using actual usage on a cause-and-effect rationale. Combination III is rarely encountered in practice.

14-18 (20–25 min.) Single-rate method, budgeted versus actual costs and quantities.

1a. $\text{Budgeted rate} = \dfrac{\text{Budgeted indirect costs}}{\text{Budgeted trips}}$ = $115,000/50 trips = $2,300 per round-trip

Indirect costs allocated to Dark C. Division = $2,300 per round trip × 30 budgeted round trips
= $69,000

Indirect costs allocated to Milk C. Division = $2,300 per round trip × 20 budgeted round trips
= $46,000

b. Budgeted rate = $2,300 per round-trip

Indirect costs allocated to Dark C. Division = $2,300 per round trip × 30 actual round trips
= $69,000

Indirect costs allocated to Milk C. Division = $2,300 per round trip × 15 actual round trips
= $34,500

c. $\text{Actual rate} = \dfrac{\text{Actual indirect costs}}{\text{Actual trips}}$ = $96,750/ 45 trips = $2,150 per round trip

Indirect costs allocated to Dark C. Division = $2,150 per round trip × 30 actual round trips
= $64,500

Indirect costs allocated to Milk C. Division = $2,150 per round trip × 15 actual round trips
= $32,250

14-18 (cont'd)

2.   When budgeted rates/budgeted quantities are used, the Dark Chocolate and Milk Chocolate Divisions know at the start of 2009 that they will be charged a total of $69,000 and $46,000 respectively for transportation. In effect, the fleet resource becomes a fixed cost for each division. Then, each may be motivated to over-use the trucking fleet, knowing that their 2009 transportation costs will not change.

When budgeted rates/actual quantities are used, the Dark Chocolate and Milk Chocolate Divisions know at the start of 2009 that they will be charged a rate of $2,300 per round trip, i.e., they know the price per unit of this resource. This enables them to make operating decisions knowing the rate they will have to pay for transportation. Each can still control its total transportation costs by minimizing the number of round trips it uses. Assuming that the budgeted rate was based on honest estimates of their annual usage, this method will also provide an estimate of the excess trucking capacity (the portion of fleet costs not charged to either division). In contrast, when actual costs/actual quantities are used, the two divisions must wait until year end to know their transportation charges.

The use of actual costs/actual quantities makes the costs allocated to one division a function of the actual demand of other users. In 2009, the actual usage was 45 trips, which is 5 trips below the 50 trips budgeted. The Dark Chocolate Division used all the 30 trips it had budgeted. The Milk Chocolate Division used only 15 of the 20 trips budgeted. When costs are allocated based on actual costs and actual quantities, the same fixed costs are spread over fewer trips resulting in a higher rate than if the Milk Chocolate Division had used its budgeted 20 trips. As a result, the Dark Chocolate Division bears a proportionately higher share of the fixed costs.

Using actual costs/actual rates also means that any efficiencies or inefficiencies of the trucking fleet get passed along to the user divisions. In general, this will have the effect of making the truck fleet less careful about its costs, although in 2009, it appears to have managed its costs well, leading to a lower actual cost per round trip relative to the budgeted cost per round trip.

For the reasons stated above, of the three single-rate methods suggested in this problem, the budgeted rate and actual quantity may be the best one to use. (The management of Chocolat, Inc. would have to ensure that the managers of the Dark Chocolate and Milk Chocolate divisions do not systematically overestimate their budgeted use of the fleet division in an effort to drive down the budgeted rate).

14-20 (30 min.) **Support department cost allocation; direct and step-down methods.**

1.

		AS	IS	GOVT	CORP
a.	Direct method costs	$600,000	$2,400,000		
	Alloc. of AS costs				
	(40/75, 35/75)	(600,000)		$ 320,000	$ 280,000
	Alloc. of IS costs				
	(30/90, 60/90)		(2,400,000)	800,000	1,600,000
		$ 0	$ 0	$1,120,000	$1,880,000
b.	Step-down (AS first) costs	$600,000	$2,400,000		
	Alloc. of AS costs				
	(0.25, 0.40, 0.35)	(600,000)	150,000	$ 240,000	$ 210,000
	Alloc. of IS costs				
	(30/90, 60/90)		(2,550,000)	850,000	1,700,000
		$ 0	$ 0	$1,090,000	$1,910,000
c.	Step-down (IS first) costs	$600,000	$2,400,000		
	Alloc. of IS costs				
	(0.10, 0.30, 0.60)	240,000	(2,400,000)	$ 720,000	$1,440,000
	Alloc. of AS costs				
	(40/75, 35/75)	(840,000)		448,000	392,000
		$ 0	$ 0	$1,168,000	$1,832,000

2.

	GOVT	CORP
Direct method	$1,120,000	$1,880,000
Step-down (AS first)	1,090,000	1,910,000
Step-down (IS first)	1,168,000	1,832,000

The direct method ignores any services to other support departments. The step-down method partially recognizes services to other support departments. The information systems support group (with total budget of $2,400,000) provides 10% of its services to the AS group. The AS support group (with total budget of $600,000) provides 25% of its services to the information systems support group. When the AS group is allocated first, a total of $2,550,000 is then assigned out from the IS group. Given CORP's disproportionate (2:1) usage of the services of IS, this method then results in the highest overall allocation of costs to CORP. By contrast, GOVT's usage of the AS group exceeds that of CORP (by a ratio of 8:7), and so GOVT is assigned relatively more in support costs when AS costs are assigned second, after they have already been incremented by the AS share of IS costs as well.

14-20 (cont'd)

3. Three criteria that could determine the sequence in the step-down method are:
   a. Allocate support departments on a ranking of the percentage of their total services provided to other support departments.
      1. Administrative Services   25%
      2. Information Systems   10%
   b. Allocate support departments on a ranking of the total dollar amount in the support departments.
      1. Information Systems $2,400,000
      2. Administrative Services $ 600,000
   c. Allocate support departments on a ranking of the dollar amounts of service provided to other support departments
      1. Information Systems
         $(0.10 \times \$2,400,000)$ = $240,000
      2. Administrative Services
         $(0.25 \times \$600,000)$ = $150,000

   The approach in (a) above typically better approximates the theoretically preferred reciprocal method. It results in a higher percentage of support-department costs provided to other support departments being incorporated into the step-down process than does (b) or (c), above.

14-22 (45 min.)   Allocating costs of support departments; step-down and direct methods.

	Building and Grounds	Personnel	General Plant Admin.	Cafeteria Operating Loss	Storeroom	Machining	Assembly
1. Step-down Method:	$ 10,000	$ 1,000	$ 26,090	$ 1,640	$ 2,670	$34,700	$48,900
(1) Building & grounds at $0.10/sq. m. ($10,000 ÷ 100,000)	$(10,000)	200	700	400	700	3,000	5,000
(2) Personnel at $6/employee ($1,200 ÷ 200)		$(1,200)	210	60	30	300	600
(3) General plant administration at $1/labour-hour ($27,000 ÷ 27,000)			$(27,000)	1,000	1,000	8,000	17,000
(4) Cafeteria at $20/employee ($3,100 ÷ 155)				$(3,100)	100	1,000	2,000
(5) Storeroom at $1.50/requisition ($4,500 ÷ 3,000)					$(4,500)	3,000	1,500
(6) Costs allocated to operating depts.						$50,000	$75,000
(7) Divide (6) by dir. manuf. labour-hrs.						÷ 5,000	÷15,000
(8) Overhead rate per direct manuf. labour-hour						$ 10	$ 5
2. Direct method:	$10,000	$1,000	$26,090	$1,640	$2,670	$34,700	$48,900
(1) Building and grounds, 30,000/80,000; 50,000/80,000	(10,000)					3,750	6,250
(2) Personnel, 50/150; 100/150		(1,000)				333	667
(3) General plant administration, 8,000/25,000; 17,000/25,000			(26,090)			8,349	17,741
(4) Cafeteria, 50/150; 100/150				(1,640)		547	1,093
(5) Storeroom: 2,000/3,000; 1,000/3,000					(2,670)	1,780	890
(6) Costs allocated to operating depts.						$49,459	$75,541
(7) Divide (6) by direct manufacturing labour-hours						÷ 5,000	÷15,000
(8) Overhead rate per direct manufacturing labour-hour						$ 9.892	$ 5.036

14-22 (cont'd)

3. Comparison of methods:

Step-down method:	Job 88:	18 × $10	$180	
		2 × $ 5	10	$190.00
	Job 89:	3 × $10	$ 30	
		17 × $ 5	85	115.00
Direct method:	Job 88:	18 × $9.892	$178.06	
		2 × $5.036	10.07	$188.13
	Job 89:	3 × $9.892	$ 29.68	
		17 × $5.036	85.61	115.29

4. The manager of the Machining Department would prefer the direct method. The direct method results in a lower amount of support departments' costs being allocated to the Machining Department than the step-down method. This is clear from a comparison of the overhead rate, per direct manufacturing labour-hour, for the Machining Department under the two methods.

14-24 (40 min.) Direct and step-down allocation.

1.

	Support Departments		Operating Departments		
	HR	IS	Corporate	Consumer	Total
Costs Incurred	$72,700	$234,400	$ 998,270	$489,860	$1,795,230
Alloc. of HR costs					
(42/70, 28/70)	(72,700)		43,620	29,080	
Alloc. of IS costs					
(1,920/3,520, 1,600/3,520)		(234,400)	127,855	106,545	
	$ 0	$ 0	$1,169,745	$625,485	$1,795,230

2. Rank on percentage of services rendered to other support departments.

Step 1: HR provides 23.077% of its services to Information Systems:

$$\frac{21}{42 + 28 + 21} = \frac{21}{91} = 23.077\%$$

This 23.077% of $72,700 HR department costs is $16,777.

Step 2: Information Systems provides 8.333% of its services to HR:

$$\frac{320}{1,920 + 1,600 + 320} = \frac{320}{3,840} = 8.333\%$$

This 8.333% of $234,400 Information Systems department costs is $19,533.

	Support Departments		Operating Departments		
	HR	IS	Corporate	Consumer	Total
Costs Incurred	$72,700	$234,400	$ 998,270	$489,860	$1,795,230
Alloc. of HR costs					
(21/91, 42/91, 28/91)	(72,700)	16,777	33,554	22,369	
	$ 0	251,177			
Alloc. of IS costs					
(1,920/3,520, 1,600/3,520)		(251,177)	137,006	114,171	
		$ 0	$1,168,830	$626,400	$1,795,230

14-24 (cont'd)

3. An alternative ranking is based on the dollar amount of services rendered to other support departments. Using numbers from requirement 2, this approach would use the following sequence:

    Step 1: Allocate Information Systems first ($19,533 provided to HR).

    Step 2: Allocate HR second ($16,777 provided to Information Systems).

14-26 (20 min.) Single-rate, dual-rate, and practical capacity allocation.

Budgeted number of gifts wrapped = 6,750
Budgeted fixed costs = $6,750
Fixed cost per gift based on budgeted volume = $6,750 ÷ 6,750 = $1.00
Average budgeted variable cost per gift =   0.50
Total cost per gift wrapped $1.50

1.a. Allocation based on budgeted usage of gift-wrapping services:

Women's Face Wash (2,475 × $1.50)	$ 3,712.50
Men's Face Wash (825 × $1.50)	1,237.50
Fragrances (1,800 × $1.50)	2,700.00
Body Wash (450 × $1.50)	675.00
Hair Products (1,200 × $1.50)	1,800.00
Total	$10,125.00

1.b. Allocation based on actual usage of gift-wrapping services:

Women's Face Wash (2,100 × $1.50)	$3,150.00
Men's Face Wash (750 × $1.50)	1,125.00
Fragrances (1,575 × $1.50)	2,362.50
Body Wash (525 × $1.50)	787.50
Hair Products (1,050 × $1.50)	1,575.00
Total	$9,000.00

1.c. Practical gift-wrapping capacity = 7,500
Budgeted fixed costs = $6,750
Fixed cost per gift based on practical capacity = $6,750 ÷ 7,500 = $0.90
Average budgeted variable cost per gift =   0.50
Total cost per gift wrapped $1.40

14-26 (cont'd)

Allocation based on actual usage of gift-wrapping services:

Women's Face Wash (2,100 × $1.40)	$2,940
Men's Face Wash (750 × $1.40)	1,050
Fragrances (1,575 × $1.40)	2,205
Body Wash (525 × $1.40)	735
Hair Products (1,050 × $1.40)	1,470
Total	$8,400

2. Budgeted rate for fixed costs $= \dfrac{\text{Budgeted fixed costs}}{\text{Practical capacity}}$

$= \$6,750 \div 7,500 \text{ gifts} = \$0.90 \text{ per gift}$

Fixed costs allocated on budgeted usage.

Rate for variable costs $=$ $0.50 per item
Variable costs based on actual usage.

Allocation:

Department	Variable Costs	Fixed Costs	Total
Women's Face Wash	2,100 × $0.50 =$1,050.00	2,475 × $0.90 = $2,227.50	$3,277.50
Men's Face Wash	750 × $0.50 = 375.00	825 × $0.90 = 742.50	1,117.50
Fragrances	1,575 × $0.50 = 787.50	1,800 × $0.90 = 1,620.00	2,407.50
Body Wash	525 × $0.50 = 262.50	450 × $0.90 = 405.00	667.50
Hair Products	1,050 × $0.50 = 525.00	1,200 × $0.90 = 1,080.00	1,605.00
Total	$3,000.00	$6,075.00	$9,075.00

3. The dual-rate method has three major advantages over the single-rate method:
    a. Fixed costs and variable costs can be allocated differently—fixed costs based on rates calculated using practical capacity and budgeted usage, and variable costs based on budgeted rates and actual usage.
    b. Fixed costs are allocated proportionately to the departments causing the incurrence of those costs based on the capacity of each department.
    c. The costs allocated to a department are not affected by the usage by other departments.

Note: If capacity costs are the result of a long-term decision by top management, it may be desirable to allocate to each department the cost of capacity used based on actual usage. The users are then not allocated the costs of unused capacity.

14-28 (40–60 min.) **Support-department cost allocations; single-department cost pools; direct, step-down, and reciprocal methods.**

All the following computations are in dollars.
1.

Direct method:	To X	To Y
A	250/400 × $100,000 = $62,500	150/400 × $100,000 = $37,500
B	100/500 × $ 40,000 = 8,000	400/500 × $ 40,000 = 32,000
Total	$70,500	$69,500

Step-down method, allocating A first:

	A	B	X	Y
Costs to be allocated	$100,000	$40,000	–	–
Allocate A: (100; 250; 150 ÷ 500)	(100,000)	20,000	$50,000	$30,000
Allocate B: (100; 400 ÷ 500)	–	(60,000)	12,000	48,000
Total	$ 0	$ 0	$62,000	$78,000

Step-down method, allocating B first:

	A	B	X	Y
Costs to be allocated	$100,000	$ 40,000	–	–
Allocate B: (500; 100; 400 ÷ 1,000)	20,000	(40,000)	$ 4,000	$16,000
Allocate A: (250/400, 150/400)	(120,000)	–	75,000	45,000
Total	$ 0	$ 0	$79,000	$61,000

Note that these methods produce significantly different results, so the choice of method may frequently make a difference in the budgeted department overhead rates.

14-28 (cont'd)

Reciprocal method:

Stage 1: Let   A   =   total costs of materials-handling department
                B   =   total costs of power-generating department

(1)   A   = $100,000 + 0.5B
(2)   B   = $ 40,000 + 0.2A

Stage 2: Substituting in (1):   A   = $100,000 + 0.5($40,000 + 0.2A)
                             A   = $100,000 + $20,000 + 0.1A
                        0.9A   = $120,000
                             A   = $133,333

Substituting in (2):   B   = $40,000 + 0.2($133,333)
                          B   = $66,666

Stage 3:

	A	B	X	Y
Original amounts	$100,000	$40,000	—	—
Allocation of A	(133,333)	26,666(20%)	$66,667(50%)	$40,000(30%)
Allocation of B	33,333(50%)	(66,666)	6,667(10%)	26,666(40%)
Totals accounted for	$ 0	$ 0	$73,334	$66,666

14-28 (cont'd)

SOLUTION EXHIBIT 14-28

Reciprocal Method of Allocating Support Department Costs for Manes Company Using Repeated Iterations.

	Support Departments		Operating Departments	
	A	B	X	Y
Budgeted manufacturing overhead costs before any interdepartmental cost allocations	$100,000	$40,000		
1st Allocation of Dept. A: (2/10, 5/10, 3/10)[a]	(100,000)	20,000 ___ 60,000	$50,000	$30,000
1st Allocation of Dept. B (5/10, 1/10, 4/10)[b]	30,000	(60,000)	6,000	24,000
2nd Allocation of Dept. A (2/10, 5/10, 3/10)[a]	(30,000)	6,000	15,000	9,000
2nd Allocation of Dept B: (5/10, 1/10, 4/10)[b]	3,000	(6,000)	600	2,400
3rd Allocation of Dept A: (2/10, 5/10, 3/10)[a]	(3,000)	600	1,500	900
3rd Allocation of Dept. B: (5/10, 1/10, 4/10)[b]	300	(600)	60	240
4th Allocation of Dept. A (2/10, 5/10, 3/10)[a]	(300)	60	150	90
4th Allocation of Dept. B (5/10, 1/10, 4/10)[b]	30	(60)	6	24
5th Allocation of Dept A (2/10, 5/10, 3/10)[a]	(30)	6	15	9
5th Allocation of Dept B (5/10, 1/10, 4/10)[b]	3	(6)	1	2
6th Allocation of Dept A (2/10, 5/10, 3/10)[a]	(3)	0	2	1
Total budgeted manufacturing overhead of operating departments	$ 0	$ 0	$73,334	$66,666

Total accounts allocated and reallocated (the numbers in parentheses in first two columns)
Dept A; Materials Handling: $100,000 + $30,000 + $3,000 + $300 + $30 + $3 = $133,333
Dept B; Power Generation: $60,000 + $6,000 + $600 + $60 + $6 = $66,666

[a]Base is (100 + 250 +150) or 500 labour-hours; 100 ÷ 500 = 2/10, 250 ÷ 500 = 5/10, 150 ÷ 500 = 3/10.
[b]Base is (500 + 100 + 400) or 1,000 kWh ; 500 ÷ 1,000 = 5/10, 100 ÷ 1,000 = 1/10, 400 ÷ 1,000 = 4/10.

14-28 (cont'd)

Comparison of methods:

Method of Allocation	X	Y
Direct method	$70,500	$69,500
Step-down: A first	62,000	78,000
Step-down: B first	79,000	61,000
Reciprocal method	73,334	66,666

Note that *in this case* the direct method produces answers that are the closest to the "correct" answers (that is, those from the reciprocal method), step-down allocating B first is next, and step-down allocating A first is least accurate.

2. At first glance, it appears that the cost of power is $40 per unit plus the material handling costs. If so, Manes would be better off by purchasing from the power company. However, the decision should be influenced by the effects of the interdependencies and the fixed costs. Note that the power needs would be less (students frequently miss this) if they were purchased from the outside:

	Outside Power Units Needed
X	100
Y	400
A (500 units minus 20% of 500 units, because there is no need to service the nonexistent power department)	400
Total units	900

Total costs, 900 × $40 = $36,000

14-28 (cont'd)

In contrast, the total costs that would be saved by not producing the power inside would depend on the effects of the decision on various costs:

	Avoidable Costs of 1,000 Units of Power Produced Inside
Variable indirect labour and indirect material costs	$10,000
Supervision in power department	10,000
Materials handling, 20% of $70,000*	14,000
Probable minimum cost savings	$34,000
Possible additional savings:	
a. Can any supervision in materials handling be saved because of overseeing less volume? Minimum savings is probably zero; the maximum is probably 20% of $10,000 or $2,000.	?
b. Is any depreciation a truly variable, wear-and-tear type of cost?	?
Total savings by not producing 1,000 units of power	$34,000 + ?

* Materials handling costs are higher because the power department uses 20% of materials handling. Therefore, materials-handling costs will decrease by 20%.

In the short run (at least until a capital investment in equipment is necessary), the data suggest continuing to produce internally because the costs eliminated would probably be less than the comparable purchase costs.

14-30 (25 min.) Cost allocation to divisions.

Percentages for various allocation bases (old and new):

	Pulp	Paper	Fibres	Total
(1) Division margin percentages $2,400,000; $7,100,000; $9,500,000 ÷ $19,000,000	12.63157%	37.36843%	50.0%	100.0%
(2) Share of employees $350; 250; 400 ÷ 1,000	35.0	25.0	40.0	100.0
(3) Share of floor space 35,000; 24,000; 66,000 ÷ 125,000	28.0	19.2	52.8	100.0
(4) Share of total division administrative costs $2,000,000; $1,800,000; $3,200,000 ÷ $7,000,000	28.57142	25.71428	45.71428	100.0

1.

	Pulp	Paper	Fibres	Total
(5) Division margin	$2,400,000	$ 7,100,000	$ 9,500,000	$19,000,000
(6) Corporate overhead allocated on segment margins = (1) × $9,000,000	1,136,842	3,363,158	4,500,000	9,000,000
(7) Operating margin with division margin-based allocation = (5) – (6)	$1,263,158	$ 3,736,842	$ 5,000,000	$10,000,000
(8) Revenues	$8,500,000	$17,500,000	$24,000,000	$50,000,000
Operating margin as a percentage of revenues	14.9%	21.3%	20.8%	20.0%

2.

	Pulp	Paper	Fibres	Total
(5) Division margin	$2,400,000	$ 7,100,000	$ 9,500,000	$19,000,000
HRM costs (alloc. base: no. of employees) = (2) × $1,800,000	630 ,000	450,000	720,000	1,800,000
Facility costs (alloc. base: floor space) = (3) × $2,700,000	756,000	518,400	1,425,600	2,700,000
Corp. admin (alloc. base: div. admin costs) = (4) × $4,500,000	1,285,714	1,157,143	2,057,143	4,500,000
Corp. overhead allocated to each division	2,671,714	2,125,543	4,202,743	9,000,000
Operating margin with cause-and-effect allocation	$ (271,714)	$ 4,974,457	$ 5,297,257	$10,000,000
(8) Revenues	$8,500,000	$17,500,000	$24,000,000	$50,000,000
Operating margin as a percentage of revenues	-3.2%	28.4%	22.1%	20.0 %

14-30 (cont'd)

3. When corporate overhead is allocated to the divisions on the basis of division margins (requirement 1), each division is profitable (has positive operating margin) and the Paper division is the most profitable (has the highest operating margin percentage) by a slim margin, while the Pulp division is the least profitable. When Bardem's suggested bases are used to allocate the different types of corporate overhead costs (requirement 2), we see that, in fact, the Pulp division is not profitable (it has a negative operating margin). Paper continues to be the most profitable and, in fact, it is significantly more profitable than the Fibres division.

    If division performance is linked to operating margin percentages, Pulp will resist this new way of allocating corporate costs, which causes its operating margin of nearly 15% (in the old scheme) to be transformed into a -3.2% operating margin. The new cost allocation methodology reveals that, if the allocation bases are reasonable, the Pulp division consumes a greater share of corporate resources than its share of segment margins would indicate. Pulp generates 12.6% of the segment margins, but consumes almost 29.7% ($2,671,714 ÷ $9,000,000) of corporate overhead resources. Paper will welcome the change—its operating margin percentage rises the most, and Fibres' operating margin percentage remains practically the same.

    Note that in the old scheme, Paper was being penalized for its efficiency (smallest share of administrative costs), by being allocated a larger share of corporate overhead. In the new scheme, its efficiency in terms of administrative costs, employees, and square metres is being recognized.

4. The new approach is preferable because it is based on cause-and-effect relationships between costs and their respective cost drivers in the long run.

    Human resource management costs are allocated using the number of employees in each division because the costs for recruitment, training, etc., are mostly related to the number of employees in each division. Facility costs are mostly incurred on the basis of space occupied by each division. Corporate administration costs are allocated on the basis of divisional administrative costs because these costs are incurred to provide support to divisional administrations.

    To overcome objections from the divisions, Bardem may initially choose not to allocate corporate overhead to divisions when evaluating performance. He could start by sharing the results with the divisions, and giving them—particularly the Pulp division—adequate time to figure out how to reduce their share of cost drivers. He should also develop benchmarks by comparing the consumption of corporate resources to competitors and other industry standards.

14-32 Cost allocation to divisions.

1.

	Bread	Cake	Doughnuts	Total
Segment margin	$6,400,000	$1,300,000	$6,150,000	$13,850,000
Allocated headquarters costs ($5,100,000 ÷ 3)	1,700,000	1,700,000	1,700,000	5,100,000
Operating income	$4,700,000	$ (400,000)	$4,450,000	$ 8,750,000

2.

	Bread	Cake	Doughnuts	Total
Segment margin	$6,400,000	$1,300,000	$6,150,000	$13,850,000
Allocated headquarters costs, Human resources[1] (50%; 12.5%; 37.5% × $1,900,000)	950,000	237,500	712,500	1,900,000
Accounting department[2] (53.9%; 11.6%; 34.5% × $1,400,000)	754,600	162,400	483,000	1,400,000
Rent and depreciation[3] (50%; 20%; 30% × $1,200,000)	600,000	240,000	360,000	1,200,000
Other ($\frac{1}{3}$ × $600,000)	200,000	200,000	200,000	600,000
Total	2,504,600	839,900	1,755,500	5,100,000
Operating income	$3,895,400	$ 460,100	$4,394,500	$ 8,750,000

[1]HR costs: 400 ÷ 800 = 50%; 100 ÷ 800 = 12.5%; 300 ÷ 800 = 37.5%

[2]Accounting: $20,900,000 ÷ $38,800,000 = 53.9%; $4,500,000 ÷ $38,800,000 = 11.6%; $13,400,000 ÷ $38,800,000 = 34.5%

[3] Rent and depreciation: 10,000 ÷ 20,000 = 50%; 4,000 ÷ 20,000 = 20%; 6,000 ÷ 20,000 = 30%

A cause-and-effect relationship may exist between Human Resources costs and the number of employees at each division. Rent and depreciation costs may be related to square metres, except that very expensive machines may require few square metres, which is inconsistent with this choice of allocation base. The Accounting Department costs are probably related to the revenues earned by each division—higher revenues mean more transactions and more accounting. Other overhead costs are allocated arbitrarily.

14-32 (cont'd)

3. The manager suggesting the new allocation bases probably works in the Cake Division. Under the old scheme, the Cake Division shows an operating loss after allocating headquarters costs because it is smaller, yet was charged an equal amount (a third) of headquarters costs. The new allocation scheme shows an operating profit in the Cake Division, even after allocating headquarters costs. The ABC method is a better way to allocate headquarters costs because it uses cost allocation bases that, by and large, represent cause-and-effect relationships between various categories of headquarters costs and the demands that different divisions place on these costs.

14-34 Matrix algebra.

1.

1.11016	0.17167	0.30329
0.27182	1.07296	0.22890
0.33190	0.25751	1.12160

2.

Artificial
Costs
$ 162.30043
114.37768
219.45064

3.

Total Costs including reciprocal allocation costs		
Service groups: Artificial costs		
Corporate Treasury	$ 162.30043	
CHRM	114.37768	
IT	219.45064	
Total Costs Operating Groups; after reciprocal allocation of costs		
Sales and Marketing	$ 180.82961	
Purchasing	$ 307.94464	
Consumer Services & Returns	$ 135.22575	
Total (check)	$ 624.00000	

CHAPTER 15
COST ALLOCATION: JOINT PRODUCTS AND BYPRODUCTS

15-2 A *joint cost* is a cost of a production process that yields multiple products simultaneously. A *separable cost* is a cost incurred beyond the splitoff point that is assignable to each of the specific products identified at the splitoff point.

15-4 A *product* is any output that has a positive sales value (or an output that enables an organization to avoid incurring costs). In some joint-cost settings, outputs can occur that do not have a positive sales value. The offshore processing of hydrocarbons yields water that is recycled back into the ocean while yielding oil and gas. The processing of mineral ore to yield gold and silver also yields dirt as an output, which is recycled back into the ground.

15-6 The joint production process yields individual products that are either sold this period or held as inventory to be sold in subsequent periods. Hence the joint costs need to be allocated between total production rather than just those sold this period.

15-8 Both methods use market selling-price data in allocating joint costs, but they differ in which sales-price data they use. The *sales value at splitoff method* allocates joint costs on the basis of each product's relative sales value at the splitoff point. The *estimated net realizable value method* allocates joint costs on the basis of the relative estimated net realizable value (expected final sales value in the ordinary course of business minus the expected separable costs of production and marketing).

15-10 The estimated NRV method can be simplified by assuming (a) a standard set of post-splitoff point processing steps and (b) a standard set of selling prices. The use of (a) and (b) achieves the same benefits that the use of standard costs does in costing systems.

15-12 No. Any method used to allocate joint costs to individual products that is applicable to the problem of joint product-cost allocation should not be used for management decisions regarding whether a product should be sold or processed further. When a product is an inherent result of a joint process, the decision to process further should not be influenced by either the size of the total joint costs or the portion of the joint costs assigned to particular products. Joint costs are irrelevant for these decisions. The only relevant items for these decisions are the incremental revenue and the incremental costs beyond the splitoff point.

15-14 Two methods to account for byproducts are:
a. Production method—recognizes byproducts in the financial statements at the time production is completed.
b. Sales method—delays recognition of byproducts until the time of sale.

15-16 (20-30 min.) **Joint-cost allocation, insurance settlement.**

1.   a.   Sales value at splitoff method:

	Kg of Product	Wholesale Selling Price per kg	Sales Value at Splitoff	Weighting: Sales Value at Splitoff	Joint Costs Allocated	Allocated Costs per kg
Breasts	100	$0.55	$55.00	0.675	$33.75	0.3375
Wings	20	0.20	4.00	0.049	2.45	0.1225
Thighs	40	0.35	14.00	0.172	8.60	0.2150
Bones	80	0.10	8.00	0.098	4.90	0.0613
Feathers	10	0.05	0.50	0.006	0.30	0.0300
	250		$81.50	1.000	$50.00	

Costs of Destroyed Product

Breasts: $0.3375 per kilogram × 40 kilograms = $13.50

Wings: $0.1225 per kilogram × 15 kilograms =   1.84

$15.34

b.   Physical measure method:

	Kg of Product	Weighting: Physical Measures	Joint Costs Allocated	Allocated Costs per kg
Breasts	100	0.400	$20.00	$0.200
Wings	20	0.080	4.00	0.200
Thighs	40	0.160	8.00	0.200
Bones	80	0.320	16.00	0.200
Feathers	10	0.040	2.00	0.200
	250	1.000	$50.00	

Costs of Destroyed Product

Breast: $0.20 per kilogram × 40 kilograms = $ 8

Wings: $0.20 per kilogram × 15 kilograms =   3

$11

15-16 (cont'd)

Note: Although not required, it is useful to highlight the individual product profitability figures:

Product	Sales Value	Sales Value at Splitoff Method		Physical Measures Method	
		Joint Costs Allocated	Gross Income	Joint Costs Allocated	Gross Income
Breasts	$55.00	$33.75	$21.25	$20.00	$35.00
Wings	4.00	2.45	1.55	4.00	0.00
Thighs	14.00	8.60	5.40	8.00	6.00
Bones	8.00	4.90	3.10	16.00	(8.00)
Feathers	0.50	0.30	0.20	2.00	(1.50)

2. The sales-value at splitoff method captures the benefits-received criterion of cost allocation and is the preferred method. The costs of processing a chicken are allocated to products in proportion to the ability to contribute revenue. Quality Chicken's decision to process chicken is heavily influenced by the revenues from breasts and thighs. The bones provide relatively few benefits to Quality Chicken despite their high physical volume.

The physical measures method shows profits on breasts and thighs and losses on bones and feathers. Given that Quality Chicken has to jointly process all the chicken products, it is non-intuitive to single out individual products that are being processed simultaneously as making losses while the overall operations make a profit. Quality Chicken is processing chicken mainly for breasts and thighs and not for wings, bones, and feathers, while the physical measure method allocates a disproportionate amount of costs to wings, bones, and feathers.

15-18 (20-30 min.) **Net realizable value cost-allocation method, further process decision.**

A diagram of the situation is in Solution Exhibit 15-18.

1.

	Quantity in Kilograms	Sales Price per Kilogram	Final Sales Value	Separable Processing Costs	Estimated Net Realizable Value at Splitoff	Weighting
Alco	20,000	$24.00	$ 480,000	$120,000	$360,000	360/672
Devo	60,000	7.20	432,000	240,000	192,000	192/672
Holo	100,000	1.20	120,000	0	120,000	120/672
Totals			$1,032,000	$360,000	$672,000	

Allocation of $504,000 joint costs:

Alco 360/672 × $504,000 = $270,000
Devo 192/672 × $504,000 = 144,000
Holo 120/672 × $504,000 =   90,000
                               $504,000

	Joint Costs Allocated	Separable Processing Costs	Total Costs	Units	Unit Cost
Alco	$270,000	$120,000	$390,000	20,000	$19.50
Devo	144,000	240,000	384,000	60,000	6.40
Holo	90,000	0	90,000	100,000	0.90
Totals	$504,000	$360,000	$864,000	180,000	

The ending inventory is:

Alco 1,000 × $19.50 = $19,500
Devo 1,000 × $6.40   =   6,400
Holo 1,000 × $0.90   =   900
                          $26,800

15-18 (cont'd)

2.

	Unit Sales Price	Unit Cost	Gross Margin	Gross-Margin Percentage
Alco	$24.00	$19.50	$4.50	18.75%
Devo	7.20	6.40	0.80	11.11%
Holo	1.20	0.90	0.30	25.00%

3. Further processing of Devo yields incremental income of $48,000:

Incremental revenue of further processing Devo, ($7.20 – $2.40) × 60,000	$288,000
Incremental processing costs	240,000
Incremental operating income from further processing	$ 48,000

Montore should process Devo further. Note that joint costs are irrelevant to this decision; they remain the same, whichever alternative (sell at splitoff or process further) is selected.

SOLUTION EXHIBIT 15-18

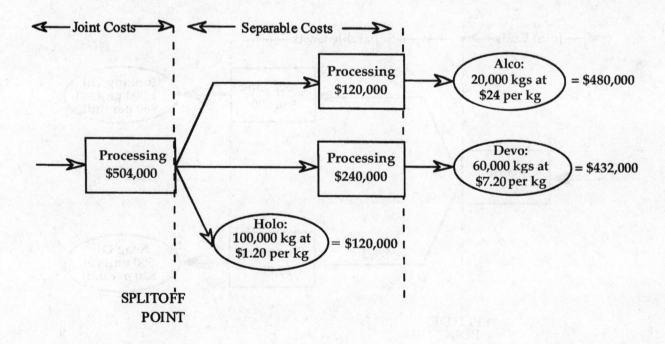

15-20 (10 min.) Estimated net realizable value method.

A diagram of the situation is in Solution Exhibit 15-20 (all numbers are in thousands, other than per-unit costs).

	Cooking Oil	Soap Oil	Total
Expected final sales value of production, CO, 1,000 × $60; SO, 500 × $30	$60,000	$15,000	$75,000
Deduct expected separable costs to complete and sell	36,000	9,000	45,000
Estimated net realizable value at splitoff point	$24,000	$ 6,000	$30,000
Weighting	$\dfrac{\$24,000}{\$30,000}=0.8$	$\dfrac{\$6,000}{\$30,000}=0.2$	
Joint costs allocated, CO, 0.8 × $28,800; SO, 0.2 × $28,800	$23,040	$ 5,760	$28,800

SOLUTION EXHIBIT 15-20

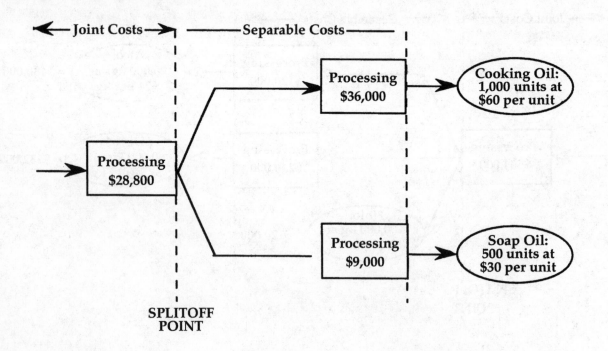

318

15-22 (30 min.) Joint-cost allocation, sales value, physical measure, NRV methods.

1 a.

PANEL A: Allocation of Joint Costs Using Sales Value at Splitoff Method	Special B/ Beef Ramen	Special S/ Shrimp Ramen	Total
Sales value of total production at splitoff point (10,000 tonnes × $10 per tonne; 20,000 × $15 per tonne)	$100,000	$300,000	$400,000
Weighting ($100,000; $300,000 ÷ $400,000)	0.25	0.75	
Joint costs allocated (25; 0.75 × $240,000)	$60,000	$180,000	$240,000

PANEL B: Product-Line Income Statement for June 2009	Special B	Special S	Total
Revenues (12,000 tonnes × $18 per tonne; 24,000 × $25 per tonne)	$216,000	$600,000	$816,000
Deduct joint costs allocated (from Panel A)	60,000	180,000	240,000
Deduct separable costs	48,000	168,000	216,000
Gross margin	$108,000	$252,000	$360,000
Gross margin percentage	50%	42%	44%

1 b.

PANEL A: Allocation of Joint Costs Using Physical-Measure Method	Special B/ Beef Ramen	Special S/ Shrimp Ramen	Total
Physical measure of total production (tonnes)	10,000	20,000	30,000
Weighting (10,000 tonnes; 20,000 tonnes ÷ 30,000 tonnes)	33%	67%	
Joint costs allocated (0.33 × $240,000; 0.67 × $240,000)	$79,200	$160,800	$240,000

PANEL B: Product-Line Income Statement for June 2009	Special B	Special S	Total
Revenues (12,000 tonnes × $18 per tonne; 24,000 × $25 per tonne)	$216,000	$600,000	$816,000
Deduct joint costs allocated (from Panel A)	79,200	160,800	240,000
Deduct separable costs	48,000	168,000	216,000
Gross margin	$ 88,800	$271,200	$360,000
Gross margin percentage	41%	45%	44%

15-22 (cont'd)

1 c.

PANEL A: Allocation of Joint Costs Using Net Realizable Value Method	Special B	Special S	Total
Final sales value of total production during accounting period			
(12,000 tonnes × $18 per tonne; 24,000 tonnes × $25 per tonne)	$216,000	$600,000	$816,000
Deduct separable costs	48,000	168,000	216,000
Net realizable value at splitoff point	$168,000	$432,000	$600,000
Weighting ($168,000; $432,000 ÷ $600,000)	28%	72%	
Joint costs allocated (0.28; 0.72 × $240,000)	$67,200	$172,800	$240,000

PANEL B: Product-Line Income Statement for June 2009	Special B	Special S	Total
Revenues (12,000 tonnes × $18 per tonne; 24,000 tonnes × $25 per tonne)	$216,000	$600,000	$816,000
Deduct joint costs allocated (from Panel A)	67,200	172,800	240,000
Deduct separable costs	48,000	168,000	216,000
Gross margin	$100,800	$259,200	$360,000
Gross margin percentage	46.7%	43.2%	44.1%

2. Sherrie Dong probably performed the analysis shown below to arrive at the net loss of $2,228 from marketing the stock:

PANEL A: Allocation of Joint Costs Using Sales Value at Splitoff	Special B/ Beef Ramen	Special S/ Shrimp Ramen	Stock	Total
Sales value of total production at splitoff point				
(10,000 tonnes × $10 per tonne; 20,000 × $15 per tonne; 4,000 × $5 per tonne)	$100,000	$300,000	$20,000	$420,000
Weighting				
($100,000; $300,000; $20,000 ÷ $420,000)	23.8095%	71.4286%	4.7619%	100%
Joint costs allocated				
(0.238095; 0.714286; 0.047619 × $240,000)	$57,143	$171,429	$11,428	$240,000

PANEL B: Product-Line Income Statement for June 2009	Special B	Special S	Stock	Total
Revenues				
(12,000 tonnes ×$18 per tonne; 24,000 × $25 per tonne; 4,000 ×$5 per tonne)	$216,000	$600,000	$20,000	$836,000
Separable processing costs	48,000	168,000	0	216,000
Joint costs allocated (from Panel A)	57,143	171,429	11,428	240,000
Gross margin	$110,857	$260,571	8,572	380,000
Deduct marketing costs			10,800	10,800
Operating income			$ (2,228)	$369,200

15-22 (cont'd)

In this (misleading) analysis, the $240,000 of joint costs are re-allocated between Special B, Special S, and the stock. Irrespective of the method of allocation, this analysis is wrong. Joint costs are always irrelevant in a process-further decision. Only incremental costs and revenues past the splitoff point are relevant. In this case, the correct analysis is much simpler: the incremental revenues from selling the stock are $20,000, and the incremental costs are the marketing costs of $10,800. So, Instant Foods should sell the stock—this will increase its operating income by $9,200 ($20,000 – $10,800).

15-24 (40 min.) Alternative methods of joint-cost allocation, ending inventories.

Total production for the year was:

	Sold	Ending Inventories	Total Production
X	120	180	300
Y	340	60	400
Z	475	25	500

A diagram of the situation is in Solution Exhibit 15-24.

1. a. Net realizable value (NRV) method:

	X	Y	Z	Total
Final sales value of total production, 300 × $1,500; 400 × $1,000; 500 × $700	$450,000	$400,000	$350,000	$1,200,000
Deduct separable costs	--	--	200,000	200,000
Net realizable value at splitoff point	$450,000	$400,000	$150,000	$1,000,000
Weighting, $450; $400; $150 ÷ $1,000	0.45	0.40	0.15	
Joint costs allocated, 0.45, 0.40, 0.15 × $400,000	$180,000	$160,000	$60,000	$400,000

15-24 (cont'd)

Ending Inventory Percentages:

	X	Y	Z
Ending inventory	180	60	25
Total production	300	400	500
Ending inventory percentage	60%	15%	5%

Income Statement

	X	Y	Z	Total
Revenues,				
120 × $1,500; 340 × $1,000; 475 × $700	$180,000	$340,000	$332,500	$852,500
Cost of goods sold:				
Joint costs allocated	180,000	160,000	60,000	400,000
Separable costs	--	--	200,000	200,000
Production costs	180,000	160,000	260,000	600,000
Deduct ending inventory,				
60%; 15%; 5% of production costs	108,000	24,000	13,000	145,000
Cost of goods sold	72,000	136,000	247,000	455,000
Gross margin	$108,000	$204,000	$ 85,500	$397,500
Gross-margin percentage	60%	60%	25.71%	

b. Constant gross-margin percentage NRV method:

Step 1:

Final sales value of prodn., (300 × $1,500) + (400 × $1,000) + (500 × $700)	$1,200,000
Deduct joint and separable costs, $400,000 + $200,000	600,000
Gross margin	$ 600,000
Gross-margin percentage, $600,000 ÷ $1,200,000	50%

Step 2:

	X	Y	Z	Total
Final sales value of total production,				
300 × $1,500; 400 × $1,000; 500 × $700	$450,000	$400,000	$350,000	$1,200,000
Deduct gross margin, using overall				
gross-margin percentage of sales, 50%	225,000	200,000	175,000	600,000
Total production costs	225,000	200,000	175,000	600,000

Step 3:

	X	Y	Z	Total
Deduct separable costs	–	–	200,000	200,000
Joint costs allocated	$225,000	$200,000	$(25,000)	$ 400,000

15-24 (cont'd)

The negative joint-cost allocation to Product Z illustrates one "unusual" feature of the constant gross-margin percentage NRV method: some products may receive negative cost allocations so that all individual products have the same gross-margin percentage.

Income Statement

	X	Y	Z	Total
Revenues, 120 × $1,500; 340 × $1,000; 475 × $700	$180,000	$340,000	$332,500	$852,500
Cost of goods sold:				
Joint costs allocated	225,000	200,000	(25,000)	400,000
Separable costs	-	-	200,000	200,000
Production costs	225,000	200,000	175,000	600,000
Deduct ending inventory,				
60%; 15%; 5% of production costs	135,000	30,000	8,750	173,750
Cost of goods sold	90,000	170,000	166,250	426,250
Gross margin	$ 90,000	$170,000	$166,250	$426,250
Gross-margin percentage	50%	50%	50%	50%

Summary

	X	Y	Z	Total
a. NRV method:				
Inventories on balance sheet	$108,000	$ 24,000	$ 13,000	$145,000
Cost of goods sold on income statement	72,000	136,000	247,000	455,000
				$600,000
b. Constant gross-margin percentage NRV method				
Inventories on balance sheet	$135,000	$ 30,000	$ 8,750	$173,750
Cost of goods sold on income statement	90,000	170,000	166,250	426,250
				$600,000

2. Gross-margin percentages:

	X	Y	Z
NRV method	60%	60%	25.71%
Constant gross-margin percentage NRV	50%	50%	50.00%

15-24 (cont'd)

SOLUTION EXHIBIT 15-24

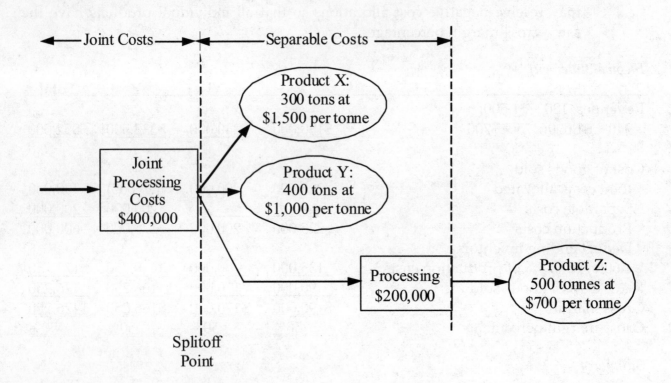

15-26 (30 min.) Accounting for a main product and a byproduct.

		Production Method	Sales Method
1.	Revenues		
	Main product	$640,000[a]	$640,000
	Byproduct	–	28,000[d]
	Total revenues	640,000	668,000
	Cost of goods sold		
	Total manufacturing costs	480,000	480,000
	Deduct value of byproduct production	40,000[b]	0
	Net manufacturing costs	440,000	480,000
	Deduct main product inventory	88,000[c]	96,000[e]
	Cost of goods sold	352,000	384,000
	Gross margin	$288,000	$284,000

[a] 32,000 × $20.00
[b] 8,000 × $5.00
[c] (8,000/40,000) × $440,000 = $88,000

[d] 5,600 × $5.00
[e] (8,000/40,000) × $480,000 = $96,000

		Production Method	Sales Method
2.	Main Product	$88,000	$96,000
	Byproduct	12,000[a]	0

[a] Ending inventory shown at unrealized selling price.
BI + Production – Sales = EI
0 + 8,000 – 5,600 = 2,400 kilograms
Ending inventory = 2,400 kilograms × $5 per kilogram = $12,000

15-28 (40–60 min.) **Comparison of alternative joint-cost allocation methods, further-processing decision, chocolate products.**

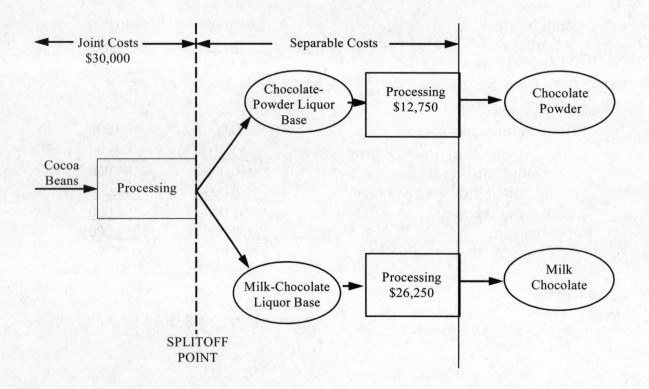

1   a. Sales value at splitoff method:

	Chocolate-Powder/ Liquor Base	Milk-Chocolate/ Liquor Base	Total
Sales value of total production at splitoff,			
600 × $21; 900 × $26	$12,600	$23,400	$36,000
Weighting, $12,600; $23,400 ÷ $36,000	0.35	0.65	
Joint costs allocated,			
0.35; 0.65 × $30,000	$10,500	$19,500	$30,000

15-28 (cont'd)

b.

Physical-measure method:

Physical measure of total production

	600 litres	900 litres	1,500 litres
(15,000 ÷ 1,500) × 60; 90	600 litres	900 litres	1,500 litres
Weighting, 600; 900 ÷ 1,500	0.40	0.60	
Joint costs allocated,			
0.40; 0.60 × $30,000	$12,000	$18,000	$30,000

c.   Net realizable value method:

	Chocolate Powder	Milk Chocolate	Total
Final sales value of total production,			
6,000 × $4; 10,200 × $5	$24,000	$51,000	$75,000
Deduct separable costs	12,750	26,250	39,000
Net realizable value at splitoff point	$11,250	$24,750	$36,000
Weighting, $11,250; $24,750 ÷ $36,000	0.3125	0.6875	
Joint costs allocated,			
0.3125; 0.6875 × $30,000	$ 9,375		$30,000
		$20,625	

d.   Constant gross-margin percentage NRV method:

Step 1:

Final sales value of total production, (6,000 × $4) + (10,200 × $5)	$75,000
Deduct joint and separable costs, ($30,000 + $12,750 + $26,250)	69,000
Gross margin	$ 6,000
Gross-margin percentage ($6,000 ÷ $75,000)	8%

Step 2:

	Chocolate Powder	Milk Chocolate	Total
Final sales value of total production,			
6,000 × $4; 10,200 × $5	$24,000	$51,000	$75,000
Deduct gross margin, using overall			
gross-margin percentage of sales (8%)	1,920	4,080	6,000
Total production costs	22,080	46,920	69,000

15-28 (cont'd)

Step 3:

	Chocolate Powder	Milk Chocolate	Total
Deduct separable costs	12,750	26,250	39,000
Joint costs allocated	$ 9,330	$20,670	$30,000

2.		Chocolate Powder	Milk Chocolate	Total
a.	Revenues	$24,000	$51,000	$75,000
	Joint costs	10,500	19,500	30,000
	Separable costs	12,750	26,250	39,000
	Total cost of goods sold	23,250	45,750	69,000
	Gross margin	$ 750	$ 5,250	$ 6,000
	Gross-margin percentage	3.125%	10.294%	8%
b.	Revenues	$24,000	$51,000	$75,000
	Joint costs	12,000	18,000	30,000
	Separable costs	12,750	26,250	39,000
	Total cost of goods sold	24,750	44,250	69,000
	Gross margin	$ (750)	$ 6,750	$ 6,000
	Gross-margin percentage	(3.125)%	13.235%	8%
c.	Revenues	$24,000	$51,000	$75,000
	Joint costs	9,375	20,625	30,000
	Separable costs	12,750	26,250	39,000
	Total cost of goods sold	22,125	46,875	69,000
	Gross margin	$ 1,875	$ 4,125	$ 6,000
	Gross-margin percentage	7.813%	8.088%	8%
d.	Revenues	$24,000	$51,000	$75,000
	Joint costs	9,330	20,670	30,000
	Separable costs	12,750	26,250	39,000
	Total cost of goods sold	22,080	46,920	69,000
	Gross margin	$ 1,920	$ 4,080	$ 6,000
	Gross-margin percentage	8%	8%	8%

15-28 (cont'd)

3.   Further processing of chocolate-powder liquor base into chocolate powder:

Incremental revenue, $24,000 – $12,600	$11,400
Incremental costs	12,750
Incremental operating income from further processing	$ (1,350)

Further processing of milk-chocolate liquor base into milk chocolate:

Incremental revenue, $51,000 – $23,400	$27,600
Incremental costs	26,250
Incremental operating income from further processing	$ 1,350

Chocolate Factory could increase operating income by $1,350 (to $7,350) if chocolate-powder liquor base is sold at the splitoff point and if milk-chocolate liquor base is further processed into milk chocolate.

15-30 (40 min.)   Alternative methods of joint-cost allocation, product-mix decision.

1.   Joint costs = $360,000

a.   **Sales value at splitoff method**

		Select	White	Knotty	Total
1.	Sales value at splitoff (30,000 × $9.60, 50,000 × $4.80, 20,000 × $3.60)	$288,000	$240,000	$72,000	$600,000
2.	Weighting (288/600, 240/600, 72/600)	0.48	0.40	0.12	1.00
3.	Joint cost allocated (0.48, 0.40, 0.12 × 360,000)	$172,800	$144,000	$43,200	$360,000
4.	Total cost computation				
	Joint costs	$172,800	$144,000	$43,200	$360,000
	Separable processing	72,000	108,000	18,000	198,000
	Total costs	$244,800	$252,000	$61,200	$558,000
	Total units	25,000	40,000	15,000	
Unit cost		$9.792	$6.30	$4.08	

15-30 (cont'd)

b. **Physical-measure method**

		Select	White	Knotty	Total
1.	Physical measure of production (board feet)	30,000	50,000	20,000	100,000
2.	Weighting (30/100, 50/100, 20/100)	0.30	0.50	0.20	1.00
3.	Joint costs allocated (0.30, 0.50, 0.20 × $360,000)	$108,000	$180,000	$72,000	$360,000
4.	Total cost computation				
	Joint costs	$108,000	$180,000	$72,000	$360,000
	Separable processing	72,000	108,000	18,000	198,000
	Total costs	$180,000	$288,000	$90,000	$558,000
	Total units	25,000	40,000	15,000	
	Unit cost	$7.20	$7.20	$6.00	

c. **Estimated net realizable value method**

		Select	White	Knotty	Total
1.	Expected final sales value of production (25,000 × $19.20, 40,000 × $10.80, 15,000 × $8.40)	$480,000	$432,000	$126,000	$1,038,000
2.	Deduct expected separable costs	72,000	108,000	18,000	198,000
3.	Estimated NRV at splitoff	$408,000	$324,000	$108,000	$ 840,000
4.	Weighting (408/840, 324/840, 108/840)	0.4857	0.3857	0.1286	1.0000
5.	Joint costs allocated (0.4857, 0.3857, 0.1286 × $360,000)	$174,852	$138,852	$46,296	$360,000
	Total cost computation				
	Joint costs	$174,852	$138,852	$46,296	$360,000
	Separable processing	72,000	108,000	18,000	198,000
	Total costs	$246,852	$246,852	$64,296	$558,000
	Total units	25,000	40,000	15,000	
	Unit cost	$9.87	$6.17	$4.29	

15-30 (cont'd)

2.

		Select	White	Knotty	Total
a.	Sales value at splitoff ($9.792 × 1,000, $6.30 × 2,000, $4.08 × 500)	$9,792	$12,600	$2,040	$24,432
b.	Physical measure ($7.20 × 1,000, $7.20 × 2,000, $6.00 × 500)	7,200	14,400	3,000	24,600
(c)	Estimated NRV ($9.87 × 1,000), $6.17 × 2,000, $4.29 × 500)	9,870	12,340	2,145	24,355

3. **Raw to Select Oak**

Incremental revenues: $480,000 – $288,000	$192,000
Deduct incremental processing costs	72,000
Increase in operating income	$120,000

Raw to White Oak

Incremental revenues: $432,000 – $240,000	$192,000
Deduct incremental processing costs	108,000
Increase in operating income	$ 84,000

Raw to Knotty Oak

Incremental revenues: $126,000 – $72,000	$54,000
Deduct incremental processing costs	18,000
Increase in operating income	$36,000

Northwest Forestry is maximizing its total August 2010 operating income by fully processing each raw oak product into its finished product form.

15-32 (25 min.) Joint-cost allocation, relevant costs (R. Capettini, adapted).

1. The "four-day progressive product trimming" ignores the fundamental point that the $360 cost to buy the pig is a joint cost. A pig is purchased as a whole. The butcher's challenge is to maximize the total revenues minus incremental costs (assumed zero) from the sale of all products.

At each stage, the decision made ignores the general rule that product emphasis decisions should consider relevant revenues and relevant costs. Allocated joint costs are not relevant. For example, the Day 2 decision to drop bacon ignores the fact that the $360 joint cost has been paid to acquire the whole pig. The $172.80 of revenues are relevant inflows. This same position also holds for the Day 3 and Day 4 decisions.

15-32 (cont'd)

2. The revenue amounts are the figures to use in the sales value at splitoff method:

Product	Revenue	Joint Costs Weighting	Allocated
Pork chops	$144.00	0.2899	$104.36
Ham	180.00	0.3623	130.43
Bacon	172.80	0.3478	125.21
	$496.80	1.0000	$360.00

3. No. The decision to sell or not sell individual products should consider relevant revenues and relevant costs. In the butcher's context, the relevant costs would be the additional time and other incidentals to take each pig part and make it a salable product. The relevant revenues would be the difference between the selling price at the consumer level for the pig parts and what the butcher may receive for the whole pig.

15-34 (40 min.) **Joint-cost allocation.**

1.

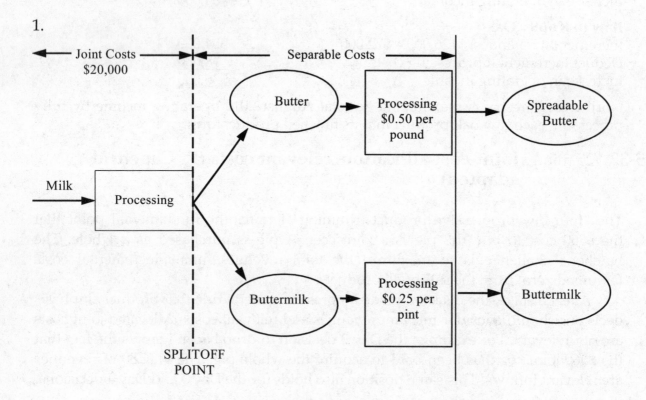

15-34 (cont'd)

a.
Physical-measure method:

	Butter	Buttermilk	Total
Physical measure of total production (10,000 lbs × 2; 20,000 qts × 4)	20,000 cups	80,000 cups	100,000 cups
Weighting, 20,000; 80,000 ÷ 100,000	0.20	0.80	
Joint costs allocated, 0.20; 0.80 × $20,000	$4,000	$16,000	$20,000

b. Sales value at splitoff method:

	Butter	Buttermilk	Total
Sales value of total production at splitoff, 10,000 × $2; 20,000 × $1.5	$20,000	$30,000	$50,000
Weighting, $20,000; $30,000 ÷ $50,000	0.40	0.60	
Joint costs allocated, 0.40; 0.60 × $20,000	$ 8,000	$12,000	$20,000

c. Net realizable value method:

	Butter	Buttermilk	Total
Final sales value of total production, 20,000 × $2.50; 20,000 × $1.50	$50,000	$30,000	$80,000
Deduct separable costs	5,000	0	5,000
Net realizable value	$45,000	$30,000	$75,000
Weighting, $45,000; $30,000 ÷ $75,000	0.60	0.40	
Joint costs allocated, 0.60; 0.40 × $20,000	$12,000	$ 8,000	$20,000

d. Constant gross-margin percentage NRV method:

Step 1:

Final sales value of total production,	$80,000
Deduct joint and separable costs, ($20,000 + $5,000)	25,000
Gross margin	$55,000
Gross-margin percentage ($55,000 ÷ $80,000)	68.75%

15-34 (cont'd)

Step 2:

	Butter	Buttermilk	Total
Final sales value of total production (see 1c.)	$50,000	$30,000	$80,000
Deduct gross margin, using overall gross-margin percentage of sales (68.75%)	34,375	20,625	55,000
Total production costs	15,625	9,375	25,000

Step 3:

Deduct separable costs	5,000	0	5,000
Joint costs allocated	$10,625	$ 9,375	$20,000

2. Advantages and disadvantages:

Physical-Measure
  Advantage: Low information needs. Only knowledge of joint cost and physical distribution is needed.
  Disadvantage: Allocation is unrelated to the revenue-generating ability of products.

Sales Value at Splitoff
  Advantage: Considers market value of products as basis for allocating joint cost. Relative sales value serves as a proxy for relative benefit received by each product from the joint cost.
  Disadvantage: Uses selling price at the time of splitoff even if product is not sold by the firm in that form. Selling price may not exist for product at splitoff.

Net Realizable Value
  Advantages: Allocates joint costs using ultimate net value of each product; applicable when the option to process further exists.
  Disadvantages: High information needs. Makes assumptions about expected outcomes of future processing decisions.

15-34 (cont'd)

Constant Gross-Margin percentage method

Advantage: Since it is necessary to produce all joint products, they all look equally profitable.

Disadvantages: High information needs. All products are not necessarily equally profitable; method may lead to negative cost allocations so that unprofitable products are subsidized by profitable ones.

3. When selling prices for all products exist at splitoff, the sales value at splitoff method is the preferred technique. It is a relatively simple technique that depends on a common basis for cost allocation: revenues. It is better than the physical measure method because it considers the relative market values of the products generated by the joint cost when seeking to allocate it (which is a surrogate for the benefits received by each product from the joint cost). Further, the sales value at splitoff method has advantages over the NRV method and the constant gross margin percentage method because it does not penalize managers by charging more for developing profitable products using the output at splitoff, and it requires no assumptions about future processing activities and selling prices.

15-36 (20 min.) Joint-cost allocation with a byproduct.

1. Sales value at splitoff method: Byproduct recognized at time of production method

Joint cost to be charged to joint products = Joint cost − NRV of Byproduct
$$= \$10,000 - 1000 \text{ tonnes} \times 20\% \times 0.25 \text{ vats} \times \$60$$
$$= \$10,000 - 50 \text{ vats} \times \$60$$
$$= \$ 7,000$$

	Grade A Coal	Grade B Coal	Total
Sales value of coal at splitoff, 1,000 tonnes × 0.4 × $100; 1,000 tonnes × 0.4 × $60	$40,000	$24,000	$64,000
Weighting, $40,000; $24,000 ÷ $64,000	0.625	0.375	
Joint costs allocated, 0.625; 0.375 × $7,000	$ 4,375	$ 2,625	$ 7,000
Gross margin (Sales revenue − Allocated cost)	$35,625	$21,375	$57,000

15-36 (cont'd)

2. Sales value at splitoff method: Byproduct recognized at time of sale method

    Joint cost to be charged to joint products = Total joint cost = $10,000

	Grade A Coal	Grade B Coal	Total
Sales value of coal splitoff,			
1,000 tonnes × .4 × $100; 1,000 tonnes × .4 × $60	$40,000	$24,000	$64,000
Weighting, $40,000; $24,000 ÷ $64,000	0.625	0.375	
Joint costs allocated,			
0.625; 0.375 × $10,000	$ 6,250	$ 3,750	$10,000
Gross margin (Sales revenue − Allocated cost)	$33,750	$20,250	$54,000

    Since the entire production is sold during the period, the overall gross margin is the same under the production and sales methods. In particular, under the sales method, the $3,000 received from the sale of the coal tar is added to the overall revenues, so that Cumberland's overall gross margin is $57,000, as in the production method.

3. The production method of accounting for the byproduct is only appropriate if Cumberland is positive they can sell the byproduct and positive of the selling price. Moreover, Cumberland should view the byproduct's contribution to the firm as material enough to find it worthwhile to record and track any inventory that may arise. The sales method is appropriate if either the disposition of the byproduct is unsure or the selling price is unknown, or if the amounts involved are so negligible as to make it economically infeasible for Cumberland to keep track of byproduct inventories.

15-38 (30 min.)   Accounting for a byproduct.

1.   Byproduct recognized at time of production:
      Joint cost = ($300 × 50) + $10,000 = $25,000
      Joint cost charged to main product = Joint cost – NRV of byproduct
                                        = $25,000 – (6 × 50 scarves × $25)
                                        = $25,000 – (300 scarves × $25)
                                        = $17,500

Inventoriable cost of main product = $\dfrac{\$17,500}{1,500 \text{ blouses}}$ = $11.67 per blouse

Inventoriable cost of byproduct = NRV = $25 per scarf

Gross Margin Calculation under Production Method

Revenues	
Main product: Blouses (1,200 blouses × $90)	$108,000
Byproduct: Scarves	0
	108,000
Cost of goods sold	
Main product: Blouses (1,200 blouses × $11.67)	14,000
Gross margin	$ 94,000
Gross-margin percentage ($94,000 ÷ $108,000)	87.04%

Inventoriable costs (end of period):
   Main product: Blouses (300 blouses × $11.67) = $3,500
   Byproduct: Scarves (40 scarves × $25) = $1,000

15-38 (cont'd)

2. Byproduct recognized at time of sale:

    Joint cost to be charged to main product = Total joint cost = $25,000

    Inventoriable cost of main product = $\dfrac{\$25,000}{1,500 \text{ blouses}}$ = $16.67 per blouse

    Inventoriable cost of byproduct = $0

Gross Margin Calculation under Sales Method	
Revenues	
Main product: Blouses (1,200 blouses × $90)	$108,000
Byproduct: Scarves (260 scarves × $25)	6,500
	114,500
Cost of goods sold	
Main product: Blouses (1,200 blouses × $16.67)	20,000
Gross margin	$ 94,500
Gross-margin percentage ($94,500 ÷ $114,500)	82.53%

Inventoriable costs (end of period):

    Main product: Blouses (300 blouses × $16.67) = $5,000

    Byproduct: Scarves (40 scarves × $0) = $0

3. a. Byproduct—production method journal entries

    i) At time of production:

Work-in-Process Inventory	25,000	
Accounts Payable, etc.		25,000

For byproduct:

Finished Goods Inv – Scarves	7,500	
Work-in-Process Inventory		7,500

For main product

Finished Goods Inv – Blouses	17,500	
Work-in-Process Inventory		17,500

15-38 (cont'd)

ii) At time of sale:

<u>For byproduct</u>

Cash or A/R	6,500	
Finished Goods Inv – Scarves		6,500

<u>For main product</u>

Cash or A/R	108,000	
Sales Revenue – Blouses		108,000

Cost of goods sold – Blouses	14,000	
Finished Goods Inv – Blouses		14,000

b. Byproduct — sales method journal entries

i) At time of production:

Work-in-Process Inventory	25,000	
Accounts Payable, etc.		25,000

<u>For byproduct:</u>
No entry

<u>For main product</u>

Finished Goods Inv – Blouses	25,000	
Work-in-Process Inventory		25,000

ii) At time of sale:

<u>For byproduct</u>

Cash or A/R	6,500	
Sales Revenue – Scarves		6,500

<u>For joint product</u>

Cash or A/R	108,000	
Sales Revenue – Blouses		108,000

Cost of goods sold - Blouses	20,000	
Finished Goods Inv – Blouses		20,000

339

15-40 (20-30 min.) **Joint-product/byproduct distinctions, ethics (continuation of 15-39).**

1. The 2010 method gives Princess managers relatively little discretion vis-à-vis the pre-2010 method. The 2010 method recognizes all four products in the accounting system at the time of production.

    The pre-2010 method recognizes only two products (apple slices and applesauce) at the time of production. Consider the data in the question. The $72,000 of joint costs would be allocated as follows (using the $72,000 and $43,200 estimated NRV amounts):

    Apple Slices: $\dfrac{\$72,000}{\$115,200} \times \$72,000 = \$45,000$

    Applesauce: $\dfrac{\$43,200}{\$115,200} \times \$72,000 = \$27,000$

    The gross margin on each product is:

    Apple Slices: $\dfrac{(\$85,536 - \$45,000 - \$13,536)}{\$85,536} = 31.57\%$

    Applesauce: $\dfrac{(\$53,460 - \$27,000 - \$10,260)}{\$53,460} = 30.30\%$

    The gross margins on the two "byproducts" are:

    Apple Juice: $\dfrac{\$32,400 - \$3,600}{\$32,400} = 88.89\%$

    Animal Feed: $\dfrac{\$3,240 - \$840}{\$3,240} = 74.07\%$

    With the pre-2010 method, managers have flexibility as to when to sell the apple juice and the animal feed. Both can be kept in cold storage until needed. If there is a need for a large "dose" of gross margin at year end to meet the target ratio, high gross margins from apple juice or animal feed can be drawn on to help achieve the target.

2. The controller could examine the sales patterns of apple juice and animal feed at year end. Do managers who have ratios from existing sales below the target sell apple juice and animal feed inventories to achieve the target ratio? Do managers who have ratios above the target put apple juice and animal feed production into inventory so as to provide a "cushion" for subsequent years?

15-40 (cont'd)

One piece of evidence here would be physical inventory holding patterns on a monthly basis. If there were a different pattern of inventory holding for the two byproducts than for the two joint products, there would be grounds for further investigating whether managers are abusing the bonus system.

3. Using the estimated net realizable value method with all products treated as a joint product would reduce "gaming" behaviour by managers with respect to bonus payments. The estimated net realizable value of all four products ($72,000 + $43,200 + $28,800 + $2,400 = $146,400) would be used to allocate the $72,000 joint cost:

Slices: $\dfrac{\$72,000}{\$146,400} \times \$72,000$ = $35,410

Sauce: $\dfrac{\$43,200}{\$146,400} \times \$72,000$ = $21,246

Juice: $\dfrac{\$28,800}{\$146,400} \times \$72,000$ = $14,164

Feed: $\dfrac{\$2,400}{\$146,400} \times \$72,000$ = $ 1,180

$72,000

A second method that could be used in conjunction with that discussed above is to have an inventory-holding charge. If managers build up inventory, they would be penalized. This would reduce incentives to use inventory to manipulate reported income to meet target ratios.

CHAPTER 16
REVENUES, SALES VARIANCES, AND
CUSTOMER PROFITABILITY ANALYSIS

16-2 The *stand-alone revenue-allocation method* uses information about individual products in their separate markets when allocating bundled revenues to individual products. The *incremental revenue-allocation method* ranks the individual products in a bundle and then uses this ranking to allocate the bundled revenues to these individual products.

16-4 A dispute over the allocation of revenues of a bundled product could be resolved by (a) having an agreement that outlines the preferred method in the case of a dispute or (b) having a third party (such as the company president or an independent arbitrator) make a decision.

16-6 The total sales-mix variance arises from differences in the budgeted contribution margin of the actual and budgeted sales mix. The composite unit concept enables the effect of individual product changes to be summarized in a single intuitive number by using weights based on the mix of individual units in the actual and budgeted mix of products sold.

16-8 The sales-quantity variance can be decomposed into (a) a market-size variance (the actual total market-size change from that budgeted) and (b) a market-share variance (the actual market-share change from that budgeted). Both variances use the budgeted average selling price per unit, when the focus is on revenues.

16-10 Customer profitability analysis highlights to managers how individual customers differentially contribute to total profitability. It helps managers to see whether customers who contribute sizably to total profitability are receiving a comparable level of attention from the organization.

16-12 No. A customer profitability profile highlights differences in the current period's profitability across customers. Dropping customers should be the last resort. An unprofitable customer in one period may be highly profitable in subsequent future periods. Moreover, costs assigned to individual customers need not be purely variable with respect to short-run elimination of sales to those customers. Thus, when customers are dropped, costs assigned to those customers may not disappear in the short run.

16-14 A process where the inputs are nonsubstitutable leaves workers no discretion as to the components to use. A process where the inputs are substitutable means there is discretion about the exact number and type of inputs or about the weighting of inputs where the number and type is mandated.

16-16 (10-15 min.) Allocation of Common Costs

1. a. Stand-alone method (costs are in thousands):

City	Separate Cost	Percentage	Joint Cost	Allocation
St. Anne	$2,100	$2,100 ÷ $7,000=0.3	$5,000	$1,500
St. Teresa	1,400	$1,400 ÷ $7,000=0.2	5,000	1,000
St. Steven	3,500	$3,500 ÷ $7,000=0.5	5,000	2,500
	$7,000			$5,000

b. Incremental method (cities ranked in order of most waste to least waste):

	Allocated Cost	Cost Remaining to Allocate
St. Steven	$3,500	$1,500 ($5,000 − $3,500)
St. Anne	1,500	0 ($1,500 − $1,500)
St. Teresa	0	0

2. In this situation, the stand-alone method is the better method because the weights it uses for allocation are based on the cost for each user as a separate entity. The citizens of St. Steven would not consider the incremental method fair because they would be subsidizing the other cities (especially St. Teresa). St. Anne is indifferent across the two methods; its citizens save $600,000 over the stand-alone cost in either case. While the citizens of St. Teresa would clearly prefer the incremental allocation method and might seek to justify it because they generate the least amount of waste, they should understand that citizens of the other cities would believe it is not fair.

16-18 (30–40 min.) Variance analysis, multiple products.

1.

$$\text{Sales-volume variance} = \left(\begin{array}{c} \text{Actual sales} \\ \text{quantity in units} \end{array} - \begin{array}{c} \text{Budgeted sales} \\ \text{quantity in units} \end{array} \right) \times \begin{array}{c} \text{Budgeted contribution} \\ \text{margin per ticket} \end{array}$$

Lower-tier tickets = (3,300 – 4,000) × $20 = $14,000 U
Upper-tier tickets = (7,700 – 6,000) × $ 5 = <u>8,500</u> F
All tickets <u>$ 5,500</u> U

2.

$$\text{Budgeted average contribution margin per unit} = \frac{(4,000 \times \$20) + (6,000 \times \$5)}{10,000}$$

$$= \frac{\$80,000 + \$30,000}{10,000} = \frac{\$110,000}{10,000}$$

$$= \$11 \text{ per unit (seat sold)}$$

Sales-mix percentages:

	Budgeted	**Actual**
Lower-tier	$\frac{4,000}{10,000} = 0.40$	$\frac{3,300}{11,000} = 0.30$
Upper-tier	$\frac{6,000}{10,000} = 0.60$	$\frac{7,700}{11,000} = 0.70$

16-18 (cont'd)

Solution Exhibit 16-18 presents the sales-volume, sales-quantity, and sales-mix variances for lower-tier tickets, upper-tier tickets, and in total for the Penguins in 2010.

The sales-quantity variances can also be computed as:

$$\begin{array}{l}\text{Sales-quantity}\\ \text{variance}\end{array} = \left(\begin{array}{l}\text{Actual units}\\ \text{of all tickets}\\ \text{sold}\end{array} - \begin{array}{l}\text{Budgeted units}\\ \text{of all tickets}\\ \text{sold}\end{array}\right) \times \begin{array}{l}\text{Budgeted}\\ \text{sales-mix} \\ \text{percentage}\end{array} \times \begin{array}{l}\text{Budgeted}\\ \text{cont. margin}\\ \text{per ticket}\end{array}$$

The sales-quantity variances are:

Lower-tier tickets =	(11,000 – 10,000) × 0.40 × $20	=	$ 8,000 F
Upper-tier tickets =	(11,000 – 10,000) × 0.60 × $ 5	=	3,000 F
All tickets			$11,000 F

The sales-mix variance can also be computed as:

$$\begin{array}{l}\text{Sales-mix}\\ \text{variance}\end{array} = \begin{array}{l}\text{Actual units}\\ \text{of all tickets}\\ \text{sold}\end{array} \times \left(\begin{array}{l}\text{Actual}\\ \text{sales-mix}\\ \text{percentage}\end{array} - \begin{array}{l}\text{Budgeted}\\ \text{sales-mix}\\ \text{percentage}\end{array}\right) \times \begin{array}{l}\text{Budgeted}\\ \text{contribution margin}\\ \text{per ticket}\end{array}$$

The sales-mix variances are

Lower-tier tickets =	11,000 × (0.30 – 0.40) × $20 =		$22,000 U
Upper-tier tickets =	11,000 × (0.70 – 0.60) × $ 5 =		5,500 F
All tickets			$16,500 U

3. The Penguins increased average attendance by 10% per game. However, there was a sizable shift from lower-tier seats (budgeted contribution margin of $20 per seat) to the upper-tier seats (budgeted contribution margin of $5 per seat). The net result: the actual contribution margin was $5,500 below the budgeted contribution margin.

16-18 (cont'd)

SOLUTION EXHIBIT 16-18
Columnar Presentation of Sales-Volume, Sales-Quantity, and Sales-Mix Variances for Penguins

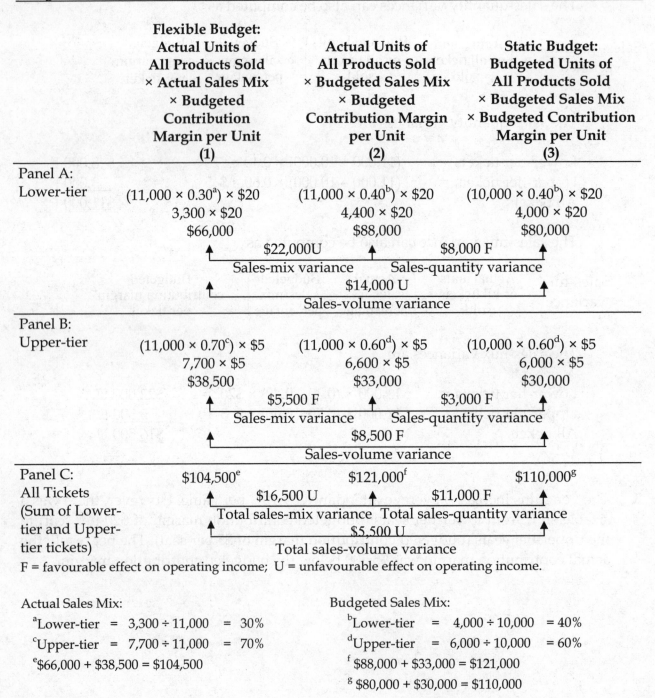

	Flexible Budget: Actual Units of All Products Sold × Actual Sales Mix × Budgeted Contribution Margin per Unit (1)	Actual Units of All Products Sold × Budgeted Sales Mix × Budgeted Contribution Margin per Unit (2)	Static Budget: Budgeted Units of All Products Sold × Budgeted Sales Mix × Budgeted Contribution Margin per Unit (3)
Panel A: Lower-tier	$(11{,}000 \times 0.30^a) \times \$20$ $3{,}300 \times \$20$ $\$66{,}000$	$(11{,}000 \times 0.40^b) \times \$20$ $4{,}400 \times \$20$ $\$88{,}000$	$(10{,}000 \times 0.40^b) \times \$20$ $4{,}000 \times \$20$ $\$80{,}000$

$\$22{,}000$U — Sales-mix variance $\$8{,}000$ F — Sales-quantity variance

$\$14{,}000$ U — Sales-volume variance

Panel B: Upper-tier	$(11{,}000 \times 0.70^c) \times \$5$ $7{,}700 \times \$5$ $\$38{,}500$	$(11{,}000 \times 0.60^d) \times \$5$ $6{,}600 \times \$5$ $\$33{,}000$	$(10{,}000 \times 0.60^d) \times \$5$ $6{,}000 \times \$5$ $\$30{,}000$

$\$5{,}500$ F — Sales-mix variance $\$3{,}000$ F — Sales-quantity variance

$\$8{,}500$ F — Sales-volume variance

Panel C: All Tickets (Sum of Lower-tier and Upper-tier tickets)	$\$104{,}500^e$	$\$121{,}000^f$	$\$110{,}000^g$

$\$16{,}500$ U — Total sales-mix variance $\$11{,}000$ F — Total sales-quantity variance

$\$5{,}500$ U — Total sales-volume variance

F = favourable effect on operating income; U = unfavourable effect on operating income.

Actual Sales Mix:
^{a}Lower-tier = $3{,}300 \div 11{,}000$ = 30%
^{c}Upper-tier = $7{,}700 \div 11{,}000$ = 70%
$^e\$66{,}000 + \$38{,}500 = \$104{,}500$

Budgeted Sales Mix:
^{b}Lower-tier = $4{,}000 \div 10{,}000$ = 40%
^{d}Upper-tier = $6{,}000 \div 10{,}000$ = 60%
$^f\$88{,}000 + \$33{,}000 = \$121{,}000$
$^g\$80{,}000 + \$30{,}000 = \$110{,}000$

16-20 (60 min.) Variance analysis, multiple products.

1. Budget for 2010

	Selling Price (1)	Variable Cost per Unit (2)	Contrib. Margin per Unit (3) = (1) – (2)	Units Sold (4)	Sales Mix (5)	Contribution Margin (6) = (3) × (4)
Kola	$6.00	$4.00	$2.00	400,000	16%	$ 800,000
Limor	4.00	2.80	1.20	600,000	24	720,000
Orlem	7.00	4.50	2.50	1,500,000	60	3,750,000
Total				2,500,000	100%	$5,270,000

Actual for 2010

	Selling Price (1)	Variable Cost per Unit (2)	Contrib. Margin per Unit (3) = (1) – (2)	Units Sold (4)	Sales Mix (5)	Contribution Margin (6) = (3) × (4)
Kola	$6.20	$4.50	$1.70	480,000	16%	$ 816,000
Limor	4.25	2.75	1.50	900,000	30	1,350,000
Orlem	6.80	4.60	2.20	1,620,000	54	3,564,000
Total				3,000,000	100%	$5,730,000

Solution Exhibit 16-20 presents the sales-volume, sales-quantity, and sales-mix variances for each product and in total for 2010.

$$\text{Sales-volume variance} = \left(\begin{array}{c} \text{Actual} \\ \text{quantity of} \\ \text{units sold} \end{array} - \begin{array}{c} \text{Budgeted} \\ \text{quantity of} \\ \text{units sold} \end{array} \right) \times \begin{array}{c} \text{Budgeted} \\ \text{contribution margin} \\ \text{per unit} \end{array}$$

Kola	= (480,000 – 400,000) × $2.00	=	$160,000 F
Limor	= (900,000 – 600,000) × $1.20	=	360,000 F
Orlem	= (1,620,000 – 1,500,000) × $2.50	=	300,000 F
Total			$820,000 F

$$\text{Sales-quantity variance} = \left(\begin{array}{c} \text{Actual units} \\ \text{of all products} \\ \text{sold} \end{array} - \begin{array}{c} \text{Budgeted units} \\ \text{of all products} \\ \text{sold} \end{array} \right) \times \begin{array}{c} \text{Budgeted} \\ \text{sales-mix} \\ \text{percentage} \end{array} \times \begin{array}{c} \text{Budgeted} \\ \text{contribution margin} \\ \text{per unit} \end{array}$$

Kola	= (3,000,000 – 2,500,000) × 0.16 × $2.00	=	$ 160,000 F
Limor	= (3,000,000 – 2,500,000) × 0.24 × $1.20	=	144,000 F
Orlem	= (3,000,000 – 2,500,000) × 0.60 × $2.50	=	750,000 F
Total			$1,054,000 F

16-20 (cont'd)

$$\begin{array}{ll}\text{Sales-mix} \\ \text{variance}\end{array} = \begin{array}{l}\text{Actual units} \\ \text{of all products} \\ \text{sold}\end{array} \times \left[\begin{array}{ll}\text{Actual} & \text{Budgeted} \\ \text{sales-mix} - \text{sales-mix} \\ \text{percentage} & \text{percentage}\end{array}\right] \times \begin{array}{l}\text{Budgeted} \\ \text{contrib. margin} \\ \text{per unit}\end{array}$$

Kola	=	$3{,}000{,}000 \times (0.16 - 0.16) \times \$2.00$	=	$ 0
Limor	=	$3{,}000{,}000 \times (0.30 - 0.24) \times \$1.20$	=	216,000 F
Orlem	=	$3{,}000{,}000 \times (0.54 - 0.60) \times \$2.50$	=	450,000 U
Total				$234,000 U

2. The breakdown of the favourable sales-volume variance of $820,000 shows that the biggest contributor is the 500,000 unit increase in sales resulting in a favourable sales-quantity variance of $1,054,000. There is a partially offsetting unfavourable sales-mix variance of $234,000 in contribution margin.

SOLUTION EXHIBIT 16-20

Sales-Mix and Sales-Quantity Variance Analysis of Soda King for 2010

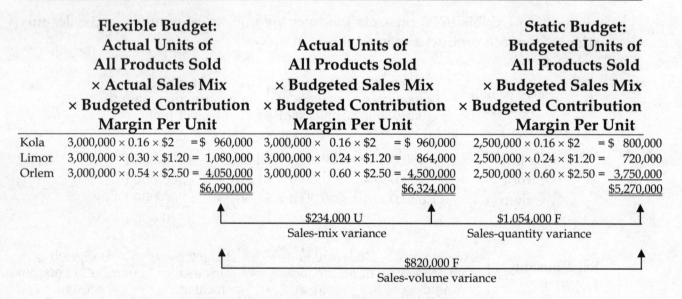

F = favourable effect on operating income; U= unfavourable effect on operating income

16-22 (20–30 min.) Customer profitability, service company.

1.

	Avery	Okie	Wizard	Grainger	Duran
Revenues	$260,000	$200,000	$322,000	$122,000	$212,000
Technician and equipment cost	182,000	175,000	225,000	107,000	178,000
Gross margin	78,000	25,000	97,000	15,000	34,000
Service call handling ($75 × 150; 240; 40; 120; 180)	11,250	18,000	3,000	9,000	13,500
Web-based parts ordering ($80 × 120; 210; 60; 150; 150)	9,600	16,800	4,800	12,000	12,000
Billing/Collection ($50 × 30; 90; 90; 60; 120)	1,500	4,500	4,500	3,000	6,000
Database maintenance ($10 × 150; 240; 40; 120; 180)	1,500	2,400	400	1,200	1,800
Customer-level operating income	$ 54,150	$ (16,700)	$ 84,300	$(10,200)	$ 700

2. Customers Ranked on Customer-Level Operating Income

Customer Code	Customer-Level Operating Income (1)	Customer Revenue (2)	Customer-Level Operating Income as a % of Revenue (3) = (1) ÷ (2)	Cumulative Customer-Level Operating Income (4)	Cumulative Customer-Level Operating Income as a % of Total Customer-Level Operating Income (5) = (4) ÷ $112,250
Wizard	$ 84,300	$ 322,000	26.18%	$ 84,300	75%
Avery	54,150	260,000	20.83%	138,450	123%
Duran	700	212,000	0.33%	139,150	124%
Grainger	(10,200)	122,000	-8.36%	128,950	115%
Okie	(16,700)	200,000	-8.35%	112,250	100%
	$112,250	$1,116,000			

16-22 (cont'd)

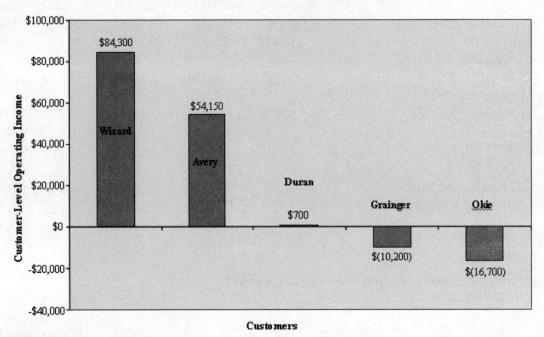

The above table and graph present the summary results. Wizard, the most profitable customer, provides 75% of total operating income. The three best customers provide 124% of IS's operating income, and the other two, by incurring losses for IS, erode the extra 24% of operating income down to IS's operating income.

3.   The options that Instant Service should consider include:
a.   Increase the attention paid to Wizard and Avery. These are "key customers," and every effort has to be made to ensure they are retained by IS. IS may well want to suggest a minor price reduction to signal how important it is in their view to provide a cost-effective service to these customers.
b.   Seek ways of reducing the costs or increasing the revenues of the problem accounts—Okie and Grainger. For example, are the copying machines at those customer locations outdated and in need of repair? If yes, an increased charge may be appropriate. Can IS provide better on-site guidelines to users about ways to reduce breakdowns?
c.   As a last resort, IS may want to consider dropping particular accounts. For example, if Grainger (or Okie) will not agree to a fee increase but has machines continually breaking down, IS may well decide that it is time not to bid on any more work for that customer. But care must then be taken to otherwise use or get rid of the excess fixed capacity created by "firing" unprofitable customers.

16-24 (20-25 min.) Direct materials efficiency, mix, and yield variances.

1 and 2.   Actual total quantity of all inputs used and actual input mix percentages for each input are as follows:

Chemical	Actual Quantity	Actual Mix Percentage		
Echol	24,080	24,080 ÷ 86,000	=	0.28
Protex	15,480	15,480 ÷ 86,000	=	0.18
Benz	36,120	36,120 ÷ 86,000	=	0.42
CT-40	10,320	10,320 ÷ 86,000	=	0.12
Total	86,000			1.00

Budgeted total quantity of all inputs allowed and budgeted input mix percentages for each input are as follows:

Chemical	Budget Quantity	Budget Mix Percentage		
Echol	25,200	25,200 ÷ 84,000	=	0.30
Protex	16,800	16,800 ÷ 84,000	=	0.20
Benz	33,600	33,600 ÷ 84,000	=	0.40
CT-40	8,400	8,400 ÷ 84,000	=	0.10
Total	84,000			1.00

Solution Exhibit 16-24 presents the total direct materials efficiency, yield, and mix variances for August 2010.

Total direct materials efficiency variance can also be computed as:

$$\begin{array}{l}\text{Direct materials} \\ \text{efficiency variance} \\ \text{for each input}\end{array} = \left(\begin{array}{l}\text{Actual} \\ \text{inputs}\end{array} - \begin{array}{l}\text{Budgeted inputs allowed} \\ \text{for actual outputs achieved}\end{array}\right) \times \begin{array}{l}\text{Budgeted} \\ \text{prices}\end{array}$$

Echol	=	(24,080 – 25,200) × \$0.22	=	\$246 F
Protex	=	(15,480 – 16,800) × \$0.47	=	620 F
Benz	=	(36,120 – 33,600) × \$0.17	=	428 U
CT-40	=	(10,320 – 8,400) × \$0.32	=	614 U
Total direct materials efficiency variance				\$176 U

16-24 (cont'd)

The total direct materials yield variance can also be computed as the sum of the direct materials yield variances for each input:

$$
\begin{pmatrix} \text{Direct} \\ \text{materials} \\ \text{yield variance} \\ \text{for each input} \end{pmatrix} = \begin{pmatrix} \text{Actual total} \\ \text{quantity of all} \\ \text{direct materials} \\ \text{inputs used} \end{pmatrix} - \begin{pmatrix} \text{Budgeted total quantity} \\ \text{of all direct materials} \\ \text{inputs allowed for} \\ \text{actual output achieved} \end{pmatrix} \times \begin{pmatrix} \text{Budgeted} \\ \text{direct materials} \\ \text{input mix} \\ \text{percentage} \end{pmatrix} \times \begin{pmatrix} \text{Budgeted} \\ \text{price of} \\ \text{direct materials} \\ \text{inputs} \end{pmatrix}
$$

Echol	=	(86,000 – 84,000)	× 0.30 × $0.22	= 2,000 × 0.30 × $0.22	=	$132 U
Protex	=	(86,000 – 84,000)	× 0.20 × $0.47	= 2,000 × 0.20 × $0.47	=	188 U
Benz	=	(86,000 – 84,000)	× 0.40 × $0.17	= 2,000 × 0.40 × $0.17	=	136 U
CT-40	=	(86,000 – 84,000)	× 0.10 × $0.32	= 2,000 × 0.10 × $0.32	=	64 U
Total direct materials yield variance						$520 U

The total direct materials mix variance can also be computed as the sum of the direct materials mix variances for each input:

$$
\begin{pmatrix} \text{Direct} \\ \text{materials} \\ \text{mix variance} \\ \text{for each input} \end{pmatrix} = \begin{pmatrix} \text{Actual} \\ \text{direct materials} \\ \text{input mix} \\ \text{percentage} \end{pmatrix} - \begin{pmatrix} \text{Budgeted} \\ \text{direct materials} \\ \text{input mix} \\ \text{percentage} \end{pmatrix} \times \begin{pmatrix} \text{Actual} \\ \text{quantity of all} \\ \text{direct materials} \\ \text{inputs used} \end{pmatrix} \times \begin{pmatrix} \text{Budgeted} \\ \text{price of} \\ \text{direct materials} \\ \text{inputs} \end{pmatrix}
$$

Echol	=	(0.28 – 0.30) × 86,000 × $0.22	= –0.02 × 86,000 × $0.22	=	$378 F
Protex	=	(0.18 – 0.20) × 86,000 × $0.47	= –0.02 × 86,000 × $0.47	=	808 F
Benz	=	(0.42 – 0.40) × 86,000 × $0.17	= 0.02 × 86,000 × $0.17	=	292 U
CT-40	=	(0.12 – 0.10) × 86,000 × $0.32	= 0.02 × 86,000 × $0.32	=	550 U
Total direct materials mix variance					$344 F

3. Energy Products used a larger total quantity of direct materials inputs than budgeted, and so showed an unfavourable yield variance. The mix variance was favourable because the actual mix contained more of the cheapest input, Benz, and less of the most costly input, Protex, than the budgeted mix. The favourable mix variance offset some, but not all, of the unfavourable yield variance—the overall efficiency variance was unfavourable. Energy Products will find it profitable to shift to the cheaper mix only if the yield from this cheaper mix can be improved. Energy Products must also consider the effect on output quality of using the cheaper mix, and the potential consequences for future revenues.

16-24 (cont'd)

SOLUTION EXHIBIT 16-24
Columnar Presentation of Direct Materials Efficiency, Yield, and Mix Variances for The Energy Products Company for August 2010

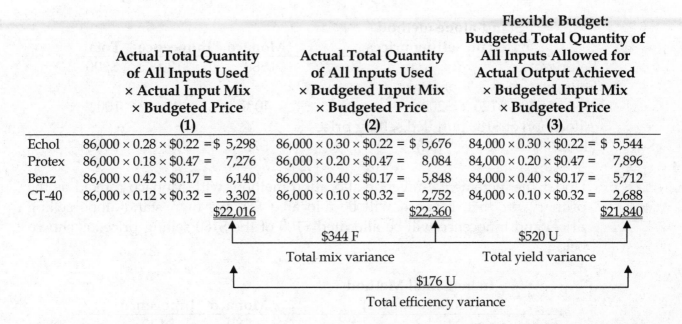

	Actual Total Quantity of All Inputs Used × Actual Input Mix × Budgeted Price (1)	Actual Total Quantity of All Inputs Used × Budgeted Input Mix × Budgeted Price (2)	Flexible Budget: Budgeted Total Quantity of All Inputs Allowed for Actual Output Achieved × Budgeted Input Mix × Budgeted Price (3)
Echol	$86,000 \times 0.28 \times \$0.22 = \$ 5,298$	$86,000 \times 0.30 \times \$0.22 = \$ 5,676$	$84,000 \times 0.30 \times \$0.22 = \$ 5,544$
Protex	$86,000 \times 0.18 \times \$0.47 = 7,276$	$86,000 \times 0.20 \times \$0.47 = 8,084$	$84,000 \times 0.20 \times \$0.47 = 7,896$
Benz	$86,000 \times 0.42 \times \$0.17 = 6,140$	$86,000 \times 0.40 \times \$0.17 = 5,848$	$84,000 \times 0.40 \times \$0.17 = 5,712$
CT-40	$86,000 \times 0.12 \times \$0.32 = \underline{3,302}$	$86,000 \times 0.10 \times \$0.32 = \underline{2,752}$	$84,000 \times 0.10 \times \$0.32 = \underline{2,688}$
	$\underline{\$22,016}$	$\underline{\$22,360}$	$\underline{\$21,840}$

$344 F
Total mix variance

$520 U
Total yield variance

$176 U
Total efficiency variance

F = favourable effect on operating income; U = unfavourable effect on operating income

16-26 (20 min.) **Revenue allocation for bundled products.**

1. a. Under the stand-alone revenue-allocation method based on selling price, Monaco will be allocated 40% of all revenues, or $72 of the bundled selling price, and Innocence will be allocated 60% of all revenues, or $108 of the bundled selling price, as shown below.

Stand-alone method, based on selling prices	Monaco	Innocence	Total
Selling price	$80	$120	$200
Selling price as a % of total ($80 ÷ $200; $120 ÷ $200)	40%	60%	100%
Allocation of $180 bundled selling price (40% × $180; 60% × $180)	$72	$108	$180

b. Under the incremental revenue-allocation method, with Monaco ranked as the primary product, Monaco will be allocated $80 (its own stand-alone selling price) and Innocence will be allocated $100 of the $180 selling price, as shown below.

Incremental Method (Monaco rank 1)	Monaco	Innocence
Selling price	$80	$120
Allocation of $180 bundled selling price ($80; $100 = $180 – $80)	$80	$100

c. Under the incremental revenue-allocation method, with Innocence ranked as the primary product, Innocence will be allocated $120 (its own stand-alone selling price) and Monaco will be allocated $60 of the $180 selling price, as shown below.

Incremental Method (Innocence rank 1)	Monaco	Innocence
Selling price	$80	$120
Allocation of $180 bundled selling price ($60 = $180 – $120; $120)	$60	$120

16-26 (cont'd)

d. Under the Shapley value method, each product will be allocated the average of its allocations in 1b and 1c, i.e., the average of its allocations when it is the primary product and when it is the secondary product, as shown below.

Shapley Value Method	Monaco	Innocence
Allocation when Monaco = Rank 1; Innocence = Rank 2 (from 1b.)	$80	$100
Allocation when Innocence = Rank 1; Monaco = Rank 2 (from 1c.)	$60	$120
Average of allocated selling price ($80 + $60) ÷ 2; ($100 + $120) ÷ 2	$70	$110

2. A summary of the allocations based on the four methods in requirement 1 is shown below.

	Stand-alone (Selling Prices)	Incremental (Monaco first)	Incremental (Innocence first)	Shapley
Monaco	$ 72	$ 80	$ 60	$ 70
Innocence	108	100	120	110
Total for L'Amour	$180	$180	$180	$180

If there is no clear indication of which product is the more "important" product, or if it can be reasonably assumed that the two products are equally important to the company's strategy, the Shapley value method is the fairest of all the methods because it averages the effect of product rank. In this particular case, note that the allocations from the stand-alone method based on selling price are reasonably similar to the allocations from the Shapley value method, so the managers at Yves may well want to use the much simpler stand-alone method. The stand-alone method also does not require ranking the products in the suite, and so it is less likely to cause debates among product managers in the Men's and Women's Fragrance divisions. If, however, one of the products (Monaco or Innocence) is clearly the product that is driving sales of the bundled product, then that product should be considered as the primary product.

16-28 (20 min.) Market-share and market-size variances (continuation of 16-27).

1.

	Actual	Budgeted
Worldwide	500,000	400,000
Aussie Info.	110,000	100,000
Market share	22%	25%

Average contribution margin per unit:
Actual = $108.80 ($11,968,000 ÷ 110,000)
Budgeted = $130.75 ($13,075,000 ÷ 100,000)

$$\begin{array}{c} \text{Market-share} \\ \text{variance} \end{array} = \begin{array}{c} \text{Actual} \\ \text{market size} \\ \text{in units} \end{array} \times \left(\begin{array}{c} \text{Actual} \\ \text{market} \\ \text{share} \end{array} - \begin{array}{c} \text{Budgeted} \\ \text{market} \\ \text{share} \end{array} \right) \times \begin{array}{c} \text{Budgeted} \\ \text{contribution margin} \\ \text{per composite unit} \\ \text{for budgeted mix} \end{array}$$

= 500,000 × (0.22 – 0.25) × $130.75
= 500,000 × (–0.03) × $130.75
= $1,961,250 U

$$\begin{array}{c} \text{Market-size} \\ \text{variance} \end{array} = \left(\begin{array}{c} \text{Actual} \\ \text{market size} \\ \text{in units} \end{array} - \begin{array}{c} \text{Budgeted} \\ \text{market size} \\ \text{in units} \end{array} \right) \times \begin{array}{c} \text{Budgeted} \\ \text{market} \\ \text{share} \end{array} \times \begin{array}{c} \text{Budgeted} \\ \text{contribution margin} \\ \text{per composite unit} \\ \text{for budgeted mix} \end{array}$$

= (500,000 – 400,000) × 0.25 × $130.75
= 100,000 × 0.25 × $130.75
= $3,268,750 F

16-28 (cont'd)

Solution Exhibit 16-28 presents the market-share variance, the market-size variance, and the sales-quantity variance for the third quarter 2010.

SOLUTION EXHIBIT 16-28

Market-Share and Market-Size Variance Analysis of Aussie Infonautics for the Third Quarter 2010.

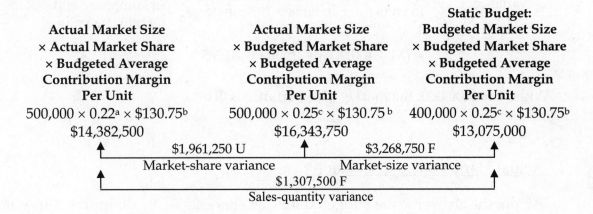

Actual Market Size × Actual Market Share × Budgeted Average Contribution Margin Per Unit	Actual Market Size × Budgeted Market Share × Budgeted Average Contribution Margin Per Unit	Static Budget: Budgeted Market Size × Budgeted Market Share × Budgeted Average Contribution Margin Per Unit
500,000 × 0.22[a] × $130.75[b]	500,000 × 0.25[c] × $130.75[b]	400,000 × 0.25[c] × $130.75[b]
$14,382,500	$16,343,750	$13,075,000

$1,961,250 U — Market-share variance $3,268,750 F — Market-size variance

$1,307,500 F — Sales-quantity variance

F = favourable effect on operating income; U = unfavourable effect on operating income

[a]Actual market share: 110,000 units ÷ 500,000 units = 0.22, or 22%
[b]Budgeted average contribution margin per unit $13,075,000 ÷ 100,000 units = $130.75 per unit
[c]Budgeted market share: 100,000 units ÷ 400,000 units = 0.25, or 25%

2. While the market share declined (from 25% to 22%), the overall increase in the total market size meant a favourable sales-quantity variance:

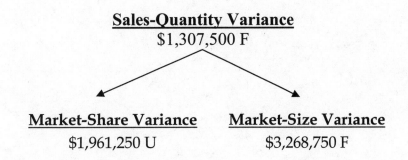

Sales-Quantity Variance
$1,307,500 F

Market-Share Variance   **Market-Size Variance**
$1,961,250 U $3,268,750 F

16-28 (cont'd)

3. The required actual market size is the budgeted market size, i.e., 400,000 units. This can easily be seen by setting up the following equation:

$$
\begin{matrix} \text{Market - size} \\ \text{variance} \end{matrix} = \left(\begin{matrix} \text{Actual} \\ \text{market size} \\ \text{in units} \end{matrix} - \begin{matrix} \text{Budgeted} \\ \text{market size} \\ \text{in units} \end{matrix} \right) \times \begin{matrix} \text{Budgeted} \\ \text{market} \\ \text{share} \end{matrix} \times \begin{matrix} \text{Budgeted} \\ \text{contribution margin} \\ \text{per composite unit} \\ \text{for budgeted mix} \end{matrix}
$$

$$
= (M - 400{,}000) \times 0.25 \times \$130.75
$$

When M = 400,000, the market-size variance is \$0.

Actual Market-Share Calculation

Again, the answer is the budgeted market share, 25%. By definition, this will hold irrespective of the actual market size. This can be seen by setting up the appropriate equation:

$$
\begin{matrix} \text{Market-share} \\ \text{variance} \end{matrix} = \begin{matrix} \text{Actual} \\ \text{market size} \\ \text{in units} \end{matrix} \times \left(\begin{matrix} \text{Actual} \\ \text{market} \\ \text{share} \end{matrix} - \begin{matrix} \text{Budgeted} \\ \text{market} \\ \text{share} \end{matrix} \right) \times \begin{matrix} \text{Budgeted} \\ \text{contribution margin} \\ \text{per composite unit} \\ \text{for budgeted mix} \end{matrix}
$$

$$
= \text{Actual market size} \times (M - 25\%) \times \$130.75
$$

When M = 25%, the market-share variance is \$0.

16-30 (15 min.) Market-share and market-size variances (continuation of 16-29).

	Actual	Budgeted
Calgary Market	960,000	1,000,000
Debbie's Delight	120,000	100,000
Market share	0.125	0.100

The budgeted average contribution margin per unit (also called budgeted contribution margin per composite unit for budgeted mix) is $2.35:

	Budgeted Contribution Margin per kg	Budgeted Sales Volume in kg	Budgeted Contribution Margin
Chocolate chip	$2.00	45,000	$ 90,000
Oatmeal raisin	2.30	25,000	57,500
Coconut	2.60	10,000	26,000
White chocolate	3.00	5,000	15,000
Macadamia nut	3.10	15,000	46,500
All cookies		100,000	$235,000

$$\text{Budgeted average contribution margin per unit} = \frac{\$235,000}{100,000} = \$2.35$$

$$\begin{pmatrix}\text{Market-size variance in contribution margin}\end{pmatrix} = \begin{pmatrix}\text{Actual market size in units} - \text{Budgeted market size in units}\end{pmatrix} \times \begin{pmatrix}\text{Budgeted market share}\end{pmatrix} \times \begin{pmatrix}\text{Budgeted average contrib. margin per unit}\end{pmatrix}$$

$$= (960,000 - 1,000,000) \times 0.100 \times \$2.35$$
$$= \$9,400 \text{ U}$$

$$\begin{pmatrix}\text{Market-share variance in contribution margin}\end{pmatrix} = \begin{pmatrix}\text{Actual market size in units}\end{pmatrix} \times \begin{pmatrix}\text{Actual market share} - \text{Budgeted market share}\end{pmatrix} \times \begin{pmatrix}\text{Budgeted average contrib. margin per unit}\end{pmatrix}$$

$$= 960,000 \times (0.125 - 0.100) \times \$2.35$$
$$= \$56,400 \text{ F}$$

16-30 (cont'd)

By increasing its actual market share from the 10% budgeted to the actual 12.5%, Debbie's Delight has a favourable market-share variance of $56,400. There is a smaller offsetting unfavourable market-size variance of $9,400 due to the 40,000 unit decline in the Calgary market (from 1,000,000 budgeted to an actual of 960,000).

Solution Exhibit 16-30 presents the sales-quantity, market-share, and market-size variances for Debbie's Delight, Inc. in August 2010.

SOLUTION EXHIBIT 16-30

Market-Share and Market-Size Variance Analysis of Debbie's Delight for August 2010

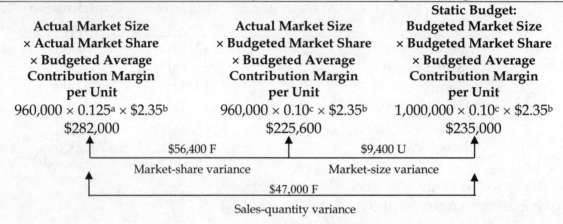

F = favourable effect on operating income; U = unfavourable effect on operating income
[a]Actual market share: 120,000 units ÷ 960,000 units = 0.125, or 12.5%
[b]Budgeted average contribution margin per unit: $235,000 ÷ 1,000,000 units = $2.35 per unit
[c]Budgeted market share: 100,000 units ÷ 1,000,000 units = 0.10, or 10%

An overview of Problems 16-29 and 16-30 is:

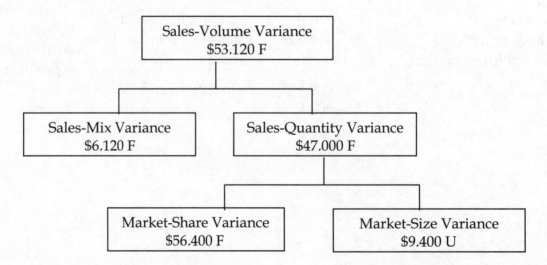

16-32 (35 min.) Materials variances: price, efficiency, mix and yield.

1.

Oak ($6 × 8 b.f.)	$	48
Pine ($2 × 12 b.f.)		24
Cost per dresser	$	72
Number of dressers		×3,000 units
Total budgeted cost		$216,000

2. Solution Exhibit 16-32A presents the total price variance ($5,246 F), the total efficiency variance ($1,280 F), and the total flexible-budget variance ($6,526 F).

Total direct materials price variance can also be computed as:

$$\begin{pmatrix} \text{Direct materials} \\ \text{price variance} \\ \text{for each input} \end{pmatrix} = \begin{pmatrix} \text{Actual} \\ \text{price of input} - \begin{array}{c}\text{Budgeted} \\ \text{price of input}\end{array} \end{pmatrix} \times \begin{array}{c}\text{Actual quantity} \\ \text{of input}\end{array}$$

Oak	=	($6.10 – $6.00) ×	23,180 =	$2,318	U
Pine	=	($1.80 – $2.00) ×	37,820 =	7,564	F
Total direct materials price variance				$5,246	F

Total direct materials efficiency variance can also be computed as:

$$\begin{pmatrix} \text{Direct materials} \\ \text{efficiency variance} \\ \text{for each input} \end{pmatrix} = \begin{pmatrix} \text{Actual quantity} \\ \text{of input} - \begin{array}{c}\text{Budgeted quantity of input} \\ \text{allowed for actual output}\end{array} \end{pmatrix} \times \begin{array}{c}\text{Budgeted} \\ \text{price of input}\end{array}$$

Oak	= (23,180 – 24,000) × $6.00	=	$4,920 F
Pine	= (37,820 – 36,000) × $2.00	=	3,640 U
Total direct materials efficiency variance			$1,280 F

16-32 (cont'd)

SOLUTION EXHIBIT 16-32A
Columnar Presentation of Direct Materials Price and Efficiency Variances for PDS Manufacturing

	Actual Costs Incurred (Actual Input Quantity × Actual Price) (1)	Actual Input Quantity × Budgeted Price (2)	Flexible Budget (Budgeted Input Quantity Allowed for Actual Output × Budgeted Price) (3)
Oak	23,180 × $6.10 = $141,398	23,180 × $6.00 = $139,080	24,000 × $6.00 = $144,000
Pine	37,820 × $1.80 = 68,076	37,820 × $2.00 = 75,640	36,000 × $2.00 = 72,000
	$209,474	$214,720	$216,000

$5,246 F
Total price variance

$1,280 F
Total efficiency variance

$6,526 F
Total flexible-budget variance

F = favourable effect on operating income; U = unfavourable effect on operating income

3.

	Actual Quantity of Input	Actual Mix	Budgeted Quantity of Input for Actual Output		Budgeted Mix
Oak	23,180 b.f.	38%	8 b.f. × 3,000 units =	24,000 b.f.	40%
Pine	37,820 b.f.	62%	12 b.f. × 3,000 units =	36,000 b.f.	60%
Total	61,000 b.f.	100%		60,000 b.f.	100%

16-32 (cont'd)

4. Solution Exhibit 16-32B presents the total direct materials yield and mix variances for PDS Manufacturing.

The total direct materials yield variance can also be computed as the sum of the direct materials yield variances for each input:

$$
\begin{pmatrix} \text{Direct} \\ \text{materials} \\ \text{yield variance} \\ \text{for each input} \end{pmatrix} = \begin{pmatrix} \text{Actual total} \\ \text{quantity of all} \\ \text{direct materials} \\ \text{inputs used} \end{pmatrix} - \begin{pmatrix} \text{Budgeted total quantity} \\ \text{of all direct materials inputs} \\ \text{allowed for actual output} \end{pmatrix} \times \begin{pmatrix} \text{Budgeted} \\ \text{direct materials} \\ \text{input mix} \\ \text{percentage} \end{pmatrix} \times \begin{pmatrix} \text{Budgeted} \\ \text{price of} \\ \text{direct materials} \\ \text{inputs} \end{pmatrix}
$$

Oak = (61,000 – 60,000) × 0.40 × \$6.00 = 1,000 × 0.40 × \$6.00 = \$2,400 U
Pine = (61,000 – 60,000) × 0.60 × \$2.00 = 1,000 × 0.60 × \$2.00 = <u>1,200</u> U

Total direct materials yield variance <u>\$3,600</u> U

The total direct materials mix variance can also be computed as the sum of the direct materials mix variances for each input:

$$
\begin{pmatrix} \text{Direct} \\ \text{materials} \\ \text{mix variance} \\ \text{for each input} \end{pmatrix} = \begin{pmatrix} \text{Actual} \\ \text{direct materials} \\ \text{input mix} \\ \text{percentage} \end{pmatrix} - \begin{pmatrix} \text{Budgeted} \\ \text{direct materials} \\ \text{input mix} \\ \text{percentage} \end{pmatrix} \times \begin{pmatrix} \text{Actual total} \\ \text{quantity of all} \\ \text{direct materials} \\ \text{inputs used} \end{pmatrix} \times \begin{pmatrix} \text{Budgeted} \\ \text{price of} \\ \text{direct materials} \\ \text{inputs} \end{pmatrix}
$$

Oak = (0.38 – 0.40) × 61,000 × \$6.00 =   0.02 × 61,000 × \$6.00 = \$7,320 F
Pine = (0.62 – 0.60) × 61,000 × \$2.00 = – 0.02 × 61,000 × \$2.00 = <u>2,440</u> U

Total direct materials mix variance <u>\$4,880</u> F

The sum of the direct materials mix variance and the direct materials yield variance equals the direct materials efficiency variance. The favourable mix variance arises from using more of the cheaper pine (and less oak) than the budgeted mix. The yield variance indicates that the dressers required more total inputs (61,000 b.f.) than expected (60,000 b.f.) for the production of 3,000 dressers. Both variances are relatively small and probably within tolerable limits. PDS should investigate whether substituting the cheaper pine for the more expensive oak caused the unfavourable yield variance. It should also be careful that using more of the cheaper pine does not reduce the quality of the dresser or how customers perceive it.

16-32 (cont'd)

SOLUTION EXHIBIT 16-32B
Columnar Presentation of Direct Materials Yield and Mix Variances for PDS Manufacturing

Actual Total Quantity of All Inputs Used × Actual Input Mix × Budgeted Price (1)	Actual Total Quantity of All Inputs Used × Budgeted Input Mix × Budgeted Price (2)	Flexible Budget: Budgeted Total Quantity of All Inputs Allowed for Actual Output × Budgeted Input Mix × Budgeted Price (3)
Oak 61,000 × 0.38 × $6.00 = $139,080	61,000 × 0.40 × $6.00 = $146,400	60,000 × 0.40 × $6.00 = $144,000
Pine 61,000 × 0.62 × $2.00 = 75,640	61,000 × 0.60 × $2.00 = 73,200	60,000 × 0.60 × $2.00 = 72,000
$214,720	$219,600	$216,000

$$\underset{\text{Total mix variance}}{4{,}880\ F} \qquad \underset{\text{Total yield variance}}{\$3{,}600\ U}$$

$$\underset{\text{Total efficiency variance}}{\$1{,}280\ F}$$

F = favourable effect on operating income; U = unfavourable effect on operating income.

16-34 Customer profitability in a manufacturing firm.

1.   Calculation of customer profitability by customer:

	Customer				
	A	**B**	**C**	**D**	**E**
Revenues at list price					
$100 × 5,000; 2,400; 1,200; 4,000; 8,000	$500,000	$240,000	$120,000	$400,000	$800,000
Price discount					
10% × $500,000; 0; 10% × $120,000; 0; 10% × $400,000	50,000	0	12,000	0	40,000
Revenues (actual price)	450,000	240,000	108,000	400,000	760,000
Cost of goods sold					
$80 × 5,000; 2,400, 1,200; 4,000; 8,000	400,000	192,000	96,000	320,000	640,000
Gross margin	50,000	48,000	12,000	80,000	120,000
Customer-level costs:					
Order taking					
$380 × 10; 12; 48; 16; 12	3,800	4,560	18,240	6,080	4,560
Product handling					
$10 × 500; 240; 144; 400; 812	5,000	2,400	1,440	4,000	8,120
Warehousing					
$55 × 13; 16; 0; 12; 120	715	880	0	660	6,600
Rush order processing					
$520 × 0; 2; 0; 0; 5	0	1,040	0	0	2,600
Exchange and repair					
$40 × 0; 30; 5; 20; 95	0	1,200	200	800	3,800
Total customer-level costs	9,515	10,080	19,880	11,540	25,680
Customer-level operating income	$ 40,485	$ 37,920	$ (7,880)	$ 68,460	$ 94,320

Customer ranking

Customer Code	Customer-Level Operating Income (1)	Customer Revenue (2)	Customer-Level Operating Income Divided by Revenue (3) = (1) ÷ (2)	Cumulative Customer-Level Operating Income (4)	Cumulative Customer-Level Operating Income as a % of Total Customer-Level Operating Income (5) = (4) ÷ $233,305
E	$ 94,320	$ 760,000	12.4%	$ 94,320	40.4%
D	68,460	400,000	17.1%	$162,780	69.8%
A	40,485	450,000	9.0%	$203,265	87.1%
B	37,920	240,000	15.8%	$241,185	103.4%
C	(7,880)	108,000	-7.3%	$233,305	100.0%
Total	$233,305	$1,958,000			

16-34 (cont'd)

2. Customer C is Bizzan's only unprofitable customer. All other customers are profitable in line with revenue, except customer A which has more revenue than D but less operating income.

    If Customer C were not being given price discounts, C would be profitable. The salesperson is giving discounts on orders even though the size of the order is small. It is costing Bizzan money to process many small orders as opposed to a few large orders. To turn Customer C into a profitable customer, Bizzan needs to encourage Customer C to place fewer, larger orders and offer a price discount only if Customer C changes behaviour, rather than as a reward for repeat business. Bizzan should also investigate why Customer C was given price discounts given the orders were small.

    Customer E has many rush orders in proportion to total number of orders. Bizzan should work with Customer E to find a production schedule that would meet its needs without having to rush the order.

    Customer E also has high warehousing needs that are costly to Bizzan. Bizzan should work with Customer E to align its production schedule to Customer E's needs.

    The exchange and repair rate for customers with rush orders is higher than for other customers. Bizzan should explore whether rushing an order reduces attention to quality. Either reducing the number of rush orders (which would also save Bizzan money) or working toward increasing the quality of rush orders would help to reduce these costs.

    The three most profitable customers (E, D, and A) generate 87% of the customer-level operating income. These customers are valued customers and should receive the highest level of customer service.

16-36 (40 min.) Customer profitability and ethics.

1. Customer-level operating income based on expected cost of orders:

	Customers					
	IHoG	**GRU**	**GM**	**GC**	**GG**	**Gmart**
Revenues at list price						
$40 × 200; 540; 300; 100; 400; 1,000	$8,000	$21,600	$12,000	$4,000	$16,000	$40,000
Price discounts						
GRU: 5% × $21,600; Gmart: 5% × $40,000	0	1,080	0	0	0	2,000
Revenues (actual price)	8,000	20,520	12,000	4,000	16,000	38,000
Cost of goods sold						
$30 × 200; 540; 300; 100; 400; 1,000	6,000	16,200	9,000	3,000	12,000	30,000
Gross margin	2,000	4,320	3,000	1,000	4,000	8,000
Customer-level operating costs:						
Order taking						
$28 × 4; 12; 6; 4; 16; 20	112	336	168	112	448	560
Product handling						
$1 × 200; 540; 300; 100; 400; 1,000	200	540	300	100	400	1,000
Delivery						
$1 × 80; 120; 72; 28; 304; 100	80	120	72	28	304	100
Expedited delivery						
$300 × 0; 4; 0; 0; 1; 3	0	1,200	0	0	300	900
Sales commissions						
$20 × 4; 12; 6; 4; 16; 20)	80	240	120	80	320	400
Total customer-level operating costs	472	2,436	660	320	1,772	2,960
Customer-level operating income	$1,528	$1,884	$2,340	$680	$2,228	$5,040

16-36 (cont'd)

2. Customer-level operating income based on actual order costs:

	Customer					
	IHoG	**GRU**	**GM**	**GC**	**GG**	**Gmart**
Revenues at list price $40 × 200; 540; 300; 100; 400; 1,000	$8,000	$21,600	$12,000	$4,000	$16,000	$40,000
Price discounts GRU: 5% × $21,600; Gmart: 5% × $40,000	0	1,080	0	0	0	2,000
Revenues (actual price)	8,000	20,520	12,000	4,000	16,000	38,000
Cost of goods sold $30 × 200; 540; 300; 100; 400; 1,000	6,000	16,200	9,000	3,000	12,000	30,000
Gross margin	2,000	4,320	3,000	1,000	4,000	8,000
Customer-level operating costs:						
Order taking $12 × 4; $28 × 12; $12 × 6; $12 × 4; $12 × 16; $12 × 20	48	336	72	48	192	240
Product handling $1 × 200; 540; 300; 100; 400; 1,000	200	540	300	100	400	1,000
Delivery $1 × 80; 120; 72; 28; 304; 100	80	120	72	28	304	100
Expedited delivery $300 × 0; 4; 0; 0; 1; 3	0	1,200	0	0	300	900
Sales commissions $20 × 4; 12; 6; 4; 16; 20	80	240	120	80	320	400
Total customer-level operating costs	408	2,436	564	256	1,516	2,640
Customer-level operating income	$1,592	$1,884	$2,436	$744	$2,484	$5,360

Comparing the answers in requirements 1 and 2, it appears that operating income is higher than expected, so the management of Glat Corporation would be very pleased with the performance of the salespeople for reducing order costs. Except for GRU, all of the customers are more profitable than originally reported.

16-36 (cont'd)

3. Customer-level operating income if larger orders

	Customer					
	IHoG	**GRU**	**GM**	**GC**	**GG**	**Gmart**
Revenues at list price						
$40 × 200; 540; 300; 100; 400; 1,000	$8,000	$21,600	$12,000	$4,000	$16,000	$40,000
Price discounts						
GRU: 5% × $21,600; Gmart: 5% ×						
$40,000	0	1,080	0	0	0	2,000
Revenues (actual price)	8,000	20,520	12,000	4,000	16,000	38,000
Cost of goods sold						
$30 × 200; 540; 300; 100; 400; 1,000	6,000	16,200	9,000	3,000	12,000	30,000
Gross margin	2,000	4,320	3,000	1,000	4,000	8,000
Customer-level operating costs:						
Order taking						
$28 × 2; 12; 2; 2; 4; 10	56	336	56	56	112	280
Product handling						
$1 × 200; 540; 300; 100; 400; 1,000	200	540	300	100	400	1,000
Delivery						
$1 × 80; 120; 72; 28; 304; 100	80	120	72	28	304	100
Expedited delivery						
$300 × 0; 4; 0; 0; 1; 3	0	1,200	0	0	300	900
Sales commissions						
$20 × 2; 12; 2; 2; 4; 10	40	240	40	40	80	200
Total customer-level operating costs	376	2,436	468	224	1,196	2,480
Customer-level operating income	$1,624	$1,884	$2,532	$776	$2,804	$5,520

4. The behaviour of the salespeople is costing Glat Corporation $640 in profit (the difference between the incomes in requirements 2 and 3). Although management thinks the salespeople are saving money based on the budgeted order costs, in reality they are costing the firm money by increasing the costs of orders ($936 in requirement 2 versus $896 in requirement 3) and at the same time increasing their sales commissions ($1,240 in requirement 2 versus $640 in requirement 3). This is not ethical.

Glat Corporation needs to change the structure of the sales commission, possibly linking commissions to the overall units sold rather than on number of orders. They could also base commissions on total revenues, which will discourage salespeople from offering discounts unless they are needed to close the sale. A negative consequence of greater reluctance to offer discounts is that salespeople will not seek larger orders but instead focus on smaller orders that do not require discounts to be offered. This behaviour will, in turn, increase order-taking costs.

CHAPTER 17
PROCESS COSTING

17-2   Process-costing systems separate costs into cost categories according to the timing of when costs are introduced into the process. Often only two cost classifications, direct materials and conversion costs, are necessary. Direct materials are frequently added at one point in time, often the start or the end of the process, and all conversion costs are added at about the same time, but in a pattern different from direct materials costs.

17-4   The key steps in process costing follow:
• Summarize the flow of physical units of output.
• Compute output in terms of equivalent units.
• Compute equivalent unit costs.
• Summarize total costs to account for.
• Assign these costs to units completed and to units in ending Work in Process.

17-6   Three inventory methods associated with process costing are:
• Weighted average.
• First-in, first-out (FIFO).
• Standard costing.

17-8   FIFO computations are distinctive because they assign the cost of the earliest equivalent units available (starting with equivalent units in beginning work-in-process inventory) to units completed and transferred out, and the cost of the most recent equivalent units worked on during the period to ending work-in-process inventory. In contrast, the weighted-average method costs units completed and transferred out and in ending work in process at the same average cost.

17-10   A major advantage of FIFO is that managers can judge the performance in the current period independently from the performance in the preceding period.

17-12   Yes. Standard-cost procedures are particularly applicable to process-costing systems where there are various combinations of materials and operations. Standard-cost procedures avoid the intricacies involved in detailed tracking with weighted-average or FIFO methods when there are frequent price variations over time.

17-14   No. Transferred-in costs or previous-department costs are costs incurred in a previous department that have been charged to a subsequent department. These costs may be costs incurred in that previous department during this accounting period or a preceding accounting period.

17-16 (25 min.) Equivalent units, zero beginning inventory.

1. Direct materials cost per unit ($750,000 ÷ 10,000) $ 75.00
    Conversion cost per unit ($798,000 ÷ 10,000)   79.80
    Assembly Department cost per unit $154.80

2. Solution Exhibit 17-16A calculates the equivalent units of direct materials and conversion costs in the Assembly Department of Nihon Inc. in February 2010.

    Solution Exhibit 17-16B computes equivalent units costs

    Direct materials cost per unit $ 75.00
    Conversion cost per unit   84.00
    Assembly Department cost per unit $159.00

3. The difference in the Assembly Department cost per unit calculated in requirements 1 and 2 arises because the costs incurred in January and February are the same but fewer equivalent units of work are done in February than in January. In January, all 10,000 units introduced are fully completed, resulting in 10,000 equivalent units of work done with respect to direct materials and conversion costs. In February, of the 10,000 units introduced, 10,000 equivalent units of work is done with respect to direct materials but only 9,500 equivalent units of work is done with respect to conversion costs. The Assembly Department cost per unit is therefore higher.

SOLUTION EXHIBIT 17-16A
Summarize Output in Physical Units and Compute Output in Equivalent Units; Assembly Department of Nihon Inc. for February 2010.

		Equivalent Units	
Flow of Production	Physical Units	Direct Materials	Conversion Costs
Work in process, beginning (given)	0		
Started during current period (given)	10,000		
To account for	10,000		
Completed and transferred out during current period	9,000	9,000	9,000
Work in process, ending* (given)	1,000		
1,000 × 100%; 1,000 × 50%		1,000	500
Accounted for	10,000		
Work done in current period		10,000	9,500

*Degree of completion in this department: direct materials, 100%; conversion costs, 50%.

17-16 (cont'd)

SOLUTION EXHIBIT 17-16B
Compute Cost per Equivalent Unit,
Assembly Department of Nihon Inc. for February 2010.

	Total Production Costs	Direct Materials	Conversion Costs
Costs added during February	$1,548,000	$750,000	$798,000
Divide by equivalent units of work done in current period (Solution Exhibit 17-16A)		÷ 10,000	÷ 9,500
Cost per equivalent unit		$ 75	$ 84

17-18 (25 min.) No beginning inventory, materials introduced in middle of process.

1. Solution Exhibit 17-18A shows equivalent units of work done in the current period of Chemical P, 50,000; Chemical Q, 35,000; Conversion costs, 45,000.

2. Solution Exhibit 17-18B summarizes the total Mixing Department costs for July 2010, (a) calculates cost per equivalent unit of work done in the current period for Chemical P, Chemical Q, and conversion costs, and (b) assigns these costs to units completed (and transferred out) and to units in ending work in process.

17-18 (cont'd)

SOLUTION EXHIBIT 17-18A
Summarize Output in Physical Units and Compute Equivalent Units;
Mixing Department of Roary Chemicals for July 2010

| | | Equivalent Units | | |
Flow of Production	Physical Units	Chemical P	Chemical Q	Conversion Costs
Work in process, beginning (given)	0			
Started during current period (given)	50,000			
To account for	50,000			
Completed and transferred out during current period	35,000	35,000	35,000	35,000
Work in process, ending* (given)	15,000			
15,000 × 100%; 15,000 × 0%;				
15,000 × 66 2/3%	_____	15,000	0	10,000
Accounted for	50,000			
Work done in current period only		50,000	35,000	45,000

*Degree of completion in this department: Chemical P, 100%; Chemical Q, 0%; conversion costs, 66 2/3%.

Note that chemical Q has not been included in the ending work in process, since the ending WIP is 66 2/3% complete and chemical Q is only added when the units are 75% or three-fourths complete.

17-18 (cont'd)

SOLUTION EXHIBIT 17-18B
Summarize Total Costs to Account for, Compute Cost per Equivalent Unit, and Assign Total Costs to Units Completed and to Units in Ending Work in Process; Mixing Department of Roary Chemicals for July 2010.

		Total Production Costs	Chemical P	Chemical Q	Conversion Costs
	Costs added during July	$455,000	$250,000	$70,000	$135,000
	Total costs to account for	$455,000	$250,000	$70,000	$135,000
	Costs added in current period		$250,000	$70,000	$135,000
	Divide by equivalent units of work done in current period (Solution Exhibit 17-l8A)		÷ 50,000	÷35,000	÷ 45,000
(a)	Cost per equivalent unit		$ 5	$ 2	$ 3

(b) Assignment of costs:

	Total Production Costs	Chemical P	Chemical Q	Conversion Costs
Completed and transferred out (35,000 units)	$350,000	(35,000* × $5) + (35,000* × $2) + (35,000* × $3)		
Work in process, ending (15,000 units)	105,000	(15,000† × $5) +	(0† × $2) +	(10,000† × $3)
Total costs accounted for	$455,000	$250,000 +	$70,000 +	$135,000

*Equivalent units completed and transferred out from Solution Exhibit 17-18A.
†Equivalent units in ending work in process from Solution Exhibit 17-18A.

17-20 (30 min.) FIFO method, assigning costs.

1. & 2.   Solution Exhibit 17-20A calculates the equivalent units of work done in the current period. Solution Exhibit 17-20B summarizes total costs to account for, calculates the cost per equivalent unit of work done in the current period for direct materials and conversion costs, and assigns these costs to units completed and transferred out and to units in ending work-in-process inventory.

SOLUTION EXHIBIT 17-20A
Summarize Output in Physical Units and Compute Output in Equivalent Units;
FIFO Method of Process Costing, Bio Doc Corporation for July 2010.

		Equivalent Units	
Flow of Production	Physical Units	Direct Materials	Conversion Costs
Work in process, beginning (given)	12,500	(work done before current period)	
Started during current period (given)	50,000		
To account for	62,500		
Completed and transferred out during current period:			
From beginning work in process[§]	12,500		
12,500 × (100% – 100%); 12,500 × (100% – 70%)		0	3,750
Started and completed	30,000[†]		
30,000 × 100%, 30,000 × 100%		30,000	30,000
Work in process, ending* (given)	20,000		
20,000 × 100%; 20,000 × 50%		20,000	10,000
Accounted for	62,500		
Work done in current period only		50,000	43,750

[§]Degree of completion in this department: direct materials, 100%; conversion costs, 70%.

[†]42,500 physical units completed and transferred out minus 12,500 physical units completed and transferred out from beginning work-in-process inventory.

*Degree of completion in this department: direct materials, 100%; conversion costs, 50%.

17-20 (cont'd)

SOLUTION EXHIBIT 17-20B

Summarize Total Costs to Account for, Compute Cost per Equivalent Unit, and Assign Total Costs to Units Completed and to Units in Ending Work in Process; FIFO Method of Process Costing, Bio Doc Corporation for July 2010.

	Total Production Costs	Direct Materials	Conversion Costs
Work in process, beginning (given)	$162,500	$ 75,000	$ 87,500
Costs added in current period (given)	813,750	350,000	463,750
Total costs to account for	$976,250	$425,000	$551,250
Costs added in current period		$350,000	$463,750
Divide by equivalent units of work done in current period (Solution Exhibit 17-20A)		$\div$ 50,000	$\div$ 43,750
Cost per equivalent unit of work done in current period		$ 7	$ 10.60
Assignment of costs:			
Completed and transferred out (42,500 units):			
Work in process, beginning (12,500 units)	$162,500	$75,000	$87,500
Cost added to beginning work in process in current period	39,750	$(0^* \times \$7)$ +	$(3,750^* \times \$10.60)$
Total from beginning inventory	202,250		
Started and completed (30,000 units)	528,000	$(30,000^\dagger \times \$7)$ +	$(30,000^\dagger \times \$10.60)$
Total costs of units completed and transferred out	730,250		
Work in process, ending (20,000 units)	246,000	$(20,000^\# \times \$7)$ +	$(10,000^\# \times \$10.60)$
Total costs accounted for	$976,250	$425,000 +	$551,250

*Equivalent units used to complete beginning work in process from Solution Exhibit 17-20A.

†Equivalent units started and completed from Solution Exhibit 17-20A.

#Equivalent units in ending work in process from Solution Exhibit 17-20A.

17-22 (15 min.) Weighted-average method, equivalent units and unit costs.

Under the weighted-average method, equivalent units are calculated as the equivalent units of work done to date. Solution Exhibit 17-22 shows equivalent units of work done to date for the Assembly Division for direct materials and conversion costs.

SOLUTION EXHIBIT 17-22
Summarize Output in Physical Units and Compute Equivalent Units;
Weighted-Average Method of Process Costing, Assembly Division for May 2010

| Flow of Production | Physical Units (given) | Equivalent Units | |
		Direct Materials	Conversion Costs
Work in process beginning	8		
Started during current period	55		
To account for	63		
Completed and transferred out during current period	51	51.0	51.0
Work in process, ending*			
(12 × 60%; 12 × 30%)	12	7.2	3.6
Accounted for	63		
Work done to date		58.2	54.6

*Degree of completion in this department: direct materials, 60%; conversion costs, 30%.

Costs per equivalent unit:

$$DM = \frac{\$5,426,960 + \$35,420,000}{58.2} = \frac{\$40,846,960}{58.2}$$

$$= \$701,837.80/ \text{ equivalent unit}$$

$$CV = \frac{\$1,001,440 + \$15,312,000}{54.6} = \frac{\$16,313,440}{54.6}$$

$$= \$298,780.95/ \text{ equivalent unit}$$

17-24 (15 min.) FIFO method, equivalent units and unit costs.

1. Under the FIFO method, equivalent units are calculated as the equivalent units of work done in the current period only. Solution Exhibit 17-24 shows equivalent units of work done in May 2010 in the Assembly Department for direct materials and conversion costs.

SOLUTION EXHIBIT 17-24
Summarize Output in Physical Units and Compute Equivalent Units using FIFO Method of Process Costing, Assembly Division for May 2010

		Equivalent Units	
Flow of Production	Physical Units	Direct Materials	Conversion Costs
Work in process, beginning (given)	8	(work done before current period)	
Started during current period (given)	55		
To account for	63		
Completed and transferred out during current period:			
From beginning work in process§	8		
8 × (100% − 90%);			
8 × (100% − 40%)		0.8	4.8
Started and completed	43†		
43 × 100%, 43 × 100%		43.0	43.0
Work in process, ending* (given)	12		
12 × 60%; 12 × 30%		7.2	3.6
Accounted for	63		
Work done in current period only		51.0	51.4

§Degree of completion in this department: direct materials, 90%; conversion costs, 40%.
†51 physical units completed and transferred out minus 8 physical units completed and transferred out from beginning work-in-process inventory.
*Degree of completion in this department: direct materials, 60%; conversion costs, 30%.

2.
Direct material costs, added May	$35,420,000
Equivalent units	51
Cost per equivalent unit	$694,510
Conversion costs, May	$15,312,000
Equivalent units	51.4
Cost per equivalent unit	$297,899

17-26 (25-30 min.) Standard-costing method, assigning costs.

1. The calculations of equivalent units for direct materials and conversion costs are identical to the calculations of equivalent units under the FIFO method. Solution Exhibit 17-24 shows the equivalent unit calculations under standard costing given by the equivalent units of work done in May 2010 in the Assembly Department.

2. Solution Exhibit 17-26 summarizes the total costs to account for, and assigns these costs to units completed and transferred out and to units in ending work in process.

3. Solution Exhibit 17-26 shows the direct materials and conversion cost variances for

Direct materials	$280,000 F
Conversion costs	$108,000 F

17-26 (cont'd)

SOLUTION EXHIBIT 17-26
Compute Equivalent Unit Costs, Summarize Total Costs to Account for, and Assign Costs to Units Completed and to Units in Ending Work in Process;
Use of Standard Costs in Process Costing, Assembly Division for May 2010.

	Total Production Costs	Direct Materials	Conversion Costs
Standard cost per equivalent unit (given)		$ 700,000	$ 300,000
Work in process, beginning (given)			
Direct materials, 7.2* × $700,000; Conversion costs, 3.2* × $300,000	$6,000,000		
Costs added in current period at standard costs: Direct materials, 51 × $700,000; Conversion costs, 51.4 × $300,000	51,120,000	$35,700,000	$15,420,000
Costs to account for	$57,120,000		
Assignment of costs at standard costs:			
Completed and transferred out (51 units):			
Work in process, beginning (8 units)	$ 6,000,000		
Direct materials added in current period	560,000	0.8* × $700,000	
Conversion costs added in current period	1,440,000		4.8* × $300,000
Total from beginning inventory	8,000,000		
Started and completed (43 units)	43,000,000	43† × $700,000 + 43† × $300,000	
Total costs of units transferred out	51,000,000		
Work in process, ending (12 units)			
Direct materials	5,040,000	7.2# × $700,000	
Conversion costs	1,080,000		3.6# × $300,000
Total work in process, ending	6,120,000		
Total costs accounted for	$57,120,000		
Summary of variances for current performance:			
Costs added in current period at standard prices (see above)		$35,700,000	$15,420,000
Actual costs incurred (given)		35,420,000	15,312,000
Variance		$ 280,000 F	$ 108,000 F

*Equivalent units to complete beginning work in process from Solution Exhibit 17-24.
†Equivalent units started and completed from Solution Exhibit 17-24.
#Equivalent units in work in process, ending from Solution Exhibit 17-24.

*Degree of completion: direct material 90%; conversion costs 40%
$$(8 \times 0.90 = 7.2) ; (8 \times 0.40 = 3.2)$$

17-28 (35-40 min.) Transferred-in costs, FIFO method.

Solution Exhibit 17-28A calculates the equivalent units of work done in the current period (for transferred-in costs, direct materials, and conversion costs) to complete beginning work-in-process inventory, to start and complete new units, and to produce ending work in process. Solution Exhibit 17-28B summarizes total costs to account for, calculates the cost per equivalent unit of work done in the current period for transferred-in costs, direct materials, and conversion costs, and assigns these costs to units completed and transferred out and to units in ending work-in-process inventory.

SOLUTION EXHIBIT 17-28A
Summarize Output in Physical Units and Compute Output in Equivalent Units
FIFO Method of Process Costing
Finishing Department of Asaya Clothing for June 2010

		Equivalent Units		
Flow of Production	Physical Units	Transferred-in Costs	Direct Materials	Conversion Costs
Work in process, beginning (given)	75	(work done before current period)		
Transferred-in during current period (given)	135			
To account for	210			
Completed and transferred out during current period:				
From beginning work in process[a]	75			
[75 × (100% – 100%); 75 × (100% – 0%); 75 × (100% – 60%)]		0	75	30
Started and completed	75[b]			
(75 × 100%; 75 × 100%; 75 × 100%)		75	75	75
Work in process, ending[c] (given)	60			
(60 × 100%; 60 × 0%; 60 × 75%)	—	60	0	45
Accounted for	210			
Work done in current period only		135	150	150

[a]Degree of completion in this department: Transferred-in costs, 100%; direct materials, 0%; conversion costs, 60%.
[b]150 physical units completed and transferred out minus 75 physical units completed and transferred out from beginning work-in-process inventory.
[c]Degree of completion in this department: transferred-in costs, 100%; direct materials, 0%; conversion costs, 75%.

17-28 (cont'd)

SOLUTION EXHIBIT 17-28B
Summarize Total Costs to Account for, Compute Cost per Equivalent Unit, and Assign Total Costs to Units Completed and to Units in Ending Work in Process; FIFO Method of Process Costing
Finishing Department of Asaya Clothing for June 2010

	Total Production Costs	Transferred-in Costs	Direct Materials	Conversion Costs
Work in process, beginning (given)	$ 90,000	$ 60,000	$ 0	$ 30,000
Costs added in current period (given)	246,300	130,800	37,500	78,000
Total costs to account for	$336,300	$190,800	$37,500	$108,000
Costs added in current period		$130,800	$37,500	$ 78,000
Divide by equivalent units of work done in current period (Solution Exhibit 17-28A)		÷ 135	÷ 150	÷ 150
Cost per equivalent unit of work done in current period		$ 968.89	$ 250	$ 520
Assignment of costs:				
Completed and transferred out (150 units):				
Work in process, beginning (75 units)	$ 90,000	$ 60,000	$ 0	$ 30,000
Costs added to BI WIP in current period	34,350	(0[a] × $968.89)	+ (75[a] × $250)	+ (30[a] × $520)
Total from beginning inventory	124,350			
Started and completed (75 units)	130,416	(75[b] × $968.89)	+ (75[b] × $250)	+ (75[b] × $520)
Total costs of units completed and transferred out	254,766			
Work in process, ending (60 units):	81,534	(60[c] × $968.89)	+ (0[c] × $250)	+ (45[c] × $520)
Total costs accounted for	$336,300	$190,800	+ $37,500	+ $108,000

[a] Equivalent units used to complete beginning work in process from Solution Exhibit 17-28A.
[b] Equivalent units started and completed from Solution Exhibit 17-28A.
[c] Equivalent units in ending work in process from Solution Exhibit 17-28A.

17-30 (20 min.) Weighted-average method, assigning costs (continuation of 17-29).

Solution Exhibit 17-30 summarizes total costs to account for, calculates cost per equivalent unit of work done to date in the Assembly Division of Fenton Watches, Inc., and assigns costs to units completed and to units in ending work-in-process inventory.

SOLUTION EXHIBIT 17-30
Summarize Total Costs to Account for, Compute Cost per Equivalent Unit, and Assign Total Costs to Units Completed and to Units in Ending Work in Process;
Weighted-Average Method of Process Costing
Assembly Division of Fenton Watches Inc. for May 2010

	Total Production Costs	Direct Materials	Conversion Costs
Work in process, beginning (given)	$ 584,400	$ 493,360	$ 91,040
Costs added in current period (given)	4,612,000	3,220,000	1,392,000
Total costs to account for	$5,196,400	$3,713,360	$1,483,040
Costs incurred to date		$3,713,360	$1,483,040
Divide by equivalent units of work done to date (Solution Exhibit 17-29)		÷ 532	÷ 496
Cost per equivalent unit of work done to date		$ 6,980	$ 2,990
Assignment of costs:			
Completed and transferred out (460 units)	$4,586,200	(460* × $6,980) + (460* × $2,990)	
Work in process, ending (120 units)	610,200	(72† × $6,980) + (36† × $2,990)	
Total costs accounted for	$5,196,400	$3,713,360 + $1,483,040	

*Equivalent units completed and transferred out from Solution Exhibit 17-29.
† Equivalent units in work in process, ending from Solution Exhibit 17-29.

17-32 (20 min.) FIFO method, assigning costs (continuation of 17-31).

Solution Exhibit 17-32 summarizes total costs to account for, calculates cost per equivalent unit of work done in May 2010 in the Assembly Division of Fenton Watches Inc., and assigns total costs to units completed and to units in ending work-in-process inventory.

SOLUTION EXHIBIT 17-32
Summarize Total Costs to Account for, Compute Cost per Equivalent Unit, and Assign Total Costs to Units Completed and to Units in Ending Work in Process;
FIFO Method of Process Costing
Assembly Division of Fenton Watches Inc. for May 2010

	Total Production Costs	Direct Materials	Conversion Costs
Work in process, beginning (given)	$ 584,400	$ 493,360	$ 91,040
Costs added in current period (given)	4,612,000	3,220,000	1,392,000
Total costs to account for	$5,196,400	$3,713,360	$1,483,040
Costs added in current period		$3,220,000	$1,392,000
Divide by equivalent units of work done in current period (Solution Exhibit 17-31)		÷ 460	÷ 464
Cost per equiv. unit of work done in current period		$ 7,000	$ 3,000
Assignment of costs:			
Completed and transferred out (460 units):			
Work in process, beginning (80 units)	$ 584,400	$493,360 +	$91,040
Costs added to beginning work in process in current period	200,000	(8* × $7,000) +	(48* × $3,000)
Total from beginning inventory	784,400		
Started and completed (380 units)	3,800,000	(380† × $7,000) +	(380† × $3,000)
Total costs of units completed and transferred out	4,584,400		
Work in process, ending (120 units)	612,000	(72# × $7,000) +	(36# × $3,000)
Total costs accounted for	$5,196,400	$3,713,360 +	$1,483,040

*Equivalent units used to complete beginning work in process from Solution Exhibit 17-31.
†Equivalent units started and completed from Solution Exhibit 17-31.
#Equivalent units in work in process, ending from Solution Exhibit 17-31.

17-34 (15-20 min.) Standard-costing method.

1. Since there was no additional work needed on the beginning inventory with respect to materials, the initial mulch must have been 100% complete with respect to materials. For conversion costs, the work done to complete the opening inventory was 434,250 ÷ 965,000 = 45%. Therefore, the unfinished mulch in opening inventory must have been 55% complete with respect to conversion costs.

2. It is clear that the ending WIP is also 100% complete with respect to direct materials (1,817,000 ÷ 1,817,000), and it is 60% (1,090,200 ÷ 1,817,000) complete with regard to conversion costs.

3. We can first obtain the total standard costs per unit. The number of units started and completed during August is 845,000, and a total cost of $6,717,750 is attached to them. The per-unit standard cost is therefore ($6,717,750 ÷ 845,000) = $7.95. If x and y represent the per-unit cost for direct materials and conversion costs, respectively, we therefore know that:

$$x + y = 7.95$$

We also know that the ending inventory is costed at $12,192,070 and contains 1,817,000 equivalent units of materials and 1,090,200 equivalent units of conversion costs. This provides a second equation:

$$1,817,000\ x + 1,090,200\ y = 12,192,070.$$

Solving these equations reveals that the direct materials cost per unit, x, is $4.85, while the conversion cost per unit, y, is $3.10.

4. Finally, the opening WIP contained 965,000 equivalent units of materials and (965,000-434,250) = 530,750 equivalent units of conversion costs. Applying the standard costs computed in step (3), the cost of the opening inventory must have been:

$$965,000 \times \$4.85\ +\ 530,750 \times \$3.10 = \$6,325,575.$$

17-36 (10 min.) Journal entries (continuation of 17-35).

1. Work in Process--Assembly Department   4,500,000
        Accounts Payable   4,500,000
    Direct materials purchased and used in
      production in October.

2. Work in Process--Assembly Department   2,337,500
        Various accounts   2,337,500
    Conversion costs incurred in October.

3. Work in Process--Testing Department   7,717,500
        Work in Process--Assembly Department   7,717,500
    Cost of goods completed and transferred out
      in October from the Assembly Department to the Testing Department.

Work in Process—Assembly Department

Beginning inventory, Oct. 1	1,652,750	3. Transferred out to	
1. Direct materials	4,500,000	Work in Process–Testing	7,717,500
2. Conversion costs	2,337,500		
Ending Inventory, October 31	772,750		

17-38 (30 min.) Transferred-in costs, weighted-average method (related to 17-35 to 17-37).

1. Transferred-in costs are 100% complete, and direct materials are 0% complete in both beginning and ending work-in-process inventory. The reason is that transferred-in costs are always 100% complete as soon as they are transferred in from the Assembly Department to the Testing Department. Direct materials in beginning or ending work in process for the Testing Department are 0% complete because direct materials are added only when the testing process is 90% complete and the units in beginning and ending work in process are only 70% and 60% complete, respectively.

2. Solution Exhibit 17-38A computes the equivalent units of work done to date in the Testing Department for transferred-in costs, direct materials, and conversion costs.

3. Solution Exhibit 17-38B summarizes total Testing Department costs for October 2010, calculates the cost per equivalent unit of work done to date in the Testing Department for transferred-in costs, direct materials, and conversion costs, and assigns these costs to units completed and transferred out and to units in ending work in process using the weighted-average method.

4.   Journal entries:

a. Work in Process—Testing Department   7,717,500
        Work in Process—Assembly Department   7,717,500
    Cost of goods completed and transferred out
        during October from the Assembly
        Department to the Testing Department

b. Finished Goods   23,459,600
        Work in Process—Testing Department   23,459,600
    Cost of goods completed and transferred out
        during October from the Testing Department
        to Finished Goods inventory

17-38 (cont'd)

SOLUTION EXHIBIT 17-38A
Summarize Output in Physical Units and Compute Output in Equivalent Units;
Weighted-Average Method of Process Costing
Testing Department of Larsen Corp. for October 2010

Flow of Production	Physical Units	Equivalent Units		
		Transferred-in Costs	Direct Materials	Conversion Costs
Work in process, beginning (given)	7,500			
Transferred in during current period	22,500*			
To account for	30,000			
Completed and transferred out during current period	26,300	26,300	26,300	26,300
Work in process, ending† (given)	3,700			
3,700 × 100%; 3,700 × 0%; 3,700 × 60%		3,700	0	2,220
Accounted for	30,000			
Work done to date		30,000	26,300	28,520

* 7,500 + 26,300 – 3,700

†Degree of completion in this department: transferred-in costs, 100%; direct materials, 0%; conversion costs, 60%

17-38 (cont'd)
SOLUTION EXHIBIT 17-38B

Summarize Total Costs to Account for, Compute Cost per Equivalent Unit, and Assign Total Costs to Units Completed and to Units in Ending Work in Process; Weighted-Average Method of Process Costing Testing Department of Larsen Corp. for October 2010

	Total Production Costs	Transferred-in Costs	Direct Materials	Conversion Costs
Work in process, beginning (given)	$ 3,767,960	$ 2,932,500	$ 0	$ 835,460
Costs added in current period (given)	21,378,100	7,717,500	9,704,700	3,955,900
Total costs to account for	$25,146,060	$10,650,000	$9,704,700	$4,791,360
Costs incurred to date		$10,650,000	$9,704,700	$4,791,360
Divide by equivalent units of work done to date (Solution Exhibit 17-38A)		÷ 30,000	÷ 26,300	÷ 28,520
Equivalent unit costs of work done to date		$ 355	$ 369	$ 168
Assignment of costs:				
Completed and transferred out (26,300 units)	$23,459,600	(26,300* × $355)	+ (26,300* × $369)	+ (26,300* × $168)
Work in process, ending (3,700 units)	1,686,460	(3,700† × $355)	+ (0† × $369)	+ (2,220† × $168)
Total costs accounted for	$25,146,060	$10,429,500	$9,704,700	$4,791,360

*Equivalent units completed and transferred out from Solution Exhibit 17-38A.
†Equivalent units in ending work in process from Solution Exhibit 17-38A.

389

17-40 (25 min.) Weighted-average method.

Solution Exhibit 17-40A shows equivalent units of work done to date of:

Direct materials	625 equivalent units
Conversion costs	525 equivalent units

Note that direct materials are added when the Assembly Department process is 10% complete. Both the beginning and ending work in process are more than 10% complete and hence are 100% complete with respect to direct materials.

Solution Exhibit 17-40B summarizes the total Assembly Department costs for April 2010, calculates cost per equivalent unit of work done to date for direct materials and conversion costs, and assigns these costs to units completed (and transferred out), and to units in ending work in process using the weighted-average method.

SOLUTION EXHIBIT 17-40A
Summarize Output in Physical Units and Compute Output in Equivalent Units;
Weighted-Average Method of Process Costing,
Assembly Department of Porter Handcraft for April 2010

		Equivalent Units	
Flow of Production	Physical Units	Direct Materials	Conversion Costs
Work in process, beginning (given)	75		
Started during current period (given)	550		
To account for	625		
Completed and transferred out during current period	500	500	500
Work in process, ending* (given)	125		
125 × 100%; 125 × 20%		125	25
Accounted for	625		
Work done to date		625	525

*Degree of completion in this department: direct materials, 100%; conversion costs, 20%.

17-40 (cont'd)

SOLUTION EXHIBIT 17-40B
Summarize Total Costs to Account For, Compute Cost per Equivalent Unit, and Assign
Total Costs to Units Completed and to Units in Ending Work in Process;
Weighted-Average Method of Process Costing
Assembly Department of Porter, April 2010

	Total Production Costs	Direct Materials	Conversion Costs
Work in process, beginning (given)	$ 1,910	$ 1,775	$ 135
Costs added in current period (given)	28,490	17,600	10,890
Total costs to account for	$30,400	$19,375	$11,025
Costs incurred to date		$19,375	$11,025
Divide by equivalent units of work done to date (Solution Exhibit 17-40A)		÷ 625	÷ 525
Cost per equivalent unit of work done to date		$ 31	$ 21
Assignment of costs:			
Completed and transferred out (500 units)	$26,000	(500* × $31) + (500* × $21)	
Work in process, ending (125 units)	4,400	(125† × $31) + (25† × $21)	
Total costs accounted for	$30,400	$19,375 + $11,025	

*Equivalent units completed and transferred out from Solution Exhibit 17-40A.
†Equivalent units in ending work in process from Solution Exhibit 17-40A.

17-42 (20 min.) FIFO method (continuation of 17-40).

The equivalent units of work done in April 2010 in the Assembly Department for direct materials and conversion costs are shown in Solution Exhibit 17-42A.

Solution Exhibit 17-42B summarizes the total Assembly Department costs for April 2010, calculates the cost per equivalent unit of work done in April 2010 in the Assembly Department for direct materials and conversion costs, and assigns these costs to units completed (and transferred out) and to units in ending work in process under the FIFO method.

The equivalent units of work done in beginning inventory is: direct materials, 75 × 100% = 75; and conversion costs 75 × 40% = 30. The cost per equivalent unit of beginning inventory and of work done in the current period are:

	Beginning Inventory	Work Done in Current Period (Calculated Under FIFO Method)
Direct materials	$23.67 ($1,775 ÷ 75)	$32
Conversion costs	$4.50 ($135 ÷ 30)	$22

The following table summarizes the costs assigned to units completed and those still in process under the weighted-average and FIFO process-costing methods for our example.

	Weighted Average (Solution Exhibit 17-40B)	FIFO (Solution Exhibit 17-42B)	Difference
Cost of units completed and transferred out	$26,000	$25,850	–$150
Work in process, ending	4,400	4,550	+$150
Total costs accounted for	$30,400	$30,400	

The FIFO ending inventory is higher than the weighted-average ending inventory by $150. This is because FIFO assumes that all the lower-cost prior-period units in work in process are the first to be completed and transferred out while ending work in process consists of only the higher-cost current-period units. The weighted-average method, however, smoothes out cost per equivalent unit by assuming that more of the higher-cost units are completed and transferred out, while some of the lower-cost units in beginning work in process are placed in ending work in process. Hence, in this case, the weighted-average method results in a higher cost of units completed and transferred out and a lower ending work-in-process inventory relative to the FIFO method.

17-42 (cont'd)

SOLUTION EXHIBIT 17-42A
Summarize Output in Physical Units and Compute Output in Equivalent Units;
FIFO Method of Process Costing
Assembly Department of Porter Handcraft for April 2010

| | | Equivalent Units | |
Flow of Production	Physical Units	Direct Materials	Conversion Costs
Work in process, beginning (given)	75	(work done before current period)	
Started during current period (given)	<u>550</u>		
To account for	<u>625</u>		
Completed and transferred out during current period:			
From beginning work in process§	75		
$75 \times (100\% - 100\%)$; $75 \times (100\% - 40\%)$		0	45
Started and completed	425†		
$425 \times 100\%$; $425 \times 100\%$		425	425
Work in process, ending* (given)	125		
$125 \times 100\%$; $125 \times 20\%$		125	25
Accounted for	<u>625</u>		
Work done in current period only		<u>550</u>	<u>495</u>

§Degree of completion in this department: direct materials, 100%; conversion costs, 40%.

†500 physical units completed and transferred out minus 75 physical units completed and transferred out from beginning work-in-process inventory.

*Degree of completion in this department: direct materials, 100%; conversion costs, 20%.

17-42 (cont'd)

SOLUTION EXHIBIT 17-42B
Summarize Total Costs to Account for, Compute Cost per Equivalent Unit, and Assign Total Costs to Units Completed and to Units in Ending Work in Process;
FIFO Method of Process Costing
Assembly Department of Porter Handcraft for April 2010

	Total Production Costs	Direct Materials	Conversion Costs
Work in process, beginning (given)	$ 1,910	$ 1,775	$ 135
Costs added in current period (given)	28,490	17,600	10,890
Total costs to account for	$30,400	$19,375	$11,025
Costs added in current period		$17,600	$10,890
Divide by equivalent units of work done in current period (Exhibit 17-37A)		÷ 550	÷ 495
Cost per equivalent unit of work done in current period		$ 32	$ 22
Assignment of costs:			
Completed and transferred out (500 units):			
Work in process, beginning (75 units)	$ 1,910	$1,775 +	$135
Costs added to begin. work in process in current period	990	(0* × $32) +	(45* × $22)
Total from beginning inventory	2,900		
Started and completed (425 units)	22,950	(425† × $32) +	(425† × $22)
Total costs of units completed & tsfd. out	25,850		
Work in process, ending (125 units)	4,550	(125# × $32) +	(25# × $22)
Total costs accounted for	$30,400	$19,375 +	$11,025

*Equivalent units used to complete beginning work in process from Solution Exhibit 17-42A.
†Equivalent units started and completed from Solution Exhibit 17-42A.
#Equivalent units in ending work in process from Solution Exhibit 17-42A.

17-44 (30 min.)   Transferred-in costs, FIFO method (continuation of 17-43).

1. Solution Exhibit 17-44A calculates the equivalent units of work done in April 2010 in the Binding Department for transferred-in costs, direct materials, and conversion costs.

Solution Exhibit 17-44B summarizes total Binding Department costs for April 2010; calculates the cost per equivalent unit of work done in April 2010 in the Binding Department for transferred-in costs, direct materials, and conversion costs; and assigns these costs to units completed and transferred out and to units in ending work in process using the FIFO method.

SOLUTION EXHIBIT 17-44A
Summarize Output in Physical Units and Compute Output in Equivalent Units;
FIFO Method of Process Costing, Binding Department of Publish Inc. for April 2010

| | | Equivalent Units | | |
| | Physical | Transferred-in | Direct | Conversion |
Flow of Production	Units	Costs	Materials	Costs
Work in process, beginning (given)	900	(work done before current period)		
Transferred-in during current period (given)	2,700			
To account for	3,600			
Completed and transferred out during current period:				
From beginning work in process[a]	900			
[900 × (100% – 100%); 900 × (100% – 0%); 900 × (100% – 40%)]		0	900	540
Started and completed	2,100[b]			
(2,100 × 100%; 2,100 × 100%; 2,100 × 100%)		2,100	2,100	2,100
Work in process, ending[c] (given)	600			
(600 × 100%; 600 x 0%; 600 × 60%)		600	0	360
Accounted for	3,600			
Work done in current period only		2,700	3,000	3,000

[a] Degree of completion in this department: transferred-in costs, 100%; direct materials, 0%; conversion costs, 40%.

[b] 3,000 physical units completed and transferred out minus 900 physical units completed and transferred out from beginning work-in-process inventory.

[c] Degree of completion in this department: transferred-in costs, 100%; direct materials, 0%; conversion costs, 60%.

17-44 (cont'd)

SOLUTION EXHIBIT 17-44B
Summarize Total Costs to Account for, Compute Cost per Equivalent Unit, and Assign Total Costs to Units Completed and to Units in Ending Work in Process; FIFO Method of Process Costing, Binding Department of Publish Inc. for April 2010

	Total Production Costs	Transferred-in Costs	Direct Materials	Conversion Costs
Work in process, beginning (given)	$ 42,855	$ 27,855	$ 0	$15,000
Costs added in current period (given)	237,450	141,750	26,700	69,000
Total costs to account for	$280,305	$169,605	$26,700	$84,000
Costs added in current period		$141,750	$26,700	$69,000
Divide by equivalent units of work done in current period (Sol. Exhibit 17-44A)		÷ 2,700	÷ 3,000	÷ 3,000
Cost per equivalent unit of work done in current period		$ 52.50	$ 8.90	$ 23.00
Assignment of costs:				
Completed and transferred out (3,000 units)				
Work in process, beginning (900 units)	$ 42,855	$27,855	$0	$15,000
Costs added to beginning work in process in current period	20,430	(0a × $52.50)	(900a × $8.90)	(540a × $23)
Total from beginning inventory	63,285			
Started and completed (2,100 units)	177,240	(2,100b × $52.50)	(2,100b × $8.90)	(2,100b × $23)
Total costs of units completed and transferred out	240,525			
Work in process, ending (600 units):	39,780	(600c × $52.50)	(0c × $8.90)	(360c × $23)
Total costs accounted for	$280,305	$169,605	$26,700	$84,000

a Equivalent units used to complete beginning work in process from Solution Exhibit 17-44A.
b Equivalent units started and completed from Solution Exhibit 17-44A.
c Equivalent units in ending work in process from Solution Exhibit 17-44A.

Problem 17-44 (cont'd)

Journal entries:

a.   Work in Process-- Binding Department   141,750
           Work in Process--Printing Department   141,750
     Cost of goods completed and transferred out
         during April from the Printing Department to
         the Binding Department.

b.   Finished Goods   240,525
           Work in Process-- Binding Department   240,525
     Cost of goods completed and transferred out
         during April from the Binding Department
         to Finished Goods inventory.

2.   The equivalent units of work done in beginning inventory is: transferred-in costs, 900 × 100% = 900; direct materials, 900 × 0% = 0; and conversion costs, 900 × 40% = 360. The cost per equivalent unit of beginning inventory and of work done in the current period are:

	Beginning Inventory	Work Done in Current Period
Transferred-in costs (weighted average)	$36.42 ($32,775 ÷ 900)	$53.33 ($144,000 ÷ 2,700)
Transferred-in costs (FIFO)	$30.95 ($27,855 ÷ 900)	$52.50 ($141,750 ÷ 2,700)
Direct materials	—	$ 8.90
Conversion costs	$41.67 ($15,000 ÷ 360)	$23.00

The following table summarizes the costs assigned to units completed and those still in process under the weighted-average and FIFO process-costing methods for the Binding Department.

	Weighted Average (Solution Exhibit 17-43B)	FIFO (Solution Exhibit 17-44B)	Difference
Cost of units completed and transferred out	$249,012	$240,525	−$8,487
Work in process, ending	38,463	39,780	+$1,317
Total costs accounted for	$287,475	$280,305	

Problem 17-44 (cont'd)

The FIFO ending inventory is higher than the weighted-average ending inventory by $1,317. This is because FIFO assumes that all the lower-cost prior-period units in work in process (as evidenced by the lower transferred-in costs in beginning inventory) are the first to be completed and transferred out while ending work in process consists of only the higher-cost current-period units. The weighted-average method, however, smooths out cost per equivalent unit by assuming that more of the higher-cost units are completed and transferred out, while some of the lower-cost units in beginning work in process are placed in ending work in process. Hence, in this case, the weighted-average method results in a higher cost of units completed and transferred out and a lower ending work-in-process inventory relative to FIFO. Note that the difference in cost of units completed and transferred out (–$8,487) does not fully offset the difference in ending work-in-process inventory (+$1,317). This is because the FIFO and weighted-average methods result in different values for transferred-in costs with respect to both beginning inventory and costs transferred in during the period.

17-46 (30-35 min.) Standard costing with beginning and ending work in process.

1. Solution Exhibit 17-46A computes the equivalent units of work done in November 2010 by Paquita's Pearls Company for direct materials and conversion costs.

2. and 3. Solution Exhibit 17-46B summarizes total costs of the Paquita's Pearls Company for November 30, 2010 and, using the standard cost per equivalent unit for direct materials and conversion costs, assigns these costs to units completed and transferred out and to units in ending work in process. The exhibit also summarizes the cost variances for direct materials and conversion costs for November 2010.

SOLUTION EXHIBIT 17-46A
Summarize Output in Physical Units and Compute Output in Equivalent Units;
Standard Costing Method of Process Costing,
Paquita's Pearls Company for the month ended November 30, 2010.

| | | Equivalent Units | |
Flow of Production	Physical Units	Direct Materials	Conversion Costs
Work in process, beginning (given)	25,000	(work done before current period)	
Started during current period (given)	126,250		
To account for	151,250		
Completed and transferred out during current period:			
From beginning work in process§	25,000		
25,000 × (100% − 100%); 25,000 × (100% − 75%)		0	6,250
Started and completed	100,000†		
100,000 × 100%, 100,000 × 100%		100,000	100,000
Work in process, ending* (given)	26,250		
26,250 × 100%; 26,250 × 50%		26,250	13,125
Accounted for	151,250		
Work done in current period only		126,250	119,375

§Degree of completion in this department: direct materials, 100%; conversion costs, 75%.
†125,000 physical units completed and transferred out minus 25,000 physical units completed and transferred out from beginning work-in-process inventory.
*Degree of completion in this department: direct materials, 100%; conversion costs, 50%.

17-46 (cont'd)

SOLUTION EXHIBIT 17-46B

Summarize Total Costs to Account for, Compute Cost per Equivalent Unit, and Assign Total Costs to Units Completed and to Units in Ending Work in Process; Standard-Costing Method of Process Costing

Paquita's Pearls Company for the month ended November 30, 2010

	Total Production Costs	Direct Materials		Conversion Costs
Work in process, beginning (given)	$ 250,000	$ 62,500	+	$ 187,500
Costs added in current period at standard costs	1,509,375	(126,250 × 2.50)	+	(119,375 × $10.00)
Total costs to account for	$1,759,375	$378,125	+	$1,381,250
Standard cost per equivalent unit (given)		$ 2.50		$ 10.00
Assignment of costs at standard costs:				
Completed and transferred out (125,000 units):				
Work in process, beginning (25,000 units)	$ 250,000	$62,500	+	$187,500
Costs added to beg. WIP in current period	62,500	(0* × $2.50)	+	(6,250* × $10.00)
Total from beginning inventory	312,500			
Started and completed (100,000 units)	1,250,000	(100,000† × $2.50)	+	(100,000† × $10.00)
Total costs of units transferred out	1,562,500			
Work in process, ending (26,250 units)	196,875	(26,250# × $2.50)	+	(13,125# × $10.00)
Total costs accounted for	$1,759,375	$378,125	+	$1,381,250

Summary of variances for current performance:

		Direct Materials	Conversion Costs
Costs added in current period at standard costs (see above)		$315,625	$1,193,750
Actual costs incurred (given)		327,500	1,207,415
Variance		$ 11,875 U	$ 13,665 U

*Equivalent units to complete beginning work in process from Solution Exhibit 17-46A.

†Equivalent units started and completed from Solution Exhibit 17-46A.

#Equivalent units in ending work in process from Solution Exhibit 17-46A.

17-48 (15-30 min.) Operation costing, equivalent units.

1. Materials and conversion costs of each operation, the total units produced, and the material and conversion cost per unit for the month of May are as follows:

	Extrusion	Form	Trim	Finish
Units produced	18,000	12,500	6,000	2,500
Materials costs	$192,000	$44,000	$15,000	$12,000
Materials cost per unit	10.67	3.52	2.50	4.80
Conversion costs*	392,000	132,000	69,000	42,000
Conversion cost per unit	21.78	10.56	11.50	16.80

*Direct manufacturing labour and manufacturing overhead.

The unit cost and total costs in May for each product are as follows:

Cost Elements	Plastic Sheets	Standard Model	Deluxe Model	Executive Model
Extrusion materials (EM)	$10.67	$10.67	$10.67	$10.67
Form materials (FM)	—	3.52	3.52	3.52
Trim materials (TM)	—	—	2.50	2.50
Finish materials	—	—	—	4.80
Extrusion conversion (EC)	21.78	21.78	21.78	21.78
Form conversion (FC)	—	10.56	10.56	10.56
Trim conversion (TC)	—	—	11.50	11.50
Finish conversion	—	—	—	16.80
Total unit cost	$ 32.45	$ 46.53	$ 60.53	$ 82.13
Multiply by units produced	× 5,500	× 6,500	× 3,500	× 2,500
Total product costs	$178,475	$302,445	$211,855	$205,325

17-48 (cont'd)

2.

	Equivalent Units			
	Materials		Conversion Costs	
	Percent Complete	Quantity	Percent Complete	Quantity
Entering trim operation:				
2,000 Deluxe units	100	2,000	100	2,000
1,500 Deluxe units	100	1,500	60	900
2,500 Executive units	100	2,500	100	2,500
Total equivalent units		6,000		5,400

Conversion cost per equivalent unit in trim operation: ($30,000 + $39,000) ÷ 5,400 units = $12.78 per unit

Materials cost per equivalent unit in trim operation (as before) $15,000 ÷ 6,000 units = $2.50 per unit

	Unit Cost	Equivalent Units	Total Costs
Deluxe model work-in-process costs at the trim operation			
Extrusion material (100% complete when transferred in)	$10.67	1,500	$16,005
Extrusion conversion (100% complete when transferred in)	21.78	1,500	32,670
Form material (100% complete when transferred in)	3.52	1,500	5,280
Form conversion (100% complete when transferred in)	10.56	1,500	15,840
Trim material (100% complete)	2.50	1,500	3,750
Trim conversion (60% complete)	12.78	900	11,502
Work-in-process costs	$61.81		$85,047

CHAPTER 18
SPOILAGE, REWORK, AND SCRAP

18-2 Spoilage—unacceptable units of production that are discarded or sold for net disposal proceeds.

Reworked units—unacceptable units of production that are subsequently reworked and sold as acceptable finished goods.

Scrap—residual material that has minimal (frequently zero) sales value compared with the sales value of the main or joint product(s).

18-4 Abnormal spoilage is spoilage that is not expected to arise under efficient operating conditions. Costs of abnormal spoilage are losses, measures of inefficiency that should be written off directly as losses for the accounting period.

18-6 Normal spoilage typically is expressed as a percentage of good units passing the inspection point. Given actual spoiled units, we infer abnormal spoilage as follows:

Abnormal spoilage = Actual spoilage − Normal spoilage

18-8 Yes. Normal spoilage rates should be computed from the good output or from the <u>normal</u> input, not the <u>total</u> input. Normal spoilage is a given percentage of a certain output base. This base should never include abnormal spoilage, which is included in total input. Abnormal spoilage does not vary in direct proportion to units produced, and to include it would cause the normal spoilage count to fluctuate irregularly but not vary in direct proportion to the output base.

18-10 No. If abnormal spoilage is detected at a different point in the production cycle than normal spoilage, then unit costs would differ. If, however, normal and abnormal spoilage are detected at the same point in the production cycle, their unit costs would be the same.

18-12 No. Unless there are special reasons for charging rework to jobs that contained the bad units, the costs of extra materials, labour, and so on are usually charged to manufacturing overhead and allocated to all jobs.

18-14 A company is justified in inventorying scrap when its estimated net realizable value is significant and the time between storing it and selling or reusing it may be quite long.

18-16 (5-10 min.) **Normal and abnormal spoilage in units.**

1. | Total spoiled units | 12,000 |
   |---|---|
   | Normal spoilage in units 5% × 132,000 | 6,600 |
   | Abnormal spoilage in units | 5,400 |

2. | Abnormal spoilage, 5,400 × $10.00 | $ 54,000 |
   |---|---|
   | Normal spoilage, 6,600 × $10.00 | 66,000 |
   | Potential savings, 12,000 × $10.00 | $120,000 |

Regardless of the targeted normal spoilage, abnormal spoilage is non-recurring and avoidable. The targeted normal spoilage rate is subject to change. Many companies have reduced their spoilage to almost zero, which would realize all potential savings. Of course, zero spoilage usually means higher-quality products, more customer satisfaction, more employee satisfaction, and various effects on nonmanufacturing (for example, purchasing) costs of direct materials.

18-18 (20-25 min.) **Weighted-average method, assigning costs (continuation of Exercise 18-17)**

Solution Exhibit 18-18 summarizes total costs to account for, calculates the costs per equivalent unit for direct materials and conversion costs, and assigns total costs to units completed and transferred out (including normal spoilage), to abnormal spoilage, and to units in ending work in process.

SOLUTION EXHIBIT 18-18
Summarize Total Costs to Account for, Compute Cost per Equivalent Unit, and Assign Total Costs to Units Completed, to Spoiled Units, and to Units in Ending Work in Process; Weighted-Average Method of Process Costing
Grey Manufacturing Company, November 2010

	Total Production Costs	Direct Materials	Conversion Costs
Work in process, beginning (given)	$ 2,533	$ 1,423	$ 1,110
Costs added in current period (given)	39,930	12,180	27,750
Total costs to account for	$42,463	$13,603	$28,860
Costs incurred to date		$13,603	$28,860
Divided by equivalent units of work done to date		÷11,150	÷ 9,750
Cost per equivalent unit		$ 1.22	$ 2.96
Assignment of costs:			
Good units completed and transferred out (9,000 units)			
Costs before adding normal spoilage	$37,620	(9,000# × $1.22) + (9,000# × $2.96)	
Normal spoilage (100 units)	418	(100# × $1.22) + (100# × $2.96)	
(A) Total cost of good units completed & transf. out	38,038		
(B) Abnormal spoilage (50 units)	209	(50# × $1.22) + (50# × $2.96)	
(C) Work in process, ending (2,000 units)	4,216	(2,000# × $1.22) + (600# × $2.96)	
(A)+(B)+(C) Total costs accounted for	$42,463	$13,603 + $28,860	

#Equivalent units of direct materials and conversion costs calculated in Solution Exhibit 18-17.

18-20 (20-25 min.) **FIFO method, assigning costs (continuation of Exercise 18-19).**

Solution Exhibit 18-20 summarizes total costs to account for, calculates the costs per equivalent unit for direct materials and conversion costs, and assigns total costs to units completed and transferred out (including normal spoilage), to abnormal spoilage, and to units in ending work in process.

SOLUTION EXHIBIT 18-20
Summarize Total Costs to Account For, Compute Cost per Equivalent Unit, and Assign Total Costs to Units Completed, to Spoiled Units, and to Units in Ending Work in Process; FIFO Method of Process Costing
Grey Manufacturing Company, November 2010

	Total Production Costs	Direct Materials		Conversion Costs
Work in process, beginning (given)	$ 2,533	$ 1,423		$ 1,110
Costs added in current period (given)	39,930	12,180		27,750
Total costs to account for	$42,463	$13,603		$28,860
Costs added in current period:		$12,180		$27,750
Divided by equivalent units of work done in current period		÷10,150		÷ 9,250
Cost per equivalent unit		$ 1.20		$ 3
Assignment of costs:				
Good units completed and transferred out (9,000 units):				
Work in process, beginning (1,000 units)	$ 2,533	$1,423	+	$1,110
Costs added to beg. work in process in current period	1,500	(0[a] × $1.20)	+	(500[a] × $3)
Total from beginning inventory before normal spoilage	4,033			
Started and completed before normal spoilage (8,000 units)	33,600	(8,000[a] × $1.20)	+	(8,000[a] × $3)
Normal spoilage (100 units)	420	(100[a] × $1.20)	+	(100[a] × $3)
(A) Total costs of good units completed and transferred out	38,053			
(B) Abnormal spoilage (50 units)	210	(50[a] × $1.20)	+	(50[a] × $3)
(C) Work in process, ending (2,000 units)	4,200	(2,000[a] × $1.20)	+	(600[a] × $3)
(A)+(B)+(C) Total costs accounted for	$42,463	$13,603	+	$28,860

[a] Equivalent units of direct materials and conversion costs calculated in Solution Exhibit 18-19.

18-22 (10 min.) **Standard-costing method, spoilage, journal entries.**

Spoilage represents the amount of resources that go into the process, but do not result in finished product. A simple way to account for spoilage in process costing is to calculate the amount of direct material that was spoiled. The journal entry to record the spoilage incurred in Aaron's production process is:

Manufacturing Overhead Control (normal spoilage)	250	
Work-in-Process Inventory (cost of spoiled sheet metal)		250

18-24 (25 min.) FIFO method, spoilage.

1. Solution Exhibit 18-24, Panel A, calculates the equivalent units of work done in the current period for each cost category in September 2010.
2. Solution Exhibit 18-24, Panel B, summarizes the total Chip Department costs for September 2010, calculates the costs per equivalent unit for each cost category, and assigns total costs to units completed and transferred out (including normal spoilage), to abnormal spoilage, and to units in ending work in process under the FIFO method.

SOLUTION EXHIBIT 18-24

First-in, First-out (FIFO) Method of Process Costing with Spoilage; Chipcity, Sept. 2010.

PANEL A: Summarize Output in Physical Units and Compute Output in Equivalent Units

		Equivalent Units	
Flow of Production	Physical Units	Direct Materials	Conversion Costs
Work in process, beginning (given)	600		
Started during current period (given)	2,550		
To account for	3,150		
Good units completed and transferred out during current period:			
From beginning work in process‖	600		
600 × (100% −100%); 600 × (100% − 30%)		0	420
Started and completed	1,500#		
1,500 × 100%; 1,500 × 100%		1,500	1,500
Normal spoilage*	315		
315 × 100%; 315 × 100%		315	315
Abnormal spoilage†	285		
285 × 100%; 285 × 100%		285	285
Work in process, ending‡	450		
450 × 100%; 450 × 40%		450	180
Accounted for	3,150		
Work done in current period only		2,550	2,700

‖Degree of completion in this department: direct materials, 100%; conversion costs, 30%.

#2,100 physical units completed and transferred out minus 600 physical units completed and transferred out from beginning work in process inventory.

*Normal spoilage is 15% of good units transferred out: 15% × 2,100 = 315 units. Degree of completion of normal spoilage in this department: direct materials, 100%; conversion costs, 100%.

†Abnormal spoilage = Actual spoilage − Normal spoilage = 600 − 315 = 285 units. Degree of completion of abnormal spoilage in this department: direct materials, 100%; conversion costs, 100%.

‡Degree of completion in this department: direct materials, 100%; conversion costs, 40%.

18-24 (cont'd)

SOLUTION EXHIBIT 18-24 (cont'd)

PANEL B: Summarize Total Costs to Account for, Compute Cost per Equivalent Unit, and Assign Total Costs to Units Completed, to Spoiled Units, and to Units in Ending Work in Process

	Total Production Costs	Direct Materials	Conversion Costs
Work in process, beginning (given)	$111,300	$ 96,000	$ 15,300
Costs added in current period (given)	797,400	567,000	230,400
Total costs to account for	$908,700	$663,000	$245,700
Costs added in current period		$567,000	$230,400
Divide by equiv. units of work in current period		÷ 2,550	÷ 2,700
Cost per equivalent unit		$222.353	$ 85.333
Assignment of costs:			
Good units completed and transferred out (2,100 units):			
Work in process, beginning (600 units)	$111,300	$96,000 +	$15,300
Costs added to beg. WIP in current period	35,840	$(0^\S \times \$222.353)$ +	$(420^\S \times \$85.333)$
Total from beginning inventory before normal spoilage	147,140		
Started and completed before normal spoilage (1,500 units)	461,529	$(1,500^\S \times \$222.353)$ +	$(1,500^\S \times \$85.333)$
Normal spoilage (315 units)	96,921	$(315^\S \times \$222.353)$ +	$(315^\S \times \$85.333)$
(A) Total costs of good units completed and transferred out	705,590		
(B) Abnormal spoilage (285 units)	87,691	$(285^\S \times \$222.353)$ +	$(285^\S \times \$85.333)$
(C) Work in process, ending (450 units)	115,419	$(450^\S \times \$222.353)$ +	$(180^\S \times \$85.333)$
(A)+(B)+(C) Total costs accounted for	$908,700	$663,000 +	$245,700

§Equivalent units of direct materials and conversion costs calculated in Panel A.

18-26 (15-20 min.) Physical units, inspection at various stages of completion.

	Inspection at 15%	Inspection at 40%	Inspection at 100%
Work in process, beginning (20%)*	16,000	16,000	16,000
Started during March	129,000	129,000	129,000
To account for	145,000	145,000	145,000
Good units completed and transferred out	120,000a	120,000a	120,000a
Normal spoilage (7%)	8,190b	9,310c	8,400d
Abnormal spoilage (12,000 – normal spoilage)	3,810	2,690	3,600
Work in process, ending (70%)*	13,000	13,000	13,000
Accounted for	145,000	145,000	145,000

*Degree of completion for conversion costs of the forging process at the dates of the work in process inventories

a 16,000 beginning inventory +129,000 –12,000 spoiled – 13,000 ending inventory = 120,000 units

b 7% × (120,000 – 16,000 + 13,000) = 7% × 117,000 = 8,800

c 7% × (120,000 + 13,000) = 7% × 133,000 = 9,310

d 7% × (120,000) = 8,400

18-28 (15 min.) Reworked units, costs of rework.

1. The two alternative approaches to accounting for the materials costs of reworked units are:
   (a) To charge the costs of rework to the current period as a separate expense item. This approach would highlight to Grey Goods the costs of the supplier problem.
   (b) To charge the costs of the rework to manufacturing overhead.

2. The $50 tumbler cost is the cost of the actual tumblers included in the washing machines. The $44 tumbler units from the new supplier were never used in any washing machine and that supplier is now bankrupt. This would be included in the cost of rework.

3. The total costs of rework due to the defective tumbler units include:
   (a) The labour and other conversion costs spent on substituting the old tumbler units with the new ones.
   (b) The costs of any extra negotiations to obtain the replacement tumbler units.
   (c) Any higher price the existing supplier may have charged to do a rush order for the replacement tumbler units.

18-30 (30 min.) Weighted-average method, spoilage.

1. Solution Exhibit 18-30, Panel A, calculates the equivalent units of work done to date for each cost category in March 2010.

2. & 3. Solution Exhibit 18-30, Panel B, calculates the cost per equivalent unit for each cost category, summarizes total costs to account for, and assigns these costs to units completed (including normal spoilage), to abnormal spoilage, and to units in ending work in process using the weighted-average method.

SOLUTION EXHIBIT 18-45
First-in, First-out (FIFO) Method of Process Costing with Spoilage,
Cooking Department of Spicier Inc. for January

PANEL A: Summarize Output in Physical Units and Compute Equivalent Units

Flow of Production	Physical Units (given)	Equivalent Units Direct Materials	Conversion Costs
Work in process, beginning	30,000		
Started during current period	50,000		
To account for	80,000		
Good units completed and transferred out			
during current period:	40,000	40,000	40,000
Normal spoilage*			
6,000 × 100%; 6,000 × 100%	6,000	6,000	6,000
Abnormal spoilage†			
2,000 × 100%; 2,000 × 100%	2,000	2,000	2,000
Work in process ending‡			
32,000 × 100%; 32,000 × 75%	32,000	32,000	24,000
Accounted for	80,000		
Work done to date		80,000	72,000

*Degree of completion of normal spoilage in this department: direct materials, 100%; conversion costs, 100%.
†Degree of completion of abnormal spoilage in this department: direct materials, 100%; conversion costs, 100%.
‡Degree of completion in this department: direct materials, 100%; conversion costs, 75%.

18-30 (cont'd)

SOLUTION EXHIBIT 18-45 (cont'd)

PANEL B: Compute Equivalent Unit Costs, Summarize Total Costs to Account for, and Assign Costs to Units Completed, to Spoilage Units, and to Units in Ending Work in Process

		Total Production Costs	Direct Materials	Conversion Costs
	Work in process, beginning (given)	$504,000	$288,000	$216,000
	Costs added in current period (given)	1,203,840	504,000	699,840
	Costs incurred to date		$792,000	$915,840
	Divide by equiv. units of work to date		÷ 80,000	÷ 72,000
	Equivalent unit costs of work done to date		$ 9.90	$ 12.72
	Total costs to account for	$1,707,840		
	Assignment of costs:			
	Good units completed and transferred out (40,000 units):			
	Costs before adding normal spoilage	$ 904,800	(40,000# × $9.90) + (40,000# × $12.72)	
	Normal spoilage (6,000 units)	135,720	(6,000# × $9.90) + (6,000# × $12.72)	
(A)	Total cost of good units completed and transferred out	1,040,520		
(B)	Abnormal spoilage (2,000 units)	45,240	(2,000# × $9.90) + (2,000# × $12.72)	
	Work in process, ending (32,000 units)			
	Direct materials	316,800	32,000# × $9.90	
	Conversion costs	305,280		24,000# × $12.72
(C)	Total work in process, ending	622,080		
(A)+(B)+(C)	Total costs accounted for	$1,707,840		

#Equivalent units of direct materials and conversion costs calculated in Panel A.

18-32 (30 min.) Standard-costing method, spoilage (Refer to the information in 18-30).

1. The equivalent units of work done in the current period for direct materials and conversion costs are calculated in Solution Exhibit 18-31, Panel A.
2. The cost per equivalent unit for direct materials and conversion costs equals the standard cost per unit given in the problem: $9.60 per equivalent unit for direct materials in both beginning inventory and work done in the current period, and $12.00 per equivalent unit for conversion costs in both beginning inventory and work done in the current period.
3. Solution Exhibit 18-32 summarizes the total costs to account for and assigns these costs to units completed and transferred out (including normal spoilage), to abnormal spoilage, and to ending work in process using the standard costing method.

18-32 (cont'd)

SOLUTION EXHIBIT 18-32

Compute Equivalent Unit Costs, Summarize Total Costs to Account For, and Assign
Costs to Units Completed, to Spoilage Units, and to Units in ending Work in Process;
Standard Costing Method of Process Costing with Spoilage
Lang Manufacturing Company, March 2010

		Total Production Costs	Direct Materials	Conversion Costs
	Standard cost per equivalent unit (given)	$ 21.60	$ 9.60	$ 12.00
	Work in process, beginning*	$ 504,000		
	Costs added in current period at standard prices:			
	Direct materials 50,000 × $9.60;			
	Conversion costs 54,000 × $12	1,128,000	$480,000	$648,000
	Costs to account for	$1,632,000		
	Assignment of costs at standard costs:			
	Goods units completed and transferred out (40,000 units):			
	Work in process, beginning (30,000 units)	$504,000		
	Direct materials added in Current period	0	0§ × $9.60	
	Conversion costs added in Current period	144,000		12,000§ × $12
	Total from beginning inventory before normal spoilage	648,000		
	Started and completed before normal spoilage (10,000 units)	216,000	(10,000§ × $9.60) + (10,000§ × $12)	
	Normal spoilage (6,000 units)	129,600	(6,000§ × $9.60) + (6,000§ × $12)	
(A)	Total cost of good units transferred out	993,600		
(B)	Abnormal spoilage (2,000 units)	43,200	(2,000§ × $9.60) + (2,000§ × $12)	
	Work in process, ending (32,000 units)			
	Direct materials	307,200	32,000§ × $9.60	
	Conversion costs	288,000		24,000§ × $12
(C)	Total work in process, ending	595,200		
(A)+(B)+(C)	Total costs accounted for	$1,632,000		

*Work in process, beginning has 30,000 equivalent units (30,000 physical units × 100%) of direct materials and 18,000 equivalent units (30,000 physical units × 60%) of conversion costs. Hence work in process, beginning inventory at standard cost equals ($9.60 × 30,000) + ($12.00 × 18,000) = $288,000 + $216,000 = $504,000.

§Equivalent units of direct materials and conversion costs calculated in Solution Exhibit 18-31 Panel A.

18-34 (25 min.) FIFO method, spoilage.

For the Cleaning Department, Solution Exhibit 18-34 summarizes the total costs for May, calculates the equivalent units of work done in the current period for direct materials and conversion costs, and assigns total costs to units completed and transferred out (including normal spoilage), to abnormal spoilage, and to units in ending work in process under the FIFO method.

SOLUTION EXHIBIT 18-34
First-in, First-out (FIFO) Method of Process Costing with Spoilage;
Cleaning Department of Windsor Company for May.

PANEL A: Summarize Output in Physical Units and Compute Output in Equivalent Units

| | | Equivalent Units | |
| | Physical | Direct | Conversion |
Flow of Production	Units	Materials	Costs
Work in process, beginning (given)	2,500		
Started during current period (given)	22,500		
To account for	25,000		
Good units completed and transferred out during current period:			
From beginning work in process‖	2,500		
2,500 × (100% −100%); 2,500 × (100% − 80%)		0	500
Started and completed	16,000#		
16,000 × 100%; 16,000 × 100%		16,000	16,000
Normal spoilage*	1,850		
1,850 × 100%; 1,850 × 100%		1,850	1,850
Abnormal spoilage†	650		
650 × 100%; 650 × 100%		650	650
Work in process, ending‡	4,000		
4,000 × 100%; 4,000 × 25%		4,000	1,000
Accounted for	25,000		
Work done in current period only		22,500	20,000

‖ Degree of completion in this department: direct materials, 100%; conversion costs, 80%.

#18,500 physical units completed and transferred out minus 2,500 physical units completed and transferred out from beginning work-in-process inventory.

*Normal spoilage is 10% of good units transferred out: 10% × 18,500 = 1,850 units. Degree of completion of normal spoilage in this department: direct materials, 100%; conversion costs, 100%.

†Total spoilage = 2,500 + 22,500 − 18,500 − 4,000 = 2,500 units

Abnormal spoilage = 2,500 − 1,850 = 650 units. Degree of completion of abnormal spoilage in this department: direct materials, 100%; conversion costs, 100%.

‡Degree of completion in this department: direct materials, 100%; conversion costs, 25%.

18-34 (cont'd)

SOLUTION EXHIBIT 18-34 (cont'd)

PANEL B: Summarize Total Costs to Account for, Compute Cost per Equivalent Unit, and Assign Total Costs to Units Completed, to Spoiled Units, and to Units in Ending Work in Process

	Total Production Costs	Direct Materials	Conversion Costs
Work in process, beginning (given)	$ 4,500	$ 2,500	$ 2,000
Costs added in current period (given)	42,500	22,500	20,000
Total costs to account for	$47,000	$25,000	$22,000
Costs added in current period		$22,500	$20,000
Divided by equivalent units of work done in current period		÷22,500	÷20,000
Cost per equivalent unit		$ 1	$ 1
Assignment of costs:			
Good units completed and transferred out (18,500 units):			
Work in process, beginning (2,500 units)	$ 4,500	$2,500 +	$2,000
Costs added to beg. WIP in current period	500	(0§ × $1) +	(500§ × $1)
Total from BI before normal spoilage	5,000		
Started & completed before normal spoilage (16,000)	32,000	(16,000§ × $1) +	(16,000§ × $1)
Normal spoilage (1,850 units)	3,700	(1,850§ × $1) +	(1,850§ × $1)
(A) Total costs of good units completed and transferred out	40,700		
(B) Abnormal spoilage (650 units)	1,300	(650§ × $1) +	(650§ × $1)
(C) Work in process, ending (4,000 units)	5,000	(4,000§ × $1) +	(1,000§ × $1)
(A)+(B)+(C) Total costs accounted for	$47,000	$25,000 +	$22,000

§Equivalent units of direct materials and conversion costs calculated in Panel A.

18-36 (25 min.) FIFO method, Packaging Department.

Solution Exhibit 18-36 summarizes the total Packaging Department costs for May, shows the equivalent units of work done in the Packaging Department in the current period for transferred-in costs, direct materials, and conversion costs, and assigns total costs to units completed and transferred out (including normal spoilage), to abnormal spoilage, and to units in ending work-in-process under the FIFO method.

SOLUTION EXHIBIT 18-36
First-in, First-out (FIFO) Method of Process Costing with Spoilage;
Packaging Department of Windsor Company for May

PANEL A: Summarize Output in Physical Units and Compute Output in Equivalent Units

Flow of Production	Physical Units	Transferred-in Costs	Direct Materials	Conversion Costs
Work in process, beginning (given)	7,500			
Started during current period (given)	18,500			
To account for	26,000			
Good units completed and transferred out during current period:				
From beginning work in process‖	7,500			
7,500 × (100% − 100%); 7,500 × (100% − 0%); 7,500 × (100% − 80%)		0	7,500	1,500
Started and completed	7,500#			
7,500 × 100%; 7,500 × 100%; 7,500 × 100%		7,500	7,500	7,500
Normal spoilage*	750			
750 × 100%; 750% × 100%; 750 × 100%		750	750	750
Abnormal spoilage†	250			
250 × 100%; 250 × 100%; 250 × 100%		250	250	250
Work in process, ending‡	10,000			
10,000 × 100%; 10,000 × 0%; 10,000 × 25%		10,000	0	2,500
Accounted for	26,000			
Work done in current period only		18,500	16,000	12,500

‖Degree of completion in this department: transferred-in costs, 100%; direct materials, 0%; conversion costs, 80%.
#15,000 physical units completed and transferred out minus 7,500 physical units completed and transferred out from beginning work-in-process inventory.
*Normal spoilage is 5% of good units transferred out: 5% × 15,000 = 750 units. Degree of completion of normal spoilage in this department: transferred-in costs, 100%; direct materials, 100%; conversion costs, 100%.
†Total spoilage = 7,500 + 18,500 – 15,000 – 10,000 = 1,000 units.
 Abnormal spoilage = 1,000 – 750 = 250 units. Degree of completion of abnormal spoilage in this department: transferred-in costs, 100%; direct materials, 100%; conversion costs, 100%.
‡Degree of completion in this department: transferred-in costs, 100%; direct materials, 0%; conversion costs, 25%.

18-36 (cont'd)

SOLUTION EXHIBIT 18-36 (cont'd)

PANEL B: Summarize Total Costs to Account for, Compute Cost per Equivalent Unit, and Assign Total Costs to Units Completed, to Spoiled Units, and to Units in Ending Work in Process

	Total Production Costs	Transferred-in Costs	Direct Materials	Conversion Costs
Work in process, beginning (given)	$22,250	$16,125	$ 0	$ 6,125
Costs added in current period (given)	54,675	40,700*	1,600	12,375
Total costs to account for	$76,925	$56,825	$1,600	$18,500
Costs added in current period		$40,700	$1,600	$12,375
Divided by equivalent units of work done in current period		÷18,500	÷16,000	÷12,500
Cost per equivalent unit		$ 2.20	$ 0.10	$ 0.99
Assignment of costs:				
Good units completed and transferred out (15,000 units):				
Work in process, beginning (7,500 units)	$22,250	$16,125 + $0 + $6,125		
Costs added to beg. work in process in current period	2,235	(0× $2.20) + (7,500§× 0.10)+(1,500§×$0.99)		
Total from beginning inventory before normal spoilage	24,485			
Started and completed before normal spoilage (7,500 units)	24,675	7,500§ × ($2.20 + $0.10 + $0.99)		
Normal spoilage (750 units)	2,467	750§ × ($2.20 + $0.10 + $0.99)		
(A) Total costs of good units completed and transferred out	51,627			
(B) Abnormal spoilage (250 units)	823	250§ × ($2.20 + $0.10 + $0.99)		
(C) Work in process, ending (10,000 units)	24,475	(10,000§×$2.20)+(0§×$0.10)+(2,500§×$0.99)		
(A)+(B)+(C) Total costs accounted for	$76,925	$56,825 + $1,600 + $18,500		

*Total costs of good units completed and transferred out in Panel B of Solution Exhibit 18-34.
§Equivalent units of direct materials and conversion costs calculated in Panel A.

18-38 (25-35 min.) Weighted-average method, inspection at 80% completion.

The computation and allocation of spoilage is the most difficult part of this problem. The units in the ending inventory have passed inspection. Therefore, of the 100,000 units to account for (12,500 beginning + 87,500 started), 12,500 must have been spoiled in May [100,000 – (62,500 completed + 25,000 ending inventory)]. Normal spoilage is 8,750 [0.10 × (62,500 + 25,000)]. The 3,750 remainder is abnormal spoilage (12,500 – 8,750).

Solution Exhibit 18-38, Panel A, calculates the equivalent units of work done for each cost category. We comment on several points in this calculation:

- Ending work in process includes an element of normal spoilage since all the ending WIP have passed the point of inspection—inspection occurs when production is 80% complete, while the units in ending WIP are 95% complete.
- Spoilage includes no direct materials units because spoiled units are detected and removed from the finishing activity when inspection occurs at the time production is 80% complete. Direct materials are added only later when production is 90% complete.
- Direct materials units are included for ending work in process, which is 95% complete, but not for beginning work in process, which is 25% complete. The reason is that direct materials are added when production is 90% complete. The ending work in process, therefore, contains direct materials units; the beginning work in process does not.

Solution Exhibit 18-38, Panel B, summarizes total costs to account for, computes the costs per equivalent unit for each cost category, and assigns costs to units completed (including normal spoilage), to abnormal spoilage, and to units in ending work in process using the weighted-average method. The cost of ending work in process includes the assignment of normal spoilage costs since these units have passed the point of inspection. The costs assigned to each cost category are as follows:

Cost of good units completed and transferred out (including normal spoilage costs on good units)	$2,346,687
Abnormal spoilage	84,638
Cost of ending work in process (including normal spoilage costs on ending work in process)	917,675
Total costs assigned and accounted for	$3,349,000

18-38 (cont'd)

SOLUTION EXHIBIT 18-38
Weighted-Average Method of Process Costing with Spoilage;
Finishing Department of Ottawa Manufacturing for August.

PANEL A: Summarize Output in Physical Units and Compute Output in Equivalent Units

		Equivalent Units		
Flow of Production	**Physical Units**	**Transferred-in Costs**	**Direct Materials**	**Conversion Costs**
Work in process, beginning (given)	12,500			
Started during current period (given)	87,500			
To account for	100,000			
Good units completed and transferred out during current period:	62,500	62,500	62,500	62,500
Normal spoilage on good units*	6,250			
6,250 × 100%; 6,250 × 0%; 6,250 × 80%		6,250	0	5,000
Work in process, ending‡ (given)	25,000			
25,000 × 100%; 25,000 × 100%; 25,000 × 95%		25,000	25,000	23,750
Normal spoilage in ending WIP**	2,500			
2,500 × 100%; 2,500 × 0%; 2,500 × 80%		2,500	0	2,000
Abnormal spoilage†	3,750			
3,750 × 100%; 3,750 × 0%; 3,750 × 80%		3,750	0	3,000
Accounted for	100,000			
Work done to date		100,000	87,500	96,250

*Normal spoilage is 10% of good units that pass inspection: 10% × 62,500 = 6,250 units. Degree of completion of normal spoilage in this department: transferred-in costs, 100%; direct materials, 0%; conversion costs, 80%.

‡Degree of completion in this department: transferred-in costs, 100%; direct materials, 100%; conversion costs, 95%.

**Normal spoilage is 10% of the good units in ending WIP that have passed the inspection point, 10% × 25,000 = 2,500 units. Degree of completion of normal spoilage in this department: transferred-in costs, 100%; direct materials, 0%; conversion costs, 80%.

†Abnormal spoilage = Actual spoilage – Normal spoilage = 12,500 – 8,750 = 3,750 units. Degree of completion of abnormal spoilage in this department: transferred-in costs, 100%; direct materials, 0%; conversion costs, 80%.

18-38 (cont'd)

SOLUTION EXHIBIT 18-38 (cont'd)

PANEL B: Summarize Total Costs to Account for, Compute Cost per Equivalent Unit, and Assign Total Costs to Units Completed, to Spoiled Units, and to Units in Ending Work in Process

	Total Production Costs	Transferred-in Costs	Direct Materials	Conversion Costs
Work in process, beginning (given)	$ 156,125	$103,625	$ –	$ 52,500
Costs added in current period (given)	3,192,875	809,375	819,000	1,564,500
Total costs to account for	$3,349,000	$913,000	$819,000	$1,617,000
Costs incurred to date		$913,000	$819,000	$1,617,000
Divided by equivalent units of work done to date		÷100,000	÷ 87,500	÷ 96,250
Cost per equivalent unit		$ 9.13	$ 9.36	$ 16.80

Assignment of costs:

Good units completed and transferred out (62,500 units):

Costs before adding normal spoilage	$2,205,625	62,500# × ($9.13 + $9.36 + $16.80)		
Normal spoilage (6,250 units)	141,063	(6,250# × $9.13) +	(0# × $9.36) +	(5,000# × $16.80)
(A) Total costs of good units completed and transferred out	2,346,688			
(B) Abnormal spoilage (3,750 units)	84,638	(3,750# × $9.13) +	(0# × $9.36) +	(3,000# × $16.80)

Work in process, ending (25,000 units)

WIP ending, before normal spoilage	861,250	(25,000# × $9.13) + (25,000# × $9.36) +		
Normal spoilage on ending WIP	56,425	(23,750# × $16.80)		
(C) Total costs of ending WIP	917,675	(2,500# × $9.13) +	(0# × $9.36) +	(2,000# × $16.80)
(A)+(B)+(C) Total costs accounted for	$3,349,000	$913,000 +	$819,000 +	$1,617,000

#Equivalent units of transferred-in costs, direct materials, and conversion costs calculated in Panel A.

18-40 (15 min.) Spoilage in job costing.

1. Normal spoilage rate= Units of normal spoilage ÷ Total good units completed

$$= 5 \div 35$$

$$= 14.3\%.$$

2.

a) Journal entry for spoilage related to a specific job:

Materials Control (spoiled goods at current disposal value) 5 × $200   1,000

    Work-in-Process Control (Job #10)   1,000

Note: The costs incurred on the bad units (5 × $1,000) are already part of the balance in WIP.
    The cost of the 35 good units is (35 × $1,000) + (5 × $800) = $39,000

b) Journal entry for spoilage common to all jobs:

Materials Control (spoiled goods at current disposal value) 5 × $200   1,000

Manufacturing Overhead Control (normal spoilage)   4,000

    Work-in-Process Control (Job #10)   5,000

Note: In developing the predetermined overhead rate, the budgeted manufacturing overhead would include expected normal spoilage costs.

c) Journal entry for abnormal spoilage:

Materials Control (spoiled goods at current disposal value) 5 × $200   1,000

Loss from Abnormal Spoilage 5 × $800   4,000

    Work-in-Process Control (Job #10)   5,000

Note: If the spoilage is abnormal, the net loss is highlighted and always charged to an abnormal loss account.

18-42 (10 min.) Scrap at time of sale or at time of production, journal entries (continuation of 18-40).

a) Journal entry for recognizing immaterial scrap at time of sale:

Cash or Accounts Receivable	300	
Scrap Revenues		300

(To record other revenue sale of scrap)

b) Journal entry for recognizing material scrap related to a specific job at time of sale:

Cash or Accounts Receivable	300	
Work-in-Process Control (Job #10)		300

c) Journal entry for recognizing material scrap common to all jobs at time of sale:

Cash or Accounts Receivable	300	
Manufacturing Overhead Control		300

d) Journal entry for recognizing material scrap as inventory at time of production and recording at net realizable value:

Materials Control	300	
Work-in-Process Control (Job #10)		300

Cash or Accounts Receivable	300	
Materials Control		300

(When later sold)

18-44 (40 min.) Job costing, spoilage, governance.

1. Analysis of the 5,000 units rejected by Richmond Company for Job No. R1192-122 yields the following breakdown between normal and abnormal spoilage.

	Units
Normal spoilage*	3,000
Abnormal spoilage:	
Design defect	900
Other [5,000 – (3,000 + 900)]	1,100
Total units rejected	5,000

*Normal spoilage = 0.025 of normal input
  When output equals 117,000 units,
  Normal input = 117,000 ÷ (1 – 0.025)
              = 120,000 units
  Normal spoilage = 120,000 × 0.025
              = 3,000 units

2. The journal entries required to properly account for Job No. R1192–122 are presented below and use an average cost per unit of $68.40 ($8,344,800 ÷ 122,000).

Materials control (or A/R or cash)[1]	$34,440	
Abnormal loss[2]	129,000	
WIP control[3]		$162,000
Cash[4]		1,440

To account for 5,000 units rejected.

Finished good inventory[5]	$8,182,800	
WIP control		$8,182,800

To transfer 117,000 units to finished goods inventory.

[1]Units for sale 4,100 units sold at $8.40 each.

[2]Loss from abnormal spoilage:
2,000 units at $68.40	$136,800
Disposal cost	1,440
Cost recovery (1,100 × $8.40)	(9,240)
	$129,000

[3]WIP control:
900 defective units at $68.40	$ 61,560
1,100 other rejected units at $68.40	75,240
3,000 normal units at $8.40	25,200
	$162,000

[4]Additional cost to dispose of 900 units rejected because of design defect.

[5] Less
$8,344,800	Total manufacturing costs
162,000	WIP control
8,182,800	

18-44 (cont'd)

3. a. If all spoilage were considered normal, the journal entries to account for Job No. R1192–122 would be as follows:

Materials Control (or A/R or cash)	$34,440	
Finished Goods Inventory	8,311,800	
WIP Control		$8,344,800
Cash		1,440

To transfer 117,000 good units to finished goods inventory and to recognize the salvage value of 4,100 units of spoiled units (4,100 × $8.40 = $34,440) and the disposal cost of $1,440 of the other 900 spoiled units.

All remaining WIP costs are treated as normal costs of production and charged to finished goods.

By considering all spoilage as normal, Richmond will show no abnormal loss but instead will add $129,000 to the finished-goods inventory. Hence, showing all spoilage as normal will increase Richmond's operating income by $129,000 in the short term since abnormal spoilage is expensed immediately to the income statement.

3b. Incorrect reporting of spoilage as normal instead of abnormal with the goal of increasing operating income is unethical. In assessing the situation, the management accountant should consider the following:

- Spoilage should be accounted for using relevant and reliable information. Accounting for spoilage incorrectly to make the company's operating performance look better than it is violates competence standards. It is unethical for Rutherford to suggest that Perez change abnormal spoilage to normal spoilage in order to make operating performance look good.

- The management accountant has a responsibility to avoid actual or apparent conflicts of interest and advise all appropriate parties of any potential conflict. Rutherford's motivation for wanting Perez to revise the quality figures could well have been motivated by Rutherford's desire to please senior management. In this regard, both Rutherford's and Perez's behaviour (if Drummond agrees to modify the spoilage classification) could be viewed as unethical.

- The management accountant should require that information be fairly and objectively communicated and that all relevant information should be disclosed. From a management accountant's standpoint, showing abnormal spoilage as normal spoilage to make operating performance look good would be unethical.

Perez should indicate to Rutherford that the classification of normal and abnormal spoilage established by Richmond Company is, indeed, appropriate. If Rutherford still insists on modifying the spoilage classification for this job to report higher operating income figures, Perez should raise the matter with one of Rutherford's superiors. If, after taking all these steps, there is continued pressure to overstate operating income, Perez should consider resigning from the company, and not engage in unethical behaviour.

CHAPTER 19
COST MANAGEMENT: QUALITY, TIME, AND
THE THEORY OF CONSTRAINTS

19-2 Quality of design measures how closely the characteristics of products or services match the needs and wants of customers. Conformance quality measures whether the product has been made according to design, engineering, and manufacturing specifications.

19-4 An internal failure cost differs from an external failure cost on the basis of when the nonconforming product is detected. An internal failure is detected *before a* product is shipped to a customer whereas an external failure is detected *after* a product is shipped to a customer.

19-6 No, companies should emphasize financial as well as nonfinancial measures of quality, such as yield and defect rates. Nonfinancial measures are not directly linked to bottom-line performance but they indicate and direct attention to the specific areas that need improvement. Tracking nonfinancial measures over time directly reveals whether these areas have, in fact, improved over time. Nonfinancial measures are easy to quantify and easy to understand.

19-8 Examples of nonfinancial measures of internal performance are:
1. The number of defects for each product line.
2. Process yield (rates of good output to total output at a particular process).
3. Manufacturing lead time (the time taken to convert direct materials into finished output).
4. Employee turnover (ratio of the number of employees who left the company in a year, say, to the total number of employees who worked for the company in that year).

19-10 No. There is a trade-off between customer-response time and on-time performance. Simply scheduling longer customer-response time makes achieving on-time performance easier. Companies should, however, attempt to reduce uncertainty of arrival of orders, manage bottlenecks, reduce setup and processing time, and run smaller batches. This would have the effect of reducing both customer-response time and improving on-time performance.

19-12 No. Adding a product when capacity is constrained and the timing of customer orders is uncertain causes delays in delivering all existing products. If the revenue losses from delays in delivering existing products and the increase in carrying costs of the existing products exceed the positive contribution earned by the product that was added, then it is not worthwhile to make and sell the new product, despite its positive contribution margin. The chapter describes the negative effects that one product can have on others when products share manufacturing facilities.

19-14 The four key steps in managing bottleneck resources are:
Step 1: Recognize that the bottleneck operation determines throughput contribution.
Step 2: Search for and find the bottleneck.
Step 3: Keep the bottleneck busy and subordinate all nonbottleneck operations to the bottleneck operation.
Step 4: Increase bottleneck efficiency and capacity.

19-16 (30 min.) Costs of quality.

1. The ratios of each COQ category to revenues and to total quality costs for each period are as follows:

Costen, Inc.: Semi-annual Costs of Quality Report
(in thousands)

	6/30/2009			12/31/2009			6/30/2010			12/31/2010		
	Actual	% of Revenues	% of Total Quality Costs	Actual	% of Revenues	% of Total Quality Costs	Actual	% of Revenues	% of Total Quality Costs	Actual	% of Revenues	% of Total Quality Costs
	(1)	(2) = (1) ÷ $8,240	(3) = (1) ÷ $2,040	(4)	(5) = (4) ÷ $9,080	(6) = (4) ÷ $2,159	(7)	(8) = (7) ÷ $9,300	(9) = (7) ÷ $1,605	(10)	(11) = (10) ÷ $9,020	(12) = (10) ÷ $1,271
Prevention costs												
Machine maintenance	$ 440			$ 440			$ 390			$ 330		
Supplier training	20			100			50			40		
Design reviews	50			214			210			200		
Total prevention costs	510	6.2%	25.0%	754	8.3%	34.9%	650	7.0%	40.5%	570	6.3%	44.9%
Appraisal costs												
Incoming inspection	108			123			90			63		
Final testing	332			332			293			203		
Total appraisal costs	440	5.3%	21.6%	455	5.0%	21.1%	383	4.1%	23.9%	266	3.0%	20.9%
Internal failure costs												
Rework	231			202			165			112		
Scrap	124			116			71			67		
Total internal failure costs	355	4.3%	17.4%	318	3.5%	14.7%	236	2.5%	14.7%	179	2.0%	14.1%
External failure costs												
Warranty repairs	165			85			72			68		
Customer returns	570			547			264			188		
Total external failure costs	735	8.9%	36.0%	632	7.0%	29.3%	336	3.6%	20.9%	256	2.8%	20.1%
Total quality costs	$2,040	24.7%	100.0%	$2,159	23.8%	100.0%	$1,605	17.2%	100.0%	$1,271	14.1%	100.0%
Total revenues	$8,240			$9,080			$9,300			$9,020		

19-16 (cont'd)

2. From an analysis of the Cost of Quality Report, it would appear that Costen, Inc.'s program has been successful because:

- Total quality costs as a percentage of total revenues have declined from 24.7% to 14.1%.
- External failure costs, those costs signaling customer dissatisfaction, have declined from 8.9% of total revenues to 2.8% of total revenues and from 36% of all quality costs to 20.1% of all quality costs. These declines in warranty repairs and customer returns should translate into increased revenues in the future.
- Internal failure costs as a percentage of revenues have been halved from 4.3% to 2%.
- Appraisal costs have decreased from 5.3% to 3% of revenues. Preventing defects from occurring in the first place is reducing the demand for final testing.
- Quality costs have shifted to the area of prevention where problems are solved before production starts: total prevention costs (maintenance, supplier training, and design reviews) have risen from 25% to 44.9% of total quality costs. The $60,000 increase in these costs is more than offset by decreases in other quality costs.
- Because of improved designs, quality training, and additional pre-production inspections, scrap and rework costs have almost been halved
- Production does not have to spend an inordinate amount of time with customer service since they are now making the product right the first time and warranty repairs and customer returns have decreased.

3. To estimate the opportunity cost of not implementing the quality program and to help her make her case, Jessica Tolmy could have assumed that:

- Sales and market share would continue to decline if the quality program was not implemented and then calculated the loss in revenue and contribution margin.
- The company would have to compete on price rather than quality and calculated the impact of having to lower product prices.

Opportunity costs are not recorded in accounting systems because they represent the results of what might have happened if the company had not improved quality. Nevertheless, opportunity costs of poor quality can be significant. It is important for Costen to take these costs into account when making decisions about quality.

19-18 (15 min.) **Cost of quality analysis, ethical considerations (continuation of 19-17).**

1. Cost of improving quality of plastic = $25 × 100,000 = $2,500,000

2. Total cost of lawsuits = 2 × $750,000 = $1,500,000

3. While economically this may seem like a good decision, qualitative factors should be more important than quantitative factors when it comes to protecting customers from harm and injury. If a product can cause a customer serious harm and injury, an ethical and moral company should take steps to prevent that harm and injury. The company's code of ethics should guide this decision.

4. In addition to ethical considerations, the company should consider the societal cost of this decision, effects to reputation if word of these problems leaks out at a later date, and governmental intervention and regulation. The negative societal response could be quite strong, given infants are involved.

19-20 (25 min.) **Quality improvement, relevant costs, and relevant revenues.**

1. Relevant costs over the next year of choosing the new component = $55 × 20,000 printing presses = $1,100,000

	Relevant Benefits over the Next Year of Choosing the New Component
Costs of quality items	
Savings in rework costs	
$80 × 12,875 rework hours	$1,030,000
Savings in customer-support costs	
$40 × 900 customer-support hours	36,000
Savings in transportation costs for parts	
$360 × 200 fewer loads	72,000
Savings in warranty repair costs	
$90 × 7,000 repair hours	630,000
Opportunity costs	
Contribution margin from increased sales	1,800,000
Cost savings and additional contribution margin	$3,568,000

19-20 (cont'd)

Because the expected relevant benefits of $3,568,000 exceed the expected relevant costs of the new component of $1,100,000, Photon should introduce the new component. Note that the opportunity cost benefits in the form of higher contribution margin from increased sales is an important component for justifying the investment in the new component.

2. The incremental cost of the new component of $1,100,000 is less than the incremental savings in rework and repair costs of $1,768,000 ($1,030,000 + $36,000 + $72,000 + $630,000). Thus, it is beneficial for TechnoPrint to invest in the new component even without making any additional sales.

19-22 (20 min.) Nonfinancial quality measures, on-time delivery.

1. The data seem to support the concerns expressed by Checkers' headquarters. Store 2 has the lowest percentage of late deliveries and the highest customer satisfaction scores. On the other hand, Store 4 has the highest percentage of late deliveries and the lowest customer satisfaction scores. Both Stores 1 and 3 fall between the two extremes and have similar customer satisfaction scores.

2.

	Percentage of Late Deliveries (X)	Average Overall Satisfaction (Y)
Highest observation of late delivery percentage	25	2
Lowest observation of late delivery percentage	5	4
Difference	20	−2

Average overall satisfaction = $a + b \times$ Percentage of late deliveries

Slope coefficient $(b) = \dfrac{-2}{20} = -0.10$

Using high observation, Constant $(a) = 2 + 0.10 \times 25 = 4.5$
Using low observation, Constant $(a) = 4 + 0.10 \times 5 = 4.5$

Average overall satisfaction = $4.5 - 0.10 \times$ Percentage of late deliveries

If the percentage of late deliveries increases from 5% to 7%,
Average overall satisfaction = $4.5 - 0.10 \times 7 = 3.8$

19-22 (cont'd)

3. Checkers must estimate the profit implications of lost customer satisfaction due to failure to meet guaranteed delivery times. In addition, the company needs information about the value customers place on the delivery guarantee. Customers may choose to order from Checkers because of the guarantee. Because failure to meet the guarantee represents a cost, Checkers needs to compare this expected cost to the additional sales and profits attributable to the guarantee.

Moreover, the delivery guarantee should motivate employees to strive for on-time delivery. After all, store profits, on which store managers bonuses are based, will be lower because of the $5 discount if pizzas are not delivered on time. Store managers who view the guarantee as a "win-win" situation should also be educated on the long-term effects that late deliveries have on the company if overall customer satisfaction declines. One possibility is to modify the bonus scheme so that on-time delivery is explicitly weighted in the bonus calculation.

19-24 (25 min.) Waiting time, cost considerations, and customer satisfaction (continued from 19-23).

1. i) If SU hires two more advisors then the average wait time will be:

$$= \frac{\left(\begin{array}{c}\text{Average number} \\ \text{of students per day}\end{array}\right) \times \left(\begin{array}{c}\text{Time taken to} \\ \text{advise a student}\end{array}\right)^2}{2 \times \left[\begin{array}{c}\text{Maximum amount} \\ \text{of time available}\end{array} - \left[\left(\begin{array}{c}\text{Average amount} \\ \text{of students per day}\end{array}\right) \times \left(\begin{array}{c}\text{Time taken to} \\ \text{advise a student}\end{array}\right)\right]\right]}$$

$$= \frac{400 \times (12)^2}{2 \times [12 \text{ advisors} \times 10 \text{ hours} \times 60 \text{ minutes} - [400 \times 12]]}$$

$$= \frac{57,600}{2 \times [7,200 - 4,800]} = 12 \text{ minutes}$$

ii) If SU has its current employees work 6 days a week and has them advise 350 students a day then the average wait time will be:

$$= \frac{\left(\begin{array}{c}\text{Average number} \\ \text{of students per day}\end{array}\right) \times \left(\begin{array}{c}\text{Time taken to} \\ \text{advise a student}\end{array}\right)^2}{2 \times \left[\begin{array}{c}\text{Maximum amount} \\ \text{of time available}\end{array} - \left[\left(\begin{array}{c}\text{Average amount} \\ \text{of students per day}\end{array}\right) \times \left(\begin{array}{c}\text{Time taken to} \\ \text{advise a student}\end{array}\right)\right]\right]}$$

$$= \frac{350 \times (12)^2}{2 \times [10 \text{ advisors} \times 10 \text{ hours} \times 60 \text{ minutes} - [350 \times 12]]}$$

$$= \frac{(50,400)}{2 \times [6,000 - 4,200]} = 14 \text{ minutes}$$

2. i) Cost if SU hires 2 extra advisors for the registration period:
   Advisor salary cost = 12 advisors ×10 days × $100 = $12,000
   ii) Cost if SU has its 10 advisors work 6 days a week for the registration period:
   Advisor salary cost = 10 advisors × 10 days × $100 + 10 advisors × 2 days × $150
   = $13,000
   Alternative (i) is less costly for SU.

3. Hiring two extra advisors has a shorter waiting time and a lower cost than extending the workweek to 6 days during the registration period. However, the quality of the advising may not be as high. The temporary advisors may not be as familiar with the requirements of the university. They may also be unaware of how to work within the system (i.e., they may not be aware of alternatives that may be available to help students). Conversely, having 10 advisors work 60-hour weeks may lead to lower productivity due to fatigue.

19-26 (15 min.) **Theory of constraints, throughput contribution, quality.**

1. Cost of defective unit at machining operation which is not a bottleneck operation is the loss in direct materials (variable costs) of $32 per unit. Producing 2,000 defective units does not result in loss of throughput contribution. Despite the defective production, machining can produce and transfer 80,000 units to finishing. Therefore, cost of 2,000 defective units at the machining operation is $32 × 2,000 = $64,000.

2. A defective unit produced at the bottleneck finishing operation costs Mayfield materials costs plus the opportunity cost of lost throughput contribution. Bottleneck capacity not wasted in producing defective units could be used to generate additional sales and throughput contribution. Cost of 2,000 defective units at the finishing operation is:

Loss of direct materials $32 × 2,000	$ 64,000
Forgone throughput contribution ($72 – $32) × 2,000	80,000
Total cost of 2,000 defective units	$144,000

   Alternatively, the cost of 2,000 defective units at the finishing operation can be calculated as the lost revenue of $72 × 2,000 = $144,000. This line of reasoning takes the position that direct materials costs of $32 × 2,000 = $64,000 and all fixed operating costs in the machining and finishing operations would be incurred anyway whether a defective or good unit is produced. The cost of producing a defective unit is the revenue lost of $144,000.

19-28 (30 min.) Quality improvement, relevant costs, and relevant revenues.

1. By implementing the new method, Tan would incur additional direct materials costs on all the 200,000 units started at the moulding operation.

Additional direct materials costs = $4 per lamp × 200,000 lamps	$800,000
The relevant benefits of adding the new material are:	
Increased revenue from selling 30,000 more lamps	
$40 per lamp × 30,000 lamps	$1,200,000

Note that Tan Corporation continues to incur the same total variable costs of direct materials, direct manufacturing labour, setup labour, and materials handling labour, and the same fixed costs of equipment, rent, and allocated overhead that it is currently incurring, even when it improves quality. Since these costs do not differ among the alternatives of adding the new material or not adding the new material, they are excluded from the analysis. The relevant benefit of adding the new material is the extra revenue that Tan would get from producing 30,000 good lamps.

An alternative approach to analyzing the problem is to focus on scrap costs and the benefits of reducing scrap.

The relevant benefits of adding the new material are:

a. Cost savings from eliminating scrap:	
Variable cost per lamp, $19[a] × 30,000 lamps	$ 570,000
b. Additional contribution margin from selling another 30,000 lamps because 30,000 lamps will no longer be scrapped:	
Unit contribution margin $21[b] × 30,000 lamps	630,000
Total benefits to Tan of adding new material to improve quality	$1,200,000

[a] Note that only the variable scrap costs of $19 per lamp (direct materials, $16 per lamp; direct manufacturing labour, setup labour, and materials handling labour, $3 per lamp) are relevant because improving quality will save these costs. Fixed scrap costs of equipment, rent, and other allocated overhead are irrelevant because these costs will be incurred whether Tan Corporation adds or does not add the new material.

[b] Contribution margin per unit		
Selling price		$40.00
Variable costs:		
Direct materials costs per lamp	$16.00	
Moulding department variable manufacturing costs per lamp (direct manufacturing labour, setup labour, and materials handling labour)	3.00	
Variable costs		(19.00)
Unit contribution margin		$21.00

19-28 (cont'd)

On the basis of quantitative considerations alone, Tan should use the new material. Relevant benefits of $1,200,000 exceed the relevant costs of $800,000 by $400,000.

2. Other nonfinancial and qualitative factors that Tan should consider in making a decision include the effects of quality improvement on:

a. gaining manufacturing expertise that could lead to further cost reductions in the future;

b. enhanced reputation and increased customer goodwill which could lead to higher future revenues through greater unit sales and higher sales prices; and

c. higher employee morale as a result of higher quality.

19-30 (30–40 min.) Compensation linked with profitability, waiting time, and quality measures.

1.

	Jan.-June	July-Dec.
Philadelphia		
Add: Profitability		
1% of operating income	$106,500	$106,000
Add: Average waiting time		
$50,000 if < 15 minutes	50,000	0
Deduct: Patient satisfaction		
$50,000 if < 70	0	0
Total: Bonus paid	$156,500	$106,000
Baltimore		
Add: Profitability		
1% of operating income	$90,000	$ 9,500
Add: Average waiting time		
$50,000 if < 15 minutes	0	50,000
Deduct: Patient satisfaction		
$50,000 if < 70	(50,000)	0
Total: Bonus paid	$40,000	$59,500

2. *Operating income as a measure of profitability*

Operating income captures revenue and cost-related factors. However, there is no recognition of investment differences between the two groups. If one group is substantially bigger than the other, differences in size alone give the president of the larger group the opportunity to earn a bigger bonus. An alternative approach would be to use return on investment (perhaps relative to the budgeted ROI).

19-30 (cont'd)

15 minute benchmark as a measure of patient response time

This measure reflects the ability of Mid-Atlantic Healthcare to meet a benchmark for patient response time. Several concerns arise with this specific measure:

a. It is a yes-or-no cut-off. A 16-minute waiting time earns no bonus, but neither does a two-hour wait. Moreover, no extra bonus is paid for additional waiting time reductions below 15 minutes. An alternative is to have a bonus that increases with greater waiting time improvements.

b. It can be manipulated. Doctors might quickly make initial contact with a patient to meet the benchmark, but then leave the patient sitting in the examination room for a more detailed examination or procedure to take place.

c. It reflects performance relative only to the initial waiting time. It does not consider other time-related issues such as the wait for an appointment or the time needed to fill out forms.

Problems in (b) and (c) can be overcome by measuring total patient response time (such as how long it takes from the time a patient makes an appointment to the time the actual appointment is concluded), in addition to average waiting time to meet the doctor.

Patient satisfaction as a measure of quality

This measure represents a common method for assessing quality. However, there are several concerns with its use:

a. Patient satisfaction is likely to be influenced by a number of factors that are outside the groups' control, such as how sick the patients are when coming in or the extent to which they follow doctors' orders.

b. It is influenced by the questions asked in the survey and the survey methodology. As a result, is likely to be "noisy" or very sensitive to assumptions.

c. Patient satisfaction is not the same as patient health outcomes, an important measure of healthcare quality.

A combination of measures may work well as a composite measure of quality.

19-30 (cont'd)

3. Most companies use both financial and nonfinancial measures to evaluate performance, sometimes presented in a single report such as a balanced scorecard. Using multiple measures of performance enables top management to evaluate whether lower-level managers have improved one area at the expense of others. For example, did the better average waiting time (and patient satisfaction) between July and December in the Baltimore group result from significantly higher expenditures that contributed to the dramatic reduction in operating income?

An important issue is the relative importance to place on the different measures. If waiting time is not used for performance evaluation, managers will concentrate on increasing operating income and give less attention to waiting time, even if waiting time has a significant influence on whether customers choose Mid-Atlantic Healthcare or another healthcare provider when given the choice. However, the president of the Baltimore group received a larger bonus in the second half of the year due in part to lower average waiting time, even though operating profits dropped by nearly 90%. Companies must understand the relative importance of different financial and nonfinancial objectives when using multiple measures for performance evaluation.

19-32 (60 min.) Waiting times, relevant revenues, and relevant costs (continuation of 19-31).

1. The direct approach is to look at incremental revenues and incremental costs.

Selling price per order of Y28, which has an average manufacturing lead time of 350 hours	$ 8,000
Variable cost per order	5,000
Additional contribution per order of Y28	3,000
Multiply by expected number of orders	× 25
Increase in expected contribution from Y28	$75,000

19-32 (cont'd)

Expected loss in revenues and increase in costs from introducing Y28

Product (1)	Expected Loss in Revenues from Increasing Average Manufacturing Lead Times for All Products (2)	Expected Increase in Carrying Costs from Increasing Average Manufacturing Lead Times for All Products (3)	Expected Loss in Revenues Plus Expected Increases in Carrying Costs of Introducing Y28 (4) = (2) + (3)
Z39	$25,000.00[a]	$6,375.00[b]	$31,375.00
Y28	–	2,187.50[c]	2,187.50
Total	$25,000.00	$8,562.50	$33,562.50

[a] 50 orders × ($27,000 – $26,500)
[b] (410 hours – 240 hours) × $0.75 × 50 orders
[c] (350 hours – 0) × $0.25 × 25

Increase in expected contribution from Y28 of $75,000 is greater than increase in expected costs of $33,562.50 by $41,437.50. Therefore, SRG should introduce Y28.

Alternative calculations of incremental revenues and incremental costs of introducing Y28:

	Alternative 1: Introduce Y28 (1)	Alternative 2: Do Not Introduce Y28 (2)	Relevant Revenues and Relevant Costs (3) = (1) – (2)
Expected revenues	$1,525,000.00[a]	$1,350,000.00[b]	$175,000.00
Expected variable costs	875,000.00[c]	750,000.00[d]	125,000.00
Expected inv. carrying costs	17,562.50[e]	9,000.00[f]	8,562.50
Expected total costs	892,562.50	759,000.00	133,562.50
Expected revenues minus expected costs	$ 632,437.50	$ 591,000.00	$ 41,437.50

[a] (50 × $26,500) + (25 × $8,000)   [b] 50 × $27,000
[c] (50 × $15,000) + (25 × $5,000)   [d] 50 × $15,000
[e] (50 × $0.75 × 410) + (25 × $0.25 × 350)   [f] 50 × $0.75 × 240

2. Selling price per order of Y28, which has an average
   manufacturing lead time of more than 320 hours .... $ 6,000
   Variable cost per order 5,000
   Additional contribution per order of Y28 .... $ 1,000
   Multiply by expected number of orders .... × 25
   Increase in expected contribution from Y28 .... $25,000

19-32 (cont'd)

Expected loss in revenues and increase in costs from introducing Y28:

Product (1)	Expected Loss in Revenues from Increasing Average Manufacturing Lead Times for All Products (2)	Expected Increase in Carrying Costs from Increasing Average Manufacturing Lead Times for All Products (3)	Expected Loss in Revenues Plus Expected Increases in Carrying Costs of Introducing Y28 (4) = (2) + (3)
Z39	$25,000.00[a]	$6,375.00[b]	$31,375.00
Y28	–	2,187.50[c]	2,187.50
Total	$25,000.00	$8,562.50	$33,562.50

[a] 50 orders × ($27,000 – $26,500)
[b] (410 hours – 240 hours) × $0.75 × 50 orders
[c] (350 hours – 0) × $0.25 × 25

Increase in expected contribution from Y28 of $25,000 is less than increase in expected costs of $33,562.50 by $8,562.50. Therefore, SRG should not introduce Y28.

19-34 (20 min.) Theory of constraints, throughput contribution, relevant costs.

1. It will cost Cabano $50 per unit to reduce manufacturing time. But manufacturing is not a bottleneck operation; installation is. Therefore, manufacturing more equipment will not increase sales and throughput contribution. Cabano Industries should not implement the new manufacturing method.

2. Additional relevant costs of new direct materials, $2,000 × 320 units, $640,000
Increase in throughput contribution, $25,000 × 20 units, $500,000

    The additional incremental costs exceed the benefits from higher throughput contribution by $140,000, so Cabano Industries should not implement the new design.

    Alternatively, compare throughput contribution under each alternative.

Current throughput contribution is $25,000 × 300 $7,500,000
With the modification, throughput contribution is $23,000 × 320 $7,360,000

    The current throughput contribution is greater than the throughput contribution resulting from the proposed change in direct materials. Therefore, Cabano Industries should not implement the new design.

19-34 (cont'd)

3. Increase in throughput contribution, $25,000 × 10 units $250,000
   Increase in relevant costs $ 50,000

     The additional throughput contribution exceeds incremental costs by $200,000, so Cabano Industries should implement the new installation technique.

4. Motivating installation workers to increase productivity is worthwhile because installation is a bottleneck operation, and any increase in productivity at the bottleneck will increase throughput contribution. On the other hand, motivating workers in the manufacturing department to increase productivity is not worthwhile. Manufacturing is not a bottleneck operation, so any increase in output will result only in extra inventory of equipment. Cabano Industries should encourage manufacturing to produce only as much equipment as the installation department needs, not to produce as much as it can. Under these circumstances, it would not be a good idea to evaluate and compensate manufacturing workers on the basis of their productivity.

19-36 (30–35 min.) Governance and quality.

1.

	2010	
Revenues	$10,000,000	
Costs of Quality	**Cost (1)**	**Percentage of Revenues (2) = (1) ÷ $10,000,000**
Prevention costs		
Design engineering	$200,000	2.0%
Appraisal costs		
Inspection of production	90,000	
Product testing	210,000	
Total appraisal costs	300,000	3.0%
Internal failure costs		
Scrap	230,000	2.3%
External failure costs		
Warranty liability	260,000	2.6%
Total costs of quality	$990,000	9.9%

    The total costs of quality are less than 10% of revenues.

19-36 (cont'd)

2. Students can probably discuss both sides of this argument. Evans is obviously concerned because he expected the customer complaints calculation to be based on the number of customers who actually complained, not on Williams's survey. However, Williams's approach has the advantage of being thorough and systematic.

   Having done the survey, it would be unethical for Williams to now modify her analysis and incorrectly report the costs of quality and various nonfinancial measures of quality. In assessing the situation, the specific "Standards of Ethical Conduct for Management Accountants" (described in Exhibit 1-7) that Lindsey Williams should consider are listed below.

Competence
Clear reports using relevant and reliable information should be prepared. Preparing reports on the basis of incorrect numbers violates competence standards.

Integrity
Integrity requires that Williams report the numbers she collected. The standards of ethical conduct require the management accountant to communicate favourable as well as unfavourable information. Williams also has a responsibility to avoid actual or apparent conflicts of interest and advise all appropriate parties of any potential conflict. If Williams revises the customer complaints numbers, her action could be interpreted as being motivated by her desire to please her bosses. This would violate the responsibility for integrity.

Credibility
The management accountant's standards of ethical conduct require that information should be fairly and objectively communicated and that all relevant information should be disclosed. From a management accountant's standpoint, adjusting the customer complaints numbers to make performance look good would violate the standard of objectivity.

   Williams should indicate to Roche that the costs of quality and nonfinancial measures of quality presented in the reports are, indeed, appropriate. She could propose that she add another line item indicating the number of unsolicited complaints she received, that is, complaints she received independent of the survey. She should not, however, change the numbers she obtained in the survey. If Roche still insists on modifying the customer complaints numbers, Williams should raise the matter with one of Roche's superiors, other than Evans, who has a vested interest in this dispute. If, after taking all these steps, there is continued pressure to change survey results, Williams should consider resigning from the company and not engage in unethical behaviour.

CHAPTER 20
SUPPLY-CHAIN STRATEGIES:
JIT, MRP, AND BACKFLUSH COSTING

20-2   Five cost categories important in managing goods for sale in a retail organization are:
1.   Purchasing costs.
2.   Ordering costs.
3.   Carrying costs.
4.   Stockout costs.
5.   Quality costs.

20-4   Costs included in the carrying costs of inventory are *incremental costs* for such items as insurance, rent, obsolescence, spoilage, and breakage plus the *opportunity cost* of capital (or required return on investment).

20-6   The steps in computing the costs of a prediction error when using the EOQ decision model are:

Step 1:   Compute the monetary outcome from the best action that could have been taken, given the actual amount of the cost input.

Step 2:   Compute the monetary outcome from the best action based on the incorrect amount of the predicted cost input.

Step 3:   Compute the difference between the monetary outcomes from Steps 1 and 2.

20-8   Just-in-time (JIT) purchasing is the purchase of goods or materials such that a delivery immediately precedes demand or use. Benefits include lower inventory holdings (reduced warehouse space required and less money tied up in inventory) and less risk of inventory obsolescence and spoilage.

20-10   The sequence of activities involved in placing a purchase order can be facilitated by use of the Internet. For example, Cisco is streamlining the procurement process for its customers, e.g., having a complete price list online, information about expected shipment dates, and a service order capability that is available 24 hours a day with e-mail or fax confirmation.

20-12   Obstacles to companies adopting a supply-chain approach include:
• Communication obstacles — the unwillingness of some parties to share information.
• Trust obstacles — includes the concern that all parties will not meet their agreed-upon commitments.
• Information system obstacles — includes problems due to the information systems of different parties not being technically compatible.
• Limited resources — includes problems due to the people and financial resources given to support a supply-chain initiative not being adequate.

20-14 Traditional normal and standard costing systems use sequential tracking, which is any product-costing method where recording of the journal entries occurs in the same order as actual purchases and progress in production.

Backflush costing omits the recording of some or all of the journal entries relating to the cycle from purchase of direct materials to sale of finished goods. Where journal entries for one or more stages in the cycle are omitted, the journal entries for a subsequent stage use normal or standard costs to work backward to flush out the costs in the cycle for which journal entries were not made.

20-16 (20 min.) Economic order quantity for retailer.

1. D = 10,000, P = \$200, C = \$7

$$EOQ = \sqrt{\frac{2\,DP}{C}} = \sqrt{\frac{2 \times 10{,}000 \times \$200}{7}} = 755.93 \cong 756 \text{ jerseys}$$

2. Number of orders per year $= \dfrac{D}{EOQ} = \dfrac{10{,}000}{756} = 13.22 \cong 14$ orders

3. $\begin{aligned} \text{Demand each} \\ \text{working day} \end{aligned} = \dfrac{D}{\text{Number of working days}} = \dfrac{10{,}000}{365} = 27.40 \text{ jerseys per day}$

Purchase lead time = 7 days
    Reorder point = 27.40 × 7
              = 191.80 $\cong$ 192 jerseys

20-18 (15 min.) EOQ for a retailer.

1. D = 20,000, P = \$160, C = 20% × \$8 = \$1.60

$$EOQ = \sqrt{\frac{2DP}{C}} = \sqrt{\frac{2 \times 20,000 \times \$160}{\$1.60}} = 2,000 \text{ metres}$$

2. Number of orders per year: $\dfrac{D}{EOQ} = \dfrac{20,000}{2,000} = 10$ orders

3. Demand each working day $= \dfrac{D}{\text{Number of working days}}$

    $$= \frac{20,000}{250}$$

    = 80 metres per day

    = 400 metres per week

Purchasing lead time = 2 weeks
Reorder point = 400 metres per week × 2 weeks = 800 metres

20-20 (20 min.) Sensitivity of EOQ to changes in relevant ordering and carrying costs.

1. A straightforward approach to the requirement is to construct the following table for EOQ at relevant carrying and ordering costs. Annual demand is 10,000 units. The formula for the EOQ model is:

    $$EOQ = \sqrt{\frac{2DP}{C}}$$

    where   D = demand in units for a specified period of time
    P = relevant ordering costs per purchase order
    C = relevant carrying costs of one unit in stock for the time period
    used for D (one year in this problem).

Relevant Carrying Costs per Unit per Year	Relevant Ordering Costs per Purchase Order	
	\$300	\$200

20-20 (cont'd)

$$\$10 \qquad \sqrt{\frac{2 \times 10,000 \times \$300}{\$10}} = 775 \qquad \sqrt{\frac{2 \times 10,000 \times \$200}{\$10}} = 632$$

$$15 \qquad \sqrt{\frac{2 \times 10,000 \times \$300}{\$15}} = 632 \qquad \sqrt{\frac{2 \times 10,000 \times \$200}{\$15}} = 516$$

$$20 \qquad \sqrt{\frac{2 \times 10,000 \times \$300}{\$20}} = 548 \qquad \sqrt{\frac{2 \times 10,000 \times \$200}{\$20}} = 447$$

2. For a given demand level, as relevant carrying costs increase, EOQ becomes smaller. For a given demand level, as relevant order costs increase, EOQ increases.

20-22 (20-30 min.) **Purchase-order size for retailer, EOQ, just-in-time purchasing.**

1. $EOQ = \sqrt{\dfrac{2DP}{C}}$

    (a) $D = 7,200; P = \$36; C = \$1.20$

    $$EOQ = \sqrt{\frac{2(7,200)\,(\$36)}{\$1.20}} = \sqrt{432,000} = 657.3 \text{ cases} \cong 658 \text{ cases}$$

    (b) $D = 7,200; P = \$36; C = \$1.80$

    $$EOQ = \sqrt{\frac{2(7,200)\,(\$36)}{\$1.80}} = \sqrt{288,000} = 536.7 \text{ cases} \cong 537 \text{ cases}$$

    (c) $D = 7,200; P = \$6; C = \$1.80$

    $$EOQ = \sqrt{\frac{2(7,200)\,(\$6)}{\$1.80}} = \sqrt{48,000} = 219.1 \text{ cases} \cong 220 \text{ cases}$$

20-22 (cont'd)

2. A just-in-time purchasing policy involves the purchase of goods such that their delivery immediately precedes their demand. Given the purchase order sizes calculated in requirement 1, the number of purchase orders placed each month is (D ÷ EOQ):

(a) $\dfrac{D}{EOQ} = \dfrac{7,200}{658}$ = 11 orders per month or ≅ 1 every 2.7 days

(b) $\dfrac{D}{EOQ} = \dfrac{7,200}{537}$ = 14 orders per month or ≅ 1 every 2.15 days

(c) $\dfrac{D}{EOQ} = \dfrac{7,200}{220}$ = 33 orders per month or ≅ 1 every 0.91 days

An increase in C and a decrease in P led to increases in the optimal frequency of orders. The 24-Hour Mart has increased the frequency of delivery from every third day (1a: P = $36; C = $1.20) to a delivery every day (1c: P = $6; C = $1.80). There is a reduction of 219 cases in the average inventory level: (658 – 220) ÷ 2 = 219.

20-24 (30 min.) Backflush costing and JIT production.

1.

(a) Purchases of direct materials	Inventory: Materials and In-Process Control	2,754,000	
	Accounts Payable Control		2,754,000
(b) Incur conversion costs	Conversion Costs Control	723,600	
	Various Accounts		723,600
(c) Completion of finished goods	Finished Goods Control	3,484,000[a]	
	Inventory: Materials and In-Process Control		2,733,600
	Conversion Costs Allocated		750,400
(d) Sale of finished goods	Cost of Goods Sold	3,432,000[b]	
	Finished Goods Control		3,432,000

[a]26,800 × ($102 + $28) = $3,484,000
[b]26,400 × ($102 + $28) = $3,432,000

2.

3. Under an ideal JIT production system, there could be zero inventories at the end of each day. Entry (c) would be $3,432,000 finished goods production, not $3,484,000. Also, there would be no inventory of direct materials instead of $2,754,000 – $2,733,600 = $20,400.

20-26 (20 min.) **Backflush costing, two trigger points, completion of production and sale (continuation of 20-24).**

1.

(a)	Purchases of direct materials	No Entry	

(b)	Incur conversion costs	Conversion Costs Control	723,600	
		Various Accounts		723,600

(c)	Completion of finished goods	Finished Goods Control	3,484,000	
		Accounts Payable Control		2,733,600
		Conversion Costs Allocated		750,400

(d)	Sale of finished goods	Cost of Goods Sold	3,432,000	
		Finished Goods Control		3,432,000

(e)	Underallocated or overallocated conversion Costs	Conversion Costs Allocated	750,400	
		Costs of Goods Sold		26,800
		Conversion Costs Control		723,600

2.

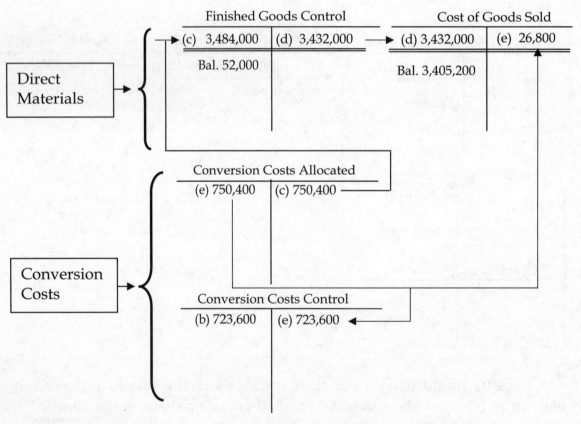

20-28 (30 min.) **Effect of different order quantities on ordering costs and carrying costs, EOQ.**

1.

	Scenario				
	1	2	3	4	5
Demand (units) (D)	234,000	234,000	234,000	234,000	234,000
Cost per purchase order (P)	$ 81.00	$ 81.00	$ 81.00	$ 81.00	$ 81.00
Annual carrying cost per package (C)	$ 11.70	$ 11.70	$ 11.70	$ 11.70	$ 11.70
Order quantity per purchase order (units) (Q)	900	1,500	1,800	2,100	2,700
Number of purchase orders per year (D ÷ Q)	260.00	156.00	130.00	111.43	86.67
Annual ordering costs (D ÷ Q) × P	$21,060	$12,636	$10,530	$ 9,026	$ 7,020
Annual carrying costs (QC ÷ 2)	$ 5,265	$ 8,775	$10,530	$12,285	$15,795
Total relevant costs of ordering and carrying inventory	$26,325	$21,411	$21,060	$21,311	$22,815

The economic order quantity is 1,800 packages. It is the order quantity at which carrying costs equal ordering costs and total relevant ordering and carrying costs are minimized.

We can also confirm this from direct calculation. Using D = 234,000; P = $81 and C = $11.70

$$EOQ = \sqrt{\frac{2 \times 234,000 \times \$81}{\$11.70}} = 1,800 \text{ packages}$$

It is interesting to note that Koala Blue faces a situation where total relevant ordering and carrying costs do not vary very much when order quantity ranges from 1,500 packages to 2,700 packages.

2.   When the ordering cost per purchase order is reduced to $49:

$$EOQ = \sqrt{\frac{2 \times 234,000 \times \$49}{\$11.70}} = 1,400 \text{ packages}$$

The EOQ drops from 1,800 packages to 1,400 packages when Koala Blue's ordering cost per purchase order decreases from $81 to $49.
The new relevant costs of ordering inventory are:

$$= \left(\frac{D}{Q} \times P\right) = \left(\frac{234,000}{1,400} \times \$49\right) = \$8,190$$

and the new relevant costs or carrying inventory are:

$$= \left(\frac{Q}{2} \times C\right) = \left(\frac{1,400}{2} \times \$11.70\right) = \$8,190$$

The total new costs of ordering and carrying inventory = $8,190 × 2 = $16,380

20-28 (cont'd)

3. As summarized below, the new Mona Lisa web-based ordering system, by lowering the EOQ to 1,400 packages, will lower the carrying and ordering costs by $4,680. Koala Blue will spend $2,000 to train its purchasing assistants on the new system. Overall, Koala Blue will still save $2,680 in the first year alone.

Total relevant costs at EOQ (from Requirement 2)	$16,380
Annual cost benefit over old system ($21,060 – $16,380)	$ 4,680
Training costs	2,000
Net benefit in first year alone	$ 2,680

20-30 (30 min.) JIT purchasing, relevant benefits, relevant costs.

1. Solution Exhibit 20-30 presents the $37,500 cash savings that would result if Margro Corporation adopted the just-in-time inventory system in 2010.

2. Conditions that should exist in order for a company to successfully adopt just-in-time purchasing include the following:
    *   Top management must be committed and provide the necessary leadership support to ensure a company-wide, coordinated effort.
    *   A detailed system for integrating the sequential operations of the manufacturing process needs to be developed and implemented. Direct materials must arrive when needed for each subassembly so that the production process functions smoothly.
    *   Accurate sales forecasts must be available for effective finished goods planning and production scheduling.
    *   Products should be designed to maximize use of standardized parts to reduce manufacturing time and costs.
    *   Reliable vendors who can deliver quality direct materials on time with minimum lead time must be obtained.

20-30 (cont'd)

SOLUTION EXHIBIT 20-30
Annual Relevant Costs of Current Purchasing Policy and JIT Purchasing Policy
for Margro Corporation

	Relevant Costs under Current Purchasing Policy	Relevant Costs under JIT Purchasing Policy
Required return on investment		
20% per year × $600,000 of average inventory per year	$120,000	
20% per year × $0 inventory per year		$ 0
Annual insurance and property tax costs	14,000	0
Warehouse rent (revenue)	60,000	(13,500)[a]
Overtime costs		
No overtime	0	
Overtime premium		40,000
Stockout costs		
No stockouts	0	
$6.50[b] contribution margin per unit ×20,000 units		130,000
Total incremental costs	$194,000	$156,500
Difference in favour of JIT purchasing		$37,500

[a]$(13,500) = Warehouse rental revenues, [(75% × 12,000) × $1.50].
[b]Calculation of unit contribution margin
Selling price
($10,800,000 ÷ 900,000 units) $12.00
Variable costs per unit :
    Variable manufacturing cost per unit
    ($4,050,000 ÷ 900,000 units) $4.50
    Variable marketing and distribution cost per unit
    ($900,000 ÷ 900,000 units) 1.00
    Total variable costs per unit 5.50
Contribution margin per unit .... $ 6.50

Note that the incremental costs of $40,000 in overtime premiums to make the additional 15,000 units are less than the contribution margin from losing these sales equal to $97,500 ($6.50 × 15,000). Margro would rather incur overtime than lose 15,000 units of sales.

20-32 (20 min.) Backflush, two trigger points, materials purchase and sale (continuation of 20-31).

1.

(a) Purchases of direct materials	Inventory Control	550,000	
	Accounts Payable Control		550,000
(b) Incur conversion costs	Conversion Costs Control	440,000	
	Various Accounts (such as Accounts Payable Control and Wages Payable Control)		440,000
(c) Completion of finished goods	No entry		
(d) Sale of finished goods	Cost of Goods Sold	900,000	
	Inventory Control		500,000
	Conversion Costs Allocated		400,000
(e) Underallocated or overallocated conversion costs	Conversion Costs Allocated	400,000	
	Cost of Goods Sold	40,000	
	Conversion Costs Control		440,000

2.

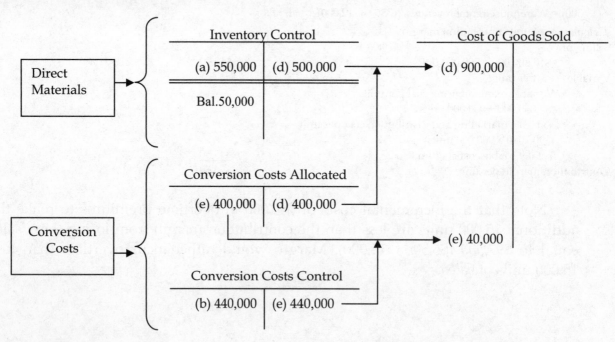

20-34 (25 min.) Relevant benefits and costs of JIT purchasing.

Solution Exhibit 20-34 presents the $869.40 cash savings that would result if Hardesty Medical Instruments adopted the just-in-time inventory system in 2010.

SOLUTION EXHIBIT 20-34
Annual Relevant Costs of Current Purchasing Policy and JIT Purchasing Policy For Hardesty Medical Instruments

	Relevant Costs Under Current Purchasing Policy	Relevant Costs Under JIT Purchasing Policy
Purchasing costs		
$12.00 per unit × 20,000 units	$240,000.00	
$12.06 per unit x 20,000 units		$241,200.00
Ordering costs		
$6 per order × 20 orders per year	120.00	
$6 per order × 200 orders per year		1,200.00
Opportunity carrying costs, required return on investment		
20% per year × $12 cost per unit × 500[a] units of average inventory per year	1,200.00	
20% per year × $12.06 cost per unit × 50[b] units of average inventory per year		120.60
Other carrying costs		
$5.40 per unit per year × 500[a] units of average inventory per year	2,700.00	
$5.40 per unit per year × 50[b] units of average inventory per year		270.00
Stockout costs		
No stockouts	0	
$3.60 per unit × 100 units per year		360.00
Total annual relevant costs	$244,020.00	$243,150.60
Annual difference in favour of JIT purchasing	$869.40	

[a]Order quantity ÷ 2 = 1,000 ÷ 2 = 500
[b]Order quantity ÷ 2 = 100 ÷ 2 = 50

2. Hardesty may benefit from Morrison managing its inventories if there is high order variability caused by randomness in when consumers purchase surgical scalpels or by trade promotions that prompt retailers to stock for the future. By coordinating their activities and sharing information about retail sales and inventory held throughout the supply chain, Morrison can plan its manufacturing activities to ensure adequate supply of product while keeping inventory low. For this to succeed, Hardesty and Morrison must have compatible information systems, build trust, and communicate freely.

20-36 (25 min.) Supplier evaluation and relevant costs of quality and timely deliveries.

Solution Exhibit 20-36 presents the $1,702 annual relevant costs difference in favour of purchasing from Quality Sports. Copeland should buy the footballs from Quality Sports.

SOLUTION EXHIBIT 20-36

Annual Relevant Costs of Purchasing from Big Red and Quality Sports

Relevant Item	Relevant Costs of Purchasing From	
	Big Red	**Quality Sports**
Purchasing costs		
$60 per unit × 12,000 units per year	$720,000	
$61.20 per unit × 12,000 units per year		$734,400
Inspection costs		
$0.02 per unit × 12,000 units	240	
No inspection necessary		0
Opportunity carrying costs, required return on investment,		
15% per year × $60 cost per unit × 100 units of		
average inventory per year;	900	
15% per year × $61.20 cost per unit × 100 units of		
average inventory per year		918
Other carrying costs (insurance, materials handling,		
and so on)		
$4 per unit × 100 units of average inventory per year	400	
$4.50 per unit × 100 units of average inventory per year		450
Stockout costs		
$24 per unit × 350 units per year	8,400	
$12 per unit × 60 units per year		720
Customer returns costs		
$30 per unit × 300 units	9,000	
$30 per unit × 25 units		750
Total annual relevant costs	$738,940	$737,238
Annual difference in favour of Quality Sports	↑ $1,702 ↑	

20-38 (25 min.) **Effect of EOQ ordering on supplier costs (continuation of Problem 20-37).**

1.

   i) Setup cost = Cost per setup × annual setups

   Alternative A: $1,000 ×50 setups = $50,000
   Alternative B: $1,000 × 250 setups = $250,000

   ii) Carrying Cost = Average inventory level × carrying cost

   Alternative A: (10,000 ÷ 2) × $50 = $250,000
   Alternative B: Assumed to be $0 (because computers are shipped on the day they are produced)

   iii) Total relevant cost

   Alternative A: $50,000 + $250,000 = $300,000
   Alternative B: $250,000 + $0 = $250,000

   Costs would be lower if IMBest produced computers every day.

2.   Let C = carrying costs per unit

   Alternative A: Total cost = $50,000 + (10,000 ÷ 2) × C
   Alternative B: Total cost = $250,000 + $0

   Equating these costs, $50,000 + $5,000C = $250,000
   $5,000C = $200,000
   C = $40

   If carrying costs fall below $40 per unit, IMBest would be better off producing the computers once a week.

20-40 (20 min.) **Lean accounting.**

1. The cost object in lean accounting is the value stream, not the individual product. FSD has identified two distinct value streams: Mechanical Devices and Electronic Devices. All direct costs are traced to the value streams. However, not all plant-level overhead costs are allocated to the value streams when computing operating income. Value streams are only charged for the percentage of space they actually use; only 85% of the $120,000 occupancy costs are charged to the two value streams. The remaining 15%, or $18,000, is not used to compute value-stream profits, nor are other plant-level overhead costs.

2. Operating income under lean accounting are the following (in thousands of dollars):

	Mechanical Devices	Electronic Devices
Sales ($700 + $500; $900 + $450)	$1,200	$1,350
Costs		
Direct materials purchased ($190 + $125; $250 + $90)	315	340
Direct manufacturing labour ($150 + $75; $200 + $60)	225	260
Equipment costs ($90 + $125; $200 + $100)	215	300
Product-line overhead ($110 + $60; $125 + $50)	170	175
Occupancy costs ($120 × 40%) ($120 × 45%)	48	54
Value-stream operating income	$ 227	$ 221

In addition to the differences discussed in Requirement 1, FSD's lean accounting system treats all direct material costs as expenses in the period they are purchased. The following factors explain the differences between traditional operating income and lean accounting income for the two value streams:

	Mechanical Devices	Electronic Devices
Traditional operating income ($100 + $105; $45 + $140)	$205	$185
Additional cost of direct materials ($315 − $300; $340 − $325)	(15)	(15)
Decrease in allocated plant-level overhead ($85 − $48; $105 − $54)	37	51
Value stream operating income	$227	$221

20-42 (30 min.) Backflush costing, income manipulation, governance.

1. Factors SVC should consider in deciding whether to adopt a version of backflush costing include:
   a. Effects on decision making by managers. There is a loss of information with backflushing. Supporters of backflushing maintain, however, that non-financial information and observation of production provide sufficient inputs to monitor production and management costs at the shop-floor level.
   b. Costs of maintaining sequential tracking vis-à-vis backflush costing.
   c. Materiality of the differences. If the production lead time is short (say, less than one day) and inventory levels are minimal (as one would anticipate with JIT), the differences between sequential tracking and backflush may be minimal.
   d. Opportunity for managers to manipulate reported numbers.

2. Strong's concerns certainly warrant consideration. Much depends on the corporate culture at SVC. If the culture is that quarterly or monthly reported numbers are pivotal to evaluations, and that managers "push the accounting system to facilitate meeting the numbers," Strong should raise these issues with Honig. Adopting an accounting system with an obvious opportunity for manipulation (backflush with sale as the trigger point) may well send managers the wrong message.

   Strong's concerns, however, are not by themselves sufficient to cause SVC not to adopt backflush costing. The factors mentioned in requirement 1 may well be compelling enough to support adoption of backflush costing. Honig has alternative ways to address Strong's quite legitimate concerns—see requirement 3.

3. Ways to motivate managers to not "artificially change" reported income include:
   a. Adopting long-term measures that reduce the importance of short-run financial targets.
   b. Increasing the weight on non-accounting-based variables—e.g., more use of stock options or customer-satisfaction measures.
   c. Penalize heavily (the "stick approach") managers who are found out to have "artificially changed" reported income. This can include withdrawal of bonuses or even termination of employment.

CHAPTER 21
CAPITAL BUDGETING: METHODS OF INVESTMENT ANALYSIS

21-2 The six parts in the capital budgeting decision process are:
1. An *identification stage* to distinguish the types of capital expenditure projects that will accomplish strategic goals for the organization.
2. A *stage to establish assumptions* that are common for exploring several potential capital expenditure investments that will achieve organization objectives.
3. An *information-acquisition stage* to consider the predicted costs and consequences of alternative capital investments through an analysis of the present value of future cash inflows and outflows and relevant qualitative factors.
4. A *selection stage* to decide on the projects to execute, timing of implementation, and performance criteria.
5. A *financing stage* to obtain project financing.
6. An *implementation and control* stage to put the projects in motion and monitor their performance throughout the investment life.

21-4 No. Only quantitative outcomes are formally analyzed in capital-budgeting decisions. Many effects of capital-budgeting decisions, however, are difficult to quantify in financial terms. These nonfinancial or qualitative factors, for example, the number of accidents in a manufacturing plant or employee morale, are important to consider in making capital-budgeting decisions.

21-6 The payback method measures the time it will take to recoup, in the form of net cash inflows, the total dollars invested in a project. The payback method is simple and easy to understand. It is a handy method when accuracy[1] in estimates of profitability is not crucial and when predicted cash flows in later years are highly uncertain. The main weakness of the payback method is its neglect of profitability and the time value of money.

[1] Accuracy is how close you are to the real-world value. Precision is reproducibility and is neither sufficient nor necessary with respect to accuracy.

21-8 No. The discounted cash-flow techniques implicitly consider amortization in rate-of-return computations; the compound interest tables automatically allow for recovery of investment. The net initial investment of an asset is usually regarded as a lump-sum outflow at time zero.

21-10 No. If managers are evaluated on the accrual accounting rate of return, they may not use the NPV method for capital-budgeting decisions. Instead, managers will choose investments that maximize the accrual accounting rate of return.

21-12 Capital investment projects typically have five major categories of cash flows:

1) *Initial investment in machine and working capital:* outflows made for purchasing plant, equipment, and machines that occur in the early periods of the project's life and include cash outflows for transporting and installing the item. Investments in plant, equipment, machines and sales promotions for product lines are invariably accompanied by incremental investments in working capital. These investments take the form of current assets, such as receivables and inventories, minus current liabilities, such as accounts payable. Working capital investments are similar to machine investments. In each case, available cash is tied up.

2) *Cash flow from current disposal of the old machine:* any cash received from disposal of the old machine is a relevant cash inflow.

3) *Recurring operating cash flows:* these inflows may result from producing and selling additional goods or services or from operating cost savings.

4) *Cash flow from terminal disposal of machine and recovery of working capital:* the disposal of the investment at the date of termination of a project generally increases cash inflow in the year of disposal. The initial investment in working capital is usually fully recouped when the project is terminated. At that time, inventories and receivables necessary to support the project are no longer needed.

5) *Income tax impacts on cash flows:* to be discussed in Chapter 22.

21-14 The Division Y manager should consider why the Division X project was accepted and the Division Y project rejected by the president. Possible explanations are:

a. The president considers qualitative factors not incorporated into the IRR computation and this leads to the acceptance of the X project and rejection of the Y project.

b. The president believes that Division Y has a history of overstating cash inflows and understating cash outflows.

c. The president has a preference for the manager of Division X over the manager of Division Y—this is a corporate politics issue.

Factor a means qualitative factors should be emphasized more in proposals. Factor b means Division Y needs to document whether its past projections have been relatively accurate. Factor c means the manager of Division Y has to play the corporate politics game better.

21-16 Exercises in compound interest.

The answers to these exercises are printed in the textbook after the last problem at the end of the chapter.

21-18 (15 min.) New assets: comparison of approaches in capital budgeting.

1. Payback period in years:
   Buy 2 Small Machines: $200,000 / ($70,000 – $10,000) = 3.33 years
   Buy 1 Large Machine: $250,000 / ($70,000 – $15,000) = 4.54 years

2. Present value and   3. Net present value

	Buy 2 small machines	Buy 1 large machine
Present value of annuities (Appendix A, Table 4)	4 periods at 5% = 3.5460	5 periods at 5% =4.3295
Present value	= ($70,000 – $10,000) x 3.5460 = $212,760	= ($70,000 – $15,000) x 4.3295 = $238,120
Net Present value	= $200,000 – $212,760 = $12,760	= $250,000 – $238,120 = ($11,880)

4. The IRR of buying 2 small machines is more than 5% because the NPV is positive. But the IRR of buying 1 large machine is less than 5% because the NPV is negative.

5. Only the project of buying 2 small machines can be accepted given the projected cash flows.

21-20 (20-25 min.) Comparison of approaches to capital budgeting.

1. Payback period = $80,000 ÷ $20,000 = 4 years

2. The table for the present value of annuities (Appendix A, Table 4) shows:
   10 periods at 12% = 5.650
   Net present value = $20,000(5.650) – $80,000
                      = $113,000 – $80,000 = $33,000

3. Internal rate of return:
   $80,000 = Present value of annuity of $20,000 at X% for 10 years, or what factor (F) in the table of present values of an annuity (Appendix A, Table 4) will satisfy the following equation.

   $80,000 = $20,000F

   $$F = \left[\frac{\$80,000}{\$20,000}\right] = 4$$

   On the ten-year line in the table for the present value of annuities (Appendix A, Table 4), find the column closest to 4.0; 4.0 is between a rate of return of 20% and 22%.

21-20 (cont'd)

Interpolation can be used to determine the exact rate:

	Present Value Factors	
20%	4.192	4.192
IRR rate	–	4.000
22%	3.923	–
Difference	0.269	0.192

$$\text{Internal rate of return} \quad = \quad 20\% + \left[\frac{0.192}{0.269}\right](2\%)$$

$$= \quad 20\% + (0.714)\,(2\%) = 21.43\%$$

4. Accrual accounting rate of return based on net initial investment:

Net initial investment	=	$80,000
Estimated useful life	=	10 years
Annual straight-line amortization	=	$80,000 ÷ 10 = $8,000

$$\text{Accrual accounting rate of return} \quad = \quad \left[\frac{\$20,000 - \$8,000}{\$80,000}\right] = 15\%$$

21-22 (15 min.) Payback period, net present value.

Criteria 1: Payback period = $250,000 ÷ $53,000 = 4.7 years

Criteria 2: Net present value:

Item	Time period	Amount	Factor	Present Value
Investment	0	$(250,000)	1.000	$(250,000)
Net Savings	t1 – t7	$65,000 - $12,000 = $53,000	4.8684	258,025
Salvage	t 7	25,000	0.5132	12,830
NPV				$ 20,855

The project is acceptable based on both criteria.

21-24 (30 min.) Equipment replacement, net present value, relevant costs, payback.

1. The cash outflows and inflows for the two alternatives are:

Year	Keep Old 53' Truck Cash Outflows	Keep Old 53' Truck Cash Inflows	Buy New 53' Truck Cash Outflows	Buy New 53' Truck Cash Inflows
0	$ 0	$ 0	$67,200	$31,200
1	42,000	0	30,000	0
2	42,000	0	30,000	0
3	42,000	0	30,000	0
4	48,000	7,200	30,000	9,600

Computations for the net present value of each alternative are:

Year	PV Discount Factor at 12%	Keep Old 53' Truck Net Cash Outflows	Keep Old 53' Truck PV of Net Cash Outflows	Buy New 53' Truck Net Cash Outflows	Buy New 53' Truck PV of Net Cash Outflows
0	1.000	$ 0	$ 0	$36,000	$36,000
1	0.893	42,000	37,506	30,000	26,790
2	0.797	42,000	33,474	30,000	23,910
3	0.712	42,000	29,904	30,000	21,360
4	0.636	40,800	25,949	20,400	12,974
			$126,833		$121,034

Edgeley Inc. should purchase the new 53' truck. The net present value difference in favour of purchase is $5,799 ($126,833 – $121,034).

The amortization on either of the trucks is irrelevant.

21-24 (cont'd)

Another approach to determine the NPV of buying a new 53' truck follows. This approach considers only the differential cash flows of purchasing the new truck.

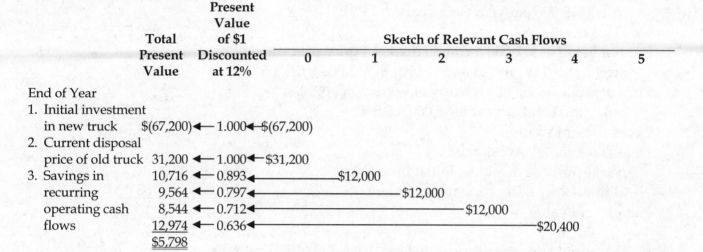

	Total Present Value	Present Value of $1 Discounted at 12%	Sketch of Relevant Cash Flows					
			0	1	2	3	4	5
End of Year								
1. Initial investment in new truck	$(67,200)	1.000 — $(67,200)						
2. Current disposal price of old truck	31,200	1.000 — $31,200						
3. Savings in	10,716	0.893		$12,000				
recurring	9,564	0.797			$12,000			
operating cash	8,544	0.712				$12,000		
flows	12,974	0.636					$20,400	
	$5,798							

2. The net initial investment for the new truck is $36,000. The difference in cash outflows between the two alternatives is:

Year	Difference in Cash Savings	Cumulative Cash Savings	Cash Investment Yet to Be Recovered at End of Year
0	—	—	$36,000
1	$12,000	$12,000	24,000
2	12,000	24,000	12,000
3	12,000	36,000	—
4	20,400	56,400	—

Payback period = 3 years

21-26 (21-30 min.) DCF, accrual accounting rate of return, working capital, evaluation of performance.

1. a.

Present value of annuity of savings in cash operating costs ($15,000 per year for 8 years at 14%): $15,000 × 4.6389		$69,583
Present value of $12,000 terminal disposal price of machine at 14% and at end of year 8: $12,000 × 0.3506		4,207
Present value of $5,000 recovery of working capital at 14% and at end of year 8: $5,000 × 0.3506		1,753
Gross present value		75,543
Deduct net initial investment:		
Special-purpose machine, initial investment	$60,000	
Additional working capital investment	5,000	65,000
Net present value		$ 10,543

1   b.   Use a trial and error approach. First, try a 20% discount rate:

$15,000 × 3.837	$57,555
($12,000 + $5,000) × 0.2326	3,954
Gross present value	61,509
Deduce net initial investment	(65,000)
Net present value	$ (3,491)

Second, try an 18% discount rate:

$15,000 × 4.078	$61,170
($12,000 + $5,000) × 0.266	4,522
Gross present value	65,692
Deduct net initial investment	(65,000)
Net present value	$ 692

By interpolation:

Internal rate of return

$$= \ 18\% + \left[\frac{\$692}{\$692 + \$3,491} \right]$$

$$= \ 18\% + (0.165)\,(2\%) = 18.33\%$$

21-26 (cont'd)

2. Accrual accounting rate of return based on net initial investment:

    Net initial investment = $60,000 + $5,000
                                       = $65,000

    Annual amortization
        [$65,000 – ($12,000 + 5,000)] ÷ 8 years   = $6,000

    $$\text{Accrual accounting rate of return} = \left[\frac{\$15,000 - \$6,000}{\$65,000}\right] = 13.85\%$$

3. If your decision is based on the DCF model, the purchase would be made because the net present value is positive, and the 18.33% internal rate of return exceeds the 14% required rate of return. However, you may believe that your performance may actually be measured using accrual accounting. This approach would show a 13.85% return on the initial investment, which is slightly below the required 14% rate. Your reluctance to make a "buy" decision may be natural, unless you are assured of reasonable consistency between the decision model and the performance evaluation method.

21-28 (20 min.) New equipment purchase.

1. The cash inflow per year is $31,250.
a. Solution Exhibit 21-28a shows the NPV computation. NPV= $50,156
   An alternative approach:
   Present value of 5-year annuity of $31,250 at 12%

$31,250 × 3.605	$ 112,656
Present value of cash outlays, $80,000 × 1.000	80,000
Net present value	$ 32,656

EXHIBIT 21-28a

	Total Present Value	Present Value Discount Factors At 12%	Sketch of Relevant Cash Flows					
			0	1	2	3	4	5
1a. Initial equipment investment	$(80,000)	1.000	$(80,000)					
1b. Initial working capital investment	0	1.000	$0					
2a. Annual cash flow from operations (excl. depr.)								
Year 1	27,906	0.893		$31,250				
Year 2	24,906	0.797			$31,250			
Year 3	22,250	0.712				$31,250		
Year 4	19,875	0.636					$31,250	
Year 5	17,719	0.567						$31,250
3 a. Terminal disposal of equipment	0	0.567						$0
3 b. Recovery of working capital	0	0.567						$0
Net present value if new equipment is purchased	$ 32,656							

b. Payback = $80,000 ÷ $31,250
              = 2.56 years

c. Let F = Present value factor for an annuity of $1 for 5 years in Appendix B, Table 4
   F = $80,000 ÷ $31,250 = 2.56

21-28 (cont'd)

The internal rate of return can be calculated by interpolation:

	Present Value Factors for Annuity of $1 for 5 years	
26%	2.635	2.635
IRR	–	2.560
28%	2.532	–
Difference	0.103	0.075

$$\text{Internal rate of return} = 26\% + \left(\frac{0.075}{0.103}\right)(2\%) = 27.46\%.$$

2.   Both the net present value and internal rate of return methods use the discounted cash flow approach in which *all* expected future cash inflows and outflows of a project are measured as if they occurred at a single point in time. The net present value approach computes the surplus generated by the project in today's dollars, while the internal rate of return attempts to measure its effective return on investment earned by the project. The payback method, by contrast, considers nominal cash flows (without discounting) and measures the time at which the project's expected future cash inflows recoup the net initial investment in a project. The payback method thus ignores the profitability of the project's entire stream of future cash flows.

3. The adjustment in discount rate made by the controller in headquarters will only change the net present value, while IRR and payback period will remain the same.

Present value of 5-year annuity of $31,250 at 20%	
$31,250 × 2.991	$ 93,469
Present value of cash outlays, $80,000 × 1.000	80,000
Net present value	$ 13,469

The project will be approved by Innovation Inc. because its NPV is positive at a 20% required rate of return. The same conclusion can be achieved if the required rate of return (20%) is compared with the internal rate of return of the project (27.46%)

21-30 (30 min.) DCF, sensitivity analysis, no income taxes.

1.

Revenues, $12 × 100,000	$1,200,000
Variable cash costs, $4.80 × 100,000	480,000
Cash contribution margin	720,000
Fixed cash costs	250,000
Cash inflow from operations	$ 470,000

Net present value:	
Cash inflow from operations	
$470,000 × 2.106	$989,820
Cash outflow for initial investment	380,000
Net present value	$ 609,820

2.
a.   10% reduction in selling prices:

Revenues, $10.80 × 100,000	$1,080,000
Variable cash costs, $4.80 × 100,000	480,000
Cash contribution margin	600,000
Fixed cash costs	250,000
Cash inflow from operations	$350,000

Net present value:	
Cash inflow from operations	
$350,000 × 2.106	$737,100
Cash outflow for initial investment	380,000
Net present value	$357,100

b.   10% reduction in unit sales:

Revenues, $12 × 90,000	$1,080,000
Variable cash costs, $4.80 × 90,000	432,000
Cash contribution margin	648,000
Fixed cash costs	250,000
Cash inflow from operations	$398,000

Net present value:	
Cash inflow from operations	
$398,000 × 2.106	$838,188
Cash outflow for initial investment	380,000
Net present value	$ 458,188

21-30 (cont'd)

c.   10% increase in the variable cost per unit.

Revenues, $12 × 100,000	$1,200,000
Variable cash costs, $4.32* × 100,000	432,000
Cash contribution margin	768,000
Fixed cash costs	250,000
Cash inflow from operations	$ 518,000

Net present value:

Cash inflow from operations	
$518,000 × 2.106	$1,090,908
Cash outflow for initial investment	380,000
Net present value	$ 710,908

3.   Sensitivity analysis enables management to see those assumptions for which input variations have sizable impact on NPV. Extra resources could be devoted to getting more informed estimates of those inputs with the greatest impact on NPV. Sensitivity analysis also enables management to have contingency plans in place if assumptions are not met. For example, if a 10% reduction in selling price is viewed as occurring with 0.40 probability, management may wish to line up bank loan facilities. At a 10% reduction in selling price, the project should simply be dropped. A bank loan would not help that.

*10% reduction in variable costs: $(1 - 0.10) \times \$4.80 = \$4.32$

21-32 (45 min.) **NPV, IRR and sensitivity analysis.**

1.   Net present value of project:

	Period 0	**Periods 1 - 10**
Cash inflows		$23,000
Cash outflows	$(42,000)	(16,000)
Net cash flows	$(42,000)	

Annual net cash inflows	$ 7,000
Present value factor for annuity, 10 periods, 6%	× 7.36
Present value of net cash inflows	$51,520
Initial investment	(42,000)
Net present value	$ 9,520

To find IRR, first divide the initial investment by the net annual cash inflow:

$$\$42,000 \div \$7,000 = 6.0.$$

The 6.0 represents the present value factor for a ten-period project with the given cash flows, so look in Table 4, Appendix B for the present value of an annuity in arrears to find the factor closest to 6.0 along the ten period row. You should find that it is between 10% and 12%.

The internal rate of return can be calculated by interpolation:

**Present Value Factors for
Annuity of $1 for 10 years**

10%	6.145	6.145
IRR	–	6.000
12%	5.650	–
Difference	0.495	0.145

Internal rate of return = $10\% + \left(\dfrac{0.145}{0.495} \right)(2\%) = 10.6\%$.

Note: You can use a calculator or excel to find the IRR, and you will get an answer of approximately 10.56%.

21-32 (cont'd)

2. If revenues are 10% higher, the new net present value will be:

	Period 0	Periods 1 - 10
Cash inflows		$25,300
Cash outflows	$(42,000)	(16,000)
Net cash inflows	$(42,000)	$ 9,300

Annual net cash inflows	$ 9,300
Present value factor for annuity, 10 periods, 6%	× 7.36
Present value of net cash inflows	$68,448
Initial investment	(42,000)
Net present value	$26,448

And the IRR will be: $42,000 ÷ $9,300 = present value factor of 4.516, yielding a return of 17.87% via interpolation (see below), or using a calculator, a return of 17.86%.

	Present Value Factors for Annuity of $1 for 10 years	
16%	4.833	4.833
IRR	–	4.516
18%	4.494	–
Difference	0.339	0.317

Internal rate of return = $16\% + \left(\dfrac{0.317}{0.339}\right)(2\%) = 17.87\%$.

If revenues are 10% lower, the new net present value will be:

	Period 0	Periods 1 – 10
Cash inflows		$20,700
Cash outflows	$(42,000)	(16,000)
Net cash inflows	$(42,000)	$ 4,700

Annual net cash inflows	$ 4,700
Present value factor for annuity, 10 periods, 6%	× 7.36
Present value of net cash inflows	$ 34,592
Initial investment	(42,000)
Net present value	$ (7,408)

21-32 (cont'd)

And the IRR will be: $42,000 ÷ $4,700 = present value factor of 8.936, yielding a return of 2.11% using interpolation (see calculations below) or, using a calculator, a return of 2.099%.

	Present Value Factors for	
	Annuity of $1 for 10 years	
2%	8.983	8.983
IRR	–	8.936
4%	8.111	–
Difference	0.872	0.047

Internal rate of return = 2% + $\left(\dfrac{0.047}{0.872}\right)$ (2%) = 2.11%.

3. If both revenues and costs are higher, the new net present value will be:

	Period 0	**Periods 1 –10**
Cash inflows		$25,300
Cash outflows	$(42,000)	(17,120)
Net cash inflows	$(42,000)	$ 8,180

Annual net cash inflows	$ 8,180
Present value factor for annuity, 10 periods, 6%	× 7.36
Present value of net cash inflows	$60,205
Initial investment	(42,000)
Net present value	$18,205

And the IRR will be: $42,000 ÷ $8,180 = present value factor of 5.134, yielding a return of 14.43% via interpolation, or using a calculator, a return of 14.406%.

	Present Value Factors for	
	Annuity of $1 for 10 years	
14%	5.216	5.216
IRR	–	5.134
16%	4.833	–
Difference	0.383	0.082

Internal rate of return = 14% + $\left(\dfrac{0.082}{0.383}\right)$ (2%) = 14.43%.

21-32 (cont'd)

If both revenues and costs are lower, the new net present value will be:

	Period 0	Periods 1 - 10
Cash inflows		$20,700
Cash outflows	$(42,000)	(14,400)
Net cash inflows	$(42,000)	$ 6,300

Annual net cash inflows	$ 6,300
Present value factor for annuity, 10 periods, 6%	× 7.36
Present value of net cash inflows	$46,368
Initial investment	(42,000)
Net present value	$ 4,368

To compute the IRR, note that the present value factor is $42,000 ÷ $6,300 = present value factor of 6.667, yielding a return of 8.15% from interpolation or, using a calculator, a return of 8.144%.

	Present Value Factors for Annuity of $1 for 10 years	
8%	6.710	6.710
IRR	–	6.667
10%	6.145	–
Difference	0.565	0.043

Internal rate of return = $8\% + \left(\dfrac{0.043}{0.565}\right)(2\%) = 8.15\%$.

4. To find the NPV with a different rate of return, use the same cash flows but with a different discount rate, this time for ten periods at 8%.

Annual net cash inflows	$ 7,000
Present value factor for annuity, 10 periods, 8%	× 6.71
Present value of net cash inflows	$46,970
Initial investment	(42,000)
Net present value	$ 4,970

The NPV is positive, so they should accept this project. Of course, this result is to be expected since in requirement 1, the IRR was determined to be 10.6%. Therefore, for any discount rate less than 10.6%, the NPV of the stream of cash flows will be positive.

21-34 (30–35 min.) NPV and AARR, goal-congruence issues.

1. Annual cash flow from operations $100,000

   Amortization: $320,000 ÷ 6 = $53,333 per year, but this is irrelevant because it has no impact on cash flows beyond moment 0.

	Year						
	0	**1**	**2**	**3**	**4**	**5**	**6**
Initial investment	$(320,000)						
Initial working capital investment	(5,000)						
Cash flow from operations (exl. deprcn.)		$100,000	$100,000	$100,000	$100,000	$100,000	$100,000
Times discount factor at 16%	× 1.000	× 0.862	× 0.743	× 0.641	× 0.552	× 0.476	× 0.410
Present value	$(325,000)	$86,200	$74,300	$64,100	$55,200	$47,600	$41,000
Net present value	$43,400						

Alternative solution using the annuity tables:

	PV Factor at i+16%, n+6	Net Cash Inflow		Total Present Value
Net present value:				
Present value of annuity of equal annual after-tax cash flows from operations	3.685 ×	$100,000 per year	=	$368,500
Net initial investment				(325,000)
Net present value				$43,500

Note: There is a difference of $100 between the two solutions due to rounding in the tables.

2. Accrual accounting rate of return (AARR): The accrual accounting rate of return takes the annual accrual net income and divides by the initial investment to get a return.

Incremental net operating income excluding amortization	$100,000
Less: amortization expense ($320,000 ÷ 6)	53,333
Income before tax	46,667

AARR = $46,667 ÷ $325,000 = 14.36%.

21-34 (cont'd)

3. Nate will not accept the project if he is being evaluated on the basis of accrual accounting rate of return, because the project does not meet the 16% threshold above which Nate earns a bonus. However, Nate should accept the project if he wants to act in the firm's best interest because the NPV is positive, implying that, based on the cash flows generated, the project exceeds the firm's required 16% rate of return. Thus, Nate will turn down an acceptable long-run project to avoid a poor evaluation based on the measure used to evaluate his performance. To remedy this, the firm could evaluate Nate instead on a project-by-project basis by looking at how well he achieves the cash flows forecasted when he chose to accept the project.

21-36 (35 min.) Recognizing cash flows for capital investment projects.

1. Partitioning relevant cash flows into categories:
    (1) Net initial investment cash flows:
    - The $98,000 cost of the new Flab-Buster 3000.
    - The disposal value of the old machine, $5,000, is a cash inflow .
    (2) Cash flow savings from operations:
    - The 30% savings in utilities cost per year of $4,320 (30% × $1,200 per month × 12 months) results in cash inflow from operations of $4,320.
    - The savings of half the maintenance costs per year of $5,000 (50% × $10,000) results in a cash inflow from operations of $5,000.
    (3) Cash flows from terminal disposal of investment:
    - The $10,000 salvage value of Flab-Buster 3000 minus the $0 salvage value of the old Fit-O-Matic is a terminal cash flow at the end of Year 10.
    (4) Data not relevant to the capital budgeting decision:
    - The $10 charge for customers, since it would not change whether or not Ludmilla got the new machine.
    - The $78,000 cost of the machine Ludmilla does not intend to buy.
    - The $50,000 original cost, nor the $46,000 in accumulated amortization of the Fit-O-Matic machine.
    - The annual amortization.

2. Net present value of the investment:

Net initial investment: Initial investment in Flab-Buster 3000	$(98,000)	
Current disposal value of Fit-O-Matic	5,000	
Net initial investment	$(93,000)	
Annual cash flow from operations: Savings in utilities costs		$ 4,320
Savings in maintenance costs		5,000
Annual cash flow from operations		$ 9,320
Cash flow from terminal disposal of machines		$ 10,000

21-36 (cont'd)

These three amounts can be combined to determine the NPV at an 8% discount rate.

Present value of net initial investment, $(93,000) × 1.000	$(93,000)
PV of 10-year annuity of cash flow from operations $9,320 × 6.710	62,537
PV of cash flow from terminal disposal of machines $10,000 × 0.463	4,630
Net present value	$(25,833)

At the required rate of return of 8%, the net present value of the investment in the Flab-Buster 3000 is substantially negative. Ludmilla should therefore not make the investment.

21-38 (30-40 min.) Equipment replacement, relevant costs, sensitivity analysis.

1. The first step is to analyze all relevant operating cash flows and align them with the appropriate alternative. This analysis follows:

	Developed Machine (1)	German Machine (2)	Increment (3)
Sales (irrelevant)	–	–	–
Costs:			
Direct materials	$300,000	$270,000	$ 30,000
Direct manufacturing labour*	120,000	60,000	60,000
Variable overhead*	240,000	120,000	120,000
Fixed overhead (irrelevant)	–	–	–
Marketing and administrative costs (irrelevant)	–	–	–
Total relevant operating cash outflows	$660,000	$450,000	$210,000

*Because the German machine produces twice as many units per hour, the direct manufacturing labour cost with the German machine would be $60,000; variable overhead, being 200% of direct manufacturing labour cost, would be $120,000.

Solution Exhibit 21-38 indicates that the German machine has a $233,260 net present value advantage over the internally developed machine.

Note: The book value of the developed machine is irrelevant and thus is completely ignored. In the light of subsequent events, nobody will deny that the original $600,000 investment could have been avoided, with a little luck or foresight. But nothing can be done to alter the past. The question is whether the company will nevertheless be better off buying the new machine. Management would have been much happier if the $600,000 had never been spent in the first place, but the original mistake should not be compounded by keeping the old machine.

21-38 (cont'd)

SOLUTION EXHIBIT 21-38
Net present value analysis of purchasing new automatic machine

End of Year	Total Present Value	Present Value Discount Factor at 16%	Sketch of Relevant Cash Flows			
			0	1	...	5
A. German Machine						
Net initial investment	$ (500,000) ◄—	1.000 ◄—	$(500,000)			
Current disposal price of old equipment	60,000 ◄—	1.000 ◄—	$60,000			
Recurring operating cash costs	(1,473,300) —	3.274 ◄—		$(450,000)		$(450,000)
Present value of net cash outflows	$(1,913,300)					
B. Internally Developed Machine						
Terminal disposal price of old equipment five years hence	$14,280 ◄—	0.476 ◄—				$30,000
Recurring operating cash costs	(2,160,840) ◄—	3.274 ◄—		$(660,000)		$(660,000)
Present value of net cash outflows	$(2,146,560)					
Difference in favour of The German machine	$ 233,260					

An alternative analysis of cash inflows and outflows (in thousands) is:

End of Year	Total Present Value	Present Value Discount Factor at 16%	Sketch of Relevant Cash Flows			
			0	1	...	5
1. Initial machine investment			$(500,000)			
2. Current disposal price of old machine			$ 60,000			
Net initial investment	$(440,000) ◄—	1.000 ◄—	$(440,000)			
3. Recurring operating cash savings	687,540 ◄—	3.274 ◄—		$210,000		$210,000
4. Difference in terminal disposal prices of machines	(14,280) ◄—	0.476 ◄—				(30,000)
Net present value	$ 233,260					

21-38 (cont'd)

Note the cash outflow of $30,000 from the difference in terminal disposal prices of machines. The relevant cash flow equals the difference in terminal disposal prices of the two machines. If the company continues to use the internally developed machine, it will receive $30,000 on disposal of its machine at the end of year 5. If it switches to the new machine, it will receive $0 on disposal at the end of year 5. Hence, by investing in the new German machine instead of continuing with the old one, the company forgoes $30,000 in terminal disposal price. Hence $30,000 appears as a cash outflow in year 5 in the sketch of relevant cash flows.

2. The uniform payback formula can be used because the operating savings are uniform:

$$\text{Payback period} = \frac{\text{Net initial investment}}{\text{Uniform increase in annual cash inflow}}$$

$$P = \left(\frac{\$500,000 - \$60,000}{\$210,000} \right) = 2.095 \text{ years}$$

The $60,000 current disposal price of the internally developed machine is deducted from the $500,000 cost of the German machine to determine the net initial investment in the automatic machine.

3. This is an example of sensitivity analysis:

Let X = annual cash savings, and let net present value = $0.

Then $0 = 3.274X – $440,000 – $14,280

Note that the net initial investment and the difference in terminal disposal prices of machines are unaffected and hence are included in the equation at the present values that we computed earlier. The present value of an annuity of $1 received at the end of each year for five years is 3.274.

$$3.274X = \$425,720$$
$$X = \$130,030$$

If the annual savings fall $79,970, from the estimated $210,000 to $130,030, the point of indifference will be reached. (Rounding errors may affect the computation slightly.)

Because the annual operating savings are equal, an alternative way to get a close answer is to divide the net present value of $233,260 by 3.274 (see Appendix A), obtaining $71,246 which is the amount of the annual difference in savings that will eliminate the $233,260 of net present value.

21-40 (25 min.) Capital budgeting, computer-integrated manufacturing, sensitivity.

1. The net present value analysis of the CIM proposal follows. We consider the differences in cash flows if the machine is replaced. All values in millions.

		Relevant Cash Flows	Present Value Discount Factors at 14%	Total Present Value
1.	Initial investment in CIM today	$(54)	1.000	$(54.000)
2a.	Current disposal price of old production line	6.0	1.000	6.000
2b.	Current recovery of working capital ($7.2 – $2.4)	4.8	1.000	4.800
3.	Recurring operating cash savings $4.8[1] each year for 10 years	4.8	5.216	25.037
4a.	Higher terminal disposal price of machines ($16.8 – $0) in year 10	16.8	0.270	4.536
4b.	Reduced recovery of working capital ($2.40 – $7.2) in year 10	(4.8)	0.270	(1.296)
Net present value of CIM investment				$(14.923)

On the basis of this formal financial analysis, Locomotive should not invest in CIM—It has a negative net present value of $(14.923) million.

[1]Recurring operating cash flows are as follows:

Cost of maintaining software programs and CIM equipment	$(1.8)
Reduction in technicians fees due to reduced maintenance requirements	1.2
Fewer product defects and reduced rework	5.4
Annual recurring operating cash flows	$ 4.8

2. Requirement 1 only looked at cost savings to justify the investment in CIM. Grass estimates additional cash revenues net of cash operating costs of $3.6 million a year as a result of higher quality and faster production resulting from CIM.

From Appendix A, the net present value of the $3.6 million annuity stream for 10 years discounted at 14% is $3.6 × 5.216 = $18.778. Taking these revenue benefits into account, the net present value of the CIM investment is $3.8546 ($18.778 – $14.923) million. On the basis of this financial analysis, Locomotive should invest in CIM.

21-40 (cont'd)

3. Let the annual cash flow from additional revenues be $X. Then we want the present value of this cash flow stream to overcome the negative NPV of $(14.923) calculated in requirement 1. Hence,

$$X (5.216) = 14.923$$
$$X = \$2.861 \text{ million}$$

An annuity stream of $2.861 million for 10 years discounted at 14% gives an NPV of $2.861 × 5.216 = $14.923 (rounded).

4.

(000,000s)	Relevant Cash Flows	Present Value Discount Factors at 14%	Total Present Value
1. Initial investment in CIM today	$(54)	1.000	$(54.000)
2a. Current disposal price of old production line	6.0	1.000	6.000
2b. Current recovery of working capital ($7.2 – $2.4)	4.8	1.000	4.800
3a. Recurring operating cash savings $4.8 each year for 5 years	4.8	3.433	16.478
3b. Recurring cash flows from additional revenues of $3.6 each year for 5 years	3.6	3.433	12.359
4a. Higher terminal disposal price of machines ($24 – $4.8) in year 5	19.2	0.519	9.965
4b. Reduced recovery of working capital ($2.4 – $7.2) in year 5	(4.8)	0.519	(2.491)
Net present value of CIM investment			$(6.889)

The use of too short a time horizon, such as 5 years, biases against the adoption of CIM projects. Before finally deciding against CIM in this case, Grass should consider other factors including{

(a) Sensitivity to different estimates of recurring cash savings or revenue gains.

(b) Accuracy of the costs of implementing and maintaining CIM.

(c) Benefits of greater flexibility that results from CIM and the opportunity to train workers for the manufacturing environment of the future.

(d) Potential obsolescence of the CIM equipment. Locomotive should consider how difficult the CIM equipment would be to modify if there is a major change in CIM technology.

(e) Alternative approaches to achieving the major benefits of CIM such as changes in process or implementation of just-in-time systems.

(f) Strategic factors. CIM may be the best approach to remain competitive against other low-cost producers in the future.

CHAPTER 22
CAPITAL BUDGETING: A CLOSER LOOK

22-2 Yes. To apply a consistent set of regulations and to provide for implementation of government initiatives, the federal government has implemented its own system of capital cost allowance (CCA). The Income Tax Act (ITA) does not permit a company to deduct amortization expense in determining taxable income but rather a company is allowed to deduct CCA. Therefore, the accounting amortization method will have no effect on taxes payable.

22-4 The total project approach calculates the present value of *all* cash outflows and inflows associated with each alternative. The incremental approach analyzes only the differences in those cash outflows and inflows that differ between alternatives.

22-6 No. Income taxes also affect the operating cash flows from an investment and the cash flows from current and terminal disposal of machines in the capital-budgeting decision. When a company has positive operating cash flows, income taxes reduce the cash flows available to the company from these sources.

22-8 The *real rate of return* is the rate of return required to cover only investment risk. This rate is made up of two elements: (a) a risk-free element and (b) a business-risk or equity element. The *nominal rate of return* is the rate of return required to cover investment risk and the anticipated decline, due to inflation, in general purchasing power of the cash that the investment generates. This rate is made up of two elements: (a) the real rate of return and (b) an inflation element.

The *nominal rate of return* and the *real rate of return* are related as follows:

a) Nominal rate (i) – Inflation rate (g) = Real rate (r) of Return
  The above is a good approximation especially when the term $r \times g$ is small.
  Real rates are the nominal rates adjusted for inflation.
  $(1 + i) = (1 + r)(1 + g) = 1 + r + g + rg$
  $i = r + g + rg$
b) Nominal rate = [(1 + Real rate)(1 + Inflation rate)] – 1

22-10 The chapter outlines five approaches used to recognize risk in capital budgeting:
1. Varying the required payback time.
2. Adjusting the required rate of return.
3. Adjusting the estimated future cash flows.
4. Sensitivity ("what-if") analysis.
5. Estimating the probability distribution of future cash inflows and outflows for each project.

22-12 No. Discounted cash-flow analysis applies to both profit-seeking and not-for-profit organizations. Not-for-profit organizations must also decide which long-term assets will accomplish various tasks at the least cost. Not-for-profit organizations incur an opportunity cost of funds.

22-14 NPV and IRR will not always rank projects identically. Different rankings occur when projects have unequal lives or unequal initial investments. The difference arises because the IRR method assumes a reinvestment rate equal to the indicated rate of return for the shortest-lived project. NPV assumes that funds can be reinvested at the required rate of return.

22-16 (30 min.) **Automated materials-handling capital project, income taxes, sensitivity analysis.**

1. (a)

	Relevant Cash Flows	Present-Value Discount Factors at 12%	Total Present Value
Initial equipment investment	$(7,375,000)	1.000	$(7,375,000)
Recurring after-tax operating savings*	1,800,000	3.037	5,466,600
Tax shield from CCA**	1,994,260	1.000	1,994,260
Net present value			$ 85,860

*$3,000,000 × (1 – 0.4) = $1,800,000
**($7,375,000 × 0.4) × (0.3/(0.3 + 0.12)) × ((2 + 0.12)/(2(1 + 0.12))) = $1,994,260

(b)

Year	CCA	Tax Shield	Operating Cash Flows	Total Cash Flows	Cumulative Cash Flows
1	$1,106,250	$442,500	$1,800,000	$2,242,500	$2,242,000
2	1,880,625	752,250	1,800,000	2,552,250	4,794,750
3	1,316,438	526,575	1,800,000	2,326,575	7,121,325
4	921,506	368,602	1,800,000	2,168,602	9,289,927

Payback period = 3 + (($7,375,000– $7,121,325)/2,168,602) = 3.12 years

2. 0   =   btocf(1 – 0.4)(3.037) – $7,375,000 + $1,994,260
btocf   = $2,952,881

22-16 (cont'd)

3. Other factors Just-in-Time Distributors should consider include:
   (a) Uncertainty regarding the annual operating cost savings of $3.0 million. Many firms have grossly underestimated the cost of maintaining and operating the automated materials-handling equipment.
   (b) Benefits to Just-in-Time Distributors from implementing the automated materials-handling system that are difficult to quantify; for example, any change in worker mentality regarding willingness to seek out other areas where automation could improve productivity.
   (c) Strategic factors. If competitors are implementing automation projects, Just-in-Time Distributors may well have to adopt automation to remain competitive in cost structure and around-the-clock service to customers.

22-18 (40 min.) Project risk, required rate of return.

1.

Drilling equipment project

	Relevant Cash Flows	Present-Value Discount Factors at 12%	Total Present Value
1. Initial drilling equipment investment	$(1,185,000)	1.000	$(1,185,000)
2. Tax shield created by CCA*	227,335	1.000	227,335
3. Recurring cash-operating flows	$ 448,000		
Additional income taxes at 30%	(134,440)		
Recurring after-tax cash-operating flows each year for 5 years (excl. amort. effects)	$ 313,560	3.605	1,130,384
Net present value			$ 172,719

*($1,185,000 × 0.3) × (0.25/(0.25 + 0.12)) × ((2 + 0.12)/2(1 + 0.12)) = $227,335

Production equipment project

Initial production equipment investment	$(850,000)	1.000	$(850,000)
Tax shield created by CCA*	163,067	1.000	163,067
Recurring operating cash flows**	248,500	3.037	754,695
Net present balue			$ 67,762

*($850,000 × 0.3) × (0.25/(0.25 + 0.12)) × ((2 + 0.12)/2(1 + 0.12)) = $163,067
**$355,000 × (1 – 0.3) = $248,500

At a 12% discount rate for both projects, the drilling equipment project has the higher NPV and would be preferred.

22-18 (cont'd)

2. We calculate the NPV of the high-risk drilling equipment project assuming a required rate of return of 18%.

	Relevant Cash Flows	Present-Value Discount Factors at 18%	Total Present Value
1. Initial drilling equipment investment	$(1,185,000)	1.000	$(1,185,000)
2. Tax shield created by CCA*	$190,922	1.000	190,922
3. Recurring cash-operating flows	$448,000		
Additional income taxes at 30%	(134,440)		
Recurring after-tax cash-operating flows each year for 5 years (excl. amort, effects)	$ 313,560	3.127	980,502
Net present value			$ (13,576)

*($1,185,000 × 0.3) × (0.25/(0.25 + 0.18)) × ((2+0.18)/2(1 + 0.18)) = $190,922

The lower-risk production equipment project for the refinery discounted at 12% has an NPV of $67,762 (requirement 1) that is greater than the NPV of $(13,576) for the higher-risk drilling equipment project for oil exploration discounted at 18%.

3. Northern should favour the investment in the production equipment for the refinery because it has a positive NPV. It should not invest in the drilling equipment because this project has a negative NPV when discounted at the risk adjusted 18% required rate of return.

22-20 (25 min.) Inflation and not-for-profit institution, no tax aspects.

1. The KopiPro official calculated the following NPV using the 18.8% discount rate and real cash-operating savings.

Year		Relevant Cash-Operating Savings in Nominal Dollars (1)	Present-Value Discount Factors at 18.8% (2)	Present Value of Cash Flows (3) = (1) × (2)
2011	1,350 x 1.1	$1,485	0.842	$ 1,250
2012	1,485 x 1.1	1,633	0.709	1,158
2013	1,633 x 1.1	1,796	0.596	1,071
2014	1,796 x 1.1	1,976	0.502	992
2015	1,976 x 1.1	2,174	0.423	919
Present value of recurring cash-operating savings				5,390
Net initial investment				5,500
Net present value				($ 110)

Inflation effects are symmetric on cash inflows and outflows. On the one hand, cash savings in inflated dollars tomorrow have lower purchasing power than cash savings in inflated dollars today. On the other hand, inflated costs today have a real value lower than uninflated costs of yesterday. Inflation helps those who owe money because they repay over time in dollars with lower purchasing power than the dollars they borrowed. Inflation hurts those who lend money, for the same reason.

Lenders factor inflation rate risk into their interest rates and, for a borrower, interest expense is a cash outflow. In the same vein, labour contracts often include escalation rates to account for anticipated inflation. It is important for managers assessing the financial viability of a project to ensure they distinguish those cash outflows that already include inflation from those that do not in order to avoid "double" discounting.

Remember that the risk-free rate of return is a lending rate. In this case the Canadian government is the borrower and hence the risk-free rate it pays to lenders must include both time-value of money, a factor for anticipated domestic inflation, and a factor for anticipated foreign exchange rate risk—otherwise lenders would not loan their money. Therefore even the risk-free rate has been adjusted for inflation and the real rate of return is:

Real rate of return = Nominal rate of return – Rate of inflation

When companies set their required rates of return, unless they anticipate higher inflation rates and higher foreign exchange rate risk than those reflected in the risk-free rate, they should avoid increasing their required rate of return based on these two factors. Therefore in 2b, the real rate of return is:

Real rate of return = 18% – 10% = 8%

22-20 (cont'd)

2. a. The real rate of return required by KopiPro can be computed using the following relationship:

$$(1 + \text{ real rate}) = \frac{1 + \text{ nominal rate}}{1 + \text{ inflation rate}} = \frac{1 + 0.188}{1 + 0.10} = \frac{1.188}{1.10} = 1.08$$

Real rate of return required $= 0.08$ or 8%

b. The net present value using real operating cash savings and real rates of return are as follows:

Year	Relevant Cash-Operating Savings in Real Dollars (1)	Present-Value Discount Factors at 8% (2)	Present Value of Cash Flows (3) = (l) × (2)
1	$1,350	0.926	$1,250
2	1,350	0.857	1,157
3	1,350	0.794	1,072
4	1,350	0.735	992
5	1,350	0.681	919
Present value of recurring cash-operating savings			5,390
Net initial investment			5,500
Net present value			($ 110)

3. Requirements 1 and 2 when correctly done give the same NPV of ($110). Consistency is key in capital budgeting. To be correct, requirement 1 should use nominal cash flows and nominal rates of return. Requirement 2 uses real cash flows and real rates of return. Both are valid approaches.

22-22 (20-30 min.) Comparison of projects with unequal lives.

1. Internal rate of return

Project 1

Let F = Present-value factor of $1 at X% received at the end of 1 year, Appendix A, Table 2.

$12,000 = PV of $14,400 at X% to be received at the end of year 1

$$F = \frac{\$12,000}{\$14,400} = 0.833$$

$$IRR = 20\%*$$

$$\frac{\$14,400}{(1+r)^1} = \$12,000$$

$$1 + r = \$14,400 \div \$12,000$$

$$1 + r = 1.20$$

$$r = 20\%$$

Project 2

Let F = Present-value factor of $1 at X% received at the end of year 4, Appendix A, Table 2.

$12,000 = PV of $21,000 at X% to be received at the end of year 4

$$F = \frac{\$12,000}{\$21,000} = 0.571$$

The internal rate of return can be calculated by interpolation:

	Present-Value Factors for $1 Received after 4 Years	
14%	0.592	0.592
IRR rate	–	0.571
16%	0.552	–
Difference	0.040	0.021

22-22 (cont'd)

$$\text{IRR rate: } 14\% + \left(\frac{0.021}{0.040}\right)(2\%) = 15.02\%*$$

$$*\frac{\$21,000}{(1+r)^4} = \$12,000$$

$$(1+r)^4 = \$21,000 \div \$12,000$$

$$(1+r) = \sqrt[4]{1.75}$$

$$1+r = 1.1502$$

$$r = 15.02\%$$

Project 1 is preferable to Project 2 using the IRR criterion.

2.   Net present value

Project 1

Gross present value	=	PV of $14,400 at 10% to be received at the end of year 1		
	=	$14,400 (0.909)	=	$13,090
Net present value	=	$13,090 – $12,000	=	$1,090

Project 2

Gross present value	=	PV of $21,000 at 10% to be received at the end of year 4		
	=	$21,000 (0.683)	=	$14,343
Net present value	=	$14,343 – $12,000	=	$2,343

Project 2 is preferable to Project 1 using the net present-value criterion.

3.   This problem contrasts the implied reinvestment rates of return under the internal rate of return and net present-value methods. Where the economic lives of mutually exclusive projects are unequal, this clash of reinvestment rates may give different conclusions under the two methods. This result occurs because the internal rate of return method assumes that the reinvestment rate is at least equal to the computed rate of return on the project. The net present-value method assumes that the funds obtainable from competing projects can be reinvested at the rate of the company's required rate of return. Comparisons follow:

22-22 (cont'd)

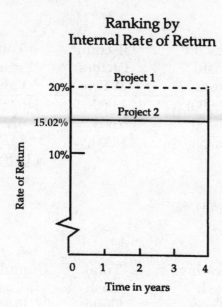

Ranking by Internal Rate of Return

Assumption: Project 1 funds can be reinvested at 20% over the life of the shorter-lived project.

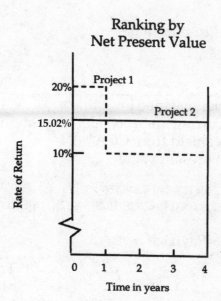

Ranking by Net Present Value

Assumption: Project 1 funds can be reinvested at 10%, the required rate of return.

22-24 (40 min.) New equipment purchase, income taxes.

1. a.

Present Value

	Relevant Cash Flows	Discount Factors at 12%	Total Present Value
Initial machine investment	$(62,500)	1.000	$(62,500)
Recurring after-tax operating savings*	18,750	3.605	67,594
Tax shield from CCA**	14,788	1.000	14,788
Net present value			$ 19,882

*31,250 × (1 – 0.4) = $18,750

**($62,500 × 0.4) × (0.20/(0.20 + 0.12)) × ((2 + 0.12)/(2(1 + 0.12))) = $14,788

b. Payback

Year	CCA	Tax Shield (CCA × 0.40)	Operating Cash Flows	Total Cash Flows	Cumulative Cash Flows
1	$6,250[a)	$2,500	$18,750	$21,250	$21,250
2	11,250[b)	4,500	18,750	23,250	44,500
3	9,000[c)	3,600	18,750	22,350	66,850
4	7,200	2,880	18,750	21,630	88,480

Payback period = 2 + (($62,500 – $47,356)/$23,819) = 3.64 years

a) 0.20 × 1/2 × 62,500 = 6,250
b) 0.20 × (62,500 – 6,250) = 11,250
c) 0.20 × (62,500 –(6,250 + 11,250)) = 9,000

c. The IRR, the discount rate at which the NPV of the cash flows is zero, must lie between 26% and 28%.

The internal rate of return can be calculated by interpolation:

	Present Value Factors for Annuity of $1 for 5 years	
26%	2.635	2.635
IRR	–	2.632
28%	2.532	–
Difference	0.103	0.003

Internal rate of return = $26\% + \left(\dfrac{0.003}{0.103}\right)(2\%) = 26.06\%$.

22-24 (cont'd)

2. Both the net present value and internal rate of return methods use the discounted cash flow approach in which *all* expected future cash inflows and outflows of a project are measured as if they occurred at a single point in time. The net present value approach computes the surplus generated by the project in today's dollars while the internal rate of return attempts to measure its effective return on investment earned by the project. The payback method, by contrast, considers nominal cash flows (without discounting) and measures the time at which the project's expected future cash inflows recoup the net initial investment in a project. The payback method thus ignores the profitability of the project's entire stream of future cash flows.

22-26 (35-40 min.) Equipment replacement, income taxes.

Microvac should not purchase the new pump because the net present value is a negative $118,664, as calculated in the chart below.

1. We compute the NPV of investing in the new pump using the incremental approach.

	Relevant Cash Flows	Present-Value Discount Factors at 16%	Total Present Value
Initial pump investment	$(807,500)	1.000	$(807,500)
Proceeds from disposal of old pump	72,600	1.000	72,600
Tax shield created by CCA*	166,882	1.000	166,882
Recurring operating savings†			293,790
Recurring cash flows from additional manufacturing@			115,517
Proceeds from disposal of pump	96,000	0.552	52,992
Lost tax shield because of disposal#	(23,415)	0.552	(12,925)
Net present value			$(118,644)

*(($807,500 – $72,600) × 0.4) × (0.25/(0.25 + 0.16)) × ((2 + 0.16)/(2(1 + 0.16))) = $166,882

†Recurring cash-operating savings	$175,000		
Additional income taxes at 40%	(70,000)		
Recurring after-tax cash-operating savings each year for 4 years	$ 105,000	2.798	$ 293,790

@Recurring after-tax cash inflow from additional units manufactured by new pump.

#($96,000 × 0.4) × (0.25/(0.25 + 0.16)) = $23,415

22-26 (cont'd)

Year (1)	Cash Inflow per Unit on Additional Units Manufactured (2)	Additional Units Manufactured (3)	Total Cash Inflow from Additional Units Manufactured (4) = (2) × (3)
2012	$[4,480 – (3,220 – 180)]	30	$43,200
2013	[4,480 – (3,220 – 180)]	50	72,000
2014	[4,480 – (3,220 – 180)]	50	72,000
2015	[4,480 – (3,220 – 180)]	70	100,800

Year (1)	Cash Inflow from Additional Units Manufactured (2)	After-Tax Cash Inflow from Additional Units Manufactured (3) = 0.60 × (2)	Present Value Discount Factors at 16%	Total Present Value
2012	$43,200	$25,920	0.862	$ 22,343
2013	72,000	43,200	0.743	32,098
2014	72,000	43,200	0.641	27,691
2015	100,800	60,480	0.552	33,385
				$115,517

2. Nonfinancial and qualitative factors that Microvac should consider before making the pump replacement decision include:
   - Availability of any necessary financing.
   - Probability of further technological changes for the vacuum pumps.
   - Leasing of the new equipment.

22-28 (35 min.) Capital budgeting, inventory changes.

1. A schedule of relevant cash flows follows:

Sketch of Relevant Cash Flows

	Year 0	Year 1	Year 2	Year 3	Year 4
Acquire machines	$(131,040)				
Sales					
6,000 × $30.00		$180,000			
6,200 × $30.00			$186,000		
7,700 × $28.80				$221,760	
3,100 × $26.40					$81,840
Manufacturing costs					
7,000 × $14.40		(100,800)			
6,500 × $15.60			(101,400)		
6,500 × $16.80				(109,200)	
3,000 × $18.00					(54,000)
Marketing, distribution, and customer-service costs					
6,000 × $3.60		(21,600)			
6,200 × $3.60			(22,320)		
7,700 × $3.60				(27,720)	
3,100 × $3.60					(11,160)
Disposal of machine					21,600
Taxes (see schedule)		(22,248)	(15,798)	(17,896)	(1,710)
Net cash flow					
after tax	($131,040)	$ 35,352	$ 46,482	$ 66,944	$36,570

	Year 1	Year 2	Year 3	Year 4
Sales	$180,000	$186,000	$221,760	$81,840
COGS*	86,400	95,520	127,800	55,680
Mkt., dist. & cust.-serv.	21,600	22,320	27,720	11,160
CCA	16,380[1]	28,665[2]	21,499[3]	10,724[4]
Taxable income	$55,620	$39,495	$44,741	$ 4,276
Tax rate	40%	40%	40%	40%
Taxes	$22,248	$15,798	$17,896	$ 1,710

*Using FIFO:
  Year 1: 6,000 × $14.40 = $86,400
  Year 2: (1,000 × $14.40) + (5,200 × $15.60) = $95,520
  Year 3: (1,300 × $15.60) + (6,400 × $16.80) = $127,800
  Year 4: (100 × $16.80) + (3,000 × $18) = $55,680

---

[1] (1/2) × 0.25 × $131,040 = $16,380
[2] 0.25 × ($131,040 − $16,380) = $28,665
[3] 0.25 × ($131,040 − $16,380 +$ 28,665)= $21,499
[4] 0.25 × ($131,040 − $16,380 + $28,665 + $21,499 − $21,600) = $10,724

22-28 (cont'd)

	Relevant Cash Flows	Present-Value Discount Factors at 16%	Total Present Value
Year 0	$(131,040)	1.000	$(131,040)
Year 1	35,352	0.862	30,473
Year 2	46,482	0.743	34,536
Year 3	66,944	0.641	42,911
Year 4	36,570	0.552	20,187
Remaining CCA tax shield*	7,847	0.476	3,735
Net present value			$ 802

*(($131,040 – $16,380 – $28,665 – $21,499 – $10,724 – $21,600) × 0.4) × (0.25/(0.25 + 0.16)) = $7,847

The NPV for adding a new line of running shoes is a positive $802.

Although the amounts arise in year 4, the income taxes are not filed until year 5.

22-30 (40-50 min.) Capital project, inflation, income taxes.

1. Nominal rate = (1 + Real rate) (1 + Inflation rate) – 1
   = (1 +0.10) (1 +0.20) – 1
   = 0.32

   Alternatively:
Real rate of interest	0.10
Inflation rate	0.20
Combination (0.10 × 0.20)	0.02
Nominal rate of interest	0.32

2.

	Relevant Cash Flows	Present-Value Discount Factors at 32%	Total Present Value
Initial robot investment	$(12,750,000)	1.000	$(12,750,000)
Tax shield created by CCA*	1,965,710	1.000	1,965,710
Recurring cash-operating savings**			9,130,000
Proceeds from disposal	2,799,000†	0.329	921,167
Lost tax shield because of disposal***	(491,210)	0.329	(161,608)
Net present value			$ (894,731)

*($12,750,000 × 0.4) × (0.25/(0.25 + 0.32)) × ((2 + 0.32)/(2(1 + 0.32) = $1,965,710

**The recurring net cash-operating savings of $8.4 million – $3.6 million = $4.80 million (in January 1, 2010 dollars) in nominal dollars are calculated in the schedule below.

†The terminal disposal price of the robots (at the end of 4 years) is: $1,350,000 × 2.074 = $2,799,000

***($2,799,000 × 0.4) × (0.25/(0.25 + 0.32)) = $491,210

Recurring Net Cash Operating Schedule (nominal dollars)

Year (1)	Cash-Operating Savings in Real Dollars (millions) (2)	Cumulative Inflation Rate (3)	Cash-Operating Savings in Nominal Dollars (4) = (2) × (3)
2010	$4.800	1.200	$5.760
2011	4.800	1.440	6.912
2012	4.800	1.728	8.294
2013	4.800	2.074	9.955

22-30 (cont'd)

Recurring cash-operating savings (nominal dollars and a nominal discount rate).

Year	(million $) Before-Tax Cash-Operating Savings	Tax Payments at 40%	After-Tax Cash-Operating Savings	Present-Value Discount Factor at 32%	(million $) Total Present Value
2010	$5.760	$2.304	$3.456	0.758	$2.620
2011	6.912	2.765	4.147	0.574	2.380
2012	8.294	3.318	4.976	0.435	2.165
2013	9.955	3.982	5.973	0.329	1.965
					$9.130

3. The nominal approach to inflation has two advantages:
    (a) Managers find it easier to understand because it uses cash-flow numbers (nominal dollars) they observe and that are recorded in their accounting systems.
    (b) It provides a planning basis that can be audited in the future in terms of the monetary units being exchanged at the time actual cash flows occur.
    (c) The nominal discount rates used are also those available and observable in the financial markets. These rates are also called market rates.

4. Other factors Pipe-it might consider are:
    (a) The sensitivity of the net present-value analysis to differences in the estimates of cost savings, disposal price, and the discount rate.
    (b) Benefits to Pipe-it that are difficult to quantify. For example, if the robots are successfully introduced, the (remaining) workers will be better able to accommodate future changes in technology.
    (c) Strategic position of Pipe-it, if competitors adopt robotics projects.
    (d) Reduction in worker accidents at Pipe-it. This factor has a human element that has motivated many businesses to use robots. It also can lead to reduced insurance payments for employee compensation.
    (e) Effect of the robots on the quality of the output.
    (f) Employment implications, especially if Pipe-it has a unionized labour force.

22-32 (20 min.) NPV and inflation.

1. Without inflation or taxes, this is a simple net present value problem using a 10% discount rate.

Present value of initial investment, $(600,000) × 1.000	$(600,000)
Present value of 6-year annuity of annual cash savings	
($140,000 × 4.355)	609,700
Net present value	$ 9,700

2. With inflation, we adjust each year's cash flow for the inflation rate to get nominal cash flows and then discount each cash flow separately using the nominal discount rate.

Nominal rate = (1 + real rate) × (1 + inflation rate) −1
Nominal rate = (1.10)(1.055) −1 = 1.16 – 1 = .16 or 16%

Period	Cash Flow (Real Dollars) (1)	Cumulative Inflation Rate (2)	Cash Inflows (Nominal Dollars) (3) = (1) × (2)	Present Value Factor, 16% (4)	Present Value (5) = (3) × (4)
1	$140,000	1.055	$147,700	0.862	$127,317
2	140,000	1.113[1]	155,824	0.743	115,777
3	140,000	1.174	164,394	0.641	105,376
4	140,000	1.239	173,435	0.552	95,736
5	140,000	1.307	182,974	0.476	87,096
6	140,000	1.379	193,038	0.410	79,146

Total present value of annual net cash inflows in nominal dollars	610,448
Present value of initial investment, $(600,000) × 1.000	(600,000)
Net present value	$ 10,448

[1]$1.113 = (1.055)^2$

3. Both the unadjusted and adjusted NPV are positive. Based on financial considerations alone, Cost-Less should buy the new cash registers. However, the effect of taxes should also be considered, as well as any pertinent non-financial issues, such as potential improvements in customer response time from moving to the new cash registers before pursuing this option.

22-34 (40-50 min.) Governance, discounted cash-flow analysis.

	Relevant Cash Flows	Present-Value Discount Factors at 12%	Total Present Value
Initial equipment investment	$(1,275,000)	1.000	$(1,275,000)
Initial working capital investment	(260,000)	1.000	(260,000)
Tax shield created by CCA*	293,521	1.000	293,521
Cash flow from canceling lease†	(26,680)	1.000	(26,680)
Additional working capital investment	(240,000)	0.797	(191,280)
Recurring rent cash flow forgone@	(38,400)	4.111	(157,862)
Recurring operating cash flows#			1,531,393
Market research and sales promotion cash flows‡	(240,000)	0.893	(214,320)
Recovery of working capital	500,000	0.507	253,500
Proceeds from disposal of equipment	360,000	0.507	182,520
Lost tax shield from disposal§	(87,568)	0.507	(44,397)
Net present value			$ 91,195

*($1,275,000 × 0.36) × (0.25/(0.25 + 0.12)) × ((2 + 0.12)/(2(1 + 0.12))) = $293,521
†$42,000 × (1 − 0.36) = $26,680
@$60,000 × (1 − 0.36) = $38,400
#Recurring after-tax cash-operating flows
‡$375,000 × (1 − 0.36) =$240,000
§($360,000 × 0.36) × (0.25/(0.25 + 0.12)) =$87,568

Year (1)	Cash-Operating Flows (2)	After-Tax Cash-Operating Flows (3) = 0.64 × (2)	Present-Value Discount Factors at 12%	Total Present Value
1	$480,000	$307,200	0.893	$ 274,330
2	480,000	307,200	0.797	244,838
3	720,000	460,800	0.712	328,090
4	720,000	460,800	0.636	293,069
5	720,000	460,800	0.567	261,274
6	400,000	256,000	0.507	129,792
				$1,531,393

Crosslink should launch the new household product because investing in the product has a positive net present value.

22-34 (cont'd)

2.

	Relevant Cash Flows	Present-Value Discount Factors at 12%	Total Present Value
Initial equipment investment	$(1,680,000)	1.000	$(1,680,000)
Initial working capital investment	(260,000)	1.000	(260,000)
Tax shield created by CCA*	386,757	1.000	386,757
Cash flow from cancelling lease**	(26,880)	1.000	(26,880)
Additional working capital investment	(240,000)	0.797	(191,280)
Recurring rent cash flow forgone***	(38,400)	4.111	(157,862)
Recurring operating cash flows (see above)			1,531,393
Market research and sales promotion cash flows****	(240,000)	0.893	(214,320)
Recovery of working capital	500,000	0.507	253,500
Proceeds from disposal of equipment	360,000	0.507	182,520
Lost tax shield from disposal*****	(87,568)	0.507	(44,397)
Net present value			$ (220,569)

*($1,680,000 × 0.36) × (0.25/(0.25 + 0.12)) × ((2 + 0.12)/(2(1 + 0.12))) = $386,757
**$42,000 × (1 − 0.36) = $26,680
***$60,000 × (1 − 0.36) = $38,400
****$375,000 × (1 − 0.36) = $240,000
*****($360,000 × 0.36) × (0.25/(0.25 + 0.12)) = $87,568

The overall NPV of the project would then be $(220,569). Marchand is unhappy with Ng's revised analysis because the NPV of the project is now negative, possibly leading to the project being rejected. He would like to resume production in the plant, and reemploy his friends who had been laid off earlier. There is also the possibility that Marchand may be hired as a consultant by the new plant management after he retires next year.

Considering the ethical issues, Ng should evaluate Marchand's directives as follows:

- Ng should present complete and clear reports and recommendations after appropriate analyses of relevant and reliable information. Marchand does not wish the report to be complete or clear, and has provided some information which is not totally reliable.
- Ng should not disclose confidential information outside of the organization, but it also appears that Marchand wants to refrain from disclosing information to senior management that it should know about.
- In evaluating Marchand's directive as it affects Ng, Ng has an obligation to communicate unfavourable as well as favourable information and professional judgments or opinions.

22-34 (cont'd)

The responsibility to communicate information fairly and objectively, as well as to disclose fully all relevant information that could reasonably be expected to influence an intended user's understanding of the reports and recommendations presented, is being hampered. Management will not have the full scope of information they should have when they are presented with the analysis.

Ng should take the following steps to resolve this situation:

- Ng should first investigate and see if Crosslink Inc. has an established policy for resolution of ethical conflicts and follow those procedures.
- If this policy does not resolve the ethical conflict, the next step would be for Ng to discuss the situation with his supervisor, Marchand, and see if he can obtain resolution. One possible solution may be to present a "base case" and sensitivity analysis of the investment. Ng should make it clear to Marchand that he has a problem and is seeking guidance.
- If Ng cannot obtain a satisfactory resolution with Marchand, he could take the situation up to the next layer of management, and inform Marchand that he is doing this. If this is not satisfactory, Ng should progress to the next, and subsequent, higher levels of management until the issue is resolved (i.e., the president, Audit Committee, or Board of Directors).
- Ng may want to have a confidential discussion with an objective advisor to clarify relevant concepts and obtain an understanding of possible courses of action.
- If Ng cannot satisfactorily resolve the situation within the organization, he may resign from the company and submit an informative memo to an appropriate person in Crosslink (i.e., the president, Audit Committee, or Board of Directors).

CHAPTER 23
MANAGEMENT CONTROL SYSTEMS, TRANSFER PRICING, AND MULTINATIONAL CONSIDERATIONS

23-2   To be effective, management control systems should be (a) closely aligned to an organization's strategies and goals, (b) designed to fit the organization's structure and the decision-making responsibility of individual managers, and (c) able to motivate managers and employees to put in effort to attain selected goals desired by top management.

23-4   The chapter cites five benefits of decentralization:
1.   Creates greater responsiveness to local needs.
2.   Leads to quicker decision making.
3.   Increases motivation of subunit managers.
4.   Aids management development and learning.
5.   Sharpens the focus of managers.

The chapter cites four costs of decentralization:
1.   Leads to suboptimal decision making.
2.   Results in duplication of activities.
3.   Decreases loyalty toward the organization as a whole.
4.   Increases costs of gathering information.

23-6   No. A transfer price is the price one subunit of an organization charges for a product or service supplied to another subunit of the same organization. The two segments can be cost centres, profit centres, or investment centres. For example, the allocation of service department costs to production departments that are set up as either cost centres or investment centres is an example of transfer pricing.

23-8   Transfer pricing systems should have the following properties. They should
1.   Promote goal congruence.
2.   Promote a sustained high level of management effort.
3.   Promote a high level of subunit autonomy in decision making.
4.   Contribute to subunit performance evaluation.

23-10   Transferring products or services at market prices generally leads to optimal decisions when (a) the intermediate market is perfectly competitive, (b) interdependencies of subunits are minimal, and (c) there are no additional costs or benefits to the corporation as a whole in using the market instead of transacting internally.

23-12 Reasons that a dual-pricing approach to transfer pricing is not widely used in practice include:

1. The manager of the division using a cost-based method does not have sufficient incentives to control costs.
2. This approach does not provide clear signals to division managers about the level of decentralization top management wants.
3. This approach tends to insulate managers from the frictions of the marketplace.

23-14 Yes. The general transfer-pricing guideline specifies that the minimum transfer price equals the additional *outlay costs* per unit incurred up to the point of transfer *plus* the *opportunity costs* per unit to the supplying division. When the supplying division has idle capacity, its opportunity costs are zero; when the supplying division has no idle capacity, its opportunity costs are positive. Hence the minimum transfer price will vary depending on whether the supplying division has idle capacity or not.

23-16 (25 min.) Decentralization, responsibility centres.

1. The manufacturing plants in the Manufacturing Division are cost centres. Senior management determines the manufacturing schedule based on the quantity of each type of stationary product specified by the sales and marketing division and detailed studies of the time and cost to manufacture each type of product. Manufacturing managers are accountable only for costs. They are evaluated based on achieving target output within budgeted costs.
2. a. If manufacturing and marketing managers were to directly negotiate the prices for manufacturing various products, Corporate Express should evaluate manufacturing plant managers as profit centres—revenues received from marketing minus the costs incurred to produce and sell output.
   b. Corporate Express would be better off decentralizing its marketing and manufacturing decisions and evaluating each division as a profit centre. Decentralization would encourage plant managers to increase total output to achieve the greatest profitability, and motivate plant managers to cut their costs to increase margins. Manufacturing managers would be motivated to design their operations according to the criteria that meet the marketing managers' approval, thereby improving cooperation between manufacturing and marketing.

   Under Corporate Express's existing system, manufacturing managers have every incentive not to improve. Manufacturing managers' incentives are to get as high a cost target as possible so that they can produce output within budgeted costs. Any significant improvements could result in the target costs being lowered for the next year, increasing the possibility of not achieving budgeted costs. By the same line of reasoning, manufacturing managers will also try to limit their production so that production quotas would not be increased in the future. Decentralizing manufacturing and marketing decisions overcomes these problems.

23-18 (25 min.) **Cost centers, profit centers, decentralization, transfer prices.**

1. The Glass Department sends its product to the Wood and Metal Departments for finishing. The Glass Department does not negotiate internal prices. The Glass, Wood, and Metal Departments are cost centers because they are only evaluated on output and cost control (cost variances).

2. The three departments are centralized because upper management dictates their production schedules.

3. A centralized department can be a profit centre. Centralization relates to the degree of autonomy that a department has for decision making. This concept is independent of the type of responsibility centre used to evaluate performance. (For example, the Glass Department could be a profit centre if upper management chooses a transfer price for the glass transferred from the Glass to the Wood and Metal Departments.) A department may be organized as a profit centre but it will be centralized if it has little freedom in making decisions.

4. a) With these changes, Fenster will be moving toward a more decentralized environment because each department will have more local decision-making authority, such as the ability to set its own production schedule, buy and sell products in the external market, and negotiate transfer prices. These changes also make all three departments profit centres (rather than cost centres) because the managers of each department are responsible for both costs and revenues.

b) I would recommend that upper management evaluate the three departments as profit centres because profits would be a good indicator of how well each department is doing.

23-20 (35 min.)   **Multinational transfer pricing, effect of alternative transfer-pricing methods, global income tax minimization.**

1.   This is a three-country, three-division transfer-pricing problem with three alternative transfer-pricing methods. Summary data in Canadian dollars are:

China Division

       Variable costs: 1,000 yuan ÷ 8 yuan per \$ = \$125 per subunit

       Fixed costs: 1,800 yuan ÷ 8 yuan per \$ = \$225 per subunit

South Korea Division

       Variable costs: 360,000 won ÷ 1,200 won per \$ = \$300 per unit

       Fixed costs: 480,000 won ÷ 1,200 won per \$ = \$400 per unit

Canadian. Division

       Variable costs: = \$100 per unit

       Fixed costs: = \$200 per unit

Market prices for private-label sale alternatives:

     China Division: 3,600 yuan ÷ 8 yuan per \$ = \$450 per subunit

     South Korea Division: 1,560,000 won ÷ 1,200 won per \$ = \$1,300 per unit

The transfer prices under each method are:

a.   Market price

-    China to South Korea = \$450 per subunit
-    South Korea to Canadian Division = \$1,300 per unit

b.   200% of full costs

-    China to South Korea

     2.0 × (\$125 + \$225) = \$700 per subunit

-    South Korea to Canadian Division

     2.0 × (\$700 + \$300 + \$400) = \$2,800 per unit

c.   300% of variable costs

-    China to South Korea

     3.0 × \$125 = \$375 per subunit

-    South Korea to Canadian Division

     3.0 × (\$375 + \$300) = \$2,025 per unit

23-20 (cont'd)

	Method A Internal Transfers at Market Price	Method B Internal Transfers at 200% of Full Costs	Method C Internal Transfers at 300% of Variable Costs
1. *China Division*			
Division revenue per unit	$ 450	$ 700	$ 375
Cost per unit:			
Division variable cost per unit	125	125	125
Division fixed cost per unit	225	225	225
Total division cost per unit	350	350	350
Division operating income per unit	100	350	25
Income tax at 40%	40	140	10
Division net income per unit	$ 60	$ 210	$ 15
2. *South Korea Division*			
Division revenue per unit	$1,300	$2,800	$2,025
Cost per unit:			
Transferred-in cost per unit	450	700	375
Division variable cost per unit	300	300	300
Division fixed cost per unit	400	400	400
Total division cost per unit	1,150	1,400	1,075
Division operating income per unit	150	1,400	950
Income tax at 20%	30	280	190
Division net income per unit	$ 120	$1,120	$ 760
3. *Canadian Division*			
Division revenue per unit	$3,200	$3,200	$3,200
Cost per unit:			
Transferred-in cost per unit	1,300	2,800	2,025
Division variable cost per unit	100	100	100
Division fixed cost per unit	200	200	200
Total division cost per unit	1,600	3,100	2,325
Division operating income per unit	1,600	100	875
Income tax at 30%	480	30	262.5
Division net income per unit	$1,120	$ 70	$ 612.5

23-20 (cont'd)

2. Division net income:

	Market Price	200% of Full Costs	300% of Variable Cost
China Division	$ 60	$ 210	$ 15.00
South Korea Division	120	1,120	760.00
Canadian Division	1,120	70	612.50
User Friendly Computer, Inc.	$1,300	$1,400	$1,387.50

User Friendly will maximize its net income by using 200% of full costs as the transfer-price. This is because Method B sources the largest proportion of income in Korea, the country with the lowest income tax rate.

23-22 (30 min.) Transfer-pricing methods, goal congruence.

1. *Alternative 1:* Sell as raw lumber for $200 per 100 board-feet:

> Revenue $200
> Variable costs   100
> Contribution margin $100 per 100 board-feet

Alternative 2: Sell as finished lumber for $275 per 100 board-feet:

> Revenue $275
> Variable costs:
>   Raw lumber $100
>   Finished lumber   125   225
> Contribution margin $ 50 per 100 board-feet

British Columbia Lumber will maximize its total contribution margin by selling lumber in its raw form.

An alternative approach is to examine the incremental revenues and incremental costs in the Finished Lumber Division:

> Incremental revenues, $275 – $200 $ 75
> Incremental costs   125
> Incremental loss $ (50) per 100 board-feet

23-22 (cont'd)

2. Transfer price at 110% of variable costs:
    = $100 + ($100 × 0.10)
    = $110 per 100 board-feet

	Sell as Raw Lumber	Sell as Finished Lumber
Raw Lumber Division		
Division revenues	$200	$110
Division variable costs	100	100
Division operating income	$100	$ 10
Finished Lumber Division		
Division revenues	$ 0	$275
Transferred-in costs	—	110
Division variable costs		125
Division operating income	$ 0	$ 40

23-22 (cont'd)

The Raw Lumber Division will maximize reported division operating income by selling raw lumber, which is the action preferred by the company as a whole. The Finished Lumber Division will maximize divisional operating income by selling finished lumber, which is contrary to the action preferred by the company as a whole.

3.   Transfer price at market price = $200 per 100 board-feet.

	Sell as Raw Lumber	Sell as Finished Lumber
Raw Lumber Division		
Division revenues	$200	$200
Division variable costs	100	100
Division operating income	$100	$100
Finished Lumber Division		
Division revenues	$ 0	$275
Transferred-in costs	–	200
Division variable costs	–	125
Division operating income	$ 0	$ (50)

Since the Raw Lumber Division will be indifferent between selling the lumber in raw or finished form, it would be willing to maximize division operating income by selling raw lumber, which is the action preferred by the company as a whole. The Finished Lumber Division will maximize division operating income by not further processing raw lumber and this is preferred by the company as a whole. Thus, transfer at market price will result in division actions that are also in the best interest of the company as a whole.

23-24 (25 min.) Multinational transfer pricing, global tax minimization.

1. Solution Exhibit 23-24 shows the after-tax operating incomes earned by the Canadian and Moroccan divisions from transferring 1,000 units using (a) full manufacturing cost per unit and (b) market price of comparable imports as transfer prices.

2. There are many ways to proceed but the first thing to note is that the transfer price that minimizes the total company import duties and income taxes will be either the full manufacturing cost or the market price of comparable imports.
    Consider what happens every time the transfer price is increased by $1 over, say, the full manufacturing cost of $600. This results in the following

(a)	an increase in Moroccan taxes of 40% × $1	$0.400
(b)	an increase in import duties paid in Canada 10% × $1	0.100
(c)	a decrease in Canadian taxes of 44% × $1.10	
	(the $1 increase in transfer price + $0.10 paid by	
	way of import duty)	(0.484)
	Net effect is an increase in import duty and tax payments of	$0.016

    Hence, Kasba Inc. will minimize import duties and income taxes by setting the transfer price at its minimum level of $600, the full manufacturing cost.

23-24 (cont'd)

SOLUTION EXHIBIT 23-24
Division Incomes of Canadian and Moroccan Divisions from Transferring 1,000 Units

	Method A: Internal Transfers at Full Manufacturing Cost	Method B: Internal Transfers at Market Price
MOROCCAN DIVISION		
Revenues:		
$600, $780 × 1,000 units	$600,000	$780,000
Deduct:		
Full manufacturing cost:		
$600 × 1,000 units	600,000	600,000
Division operating income	0	180,000
Division income taxes at 40%	0	72,000
Division after-tax operating income	$ 0	$108,000
CANADIAN DIVISION		
Revenues:		
$900 × 1,000 units	$900,000	$900,000
Deduct:		
Transferred-in costs:		
$600, $780 × 1,000 units	600,000	780,000
Import duties at 10% of transferred-in		
price $60, $78 × 1,000 units	60,000	78,000
Division operating income	240,000	42,000
Division income taxes at 44%	105,600	18,480
Division after-tax operating income	$134,400	$ 23,520

23-26 (20 min.) Dual Pricing.

1.

	Bottle Division			Mixing Division			Company
		Units	Total		Units	Total	
Revenue External	$5.00	150,000	$750,000	$ 11.50	40,000	$460,000	$1,210,000
Internal	$4.20	40,000	$168,000				$ 168,000
			$918,000			$460,000	$1,378,000
Variable costs	$3.00	190,000	$570,000	$ 2.50	40,000	$100,000	$ 670,000
				$ 3	40,000	$120,000	$ 120,000
			$570,000			$220,000	$ 790,000
Contribution margin			$348,000			$240,000	$ 588,000
Fixed costs			$125,000			$ 85,000	$ 210,000
Divisional operating income			$223,000			$155,000	$ 378,000
Internal transfer adjustment: $3 x 0.40 x 40,000							$ 48,000
Operating income							$ 330,000

2. The internal sales are included in the company's statement because the company cannot sell to itself. Therefore, it has to adjust $48,000 of dual pricing out of its income.

23-28 (30 min.) Transfer pricing, general guideline, goal congruence.

1. Using the general guideline presented in the chapter, the minimum price at which the Airbag Division would sell airbags to the Tivo Division is $90, the incremental costs. The Airbag Division has idle capacity (it is currently working at 80% of capacity). Therefore, its opportunity cost is zero — the Airbag Division does not forgo any external sales and, as a result, does not forgo any contribution margin from internal transfers. Transferring airbags at incremental cost achieves goal congruence.

2. Transferring products internally at incremental cost has the following properties:
    a. Achieves goal congruence — Yes, as described in requirement 1 above.
    b. Useful for evaluating division performance — No, because this transfer price does not cover or exceed full costs. By transferring at incremental costs and not covering fixed costs, the Airbag Division will show a loss. This loss, the result of the incremental cost-based transfer price, is not a good measure of the economic performance of the subunit.
    c. Motivating management effort — Yes, if based on budgeted costs (actual costs can then be compared to budgeted costs). If, however, transfers are based on actual costs, Airbag Division management has little incentive to control costs.
    d. Preserves division autonomy — No. Because it is rule-based, the Airbag Division has no say in the setting of the transfer price.

3. If the two divisions were to negotiate a transfer price, the range of possible transfer prices would be between $90 and $125 per unit. The Airbag Division has excess capacity that it can use to supply airbags to the Tivo Division. The Airbag Division will be willing to supply the airbags only if the transfer price equals or exceeds $90, its incremental cost of manufacturing the airbags. The Tivo Division will be willing to buy airbags from the Airbag Division only if the price does not exceed $125 per airbag, the price at which the Tivo division can buy airbags in the market from external suppliers. Within the price range of $90 and $125, each division will be willing to transact with the other and maximize overall income of Quest Motors. The exact transfer price between $90 and $125 will depend on the bargaining strengths of the two divisions. The negotiated transfer price has the following properties.
    a. Achieves goal congruence — Yes, as described above.
    b. Useful for evaluating division performance — Yes, because the transfer price is the result of direct negotiations between the two divisions. Of course, the transfer prices will be affected by the bargaining strengths of the two divisions.
    c. Motivating management effort — Yes, because once negotiated, the transfer price is independent of actual costs of the Airbag Division. Airbag Division management has every incentive to manage efficiently to improve profits.

23-28 (con'td)

    d.   Preserves subunit autonomy—Yes, because the transfer price is based on direct negotiations between the two divisions and is not specified by headquarters on the basis of some rule (such as Airbag Division's incremental costs).

4.   Neither method is perfect, but negotiated transfer pricing (requirement 3) has more favourable properties than the cost-based transfer pricing (requirement 2). Both transfer-pricing methods achieve goal congruence, but negotiated transfer pricing facilitates the evaluation of division performance, motivates management effort, and preserves division autonomy, whereas the transfer price based on incremental costs does not achieve these objectives.

23-30 (5 min.) Transfer-pricing problem (continuation of 23-29).

The company as a whole would benefit in this situation if Coffee Machines purchased from outside suppliers. The $2,500 disadvantage to the company as a whole by purchasing from the outside supplier would be more than offset by the $3,500 contribution margin of Timers and Thermostats' sale of 1,000 units to other customers.

Purchase costs from outside supplier, 1,000 units × $8.50		$8,500
Deduct variable cost savings, 1,000 units × $6		6,000
Net cost to company as a whole by buying from outside		$ 2,500
Timers and Thermostats sales to other customers, 1,000 units × $10		$10,000
Deduct:		
Variable manufacturing costs, $6 × 1,000 units	$6,000	
Variable marketing costs, $0.50 × 1,000 units	500	
Variable costs		6,500
Contribution margin from selling Timers to other customers		$ 3,500

23-32 (30–35 min.) Effect of alternative transfer-pricing methods on division operating income.

1.

Kg of cranberries harvested	400,000
Litres of juice processed (500 litres per 1,000 kg)	200,000
Revenues (200,000 litres × $2.10 per litre)	$420,000
Costs	
Harvesting Division	
Variable costs (400,000 kg × $0.10/kg)	$ 40,000
Fixed costs (400,000 kg × $0.25/kg)	100,000
Total Harvesting Division costs	140,000
Processing Division	
Variable costs (200,000 litres × $0.20/litre)	$ 40,000
Fixed costs (200,000 litres × $0.40/litre)	80,000
Total Processing Division costs	120,000
Total costs	260,000
Operating income	$160,000

2.

	200% of Full Costs	Market Price
Transfer price per kg (($0.10 + $0.25) × 2; $0.60)	$0.70	$0.60
1. Harvesting Division		
Revenues (400,000 kg × $0.70; $0.60)	$280,000	$240,000
Costs		
Division variable costs (400,000 kg ×$0.10/kg)	40,000	40,000
Division fixed costs (400,000 kg × $0.25/kg)	100,000	100,000
Total division costs	140,000	140,000
Division operating income	$140,000	$100,000
Harvesting Division manager's bonus (5% of operating income)	$7,000	$5,000
2. Processing Division		
Revenues (200,000 litres × $2.10/litre)	$420,000	$420,000
Costs		
Transferred-in costs	280,000	240,000
Division variable costs (200,000 litres × $0.20/litre)	40,000	40,000
Division fixed costs (200,000 litres × $0.40/litre)	80,000	80,000
Total division costs	400,000	360,000
Division operating income	$ 20,000	$ 60,000
Processing Division manager's bonus (5% of operating income)	$1,000	$3,000

23-32 (cont'd)

3. Bonus paid to division managers at 5% of division operating income is computed above and summarized below:

	Internal Transfers at 200% of Full Costs	Internal Transfers at Market Prices
Harvesting Division manager's bonus (5% × $140,000; 5% × $100,000)	$7,000	$5,000
Processing Division manager's bonus (5% × $20,000; 5% × $60,000)	$1,000	$3,000

The Harvesting Division manager will prefer to transfer at 200% of full costs because this method gives a higher bonus. The Processing Division manager will prefer transfer at market price for its higher resulting bonus.

Crango may resolve or reduce transfer pricing conflicts by:

- Basing division managers' bonuses on overall Crango profits in addition to division operating income. This will motivate each manager to consider what is best for Crango overall and not be concerned with the transfer price alone.
- Letting the two divisions negotiate the transfer price between themselves. However, this may result in constant re-negotiation between the two managers each accounting period.
- Using dual transfer prices. However, a cost-based transfer price will not motivate cost control by the Harvesting Division manager. It will also insulate that division from the discipline of market prices.

23-34 (30 min.)   Effect of market prices oscillations.

1. Divisional Operating Income (in thousands)

	Corn Div.	Ethanol Div.
Revenues		
Corn: 200,000 tonnes x $250	50,000	
Ethanol: 200,000 tonnes x 500 litres x $1.50		150,000
Variable costs		
Corn transferred in to Ethanol Division		50,000
Corn: ($60 + $50 + $100 x 75%) x 200,000 tonnes	37,000	
Ethanol: ($0.10 + $0.80 x 25%) x 200,000 tonnes x 500 litres		30,000
Contribution margin	13,000	70,000
Fixed costs		
Corn: $100 x 25% x 200,000 tonne	5,000	
Ethanol: $0.80 x 75% x 200,000 tonne x 500 litres		60,000
Operating income	8,000	10,000

2. Corn Division: $8,000,000 x 1% = $80,000
    Ethanol Division: $10,000,000 x 1% = $100,000

3. If an independent farmer offers to sell corn at $220 per tonne and the Corn Division can sell in the open market at a price of $220 minus the variable distribution costs, the operating income for each division would be as follows.

Divisional Operating Income (in thousands)	Corn Div.	Ethanol Div.
Revenues		
Corn: 150,000 tonnes x $250	37,500	
Corn: 50,000 tonnes x ($220 - $5)	10,750	
Ethanol: 200,000 tonnes x 500 litres x $1.50		150,000
Variable costs		
Corn transferred in to Ethanol Division		37,500
Corn bought outside by the Ethanol Division at $220		11,000
Corn: ($60 + $50 + $100 x 75%) x 200,000 tonnes	37,000	
Ethanol: ($0.10 + $0.80 x 25%) x 200,000 tonnes x 500 litres		30,000
Contribution margin	11,250	71,500
Fixed costs		
Corn: $100 x 25% x 200,000 ton	5,000	
Ethanol: $0.80 x 75% x 200,000 tonne x 500 litres		60,000
Operating income	6,250	11,500

Bonus calculation: Corn Division: $6,250,000 x 1% = $62,500
                     Ethanol Division: $11,500,000 x 1% = $115,000

It is not beneficial for Green Energy Corp. to accept the offer because its operating income is reduced from $18,000,000 to $17,750,000. However, the Ethanol Division manager will be highly interested in accepting the offer because his/her bonus will be increased by $1,500.

23-36 (30-40 min.) **Multinational transfer pricing and taxation.**

1. Deutschland Machines and its subsidiaries' operating income if it manufactures the machine and sells it in Vietnam or in Spain follows:

	If Sold in Vietnam	If Sold in Spain
Revenue	$1,200,000	$1,140,000
Costs		
Manufacturing costs	600,000	600,000
Transportation and modification costs	240,000	300,000
Total costs	840,000	900,000
Operating income	$ 360,000	$ 240,000

Deutschland Machines maximizes operating income by manufacturing the machine and selling it in Vietnam.

2. <u>Deutschland Machines will not sell if the transfer price is less than $600,000</u> — its outlay costs of manufacturing the machine.

   <u>The Vietnamese subsidiary will not agree to a transfer price of more than $960,000.</u> At a price of $960,000, the Vietnamese subsidiary's incremental operating income from purchasing and selling the milling machine will be $0 ($1,200,000 – $240,000 – $960,000).

   <u>The Spanish subsidiary will not agree to a transfer price of more than $840,000.</u> At a price of $840,000, the Spanish subsidiary's incremental operating income from purchasing and selling the special purpose machine will be $0 ($1,140,000 – $300,000 – $840,000).

   Any transfer price between $840,000 and $960,000 will achieve the optimal actions determined in requirement 1. For prices in this range, Deutschland Machines will be willing to sell, the Vietnamese subsidiary willing to buy, and the Spanish subsidiary won't be interested in acquiring the machine.

   Where within the range of $840,000 to $960,000 the transfer price will be set depends on the bargaining powers of the Deutschland Machines and the Vietnamese subsidiary managers. Deutschland Machines' main source of bargaining power comes from the threat of selling the machine to the Spanish subsidiary. If the transfer price is set at $840,000, then

Deutschland Machines' operating income, $840,000 – $600,000	$240,000
Vietnamese subsidiary's operating income, $1,200,000 – $840,000 – $240,000	$120,000
Overall operating income of Deutschland Machines and subsidiaries	$360,000

   Note that the general guideline could be used to derive the minimum transfer price.

23-36 (cont'd)

$$\begin{aligned} \text{Minimum} \atop \text{transfer price} &= \left(\begin{array}{c} \text{Additional } incremental\ costs \\ \text{per unit incurred up} \\ \text{to the point of transfer} \end{array} \right) + \left(\begin{array}{c} Opportunity\ costs \\ \text{per unit to the} \\ \text{supplying division} \end{array} \right) \\ &= \quad\quad \$600{,}000 \quad + \quad \$240{,}000 \quad = \quad \$840{,}000 \end{aligned}$$

Deutschland Machines' opportunity cost of supplying the machine to the Vietnamese subsidiary is the $240,000 in operating income it forgoes by not supplying the machine to the Spanish subsidiary. Note that competition between the Vietnamese and Spanish subsidiaries means that the transfer price will be at least $840,000.

3. Consider the optimal transfer prices that can be set to minimize taxes (for Deutschland Machines and its subsidiaries) (a) for transfers from Deutschland Machines to the Vietnamese subsidiary and (b) for transfers from Deutschland Machines to the Spanish subsidiary.

(a) Transfers from Deutschland Machines to the Vietnamese subsidiary should "allocate" as little of the operating income to Deutschland Machines' Canadian operation as possible, since the tax rate in Canada is higher than in Vietnam for this transaction. Therefore, these transfers should be priced at the lowest allowable transfer price of $600,000 to minimize overall company taxes.

Taxes paid:

Deutschland Machines, 0.40 ($600,000 – $600,000)	$ 0
Vietnamese subsidiary, 0.20 ($1,200,000 – $600,000 – $240,000)	72,000
Total taxes paid by Deutschland Machines and its subsidiaries on transfers to Vietnam	$72,000

After-tax operating income

Deutschland Machines,($600,000 – $600,000) – $0	$ 0
Vietnamese subsidiary ($1,200,000 – $600,000 – $240,000) – $72,000	288,000
Total net income for Deutschland Machines and its subsidiaries on transfers to Vietnam	$288,000

(b) Transfers from Deutschland Machines to the Spanish subsidiary should "allocate" as much of the operating income to Deutschland Machines' Canadian operation as possible, since the tax rate in Canada is lower than in Spain for this transaction. Therefore, these transfers should be priced at the highest allowable transfer price of $840,000 to minimize overall company taxes.

Taxes paid:

Deutschland Machines, 0.40 ($840,000 – $600,000)	$	96,000
Spanish subsidiary, 0.60 ($1,140,000 – $840,000 – $300,000)		0
Total taxes paid by Deutschland Machines and its subsidiaries on transfers to Spain		$96,000

23-36 (cont'd)

After-tax operating income:

Deutschland Machines, ($840,000 – $600,000) – $96,000	$144,000
Spanish subsidiary ($1,140,000 – $840,000 – $300,000) – $0	0
Total after-tax operating income for Deutschland Machines and its subsidiaries on transfers to Spain	$144,000

From the viewpoint of Deutschland Machines and its subsidiaries together, overall after-tax operating income is maximized if the machine is transferred to the Vietnamese subsidiary (after-tax operating income of $288,000 versus after-tax operating income of $144,000 if the machine is transferred to the Spanish subsidiary). Hence (a) the equipment should be manufactured by Deutschland Machines and (b) it should be transferred to the Vietnamese subsidiary at a price of $600,000.

4.   As in requirement 2, the Vietnamese subsidiary would be willing to bid up the price to $960,000, while the Spanish subsidiary would only be willing to pay up to $840,000. Deutschland Machines acting autonomously would like to maximize its own after-tax operating income by transferring the machine at as high a transfer price as possible. As in requirement 2, the price would end up being at least $840,000. Since the taxing authorities will not allow prices above $840,000, the transfer price will be $840,000. At this transfer price, the Spanish subsidiary makes zero operating income and will not be interested in the machine. Hence Deutschland Machines will sell the machine to the Vietnamese subsidiary at a price of $840,000.

The answer is not the same as in requirement 3 since, acting autonomously, the objective of each manager is to maximize after-tax operating income of his or her own company rather than after-tax operating income of Deutschland Machines and its subsidiaries as a whole. Goal congruence is not achieved in this setting.

Can the company induce the managers to take the right actions without infringing on their autonomy? This outcome is probably not going to be easy.

One possibility might be to implement a dual pricing scheme in which the machine is transferred at cost ($600,000), but under which Deutschland Machines is credited with after-tax operating income earned on the machine by the subsidiary it ships the machine to (in this example, $360,000 of net income earned by the Vietnamese subsidiary). A negative feature of this arrangement is that the $360,000 of after-tax operating income will be "double counted" and recognized on the books of both Deutschland Machines and the Vietnamese subsidiary.

Another possibility might be to evaluate the managers on the basis of overall after-tax operating income of Deutschland Machines and its subsidiaries. This approach will induce a more global perspective, but at the cost of inducing a larger noncontrollable element in each manager's performance measure.

23-38 (20-30 min.) **Pertinent transfer price.**

This problem explores the "general transfer-pricing guideline" discussed in the chapter.

1. No, transfers should not be made to Seats Division if there is no excess capacity in Frames Division. An incremental (outlay) cost approach shows a positive contribution for the company as a whole.

Selling price of the assembled seat (final product)		$360
Incremental costs in Frames Division	$144	
Incremental costs in Seats Division	180	324
Contribution (loss)		$ 36

    However, if there is no excess capacity in Frames Dvivision, any transfer will result in diverting product from the market for the intermediate product. Sales in this market result in a greater contribution for the company as a whole. Seats Division should not assemble the seat since the incremental revenue ITS Automotive can earn, $120 per unit ($360 from selling the final product – $240 from selling the intermediate product) is less than the incremental costs of $180 to assemble the seat in the Seats Division.

Selling price of intermediate products	$240
Incremental (outlay) costs in Frames Division	144
Contribution (loss)	$ 96

    The general guideline described in the chapter is

    $$\text{Minimum transfer price} = \left(\begin{array}{c} \text{Additional } \textit{incremental costs} \\ \text{per unit incurred up} \\ \text{to the point of transfer} \end{array} \right) + \left(\begin{array}{c} \textit{Opportunity costs} \\ \text{per unit to the} \\ \text{supplying division} \end{array} \right)$$

    $$= \quad \$144 + (\$240 - \$144)$$
    $$= \quad \$240, \text{ which is the market price}$$

    Market price is the transfer price that leads to the correct decision; that is, do not transfer to Seats Division unless there are extenuating circumstances for continuing to market the final product. Therefore, Seats Division must either drop the product or reduce the incremental costs of assembly from $180 per seat to less than $120.

2. If (i) Frames Division has excess capacity, (ii) there is intermediate external demand for only 800 units at $240, and (iii) the $240 price is to be maintained, then the opportunity costs per unit to the supplying division are $0. The general guideline indicates a minimum transfer price of: $144 + $0 = $144, which is the incremental or outlay costs for the first 200 units. The Seats Division would buy 200 units from the Frames Division at a transfer price of $144 because the Seats Division can earn a contribution of $36 per unit [$360 – ($144 + $180)]. In fact, the Seats Division would be willing to buy units from the Frames Division at any price up to $180 per unit because any transfers at a price of up to $180 will still yield the Seats Division a positive contribution margin.

23-38 (cont'd)

Note, however, that if the Seats Division wants more than 200 units, the minimum transfer price will be $240 as computed in requirement 1 because the Frames Division will incur an opportunity cost in the form of lost contribution of $96 (market price, $240 – outlay costs of $144) for every unit above 200 units that is transferred to the Seats Division.

The following schedule summarizes the transfer prices for units transferred from Frames to Seats Divisions.

Units	Transfer Price
0–200	$144–$180
200–1,000	$240

For an exploration of this situation when imperfect markets exist, see the next problem.

3. The Seats Division would show zero contribution, but the company as a whole would generate a contribution of $36 per unit on the 200 units transferred. Any price between $144 and $180 would induce the transfer that would be desirable for the company as a whole. A motivational problem may arise regarding how to split the $36 contribution between both divisions. Unless the price is below $180, the Seats Division would have little incentive to buy.

Note: The transfer price that may appear optimal in an economic analysis may, in fact, be totally unacceptable from the viewpoints of (1) preserving autonomy of the managers and (2) evaluating the performance of the divisions as economic units. For instance, consider the simplest case discussed above, where there is idle capacity and the $240 intermediate price is to be maintained. To direct that Frames should sell to Seats at Frames Division's variable cost of $144 may be desirable from the viewpoint of the Seats Division and the company as a whole. However, the autonomy (independence) of the manager of Frames Division is eroded. The Frames Division will earn nothing, although it could argue that it is contributing to the earning of income on the final product.

If the manager of the Frames Division wants a portion of the total company contribution of $36 per unit, the question is: How is an appropriate amount determined? This is a difficult question in practice. The price can be negotiated upward to somewhere between $144 and $180 so that some "equitable" split is achieved. A dual transfer pricing scheme has also been suggested whereby the supplier gets credit for the full intermediate market price and the buyer is charged only with variable or incremental costs. In any event, when there is heavy interdependence between divisions, as in this case, some system of subsidies may be needed to deal with the three problems of goal congruence, management effort, and subunit autonomy. Of course, where heavy subsidies are needed, a question can be raised as to whether the existing degree of decentralization is optimal.

23-40 (30 min.) Transfer pricing, goal congruence.

1a. and b. As the following calculations show, if Molson Corporation offers a price of $444 per wheel, Johnson Corporation should purchase the wheels from Molson. If Molson Corporation offers a price of $516 per wheel, Johnson Corporation should manufacture the wheels in-house.

	Transfer 1,000 wheels to Tractor. Sell 200 in outside market (1)	Buy 1,000 wheels from Molson at $444. Sell 1,200 wheels in outside market (2)	Buy 1,000 wheels from Molson at $516. Sell 1,200 wheels in outside market (3)
Incremental cost of Wheels Division supplying 1,000 wheels to Tractors $300 × 1,000; 0; 0	$(300,000)	$ 0	$ 0
Incremental costs of buying 1,000 Wheels from Molson $0; $444 × 1,000; $516 × 1,000	0	(444,000)	(516,000)
Revenue from selling wheels in outside market $420 × 200; 1,200; 1,200	84,000	504,000	504,000
Incremental costs of manufacturing Wheels for sale in outside market $300 × 200; 1,200; 1,200	(60,000)	(360,000)	(360,000)
Revenue from supplying rubber component to Molson $216 × 0; 1,000; 1,000	0	216,000	216,000
Incremental costs of supplying rubber component to Molson $144 × 0; 1,000; 1,000	0	(144,000)	(144,000)
Net costs	$(276,000)	$(228,000)	$(300,000)

At a price of $444 per wheel, the net cost of $228,000 is less than the net cost of $276,000 if Johnson Corporation made the wheels in-house. Hence, Johnson Corporation should outsource to Molson.

At a price of $516 per wheel, the net cost of $300,000 is greater than the net cost of $276,000 if Johnson Corporation made the wheels in-house. Hence, Johnson Corporation should reject Molson's offer.

23-40 (cont'd)

2.   For the Wheels Division and the Tractor Division to take actions that are optimal for Johnson Corporation as a whole, the transfer price should be set at $492, calculated as follows:

The Wheels Division can manufacture at most 1,200 wheels and is currently operating at capacity. The incremental costs of manufacturing a wheel are $300 per wheel. The opportunity cost of manufacturing wheels for the Wheels Division is (1) the contribution margin of $120 (selling price, $420 minus incremental costs, $300) that the Wheels Division would forgo by not selling wheels in the outside market and (2) the contribution margin of $72 (selling price, $216 minus incremental costs, $144) that the Wheels Division would forgo by not being able to sell the wheels rubber component to outside suppliers of wheels (such as Molson). Thus, the total opportunity cost of the Wheels Division of supplying wheels to Tractors is $120 + $72 = $192 per unit.

Using the general guideline,

$$\text{Minimum transfer price per wheel} = \left(\begin{array}{c} \text{Incremental cost per} \\ \text{wheel up to the} \\ \text{point of transfer} \end{array} + \begin{array}{c} \text{Opportunity costs} \\ \text{per wheel to the} \\ \text{selling division} \end{array} \right)$$

$$= \$300 + \$192 = \$492$$

Note that, at a price of $492, Johnson is indifferent between manufacturing wheels in-house or purchasing them from an outside supplier. Each results in a net cost of $276,000. For an outside price per wheel below $492, the Tractor Division would prefer to purchase from outside; above it, the Tractor Division would prefer to purchase from the Wheels Division.

When selling prices are uncertain, the transfer price should be set at the minimum acceptable transfer price. For example, if the transfer price were set above the minimum transfer price at $504 per wheel, say, and an outside supplier offered to supply the wheel decks at $498 per unit, the Tractor Division would purchase the wheels from the outside supplier. In fact, as the following calculations show, Johnson Corporation, as a whole, would be better off had the Tractor Division purchased the wheels from the Wheels Division. The net cost to Johnson Corporation if the Wheels Division transfers 1,000 wheels to the Tractor Division is $276,000 as calculated in Column 1 of the table presented in requirement 1. If an outside supplier supplies wheels at $498 each, we simply substitute $498 × 1,000 = $498,000 for the incremental costs of buying 1,000 wheels in column 2 or 3 and leave everything else unchanged. This gives a higher net cost of $282,000 to Johnson Corporation as a whole.

It is only if the price charged by the outside supplier falls below $492 that Johnson Corporation as a whole is better off purchasing from the outside market. Setting the transfer price at $492 per unit achieves goal congruence.

CHAPTER 24
PERFORMANCE MEASUREMENT, COMPENSATION, AND MULTINATIONAL CONSIDERATIONS

24-2 The six steps in designing an accounting-based performance measure are:
1. Choosing the variable(s) that represent(s) top management's financial goal(s).
2. Choosing the time horizon of each performance measure in Step 1.
3. Choosing definitions of the items included in the variables in Step 1.
4. Choosing measures for the items included in the variables in Step 1.
5. Choosing a target against which to gauge performance.
6. Choosing the timing of feedback.

24-4 Yes. Residual income is not identical to ROI. ROI is a percentage with investment as the denominator of the computation. Residual income is an absolute amount in which investment is used to calculate an imputed interest charge.

24-6 Definitions of investment used in practice when computing ROI are:
1. Total assets available.
2. Total assets employed.
3. Working capital (current assets minus current liabilities) plus other assets.
4. Shareholders' equity.

24-8 Special problems arise when evaluating the performance of divisions in multinational companies because:
(a) The economic, legal, political, social, and cultural environments differ significantly across countries.
(b) Governments in some countries may impose controls and limit selling prices of products.
(c) Availability of materials and skilled labour, as well as costs of materials, labour, and infrastructure may differ significantly across countries.
(d) Divisions operating in different countries keep score of their performance in different currencies.

24-10 Moral hazard describes contexts in which an employee is tempted to put in less effort (or report distorted information) because the employee's interests differ from the owner's and because the employee's effort cannot be accurately monitored and enforced.

24-12 Benchmarking or relative performance evaluation is the process of evaluating a manager's performance against the performance of other similar operations' managers. The ideal benchmark is another operation that is affected by the same noncontrollable factors that affect the manager's performance. Benchmarking cancels the effects of the common noncontrollable factors and provides better information about the manager's performance.

24-14 Four components of executive compensation plans are:
1. Base salary.
2. Annual cash incentives.
3. Long-term incentives.
4. Fringe benefits.

24-16 (30 min.)   **Return on investment; comparisons of three companies.**

1. The separate components highlight several features of return on investment not revealed by a single calculation:
   (a) The importance of investment turnover as a key to income is stressed.
   (b) The importance of revenues is explicitly recognized.
   (c) The important components are expressed as ratios or percentages instead of dollar figures. This form of expression often enhances comparability of different divisions, businesses, and time periods.
   (d) The breakdown stresses the possibility of trading off investment turnover for income as a percentage of revenues so as to increase the average ROI at a given level of output.

2. (Filled-in blanks are in bold face.)

	Companies in Same Industry		
	Blue	**Green**	**Orange**
Revenue	**$1,200,000**	$ 600,000	$12,000,000
Income	**$ 120,000**	$ 60,000	$ 60,000
Investment	$ 600,000	$6,000,000	**$ 6,000,000**
Income as a % of revenue	10%	**10%**	0.5%
Investment turnover	2.0	**0.1**	2.0
Return on investment	**20%**	**1%**	1%

Income and investment alone shed little light on comparative performances because of disparities in size between Company Blue and the other two companies. Thus, it is impossible to say whether Green's low return on investment in comparison with Blue's is attributable to its larger investment or to its lower income. Furthermore, the fact that Companies Green and Orange have identical income and investment may suggest that the same conditions underlie the low ROI, but this conclusion is erroneous. Green has higher margins but a lower investment turnover. Orange has very small margins (1/20th of Green) but turns over investment 20 times faster.

24-16 (cont'd)

I.M.A. Report No. 35 (p. 35) states:

"Introducing revenues to measure level of operations helps to disclose specific areas for more intensive investigation. Company Green does as well as Company Blue in terms of income margin, for both companies earn 10% on revenues. But Company Green has a much lower turnover of investment than does Company Blue. Whereas a dollar of investment in Company Blue supports two dollars in revenues each period, a dollar investment in Company Green supports only ten cents in revenues each period. This suggests that the analyst should look carefully at Company Green's investment. Is the company keeping an inventory larger than necessary for its revenue level? Are receivables being collected promptly? Or did Company Blue acquire its fixed assets at a price level that was much lower than that at which Company Green purchased its plant?

"On the other hand, Orange's investment turnover is as high as Blue's, but Orange's income as a percentage of revenue is much lower. Why? Are its operations inefficient, are its material costs too high, or does its location entail high transportation costs?

"Analysis of ROI raises questions such as the foregoing. When answers are obtained, basic reasons for differences between rates of return may be discovered. For example, in Company Green's case, it is apparent that the emphasis will have to be on increasing turnover by reducing investment or increasing revenues. Clearly, Green cannot appreciably increase its ROI simply by increasing its income as a percent of revenue. In contrast, Company Orange's management should concentrate on increasing the percent of income on revenue."

24-18 (10-15 min.) ROI and RI.

$$\text{ROI} = \frac{\text{Operating income}}{\text{Investment}}$$

$$\text{Operating income} = \text{ROI} \times \text{Investment}$$

[No. of kilometres (Selling price per km– Var. cost per km)] – Fixed costs = ROI × Investment

Let X = minimum selling price per km to achieve a 20% ROI

1. 1,000,000 (X – $3.60) – $1,200,000 = 20% ($1,920,000)

          1,000,000X = $384,000 + $3,600,000 + $1,200,000 = $5,184,000

               X = $5.184

2. 1,000,000 (X – $3.60) – $1,200,000 = 15% ($1,920,000)

          1,000,000X = $288,000 + $3,600,000 + $1,200,000 = $5,088,000

               X = $5.088

24-20 (25 min.) Goal congruence and ROI.

1. Bleefl would be better off if the machine is replaced. Its cost of capital is 6% and the IRR of the investment is 11%, indicating that this is a positive net present value project.

2. The ROIs for the first five years are:

	Year 1	Year 2	Year 3	Year 4	Year 5
Operating income [1]	$2,000	$2,000	$2,000	$2,000	$2,000
End of year net assets	27,000	24,000	21,000	18,000	15,000
Average net assets	28,500 [2]	25,500	22,500	19,500	16,500
ROI	7.02%	7.84%	8.89%	10.26%	12.12%

[1] Income is cash savings of $5,000 less $3,000 annual depreciation expense.
[2] ($30,000 + $27,000) ÷ 2 = $28,500

The manager would not want to replace the machine before retiring because the division is currently earning a ROI of 11%, and replacement of the machine will lower the ROI every year until the fifth year, when the manager would be long gone.

3. Bleefl could use long-term rather than short-term ROI, or use ROI and some other long-term measures to evaluate the Patio Furniture division to create goal congruence. Evaluating the managers on residual income rather than ROI would also achieve goal congruence. For example, replacing the machine increases residual income in Year 1.

    Residual income = Operating income – (6% × Average net assets)

                = $2,000 – (6% × 28,500)

                = $2,000 – $1,710 = $290

24-22 (15 min.) **ROI, RI, EVA®.**

1 and 2.

	Railway Division	Maritime Division
Total assets	$6,000,000	$1,200,000
Operating income	$ 900,000	$ 240,000
Return on investment	$900,000 ÷ 6,000,000 = 15%	$240,000 ÷ $1,200,000 = 20%
Residual income at 12% required rate of return*	$ 180,000	$ 96,000

*$900,000 – (0.12 × $6,000,000) = $180,000; $240,000 – (0.12 × $1,200,000) = $96,000

The tabulation shows that, while the Maritime Division earns the higher return on investment, the Railway Division earns the higher residual income at the 12% required rate of return.

3. After-tax cost of debt financing = (1 – 0.4) × 10% = 6%
   After-tax cost of equity financing = 14%

The weighted-average cost of capital (WACC) is given by

$$\text{WACC} = \frac{(0.06 \times \$4,200,000) + (0.14 \times \$4,200,000)}{\$4,200,000 + \$4,200,000} = \frac{\$252,000 + \$588,000}{\$8,400,000} = \frac{\$840,000}{\$8,400,000} = 0.10 \text{ or } 10\%$$

Economic value added (EVA®) calculations are as follows:

Division	After-Tax Operating Income	–	Weighted-Average Cost of Capital	×	Total Assets Minus Current Liabilities	=	Economic Value Added (EVA®)
Railway	$900,000 × 0.6	–	[10% ×		($6,000,000 – $1,800,000)]	= $540,000 – $420,000 =	$120,000
Maritime	$240,000 × 0.6	–	[10% ×		($1,200,000 – $300,000)]	= $144,000 – $90,000 =	$ 54,000

24-22 (cont'd)

Agile Transportation should use the EVA® measure for evaluating the economic performance of its divisions for two reasons: (a) It is a residual income measure and so does not have the dysfunctional effects of ROI-based measures. That is, if EVA® is used as a performance evaluation measure, divisions would have incentives to make investments whenever after-tax operating income exceeds the weighted-average cost of capital employed. These are the correct incentives to maximize firm value. ROI-based performance evaluation measures encourage managers to invest only when the ROI on new investments exceeds the existing ROI. That is, managers would reject projects whose ROI exceeds the weighted average cost of capital but is less than the current ROI of the division; using ROI as a performance evaluation measure creates incentives for managers to reject projects that increase the value of the firm simply because they may reduce the overall ROI of the division. (b) EVA® calculations incorporate tax effects that are costs to the firm. It therefore provides an after-tax comprehensive summary of the effects of various decisions on the company and its shareholders.

24-24 (25-30 min.) ROI, RI, measurement of assets.

The method for computing profitability preferred by each manager follows:

Manager of	Method Chosen
Radnor	RI based on net book value
Easttown	RI based on gross book value
Marion	ROI based on either gross or net book value

Supporting Calculations:

	ROI Calculations	
Division	Operating Income / Gross Book Value	Operating Income / Net Book Value*
Radnor	$142,050 ÷ $1,200,000 = 11.84% (3)	$142,050 ÷ $555,000 = 25.59% (3)
Easttown	$137,550 ÷ $1,140,000 = 12.07% (2)	$137,550 ÷ $525,000 = 26.20% (2)
Marion	$ 92,100 ÷ $ 750,000 = 12.28% (1)	$ 92,100 ÷ $330,000 = 27.91% (1)

	RI Calculations	
Division	Operating Income – 10% Gross BV	Operating Income – 10% Net BV1
Radnor	$142,050 – $120,000 = $22,050 (2)	$142,050 – $55,500 = $86,550 (1)
Easttown	$137,550 – $114,000 = $23,550 (1)	$137,550 – $52,500 = $85,050 (2)
Marion	$ 92,100 – $ 75,000 = $17,100 (3)	$ 92,100 – $33,000 = $59,100 (3)

* Net book value is gross book value minus accumulated depreciation.

24-24 (cont'd)

The biggest weakness of ROI is the tendency to reject projects that will lower historical ROI even though the prospective ROI exceeds the required ROI. RI achieves goal congruence because subunits will make investments as long as they earn a rate in excess of the required return for investments. The biggest weakness of RI is that it favours larger divisions in ranking performance. The greater the amount of the investment (the size of the division), the more likely that larger divisions will be favoured, assuming that income grows proportionately. The strength of ROI is that it is a ratio and so does not favour larger divisions. In general, though, achieving goal congruence is very important. Therefore, the RI measure is often preferred to ROI.

24-26 (20-30 min.) **Various measures of profitability.**

The method for computing profitability preferred by each manager follows:

Manager of	Method Chosen
Ontario	Residual income based on gross book value
Quebec	Residual income based on net book value
Alberta	ROI based on either gross or net book value

The biggest weakness of ROI is the tendency to reject projects that will lower historical ROI even though the prospective ROI exceeds the required ROI. The biggest weakness of residual income is it favours larger divisions in ranking performance. The greater the amount of the investment (the size of the division), the more likely that larger divisions will be favoured, assuming that income grows proportionately as it does in the case of Ontario and Quebec divisions.

24-26 (cont'd)

Supporting Computations:

Return on Investment Calculations

Division	Operating Income / Gross Book Value			Operating Income / Net Book Value*		
Ontario	$150,000 ÷ $1,000,000	=	15% (2)	$150,000 ÷ $500,000	=	30% (2)
Quebec	$120,000 ÷ $1,000,000	=	12% (3)	$120,000 ÷ $500,000	=	24% (3)
Alberta	$55,000 ÷ $350,000	=	15.71% (1)	$55,000 ÷ $175,000	=	31.43% (1)

Residual Income Calculations

Division	Operating Income – 12% Gross BV			Operating Income – 12% Net BV*		
Ontario	$150,000 – $120,000	=	$30,000 (1)	$150,000 – $60,000	=	$90,000 (2)
Quebec	$120,000 – $120,000	=	$0 (3)	$120,000 – $60,000	=	$120,000 (1)
Alberta	$55,000 – $42,000	=	$13,000 (2)	$55,000 – $21,000	=	$34,000 (3)

*Net book value is one half of gross book value, given that all assets were purchased ten years ago and have ten years useful life remaining, zero terminal disposal price, and straight-line amortization.

24-28 (20 min.) Multinational performance measurement, ROI, RI.

1a. Canadian Division's ROI in 2011 = Operating Income ÷ Total Assets
   = Operating Income ÷ $8,000,000 = 15%
   Hence, operating income = 15% × $8,000,000 = $1,200,000.

1b. Norwegian Division's ROI in 2011 (based on kroners) =
   8,100,000 ÷ 52,500,000 = 15.43%

2. Convert total assets into dollars using the December 31, 2010 exchange rate, the rate prevailing when the assets were acquired (6 kroners = $1):
   52,500,000 ÷ 6 kroner per dollar = $8,750,000

Convert operating income into dollars at the average exchange rate prevailing during 2011 when operating income was earned (6.5 kroners = $1):

   8,100,000 ÷ 6.5 kroner per dollar = $1,246,154
   Comparable ROI for Norwegian Division = $1,246,154 ÷ $8,750,000 = 14.24%

24-28 (cont'd)

The Norwegian Division's ROI based on kroners is helped by the inflation that occurs in Norway in 2011 (that caused the Norwegian kroner to weaken against the dollar from 6 kroners = $1 on 12-31-2010 to 7 kroners = $1 on 12-31-2011). Inflation boosts the division's operating income. Since the assets are acquired at the start of the year 2011, the asset values are not increased by the inflation that occurs during the year. The net effect of inflation on ROI calculated in kroners is to use an inflated value for the numerator relative to the denominator. Adjusting for inflationary and currency differences negates the effects of any differences in inflation rates between the two countries on the calculation of ROI. After these adjustments, the Canadian Division earned a higher ROI than the Norwegian Division.

3.   Canadian Division's RI in 2011 $= \$1,200,000 - (12\% \times \$8,000,000)$
         $= \$1,200,000 - \$960,000 = \$240,000$

Norwegian Division's RI in 2011 (in dollars) is calculated as:

$\$1,246,154 - (12\% \times \$8,750,000) = \$1,246,154 - \$1,050,000 = \$196,154.$

The Canadian Division's RI also exceeds the Norwegian Division's RI in 2011 by $43,846.

24-30 (25 min.) Financial and nonfinancial performance measures, goal congruence

1. Operating income is a good summary measure of short-term financial performance. By itself, however, it does not indicate whether operating income in the short run was earned by taking actions that would lead to long-run competitive advantage. For example, Summit's divisions might be able to increase short-run operating income by producing more product while ignoring quality or rework. Harrington, however, would like to see division managers increase operating income without sacrificing quality. The new performance measures take a balanced scorecard approach by evaluating and rewarding managers on the basis of direct measures (such as rework costs, on-time delivery performance, and sales returns). This motivates managers to take actions that Harrington believes will increase operating income now and in the future. The nonoperating income measures serve as surrogate measures of future profitability.

24-30 (cont'd)

2. The semiannual installments and total bonus for the Charter Division are calculated as follows:

Charter Division Bonus Calculation
For Year Ended December 31, 2009

January 1, 2009 to June 30, 2009

Profitability	(0.02 × $462,000)	$ 9,240
Rework	(0.02 x $462,000) – $11,500	(2,260)
On-time delivery	No bonus—under 96%	0
Sales returns	[(0.015 x $4,200,000) – $84,000] x 50%	(10,500)
Semiannual installment		$ (3,520)
Semiannual bonus awarded		$ 0

July 1, 2009 to December 31, 2009

Profitability	(0.02 × $440,000)	$ 8,800
Rework	(0.02 × $440,000) – $11,000	(2,200)
On-time delivery	96% to 98%	2,000
Sales returns	[(0.015 x $4,400,000) – $70,000] x 50%	(2,000)
Semiannual installment		$ 6,600
Semiannual bonus awarded		$ 6,600
Total bonus awarded for the year		$ 6,600

24-30 (cont'd)

The semiannual installments and total bonus for the Mesa Division are calculated as follows:

Mesa Division Bonus Calculation
For Year Ended December 31, 2009

January 1, 2009 to June 30, 2009

Profitability	(0.02 × $342,000)	$ 6,840
Rework	(0.02 × $342,000) – $6,000	0
On-time delivery	Over 98%	5,000
Sales returns	[(0.015 × $2,850,000) – $44,750] × 50%	(1,000)
Semiannual bonus installment		$10,840
Semiannual bonus awarded		$10,840

July 1, 2009 to December 31, 2009

Profitability	(0.02 × $406,000)	$ 8,120
Rework	(0.02 × $406,000) – $8,000	0
On-time delivery	No bonus—under 96%	0
Sales returns	[(0.015 × $2,900,000) – $42,500] which is greater than zero, yielding a bonus	3,000
Semiannual bonus installment		$11,120
Semiannual bonus awarded		$11,120
Total bonus awarded for the year		$21,960

3. The manager of the Charter Division is likely to be frustrated by the new plan, as the division bonus has fallen by more than $20,000 compared to the bonus of the previous year. However, the new performance measures have begun to have the desired effect—both on-time deliveries and sales returns improved in the second half of the year, while rework costs were relatively even. If the division continues to improve at the same rate, the Charter bonus could approximate or exceed what it was under the old plan.

The manager of the Mesa Division should be as satisfied with the new plan as with the old plan, as the bonus is almost equivalent. On-time deliveries declined considerably in the second half of the year and rework costs increased. However, sales returns decreased slightly. Unless the manager institutes better controls, the bonus situation may not be as favourable in the future. This could motivate the manager to improve in the future but currently, at least, the manager has been able to maintain his bonus with showing improvement in only one area targeted by Harrington.

24-30 (cont'd)

Ben Harrington's revised bonus plan for the Charter Division fostered the following improvements in the second half of the year despite an increase in sales:

An increase of 1.9% in on-time deliveries.

A $500 reduction in rework costs.

A $14,000 reduction in sales returns.

However, operating income as a percentage of sales has decreased (11% to 10%).

The Mesa Division's bonus has remained at the status quo as a result of the following effects:

An increase of 2.0 % in operating income as a percent of sales (12% to 14%).

A decrease of 3.6% in on-time deliveries.

A $2,000 increase in rework costs.

A $2,250 decrease in sales returns.

This would suggest that revisions to the bonus plan are needed. Possible changes include:

- Increasing the weights put on on-time deliveries, rework costs, and sales returns in the performance measures while decreasing the weight put on operating income.

- A reward structure for rework costs that are below 2% of operating income that would encourage managers to drive costs lower; reviewing the whole year in total. The bonus plan should carry forward the negative amounts for one six-month period into the next six-month period, incorporating the entire year when calculating a bonus; developing benchmarks; and then giving rewards for improvements over prior periods and encouraging continuous improvement.

24-32 (30-40 min.) Financial performance measures with uncertainty (CMA adapted).

1. First we need to build a decision table to evaluate all the estimates:

Combinations B = Best L = Likely W = Worst	Expected sales (in thousands)	Contribution margin 55% (in thousands)	Expected fixed costs (in thousands)	Expected income (in thousands)
W(.15)xW(.20)=(.03)	0.75x100,000=75,000	0.55x75,000=41,250	1.20x25,000=30,000	0.03x11,250=337.50
W(.15)xL(.60)=(.09)	75,000	41,250	25,000	0.09x16,250=1,462.50
W(.15)xB(.20)=(.03)	75,000	41,250	0.80x25,000=20,000	0.03x21,250=637.50
L(.75)xW(.20)=(.15)	100,000	55,000	1.20x25,000=30,000	0.15x25,000=3,750
L(.75)xL(.60)=(.45)	100,000	55,000	25,000	0.45x30,000=13,500
L(.75)xB(.20)=(.15)	100,000	55,000	0.80x25,000=20,000	0.15x35,000=5,250
B(.10)xW(.20)=(.02)	1.25x100,000=125,000	68,750	1.20x25,000=30,000	0.02x38,750=775
B(.10)xL(.60)=(.06)	125,000	68,750	25,000	0.06x43,750=2,625
B(.10)xB(.20)=(.02)	125,000	68,750	0.80x25,000=20,000	0.02x48,750=975.00
Likely Outcome				29,312.50

Second we need to calculate the bonus:

Expected net income $29,312,500
Minimum required $26,500,000
Excess obtained   2,812,500
Bonus: 1% of the excess $28,125

Conclusion: the expected value of the General Manager's bonus is not enough to pay for the leisure boat.

2. The difference between the two remuneration schemes are as follows:

	Current	Proposed
Flat salary	$75,000	$100,000
Expected bonus	$28,125	- - - - -
Total remuneration	$103,125 (1)	$100,000 (2)

(1) Expected remuneration, contains some uncertainty and partially depends on the manager's effort.

(2) Remuneration with certainty but does not depend on manager's effort

The general manager's answer depends on his aversion to risk. If he is adverse to risk (dislikes risk) he will accept the change in remuneration.

The proposed change in remuneration in the long run is not in the best interest of Electric Machines' owners because the manager's compensation is independent from his effort and results obtained.

24-34 (40-50 min.) **Evaluating managers, ROI, value-chain analysis of cost structure.**

1.

	$\dfrac{\text{Revenues}}{\text{Total Assets}}$	×	$\dfrac{\text{Operating Income}}{\text{Revenues}}$	=	$\dfrac{\text{Operating Income}}{\text{Total Assets}}$
Flexible Systems					
2008	0.926		0.250		0.231
2009	0.784		0.125		0.098
Rigid Structures					
2008	1.042		0.100		0.104
2009	1.215		0.171		0.208

Flexible Systems' ROI has declined sizably from 2008 to 2009, largely because of a decline in operating income to revenues. Rigid Structures' ROI has doubled from 2008 to 2009, in large part due to an increase in operating income to revenues.

2.

	Flexible Systems		**Rigid Structures**	
Business Function	**2008**	**2009**	**2008**	**2009**
Research and development	12.0%	6.0%	10.0%	15.0%
Design	5.0	3.0	2.0	4.0
Production	34.0	40.0	46.0	34.0
Marketing	25.0	33.0	20.0	23.0
Distribution	9.0	8.0	10.0	8.0
Customer service	15.0	10.0	12.0	16.0
Total costs	100.0%	100.0%	100.0%	100.0%

24-34 (cont'd)

Business functions with increases/decreases in the % of total costs from 2008 to 2009 are:

	Flexible Systems	Rigid Structures
Increases	Production Marketing	Research and development Design Marketing Customer service
Decreases	Research and development Design Distribution Customer service	Production Distribution

Flexible Systems has decreased expenditures in several key business functions that are critical to its long-term survival—notably research and development and design. These costs are discretionary and can be reduced in the short run without any short-run effect on customers, but such action is likely to create serious problems in the long run.

3. Based on the information provided, Cross is the better candidate for president of Integrated Automatic Solutions. Both Flexible Systems and Rigid Structures are in the same industry. Cross has headed Rigid Structures at a time when it has considerably outperformed Flexible Systems:

(a) The ROI of Rigid Structures has increased from 2008 to 2009 while that of Flexible Systems has decreased.

(b) The industry publication has given the top ranking to Rigid Structures, while it has decreased the ranking of Flexible Systems.

(c) Rigid Structures has received high marks for innovative solutions (the lifeblood of a company in the business of designing, implementing, and maintaining integrated systems of process controllers), while Flexible Systems's innovative solutions have been described as "mediocre."

24-36 (25 min.) Historical cost and current-cost ROI measures.

1.

	Jane and Rutherford		Major Mackenzie and Keele		Weston and Langstaff	
ROI = $\dfrac{\text{Operating Income}}{\text{Historical cost of investment}}$	$\dfrac{28,000}{50,000}$	= 56%	$\dfrac{33,000}{100,000}$	=33%	$\dfrac{15,000}{30,000}$	= 50%
ROI = $\dfrac{\text{Operating Income}}{\text{Current cost of investment}}$	$\dfrac{28,000}{120,000}$	= 23.33%	$\dfrac{33,000}{135,000}$	=24.44%	$\dfrac{15,000}{80,000}$	=18.75%

2. Using investments at historical cost as the denominator, the location of Jane and Rutherford has the highest ROI and the location of Major Mackenzie and Keele the lowest. Using investment at current cost as the denominator, Major Mackenzie and Keele has the highest ROI and Weston and Langstaff the lowest.

The choice of an appropriate measure depends on how World of 1 Dollar Ltd. judges the performance of its dollar stores.

If World of 1 Dollar uses a single benchmark (say, 20%) in judging the performance of each store, the current cost measure will promote comparability among stores that were bought at different times or in areas with different real estate markets. Historical cost will give rise to differences in ROI among dollar stores that are unrelated to differences in operating efficiency. For example, in times of rising prices, the oldest store (Jane and Rutherford) will have a lower historical cost investment level than the newest store (Major Mackenzie and Keele) for comparable amounts of square metres of store space in comparable locations. The current cost differences of the investment in the Jane and Rutherford store and Major Mackenzie and Keele store, for example, are much smaller than the differences in historical costs, due largely to the different time periods in which the two stores were built. A drawback of current cost is that current cost estimates are difficult to obtain.

If World of 1 Dollar Ltd. tailors the performance benchmark for each convenience store in its budgeting process, then the choice of a specific investment measure is less contentious. For example, if historical cost is used, the budgeted ROI benchmark for the Major Mackenzie and Keele store could be, say, 30%, whereas the budgeted ROI benchmark for the other two stores could be, say, 50%. Another benefit of tailoring the budget to each manager is that more incentives are provided to managers who are put in charge of poorly performing stores or stores in highly competitive markets.

24-38 (30 min.)   **Relevant costs, performance evaluation, goal-congruence.**

This problem illustrates the dysfunctional behaviour that could be motivated by arbitrary allocations of corporate overhead to profit-conscious divisional managers.

1.   Without the $960,000 in sales from the low-margin product line in the Azurro Division, the second-quarter operating statements (in thousands) will be:

	Azurro	Orange	Canarhina	Total
Net sales	$1,440	$1,440	$1,920	$4,800
Cost of sales	550	648	768	1,966
Divisional overhead	180	150	192	522
Divisional contribution	710	642	960	2,312
Corporate overhead	346	345	461	1,152
Operating income	$ 364	$ 297	$ 499	$1,160

2.   The company is worse off as a result of dropping the low profitability line of products because it has lost $250,000 in gross margin from the dropped product line with no reduction in corporate overhead. Total operating income decreases $130,000 from $1,290,000 in the first quarter to $1,160,000 in the second quarter.

3.   The Azurro Division manager's performance evaluation measure (divisional operating income) is marginally higher ($364,000 in the second quarter versus $360,000 in the first quarter) as a result of dropping the low-profitability product line. The Azurro Division manager shows a $4,000 higher operating income because the $250,000 in lost contribution margin from the dropped product line is less than the total of the $134,000 reduction in corporate overhead that is charged to the Azurro Division and the $120,000 savings in avoidable division overhead. Azurro Division sales are now only 30% of corporate sales rather than the previous 41.7% of sales (so 30% of total corporate overhead costs of $1,152,000, equal to $345,600, are allocated to the Azurro Division in the second quarter, whereas 41.7% of $1,152,000 equal to $480,000 are allocated to the Azurro Division in the first quarter).

4.   The easiest solution is to not allocate fixed corporate overhead to divisions. Then, the problem of dysfunctional behaviour will not arise. But central management may want the division managers to "see" the cost of corporate operations so that they will understand that the corporation as a whole is not profitable unless the combined divisions' contribution margins exceed corporate overhead. In this case, an allocation basis should be chosen that is not manipulable or under the control of division managers. It must also have the property that the action taken by one division does not affect the corporate overhead allocations that get made to the other divisions (as occurred in the second quarter for the company).

24-38 (cont'd)

In general, a lump sum allocation based on, say, budgeted net income or budgeted assets, rather than an allocation that varies proportionately with an actual measure of activity (such as sales or actual net income) will minimize dysfunctional behavior. The allocation should be such that managers treat it as a fixed, unavoidable charge, rather than a charge that will vary with the decisions they take. Of course, a potential disadvantage of this proposal is that managers may try to underbudget the amounts that serve as the cost allocation bases, so that their divisions get less of the corporate overhead charges.

24-40 (30-40 min.) Multinational firms, differing risk, comparison of profit, ROI and RI

1. Comparisons of after-tax operating income using translated values:

	Canada	Germany	NZ
Operating revenues: $10,479,000	$10,479,000		
5,200,000 € × $1.32		$6,864,000	
4,800,000 NZD × $0.67			$3,216,000
Operating expenses: $7,510,000	7,510,000		
3,600,000 € × $1.32		4,752,000	
3,500,000 NZD × $0.67			2,345,000
Operating income	2,969,000	2,112,000	871,000
Income tax at 40%; 30%; 20%	1,187,600	633,600	174,200
After-tax operating income	$ 1,781,400	$1,478,400	$ 696,800

In terms of after-tax operating income, the Canadian division is doing best, with Germany a close second. However, the New Zealand division is far behind the other two in terms of operating income.

2. Comparison of ROI for each division.

	Canada	Germany	NZ
1. After-tax operating income	$1,781,400	$1,478,400	$696,800
2. Long-term assets: $14,845,000	$14,845,000		
9,856,000 € × $1.25;		$12,320,000	
9,072,917 NZD × $0.64			$5,806,667
3. ROI (Row 1 ÷ Row 2)	12%	12%	12%

Because of differences in the assets employed in each division, they all have the same return on investment despite the differences in after-tax operating income.

24-40 (cont'd)

3.	Canada	Germany	NZ
After-tax operating income	$ 1,781,400	$ 1,478,400	$ 696,800
Long-term assets	$14,845,000	$12,320,000	$5,806,667
Cost of capital (given)	6%	10%	13%
Imputed cost of assets (cost of capital times long-term assets)	$ 890,700	$ 1,232,000	$ 754,867
Residual income (After-tax operating income less imputed cost of assets)	$ 890,700	$ 246,400	$ (58,067)

In contrast to the same ROIs found in each division, the Canadian division is doing best using residual income, and New Zealand has negative residual income. These differences are due to differences in the cost of capital.

4. Comparison of ROI using pre-tax operating income:

	Canada	Germany	NZ
1. Operating income (from requirement 1)	$ 2,969,000	$ 2,112,000	$ 871,000
2. Long-term assets	$14,845,000	$12,320,000	$5,806,667
3. ROI (Row 1 ÷ Row 2)	20%	17.14%	15%

The ROI computed using pre-tax operating income is much higher than the 12% ROI for all divisions using after-tax income. The differences arise from the different tax rates imposed on each division. The divisions should be compared on after-tax dollars because selling prices and costs in each country reflect different expectations regarding income taxes. For instance, selling prices are likely to be higher in the Canadian division, which has the highest tax rate.

24-42 (20-30 min.) Risk sharing, incentives, benchmarking, multiple tasks.

1. An evaluation of the four proposals to compensate the new general manager of the Industrial Pumps Division follows:

(i) Paying a flat salary will not subject the manager to any risk, but will provide no incentives for undertaking extra physical and mental effort.

24-42 (cont'd)

(ii) Rewarding the manager only on the basis of Industrial Pumps Division's RI would motivate the manager to put in extra effort to increase RI because the rewards would increase with increases in RI. But compensating the divisional manager solely on the basis of RI subjects him or her to excessive risk, because the division's RI depends not only on the manager's effort but also on other random factors over which the manager has no control. For example, the new divisional manager may put in a great deal of effort, but despite this effort, the division's RI may be low because of adverse factors such as high interest rates, or a recession.

To compensate the divisional manager for taking on uncontrollable risk, Acme Inc. must pay additional amounts within the structure of the RI-based arrangement. Thus, compensating the divisional manager only on the basis of performance-based incentives will cost Acme more money, on average, than paying a flat salary. The key question is whether the benefits of motivating additional effort justify the higher costs of performance-based rewards. This has not been a problem with Cynthia Franco due to her high intrinsic motivation, but now with the candidates available the lack of intrinsic motivation requires from Acme Inc. a new incentive scheme that can extract the greater effort possible from the new manager.

Furthermore, linking the bonus to RI and not to ROI is a positive decision. The objective of maximizing ROI may induce the general manager to reject projects that, from the viewpoint of the organization as a whole, should be accepted. This would occur for projects that would reduce Industrial Pumps' overall ROI but which would earn a return greater than the required rate of return for that project.

(iii) The motivation for having some salary and some performance-based bonus in compensation arrangements is to balance the benefits of incentives against the extra costs of imposing uncontrollable risk on the manager. The only caveat of proposal 3 is that the variable portion of the bonus be tied to ROI and not to RI.

(iv) The motivation for having some salary and some performance-based bonus in compensation arrangements is to balance the benefits of incentives against the extra costs of imposing uncontrollable risk on the manager. There are two caveats in proposal 4: one is that the variable portion of the bonus is tied to ROI and not to RI, and the other is whether, in fact, Pumps-for-All Ltd. is really comparable with Industrial Pumps Division.

24-42 (cont'd)

The senior management of Acme Inc. is proposing to benchmark the division's performance using a relative performance evaluation (RPE) system. RPE controls for common uncontrollable factors that similarly affect the performance of managers operating in the same environments (for example, the same industry). If business conditions for industrial pumps are good, all businesses manufacturing and selling industrial pumps will probably perform well. A superior indicator of the manager's performance is how well the division performed relative to his peers.

2. The candidate's complaint does not appear to be valid. The senior management of Acme Inc. is proposing to benchmark Industrial Pumps Division's performance using a relative performance evaluation (RPE) system. RPE controls for common uncontrollable factors that similarly affect the performance of managers operating in the same environments (for example, the same industry). If business conditions for industrial pumps are good, all businesses manufacturing and selling industrial pumps will probably perform well. A superior indicator of the manager's performance is how well the division performed relative to his peers.

    The goal is to filter out the common noise to get a better understanding of the manager's performance. The complaint will only be valid if there are significant differences in investments, assets, and the business environment in which Pumps-for-All and Industrial Pumps Division operate. Given the information in the problem, this does not appear to be the case.

3. Superior performance measures change significantly with the manager's performance and not very much with changes in factors that are beyond the manager's control. If the divisional manager has no authority for making capital investment decisions, then ROI is not a good measure of his/her performance—it varies with the actions taken by others rather than the actions taken by him/her. Acme may wish to evaluate the divisional manager on the basis of operating income rather than ROI.

    ROI, however, may be a good measure to evaluate Industrial Pumps Division's economic viability. Senior management at Acme Inc. could use ROI to evaluate if the division's income provides a reasonable return on investment, regardless of who has authority for making capital investment decisions. That is, ROI may be an inappropriate measure of managers' performance but a reasonable measure of the economic viability of the division. If, for whatever reasons (bad capital investments, weak economic conditions, etc.), the Division shows poor economic performance, as computed by ROI, Acme Inc. management may decide to shut down the division even though they may simultaneously conclude that the manager performed well.

24-42 (cont'd)

4. There are two main concerns with Cynthia's plans. First, creating very strong sales incentives imposes excessive risk on the sales force, because a salesperson's performance is affected not only by his or her own effort, but also by random factors (such as a recession in the industry) that are beyond the salesperson's control. If salespersons are risk averse, the firm will have to compensate them for bearing this extra uncontrollable risk. Second, compensating salespersons only on the basis of sales creates strong incentives to sell, but may result in lower levels of customer service and sales support. (This was the case at Sears auto repair shops where a change in the contractual terms of mechanics to "produce" more repairs caused unobservable quality to be negatively affected.) Where employees perform multiple tasks, it may be important to "blunt" incentives on those aspects of the job that can be measured well (for example, sales) to try and achieve a better balance of the two tasks (for example, sales and customer service and support). In addition, the division should try to better monitor customer service and customer satisfaction through surveys, or through quantifying the amount of repeat business.

24-44 (15 min.) Governance, levers of control.

1. If Amy Kimbell "turns a blind eye" toward what she has just observed at the UFP log yard, she will be violating the competence, integrity, and objectivity standards for management accountants.
   Competence: Perform professional duties in accordance with technical standards.
   Integrity: Communicate unfavourable as well as favourable information and professional judgments or opinions; Refrain from engaging in or supporting any activity that would discredit the profession.
   Credibility: Communicate information fairly and objectively; Disclose fully all relevant information that could reasonably be expected to influence an intended user's understanding of the reports, comments, and recommendations.

   Kimbell should:
   a. Try to follow established UFP policies to try to bring the issue to the attention of UFP management through regular channels.
   b. Then, if necessary, discuss the problem with the immediate superior who is not involved in the understatement of quality and costs.
   c. Clarify relevant ethical issues with an objective advisor, preferably a professional person outside UFP.
   d. If all the above channels fail to lead to a correction in the organization, she may have to resign and become a "whistle-blower" to bring UFP to justice.

24-44 (cont'd)

2. UFP is clearly emphasizing profit, driving managers to find ways to keep profits strong and increasing. This is a diagnostic measure, and over-emphasis on diagnostic measures can cause employees to do whatever is necessary—including unethical actions—to keep the measures in the acceptable range, not attract negative senior management attention, and possibly improve compensation and job reviews.

    To avoid problems like this in the future, UFP needs to establish some strong boundary systems and codes of conduct. There should be a clear message from upper management that unethical behaviour will not be tolerated. Training, role-plays, and case studies can be used to raise awareness about these issues, and strong sanctions should be put in place if the rules are violated. An effective boundary system is needed to keep managers on the right path.

    UFP also needs to articulate a belief system of core values. The goal is to inspire managers and employees to do their best, exercise greater responsibility, take pride in their work, and do things the right way.

24-46 (25 min.) Governance, manager's performance evaluation.

1. a. Variable manufacturing cost per box of 48 yogurts = $16

    Fixed manufacturing cost per unit = $1,000,000 ÷ 100,000 = $10

Revenues, $30 × 100,000	$3,000,000
Variable manufacturing costs, $16 × 100,000	1,600,000
Fixed manufacturing costs, $10 × 100,000	1,000,000
Fixed administrative costs	150,000
Fixed marketing costs	300,000
Total costs	3,050,000
Operating income	$ (50,000)

    b. Variable manufacturing cost per box of 48 yogurts = $16

    Fixed manufacturing cost per unit = $1,000,000 ÷ 125,000 = $8

Revenues, $30 × 125,000	$3,750,000
Variable manufacturing costs, $16 × 125,000	2,000,000
Fixed manufacturing costs, $8 × 100,000	800,000
Fixed administrative costs	150,000
Fixed marketing costs	300,000
Total costs	3,250,000
Operating income	$ 500,000

24-46 (cont'd)

2. The general manager's behaviour is not ethical. Professional managers are expected to take actions that are in the best interests of their shareholders. The Schomberg manager's action benefited himself at the cost of shareholders. His actions are equivalent to "cooking the books," even though he achieved this by producing more inventory than was needed, rather than through fictitious accounting. Some students might argue that his behaviour is not unethical—he simply took advantage of the faulty contract the board of directors had given him when he was hired.

3. Asking distributors to take more products than they need is also equivalent to "cooking the books." In effect, distributors are being coerced into taking more product. This is a particular problem if distributors will take less product in the following quarter or alternatively return the excess inventory next quarter. Some students might argue that the Schomberg manager's behaviour is not unethical—it is up to the distributors to decide whether to take more inventory or not. So long as the manager is not forcing the product on the distributors, it is not unethical for him to push sales this year even if the excess product will sit in the distributors' inventory.